PENGUIN BOOKS

Strangers on a Bridge

Born in New York City in 1916, James B. Donovan graduated from Fordham University and Harvard Law School. A commander in the Navy during World War II, he became general counsel of the Office of Strategic Services and was associate prosecutor at the principal Nuremberg trial. Mr. Donovan subsequently acted as chief counsel in major trials and appeals in over thirty states, and was an insurance lawyer and partner at Watters and Donovan. He was Democratic candidate for United States Senator from New York in 1962; served as general counsel for the Cuban Families Committee, obtaining the release of more than 9,700 Cubans and Americans from Castro's Cuba; was president of Pratt Institute; and was president of the Board of Education of the City of New York. He died in 1970, and was survived by his wife and four children.

D0726770

30130211112428 3

James B. Donovan with President John F.
Kennedy. (Courtesy of the author's estate)

Strangers on a Bridge

The Case of Colonel Abel

JAMES B. DONOVAN

PENGUIN BOOKS

PENGUIN BOOKS

UK | USA | Canada | Ireland | Australia
India | New Zealand | South Africa

Penguin Books is part of the Penguin Random House group of companies
whose addresses can be found at global.penguinrandomhouse.com.

First published in the USA by Scribner, an imprint of Simon and Schuster, Inc. 2015
First published in Great Britain in Penguin Books 2015
001

Text copyright © Atheneum House, Inc., 1964
Foreword copyright © Jason Matthews

The moral right of the author has been asserted

Printed in Great Britain by Clays Ltd, St Ives plc

A CIP catalogue record for this book is available from the British Library

ISBN: 978-1-405-92490-0

www.greenpenguin.co.uk

MIX
Paper from
responsible sources
FSC® C018179

Penguin Random House is committed to a
sustainable future for our business, our readers
and our planet. This book is made from Forest
Stewardship Council® certified paper.

To those among the American bar
who defend the weak, the poor
and the unpopular

CONTENTS

FOREWORD

This book is a reissue of *Strangers on a Bridge*, the 1964 best-selling story of the espionage trial of Soviet intelligence officer Rudolf Abel, written by Abel's court-appointed attorney James B. Donovan. It is no less relevant—or entertaining—today than it was then, however. It will be of interest to fans of vintage Cold War intrigue, and it will attract devotees of courtroom drama. Donovan's witty descriptions of his canny legal strategy are sure to delight, even inspire. And the smoky look into the enigmatic and elaborate mind of Abel, the Soviet spy, is fascinating. But most of all, this snapshot of the 1950s spy case reminds us that espionage has been around forever, the world's second oldest profession. Lest we forget, modern headlines documenting the recent arrests of Russian spies and sleepers in America reveal that it continues to this day.

The most successful HUMINT (human intelligence) operation in the twentieth century was arguably the Soviet Union's penetration of The Manhattan Project and the acquisition of U.S. atom secrets in the 1940s and 1950s. Designated "Task Number One" by Joseph Stalin, the Russians stole this early information—"atom secrets," in the parlance of the period—from the U.S., Britain, and Canada. Scholarly debate continues regarding which and how many top secrets the Soviet Union actually filched, and whether the information materially helped the Russians solve intractable physics and design obstacles plaguing their own weapons program.

It is known that stolen U.S. information did help the Soviets solve a number of specific mechanical problems—such as the design of a barometric detonator—but Soviet physicists did most of their own work. In fact, the NKVD (predecessor to the KGB) tightly held the purloined atom secrets and never shared the information with the majority of Russia's own scientists. Rather, NKVD chief Lavrenti Beria mostly used U.S. data to slyly *corroborate* the theoretical and design work of Soviet scientists. The modern-day consensus is that Soviet espionage probably saved the Russians a year or two in the production of a bomb.

The Soviet Union had a lot to work with in the early 1940s to accomplish Task Number One. Stalin had authorized unlimited resources for the effort. Beria and the red-clawed NKVD were given primacy in managing the operation. The Manhattan Project was a sprawling, vulnerable intelligence target of multiple domestic sites, employing over 100,000 scientists, technicians, machinists, administrative and support personnel, with discordant and uncoordinated security at plants and labs, managed by diverse agencies. At that stage in WWII, the Soviet Union was viewed as a beleaguered ally of the U.S. and enjoyed domestic public favor, as well as political support in Washington. This benign view of Russia among many scientists recruited by Moscow, or "atom spies," was manifested in a philosophical conviction that sharing weapons secrets would level the postwar playing field, eliminate mistrust, and ensure world peace.

Recruiting idealistic and sympathetic Americans and émigrés working on the Manhattan Project was like picking ripe fruit for Russian intelligence officers working under diplomatic cover in the Soviet Embassy in Washington, the Soviet Consulate in San Francisco, and the Soviet delegation to the United Nations in New York. Many of these scientist-targets were ethnically Russian, or adherents of the American Communist Party, or both; among them were Klaus Fuchs, Harry Gold, David Greenglass, Theodore Hall, and Julius and Ethel Rosenberg (all members of the spy network codenamed "Volunteer").

Soviet successes against the Manhattan Project brought familiar problems, however. In 1952, as today, once any HUMINT case gets past the heady recruitment stage—that's when the real work begins. Handling a clandestine reporting source is harder than initially suborning him. Intelligence requirements pour in from Moscow—Stalin *personally* wants more info, better info, faster.

Pushing a source to produce is delicate, and it's an actuarial certainty that the longer a source spies, the more likely he will be caught. By 1950 operating in the U.S. was becoming perilous for Russian spooks. American goodwill towards the Soviet Union had largely faded, eclipsed by the Red Scare and the burgeoning Cold War. And FBI's counterintelligence divisions were active and dangerous. Observed public contact between an American scientist and a Russian diplomat no longer was advisable.

The solution to keeping the Volunteer network up and running was quintessentially Soviet: Recruit other Americans (couriers) to meet the atom spies, and deliver the information to a controller (an illegal) who would transmit reports to Moscow. The arrangement would ensure that there was no observable Russian involvement; security and compartmentation would be preserved; and communications to and from The Center (NKVD headquarters) would be undetectable.

The NKVD classically used three categories of intelligence officer working in a foreign country. The *legal* with official cover, usually operating out of a diplomatic facility; a *non-official cover* officer who poses as a foreign salesman, or academic, or technical expert to gain periodic access to a target; and an *illegal*, who poses as a resident citizen of the country, with an elaborate and backstopped personal history (called a legend). The illegal will live unobtrusively for years to establish himself, possibly including taking a quiet entry-level job of no apparent intelligence import. This kind of illegal operative might not be activated for a decade until he is needed (it's why they're sometimes called sleeper agents).

Preparing a legend (classically done by taking over the identity of a long-ago deceased person) is painstaking—living it for years must be dementing. Administrative support for an illegal is protracted, endless, and ponderous. Illegals are frightfully expensive to deploy and maintain. Their training must be rigorous. Communications and security are critical—there is no diplomatic immunity if an NKVD illegal is arrested. Less-than-fluent foreign language skills are a liability. Balanced against this inefficient, expensive, and risky method of deploying a spy is the significant advantage of a water-tight personal history, anonymity, and invisibility.

Most intelligence services don't use illegals because of the impracticalities listed above. But there's a human dimension too. Imagine consigning an intelligence officer who has a spouse, family, and friends to potentially twenty years of what amounts to exile in enemy territory, breathing, eating, and sleeping in an assumed identity. Further imagine assigning that officer a total stranger as a cover spouse (albeit one who may be *very good* in Morse code). The entire notion is inconsistent with Western ideals and predilections. It's so Russian, so 1950s Cold War, *so Soviet*, that we assume no sentient intelligence service would use illegals anymore.

That would be a wrong assumption: Eleven illegals working for Vladimir Putin and the SVR (successor to the KGB) were arrested by the FBI in June 2010 in New York, New Jersey, and Boston.

NKVD intelligence officer Colonel Rudolf Ivanovich Abel was arrested by FBI and Immigration Service agents in a Brooklyn hotel room in the early morning hours of June 1957 on charges of conspiracy and espionage. This was the pivotal chapter of the FBI's Hollow Nickel Case, which ended with Abel's conviction in a U.S. federal court in October of the same year, and a sentence of forty-five years in the federal penitentiary in Atlanta.

Rudolf Abel arrived in the U.S. in 1948, via France and Canada, using a Lithuanian identity lifted from a deceased émigré. He had been trained as an NKVD illegals officer and was ordered to re-energize the Volunteer network of atom spies which since 1942 had been providing classified materials from Manhattan Project research labs at Los Alamos, New Mexico, but whose production had slackened due to postwar security upgrades. Soon after arrival, Abel changed identities and set himself up as a small-time photographer and artist in Brooklyn. His unobtrusive photo shop was perfect for an illegal—as a freelance shutterbug Abel could travel, be gone on unspecified assignments—and it naturally explained the photographic equipment and tools in his possession.

Rudolf Abel was a textbook illegals officer. He was fluent in English, Russian, German, Polish, and Yiddish. As a youth, he showed an aptitude for engineering, music, painting, photography, and radio. He trained Red Army radio operators during WWII, was drafted by Soviet intelligence, and participated in an audacious radio deception operation against the Abwehr (German military intelligence). Abel was rewarded for his wartime performance by being selected as an illegals officer to be assigned to the most prestigious posting on the NKVD roster: the United States.

In his first two years in the U.S., Abel established himself, received money and instructions, and probably traveled to Santa Fe, New Mexico, to sort out couriers, reactivate delinquent sources, and establish new communications plans. In his shop in Brooklyn, Abel strung a wire antenna for his shortwave radio—grounded to a cold water pipe—to commence encrypted broadcasts with the Center. It appears he did a good job resuscitating the Volunteer network: In 1949 Moscow radioed Rudolf that he had been awarded the Order of the Red Banner, an important Soviet military medal normally awarded for bravery in combat. He must have reported superior intelligence that pleased none other than Uncle Joe Stalin himself.

The year 1950 brought serious problems for the Volunteer network, however. Julius and Ethel Rosenberg, important network couriers and spotters, were arrested thanks to the confession and testimony of another network source, David Greenglass (who was Ethel's brother). A Russian husband-and-wife courier team, Lona and Morris Cohen, were identified and would also have been scooped up, but they fled to Moscow via Mexico. As the foundations of the network wobbled, Rudolf Abel, the central controller known to many of the couriers, was in jeopardy. But the Cohens got clear, and the jailed Rosenbergs steadfastly would not cooperate with the FBI, not even in exchange for their lives. They were executed in June 1953.

Exhausted and operating on the edge of discovery, Abel asked for help. In 1952 the Center assigned NKVD Lt. Colonel Reino Hayhanen to the U.S. as Abel's assistant. Reino arrived in New York on the *Queen Mary* with a Finnish émigré legend and spent nearly the next two years establishing himself, retrieving money, codes, and equipment from dead drops (formerly called dead-letter boxes) in Manhattan, Brooklyn, and the Bronx. Hayhanen was not the disciplined, tech-savvy, tradecraft-conscious illegal that Rudolf Abel was. A consistently heavy drinker, he fought publicly with his "assigned" Finnish wife (his real, Russian wife remained in Moscow), attracted attention to himself in frequent domestic disputes, and neglected his duties as an illegal operative.

One of the drops Reino unloaded contained a U.S. five-cent piece which had been hollowed out to serve as a concealment device for microfilm or miniature code pads. Before the mazy Hayhanen could open the nickel he absentmindedly spent it—or used it as a subway token. The coin circulated in the New York economy for seven months until a newsboy dropped it and it popped open, revealing a tiny sheet of number groups. The FBI's Hollow Nickel Case remained unsolved for four years as the Feds were unable to decipher the coded message.

Before the advent of automatic enciphering technology, secure radio communications between an intelligence headquarters and its agents in the field were abetted by use of one-time pads (OTPs, sometimes referred to as "cut numbers"). These cipher pads were individual sheets of printed rows and columns of five-digit numerical groups. The pads were bound with rubberized adhesive on all four sides, and normally printed small for concealment purposes.

A field agent would receive a shortwave radio broadcast from headquarters via one-way-voice-link (OWVL.) These OWVL broadcasts consisted of a monotone female voice reading a series of numbers—an enciphered message. The agent would record the recited numbers in five-digit groups and subtract them on the correct OTP page. The resultant values would correspond to the 26 letters of the alphabet and reveal the message. Because each page of the OTP is randomly different and used only once, looking for patterns in cryptanalysis is futile. It is an unbreakable cipher, as the impasse in the Hollow Nickel Case proved.

Hayhanen's behavior and performance continued deteriorating, and the Volunteer network began unraveling, especially during Abel's six-month absence for a recuperative trip to Moscow. Dead drops were neglected, radio messages were botched, and Reino spent operational monies on vodka and prostitutes. Abel urged the Center to recall Hayhanen to Moscow, which it did, in early 1957. Drunk but not stupid, Hayhanen walked into the U.S. Embassy in Paris and defected. The Embassy returned him to the U.S. and into the spy-catching hands of the FBI. Reino cooperated without reservation. He began naming names, identifying drop sites, and describing Abel and the location of his shop. He broke out the message contained in the coin. The Hollow Nickel Case was out of mothballs.

After more debriefings of Hayhanen, and increasing surveillance on Abel, FBI agents arrested Rudolf in his rented room in the early morning of 21 June, 1957. Even though he knew he was well and truly lost, the adamantine Rudolf Abel stayed professional. He refused to speak to the arresting FBI special agents—he later flatly rebuffed an FBI pitch to become a double agent—then asked permission to pack his expensive and delicate equipment. Sharp-eyed FBI agents caught him trying to slip OTPs and microfilm up his shirt sleeve as he filled a suitcase. He theatrically claimed various belongings were junk, and threw them into a wastebasket. Later inspection of the discarded items revealed more concealment devices and spy paraphernalia. Federal agents also seized micro-photography cameras for making microdots, and several shortwave radios. They found hollowed-out bolts, cufflinks, brush handles, pencils, and woodblocks containing codebooks, OTPs, microfilm, contact plans, and cash. Photographs of the Cohens, the husband-and-wife courier team who had escaped via Mexico, were also found, along with recognition paroles for other network members.

(The indefatigable Cohens were recidivist spies: In 1959 they resurfaced in Britain as Peter and Helen Kroger to support the Soviet operation—dubbed the Portland Spy Ring—targeting

Royal Navy underwater warfare secrets. This time the Cohen/Krogers were arrested by Scotland Yard, sent to prison, and eventually exchanged in a spy swap in 1969.)

A curiosity: At the time of his arrest, Abel was especially concerned about the disposition of his framed artwork that he himself had painted. Through his trial and during four years in penitentiary, he continually fretted about their storage and insisted the paintings eventually be shipped to East Germany. We can only speculate whether microfilmed atom secrets were hidden in cavities in the frames, or microdots were affixed under the layers of paint.

The account of the trial, told in Donovan's droll, spare style, is compelling. A jurist reading the book recently remarked on two questions of historical interest. The first is that the jury for this headline-worthy, capital espionage case was chosen in *three hours*, a remarkably swift process. Jury selection in high-profile cases today takes weeks and even months. Was this an anomaly for the Abel trial specifically, or was it normal for cases in 1950s federal courtrooms?

The second question in the jurist's mind is how Donovan avoided the death penalty for Abel by convincing presiding Judge Mortimer W. Byers that Rudolf could be used in a future spy swap with the Soviets. It was 1957 and three years before the first spy swaps began. At the very least Donovan was prescient: U-2 pilot Francis Gary Powers was shot down in 1960 and swapped (for Abel) in 1962; Donovan negotiated the release from Cuba of thousands of captured Bay of Pigs commandoes in 1963; UPenn student and hostage Marvin Makinen was swapped for two Soviets in 1963; UK spy Gordon Lonsdale was exchanged for British operative Greville Wynne in 1964.

(Spy swaps between East and West continued until 1986, many of them across the Glienicke Bridge, which spanned the Havel River near then-East German Potsdam, at a quiet southern corner of the American sector of partitioned Berlin. The book concludes with Donovan's captivating account of the swap on this very bridge, when Rudolf Abel crossed back into East Germany into the waiting arms of the KGB, and U-2 pilot Gary Powers returned home.)

In the Atlanta penitentiary Abel painted, socialized with prisoners, learned silk-screening, and mass-produced Christmas cards each year. For Westerners held by the Soviets, including Powers, Pryor, Wynne, and Makinen, their years of captivity were spent in the unspeakable Vladimirsky Central Prison, northeast of Moscow, or in the interrogation cells of the Lubyanka (KGB headquarters), or in Butyrka or Lefortovo prisons in central Moscow, in severe conditions, with little or no food, and suffering constant psychological and physical mistreatment.

Arrest photos from 1957 of a handcuffed, wooden-faced Rudolf Abel wearing his straw hat with a broad white band is one of the evocative images of the Cold War and Soviet-era espionage. The Hollow Nickel Case, replete with blurry OTPs, curled microfilm strips, and clunky shortwave radios, is a look back into the gritty world of postwar espionage, populated by unlikely and unattractive little people using field expedient spy gear, most of which today seems primitive, chipped, and worn. And the stolid Glienicke Bridge—riveted steel and asphalt roadway—one supposes must always be cloaked in swirling fog, its trusses back-lighted by arc lights the color of old ice. The Bridge of Spies.

The poignant fact is that the spy game continues today, whether or not one accepts the premise that a New Cold War has begun. Hollow coins, and microdots, and one-time-pads have been replaced by laptops, and software with 192-bit encryption, and modern steganography. Instead of hand-drawn sketches of early atomic bomb designs, intelligence services today seek to chart a target country's electronic financial system, or to measure its energy reserves, or to identify weaknesses in its cyber defenses. Satellites and drones let us look deep into enemy territory. But all these marvels cannot divine the *plans and intentions* of foreign leaders implacably annexing the Crimean peninsula; or mullahs bent on developing nuclear weapons; or psychopaths contemplating bedlam. Only human intelligence can do that, and spies like Rudolf Abel.

Donovan's agreement to defend Abel, in an era when the Red Scare sent other prominent lawyers scurrying for cover, was the ultimate act of patriotism; it was an affirmation of the American rule of law, and fairness, and justice—ideals that were nonexistent in a Soviet Union that deployed enemy agents to spy against the United States. Donovan knew what was important, despite screaming headlines of the day.

Plain men and women in every era, armed with hollow nickels, play the game which has not changed in centuries: They steal secrets in secret, and sometimes they get caught. Then two members of this enigmatic fraternity might pass in the fog as strangers on a bridge.

—Jason Matthews

STRANGERS
ON A BRIDGE

James B. Donovan
(Courtesy of Louis Fabian
Bachrach/Bachrach Studio)

INTRODUCTION

In early morning mists we had driven through deserted West Berlin to reach Glienicke Bridge, our rendezvous. Now we were at our end of the dark-green steel span, which crosses into Soviet-occupied East Germany. Across the lake was Potsdam; the silhouette of an ancient castle was on a hill to the right. On both sides of the lake were heavily wooded parks. It was a cold but clear morning on February 10, 1962.

Beneath the bridge, on our bank of the lake, three Berliner fishermen were casting but occasionally looked up in curiosity. A few white swans were cruising.

At the other end of the narrow bridge, called "Bridge of Freedom" in 1945 by our GIs and the Russians, we could see a group of men in dark fur hats. One tall figure was Ivan A. Schischkin, a Soviet official in East Berlin who had negotiated with me the prisoner exchange which three governments were now to complete.

It was nearly 3 A.M. in Washington, but at the White House the lights burned and President Kennedy was still up, waiting for word. There was an open telephone line from Berlin to the White House.

United States military police in trench coats were moving about at our end of Glienicke Bridge. In a small sentry shack West Berlin uniformed guards, abruptly ordered to abandon their bridge posts a little while before, sipped coffee from paper cups; they looked bewildered and vaguely apprehensive. Their loaded carbines were stacked in a corner.

Two U.S. Army cars pulled up behind us. Surrounded by burly guards was Rudolf I. Abel, gaunt and looking older than his sixty-two years. Prison in America had left its mark. Now at the last moment he was drawing on ingrained self-discipline.

Rudolf Ivanovich Abel was a colonel of the KGB, Soviet secret intelligence service. Abel was believed by the United States to be the "resident agent" who for nine years directed the entire Soviet espionage network in North America, from a Brooklyn artist's studio. He was trapped in June, 1957, when a dissolute Soviet sub-agent betrayed him. Abel had been seized by the FBI, indicted and convicted of "conspiracy to commit military and atomic espionage," a crime punishable by death.

When first arraigned in Federal Court in August, 1957, Abel asked that the judge assign "counsel selected by the Bar Association." A committee of lawyers recommended me for assignment by the court as defense attorney. After four years of legal proceedings, the Supreme Court of the United States upheld Abel's conviction by a vote of 5 to 4. The Colonel meanwhile had been serving a thirty-year term in Atlanta Penitentiary.

At his sentencing on November 15, 1957, I had asked the judge in open court not to invoke the death penalty because, among other reasons:

> It is possible that in the foreseeable future an American of equivalent rank will be captured by Soviet Russia or an ally; at such time an exchange of prisoners through diplomatic channels could be considered to be in the best national interests of the United States.

Now on Glienicke Bridge, negotiated "after diplomatic channels had been unavailing," as President Kennedy later would write me, such an exchange was about to take place.

At the opposite end of the bridge was American U-2 pilot Francis Gary Powers. In a distant section of Berlin, at an East-West crossing known as "Checkpoint Charlie," the East Germans were about to release Frederic L. Pryor, an American student from Yale. He had been arrested for espionage in East Berlin in August, 1961, and publicly threatened with the death penalty by the East German government. Final pawn in the Abel-Powers-Pryor exchange was a young American, Marvin Makinen of the University of Pennsylvania. In a Soviet prison in Kiev, where he was serving an eight-year sentence for espionage, Makinen unknowingly had received a Russian pledge of his early release.

When I walked to the center of Glienicke Bridge, concluded the prearranged ceremony and brought back what I had been promised "behind the Wall" in East Berlin, it would be the end of a long road. To a lawyer in private practice, this had become more a career than a case. The legal work was time-consuming; the related nonlegal work even more so.

I was Abel's only visitor and only correspondent in the United States throughout his imprisonment of almost five years. The Colonel was an extraordinary individual, brilliant and with the consuming intellectual thirst of every lifetime scholar. He was hungry for companionship and the trading of thoughts. While in Federal prison in New York, he once was reduced to teaching French to his cellmate, a semiliterate Mafia hoodlum convicted of strong-arming garbage collectors.

So Abel and I talked. And corresponded. We agreed and we disagreed. About his case; American justice; international affairs; modern art; the companionship of animals; the theory of probabilities in higher mathematics; the education of children; espionage and counterespionage; the loneliness of all hunted men; whether he should be cremated, if he died in prison. His range of interest seemed to be as inexhaustible as his knowledge.

At the very outset I must state what Abel never told me. He never admitted to me that any of his activities in the United States had been directed by Soviet Russia. This may seem incredible, but it is true. He could have been a KGB colonel who had decided to undertake such espionage on his own. However, I always proceeded on the premise that the United States government's proof of Abel's guilt—and the guilt of the Soviet which sent him—was overwhelming. The entire defense was based on this assumption. Furthermore, he knew my belief, tacitly accepted it and never denied its truth. We even assumed it in our discussions. But he never expressly declared it, even to me.

Why was this? Did he think I was naïve, a Soviet sympathizer or confused? Not at all. In the last analysis, such an express admission not only would be against his every instinct, disciplined for thirty years, but more to the point, it was unnecessary for his legal defense. The latter was the criterion of our communication in this area. I once asked him his real name. He deliberated and then said, "Is that knowledge necessary for my defense?" I said no. He tapped his foot and said, "Then let's talk about more pertinent matters."

Moreover, he accepted from the outset the paradoxical position in which I had been placed by court assignment. He understood my conviction that by giving him an honest defense to the best of my ability, I would be serving my country and my profession. But he recognized the distinction between knowledge required to defend his legal rights and other information, not pertinent to his court defense but perhaps valuable to United States counterintelligence agencies. Candor with caution was required and observed on both sides.

This unique lawyer-client relationship has enormously aided me in writing about the case of Colonel Abel. I never would have been clear in my professional conscience if in any manner I took advantage of the fact that Abel has now disappeared behind the Iron Curtain. He knew that I intended to write this book, begun in 1960 shortly after the Supreme Court decision. Indeed, he said that since some book about the case would undoubtedly be written, he would rather have me undertake it than entrust the task to a "professional writer who might exaggerate or distort facts to increase popular consumption."

At this late date, I do not intend to have his faith in me misplaced. Even that declaration is unnecessary, for I know nothing which could be used against him, wherever he now may be. The very facts which make dangerous in American eyes a Soviet spy who will not talk must serve in his homeland as proof of patriotic devotion. Nathan Hale was executed, but respected, by the British and his memory has been revered by us.

The day I was assigned to the Abel defense, I decided to keep a

4

diary on the case. First, in so complicated a legal matter the diary could be helpful for basic review from time to time. Second, it would be reassuring in the event my client were executed and I had to face the suspicion, however unfounded, that I failed to give him an honest defense. Finally, it would be a personal notebook on what appeared to be my most challenging assignment in law since the Nuremberg Trials.

It is from the written records—the original diary expanded from contemporaneous notes, letters to and from Abel and his "family," the official transcript of court proceedings, and finally, cabled reports to the State Department on my East Berlin mission—that this book has been written. Why did I accept the defense assignment? What was Abel like? Why did our Supreme Court divide 5 to 4 in upholding his conviction? What are the feelings of an American who goes behind the Berlin Wall, without diplomatic status or immunity, to negotiate with the Soviets? Was the final exchange on the Glienicke Bridge in the best national interest of the United States? All these questions, and more, answer themselves in the written records.

Sitting alone late one night, back in 1957, I thought of my daily relationship with Abel and wrote in my diary (a little stiffly, I now think):

We are two dissimilar men drawn close by fate and American law . . . into a classic case which deserves classic treatment.

1957

"The Abel Spy Trial," copy of an original lithograph by William Sharp. (Courtesy of Dan McDermott and Ed Radzik at Marshall Dennehey Warner Coleman & Goggin)

Monday, August 19, 1957

"Jim, that Russian spy the FBI just caught. The Bar Association wants you to defend him. What do you think?"

It was Ed Gross of our law firm, calling from New York. By the tone of his voice, I could tell he thought he was bearing bad news. When I put down the phone, I turned and told Mary, my wife. She sat down on the bed and said wearily, "Oh, no!"

It was 9:30 in the morning and we were unpacking at our summer cottage in Lake Placid, New York, deep in the Adirondack Mountains. This was to be the start of a two-week vacation, delayed by a case before the Supreme Court of Wisconsin.

Like all wives, Mary felt her husband had been overworking, and she had been looking forward to our vacation. We had met in Lake Placid while still in college and we both loved the Adirondacks. For a city lawyer, it was a perfect spot to unwind.

Ed Gross said the Brooklyn Bar Association had decided that I should defend the accused spy, Col. Rudolf Ivanovich Abel. He said Lynn Goodnough, a Brooklyn neighbor, was the chairman of the selection committee. Over ten years ago Goodnough had heard a talk I gave on the Nuremberg Trials before a conservative group of Brooklyn lawyers, including some prominent German-

Americans. The discussion became heated, Lynn told Ed, and he thought I stood up for what I believed.

I had read newspaper accounts of the indictment of Abel by a Brooklyn grand jury nearly two weeks before. The stories described Abel in a sinister way as a "master spy" heading all illegal Soviet espionage in the United States.

I left our Lake Placid cottage for a walk. After a while I had a cup of coffee with a fellow vacationing lawyer, Ed Hanrahan, former chairman of the Securities and Exchange Commission, whose judgment I value. We talked it out.

"As a friend, Jim, I strongly advise you against accepting the assignment," he said. "It's bound to take a lot out of you before it's over. You've done more than your share of Bar Association work; let them find a criminal lawyer to handle the defense. But only you can make the decision."

There was another opinion I got that morning, which probably would have been that of the average layman. I walked over to the golf course for a lesson. Between shots on the practice tee, I mentioned the proffered assignment to the club professional, Jim Searle, an old friend as well as golf tutor.

"Why in hell," he asked, "would anyone want to defend that no-good bum?"

I reminded him that under our Constitution every man, however despised, is entitled to counsel and a fair trial. So, I said, the next step is simple: Who will defend him? Jim agreed with my theory, but as I walked away from the practice tee I could sense that he was certain my egghead thinking was one of the reasons for my miserable golf swing.

Just before noon, still undecided, I called Lynn Goodnough in Brooklyn. He became quite emotional in his quiet way and said, "Jim, our committee feels very strongly that American justice, along with the Soviet Colonel, will be on trial."

Goodnough frankly said that the committee had discussed the assignment with several prominent trial lawyers with political ambitions, who forcefully declined. The McCarthy era was not

10

long closed. Because of my background as wartime counsel to the Office of Strategic Services, our own secret intelligence agency, and my subsequent courtroom experience in private practice, the committee believed I was uniquely qualified to undertake the defense of Colonel Abel. I pointed out that I had done no recent criminal work in Federal Court, and as a professional necessity I would have to be promised the assignment of a young former assistant United States Attorney to help me. Goodnough agreed and an hour or so later called back to say that U.S. District Court Judge Matthew T. Abruzzo wanted to see me in his chambers the next day at 11 A.M. Abel had been arraigned before Judge Abruzzo and now he was responsible for assigning defense counsel.

In the afternoon I drove over to the village of Lake Placid and asked Dave Soden, then a local attorney and now Supreme Court justice in Essex County, for the courtesy of using his law library. I read through the espionage statutes and was surprised to learn that since the notorious Rosenberg "atom spy" case Congress had made even peacetime espionage "on behalf of a foreign power" a crime punishable by death.

Obviously, the Colonel named Abel was in deep trouble, perhaps his last.

Mary and I had a quiet dinner together and at nine o'clock I caught the old North Country sleeper train for New York. On a Monday night the train was almost empty and I sat alone in the club car, nursing a Scotch. I tried to read for a while but my thoughts kept drifting to what I could see as a fascinating legal assignment, however unpopular or hopeless. Before the train reached Utica, about one o'clock in the morning, I decided to undertake the defense of Colonel Abel.

Tuesday, August 20

That morning I kept my appointment in Federal Court, Brooklyn, with Judge Abruzzo. Although he had been on the bench many years, I had never met him.

I told him that possible reasons against the assignment were my background as a Roman Catholic, former OSS intelligence officer and American Legion Post commander. He brushed these aside and said that they were only added qualifications for such a task.

I mentioned that I then was serving as defense counsel for an insurance company in U.S. District Court in Manhattan (for the Southern District of New York), in a case where the company refused to pay life insurance proceeds to the Polish government. It claimed to represent some Polish citizens who were beneficiaries of life insurance policies taken out by a Polish-American priest. We defended the action on the ground that Poland was a police state under the military domination of Soviet Russia and that, as we believed that the government and not its citizens would actually receive the money, we wished to hold the funds here for their benefit until Poland became truly free.

Judge Abruzzo peremptorily dismissed the matter on the ground I was only a lawyer litigating these issues. He then handed me a copy of the indictment and rather formally announced that he was assigning me to the defense. In what may have been an unnecessary afterthought, I quietly stated my acceptance.

The defendant, said the judge, was considered by our government to be the most important Soviet agent ever captured in the United States. He said the trial was certain to receive international publicity and this fact was undoubtedly the reason some twenty lawyers had called or appeared in person to solicit the assignment.

"However," Judge Abruzzo added dryly, "I was not entirely satisfied with either their professional qualifications or motives."

Judge Abruzzo told me Abel had $22,886.22 in cash and bank deposits when arrested, and that while I should discuss fees with my new client, the court would approve at least a fee of $10,000, plus out-of-pocket expenses, for the trial. I told him while I would accept any such fee, I had already determined I would donate it to charity. This, he replied, was my own business, but he seemed surprised.

At 2:30 P.M. I had to meet the press. They overflowed my law office in downtown Manhattan. I opened the conference by saying that I had agreed to accept the assignment as a public service. I stressed that it was in the national interest that Abel receive a fair hearing, and asked that they distinguish between American traitors and foreign espionage agents serving their own governments.

"A careful distinction should be drawn between the position of this defendant and people such as the Rosenbergs and Alger Hiss," I said. "If the government's allegations are true, it means that instead of dealing with Americans who have betrayed their country, we have here a Russian citizen, in a quasi-military capacity, who has served his country on an extraordinarily dangerous mission. I would hope, as an American, that the United States government has similar men on similar missions in many countries of the world.

"The nature of a secret agent's work is always dangerous and unrewarding, since he is called on to accept the knowledge that if discovered he is automatically disavowed by his government. Nevertheless, there are many statues of Nathan Hale in the United States."

Someone asked, "How do you feel? Are you pleased with your assignment?"

I thought for a minute and then candidly replied, "I wouldn't say that; no. But I'm appreciative of the respect implied in my selection by the Bar Association."

As I answered this, I was thinking of what New York Supreme Court Justice Miles McDonald had said when telephoning to wish me luck, earlier in the day. He told me, "I hope you know what lies ahead. Since John Adams defended the British soldiers for the Boston Massacre in 1774, no defense lawyer has taken on a less popular client."

When I got home, much later that night, my eight-year-old daughter Mary Ellen (who must have been listening to the radio) had left a crayon drawing on my desk. It showed a black-haired, slant-eyed convict in stripes with a ball and chain, and was titled "Russian Spy in Jail." Along the side border she had printed, "Jim Donovan is working for him."

I was to meet my new client, Col. Rudolf Ivanovich Abel, for the first time. When I reached the fortresslike Federal courthouse in Brooklyn at 11 A.M. it was alive with action. As on the opening day of a big criminal trial, electricity was in the air. Court attendants, elevator operators and the blind newsdealer in the lobby—all of them felt and imparted it. Reporters, radio newsmen with their recorders, television cameras and lighting equipment were everywhere.

"Will the Colonel accept you as his lawyer? Can we get a shot of you together? Are you going to have a joint statement?"

I was introduced to Colonel Abel in the prisoners' pen, quickly shook hands, and then we walked down the corridors, past grinding TV cameras, to a small detention room which I had asked the United States marshal to set aside for this first meeting.

A posse of deputy marshals ushered us in and then closed the door. They stood guard outside. The two of us suddenly were standing alone, face to face across a table.

"These are my credentials," I said, handing him a copy of the detailed press release issued by the Bar Association, announcing my selection. "I'd like you to read this carefully, to see whether there is anything here which you believe should bar me from acting as your defense counsel."

He put on rimless spectacles. As he carefully read the release, I studied him. He looked very shabby, I thought. He was dressed in rumpled work denims and I decided that for his courtroom appearances he should have some decent clothes that would aid him in assuming a dignified posture.

I thought of descriptions of him that I had seen in the newspapers and magazines: "an ordinary-looking little man . . . a sharp patrician face . . . long nose and bright eyes that suggested a curious bird." To me, he looked like a schoolteacher. But then, I reminded myself, so had Himmler. Abel was slight, but wiry and powerful. When we had shaken hands he gripped mine powerfully.

When he finished reading he looked up and said, "None of these things influence my judgment. I am prepared to accept you as my attorney." The words were spoken in perfect English, with the accent of an upper-class Britisher who had lived in Brooklyn for some years.

I described the life insurance case I was then handling in U.S. District Court in Manhattan, involving Soviet Russia's domination of Poland. He shrugged his shoulders and replied, "That's a legal matter. After all, if the insurance companies didn't take that position and have the issues decided, they could be compelled to pay again to Polish claimants if there ever is a turnover in the Polish government." I was fascinated. This was one of the reasons why this so-called "Iron Curtain test case" had been selected by the life insurance companies.

I told him that I would accept any fee approved by the court as reasonable, but would donate it to charity. He remarked that this was my "own affair." He thought the $10,000 fee already mentioned was fair and explained that a lawyer who visited him in jail had asked for $14,000 to conduct the trial. He turned the man down, he added, because he "lacked professional dignity," was "sloppy-looking" and "had dirty fingernails." (He has the background of a gentleman, I thought.)

With such formalities out of the way, we sat down and he asked me what I thought of his situation. With a wry smile he said, "I guess they caught me with my pants down."

I laughed. The remark was made even funnier by the fact that when the FBI had pushed into his hotel room early one June morning, Abel was sleeping in the raw. The arresting officers had found complete spy paraphernalia in his Manhattan hotel room and his artist's studio in Brooklyn. There were short-wave radios with a schedule of message reception times; hollowed-out bolts, cuff links, tie clasps and other secret message containers; a code book, coded messages and microfilm equipment; and marked-up maps of major United States defense areas. On top of all this, the government claimed it had the full confession of at least one accomplice.

15

"I'm afraid, Colonel, I'm inclined to agree with you," I said and explained that from the news stories I had seen, plus a quick look at the official files in the court clerk's office, the evidence of his espionage mission appeared to be overwhelming. "Frankly, with the new penalty of capital punishment for espionage, and present cold-war relations between your country and mine, it will be a miracle if I can save your life."

He lowered his head for a second and I filled the silence by saying I hoped to bring about a more favorable climate for his trial. In this respect, I said, it would be important to see the public reaction to my first press conference. He made a gloomy observation about his chances for a fair trial in what he called "an atmosphere still poisoned by the recent McCarthyism." He also said that he thought the Department of Justice, by "propaganda" about his guilt and describing him as a "master spy," had already prosecuted and convicted him. "Judges and jurors read all that," he said. I told him that he should have confidence in the basic American devotion to fair play.

There was no question in my mind that Abel was exactly what the government claimed, and that he had decided it would be futile to argue otherwise. At a deportation hearing in Texas, where he was held in an alien detention center prior to his indictment, he swore under oath that he was a Russian citizen and asked to be deported to the Soviet Union. He further testified in Texas that he had lived nine years in the United States, mostly in New York, as an illegal alien using at least three aliases.

When I mentioned Texas he told me that during the time he was held there the FBI offered him freedom and a $10,000-a-year job in United States counterintelligence if he would "cooperate."

"They must think all of us are rats who can be bought," he said, and this led him to discuss the government's key witness, his defected assistant Hayhanen. "He's a rat," he said bitterly. "I can't understand how a man, to save his own skin, would betray his country and place his family in complete dishonor at home."

He then told me that under no circumstances would he coop-

16

erate with the United States government, or do anything else that would embarrass his country, in order to save his own life. I said that as an American I regretted this decision. Moreover, I told him, if he were convicted I would argue that it would be in the national interest to spare his life, since after some years in jail he might change his mind.

I also said he should regard living as desirable, since political events might change and there could be an improvement in United States-Soviet relations, to his benefit; or his American equivalent might fall into Russian hands and there would be the opportunity for an exchange of prisoners; or some other eventuality could occur. I was thinking that his family might die and any compulsion to remain silent for that reason would be relieved.

"I'm not going to press you on the subject," I said, "but, speaking as an American, I hope your feelings change about cooperation. We won't talk about it again, unless you reopen the discussion." I thought this was as far as I might go.

"I appreciate that," he said, "and I understand you must have mixed emotions about me, and about undertaking my defense."

We talked then about his background. I let the conversation drift, because he seemed eager to talk and I felt it important we establish a rapport in our first meeting. He told me he came from a proud family, prominent in Russia before the Revolution. He repeated his patriotic feelings and his loyalty to what he called "Mother Russia." I said that I had sought in my press interview to give fair recognition to his background and to distinguish his case from "native American traitors." He felt this was a valid distinction and thanked me for making it.

I told him that it might be important to establish his quasi-military status, since international treaties could become applicable. He said that at home he wore a uniform and that his military rank was recognized by all in Russia except the Red Army. However, unless it was necessary to his defense, he did not want to be referred to as "Colonel," since this might embarrass his country. I asked him what he would like me to call him, in our own relationship. He grinned and said, "Why not call me Rudolf? That's as good a name as any, Mr. Donovan."

It was evident, just as Judge Abruzzo had told me, that Abel was a cultured man with an exceptional background—for his chosen profession or for any other. He spoke English fluently and was completely at home with American colloquialisms ("rat," "caught with my pants down"). I also learned that he knew five other languages, was an electronics engineer, knew chemistry and nuclear physics, was an accomplished amateur musician and painter, mathematician and cryptographer.

Abel was talking openly and frankly and I had the feeling he felt at ease with me because of my OSS background. He had found someone with whom he could "talk shop" without any worry about being overheard by the couple in the next booth. At any rate, Rudolf was an intellectual and a gentleman, with a fine sense of humor. We were getting on increasingly well and I found him intriguing. As a man, you could not help but like him.

In this regard, I was not alone. He told me, with some pride, that at the Federal Detention Headquarters on New York's lower West Side, he was kept in a maximum-security cell but the other prisoners were friendly. "They address me as Colonel," he said. "They not only understand my situation but recognize that I have been serving my own country. Moreover, they always respect a man who doesn't squeal."

As for the defense, I said I'd do my best for him and see that he received due process of law each step of the way. However, I told him my conviction that it would be in the interest of justice, the bar and himself that the entire defense be conducted with the utmost decorum. "I'll make no motions just for noise," I said, "and will avoid personal publicity. I'll also reject any offer of help from vocal left-wing committees or other such groups."

Abel expressed complete acceptance of this approach. He said quietly, "I want you to do nothing that will lower the dignity of someone honorably serving a great nation." Quite a guy, I thought to myself.

I asked him if there was anything troubling him; anything I might do for him. He mentioned that in his Fulton Street studio were all his paintings. "For sentimental reasons," he said, "I value them as part of my life here. I'm afraid vandals may break into the studio and make off with them for publicity reasons." I assured him I would look out for his paintings and, if need be, store them somewhere in my own home.

"Is there anything you would like now, though?" I asked.

"Oh, yes," he said, "I would like my freedom." He smiled as he said it and then, seriously, asked to have the daily newspapers sent to him—"except for the yellow press."

We shook hands a second time and I said goodbye, to face the reporters. We had talked our way through almost three hours.

At home that night, after the family were in bed and the house was still, I sat up late in my study. I went through a score of legal texts, did research on espionage cases both here and in Europe, and took the indictment apart, paragraph by paragraph.

My conclusion was that unless the Government's case foundered on procedural or constitutional grounds, the best hope to save Abel's life would lie in attacking the testimony of Lt. Col. Reino Hayhanen, his former assistant who had betrayed him. Hayhanen's character and habits should be laid before the jury, so they could evaluate his credibility. Also, we had to drive home that this was not a trial of Soviet Russia or communism, but solely a question of whether Abel was guilty of a specific offense under our law. If the defense could achieve these points, the jury at least should convict him only if the Government proved its case beyond a reasonable doubt.

There was one encouraging discovery. In my research, I found no example in either American or modern European history of a foreign spy being executed for peacetime espionage. Ethel and Julius Rosenberg had been given the death sentence because they were American citizens whose offense was linked to World War II activities. The case of United States vs. Abel, though, would be the first peacetime prosecution of an alien spy in this country under the so-called "Rosenberg Law," making espionage a capital crime in peacetime.

The indictment filled twelve legal-sized sheets and made a formidable document to one acting alone as defense counsel. In the three-count indictment, Abel was charged with: 1) conspiracy to transmit atomic and military information to Soviet Russia (maximum penalty, death); 2) conspiracy to gather such information (maximum penalty, ten years in prison); 3) conspiracy to remain in the United States without registering with the State Department as a foreign agent (maximum penalty, five years in prison).

The indictment further charged Abel with having four co-conspirators: Reino Hayhanen, alias "Vic," his betrayer, Mikhail N. Svirin, Vitali G. Pavlov and Alekssandr Mikhailovich Korotkov. All but Hayhanen were said to be back in Russia and two of these were described by the government as "of some prominence."

Pavlov had formerly been second secretary of the Soviet Embassy in Ottawa, Canada, where he directed a postwar spy network. When the ring was broken in 1946, Dr. Klaus Fuchs had been arrested in England and the Rosenbergs were apprehended in this country. Mikhail N. Svirin, the other co-conspirator of whom something was known, had served as a member of the UN Secretariat in New York from August, 1954, to November, 1956. His salary: $10,000 a year for "services to the UN."

The text of the indictment, especially the "overt acts" alleged, read like part of a paperback thriller or a movie script. For the scenario, the setting would be shifted from Brooklyn to Vienna or Lisbon. This was how, in part, the indictment of the grand jury read:

That from in or about 1948 . . . Rudolf Ivanovich Abel, also known as "Mark" [code name] and also known as Martin Collins and Emil R. Goldfus, unlawfully, wilfully and knowingly did conspire and agree with Reino Hayhanen, also known as "Vic" . . . and with divers other persons to the Grand Jury unknown, to . . . agree to communicate, deliver and transmit to . . . the Union of

Soviet Socialist Republics . . . documents, writings, photographs, photographic negatives, plans, maps, models, notes, instruments, appliances and information relating to the national defense of the United States of America, and particularly information relating to arms, equipment and disposition of the United States Armed Forces, and information relating to the atomic energy program of the United States. . . .

It was further a part of said conspiracy that the defendant . . . would activate and attempt to activate as agents within the United States certain members of the Armed Forces who were in a position to acquire information relating to the national defense. . . .

. . . the defendant would use short-wave radios to receive instructions . . . of the Union of Soviet Socialist Republics and to send information to the said government. . . .

. . . the defendant would fashion "containers" from bolts, nails, coins, batteries, pencils, cuff links, earrings and the like . . . suitable to secrete microfilm and microdot and other secret messages.

. . . defendant and his co-conspirators would communicate with each other by enclosing messages in said "containers" and depositing them . . . in pre-arranged "drop" points in Prospect Park, Brooklyn, and in Fort Tryon Park, N.Y., and at other places. . . .

The irony of Abel's use of Prospect Park in Brooklyn intrigued me. Our home, a duplex cooperative apartment on Prospect Park West, looks over the 526-acre park, an oasis of green in the sprawling borough. As I was reading this charge in the indictment, I looked out my study window and saw lights blinking throughout Prospect Park. Down below there possibly had been a drop, selected in Moscow for international espionage. Probably it had been used some night in the dark while Mary and I were hosts at a party upstairs.

The indictment continued:

It was further a part of said conspiracy . . . defendant would receive from the Soviet government . . . large sums of money to carry on their illegal activities . . . some of which money would be stored for future use by burying it in the ground.

. . . defendant and certain of his co-conspirators would, in the event of war between the United States and the Union of Soviet Socialist Republics, set up clandestine radio transmitting and receiving posts for the purpose of continuing to furnish . . . information relating to the national defense of the U.S., and would engage in acts of sabotage against the U.S.

There were nineteen overt acts charged and they served to fill in the details, to substantiate the conspiracy accusation and to weave all co-conspirators into the shadowy operation. They traced the conspiracy from the Kremlin to the United States and showed how the central characters met surreptitiously, used the drops, and ranged far afield for information and recruits to their cause. They also served to spell out the relationship between Abel and Hayhanen.

The overt acts told this story: Abel had slipped into the United States from "an unknown point" in Canada on November 5, 1948. His mission here was joined in 1952 by Lieutenant Colonel Hayhanen, but it was eleven months before the two first met.

In the summer of 1952 Hayhanen had been called to intelligence headquarters in Moscow and told that he had been assigned to the United States. A fraudulently obtained United States passport was supplied. Co-conspirators Svirin and Pavlov attended this meeting. Hayhanen arrived in New York in October aboard the *Queen Mary* and announced his arrival to other Soviet agents by putting a white thumbtack in a sign near a bridle path in Central Park.

Meanwhile, Abel was established in his artist's studio on the top floor of 252 Fulton Street, Brooklyn, in the shadow of the Brooklyn Bridge. With what the Government later termed "sheer audacity," the Soviet resident agent had set up shop directly opposite the Federal Building, headquarters of all Federal law enforcement agencies in Brooklyn and Long Island. Outside his studio he strung radio antennas, for better short-wave reception.

Abel's espionage nerve center was also just around the corner from the neighborhood police precinct. However, the studio was perfect for his "cover" since it was on the shabbier fringe of Brooklyn Heights, where artists, writers and poets had lived their introspective, non-busybody lives for a century. So, on December 17, 1953, Emil R. Goldfus, alias Rudolf I. Abel, alias "Mark," moved into a $35-a-month dingy one-room "studio."

In the summer of 1953, Abel and Hayhanen ("Vic") had their first meeting in the men's smoking room of Keith's RKO theater in Flushing, New York. As instructed, Hayhanen wore a blue tie with red stripes and was smoking a pipe.

"Never mind the passwords," Abel said. "I know you are the right man. Let's go outside."

During the next two and a half years, "Mark" and "Vic" met from time to time. At one meeting Abel gave Hayhanen a short-wave radio; at another he gave him a coded message to decipher; and a third time he brought him $200 and a bogus birth certificate. Twice Abel sent Hayhanen on missions: to Salida, Colorado, and Quincy, Massachusetts. Together they made trips to New Hyde Park, Long Island; Atlantic City, New Jersey; and Poughkeepsie, New York. They traveled to Poughkeepsie "for the purpose of locating a suitable site for a short-wave radio transmitter," said the indictment. (Hayhanen later complained that Abel looked down on him as an intellectual inferior, and condescendingly treated him "like a chauffeur.")

Although Abel had been arrested in his Manhattan hotel room, he was indicted and would be tried in Brooklyn, where he kept his operational headquarters. Therefore, the indictment was signed by United States Attorney Leonard P. Moore (Brooklyn and Long Island) and William F. Tompkins, Assistant Attorney General in charge of the Internal Security Division of the Department of Justice. Tompkins had come on from Washington to direct the final stages of the grand jury investigation and would remain to prosecute the case.

It was past 2 A.M. when I put down the indictment. It had been a long, grueling day since I had first met Abel in the morning.

By my invitation, I met for lunch United States Attorney Moore (now a judge of the U.S. Court of Appeals for the Second Circuit) and Assistant Attorney General Tompkins (then from Washington, D.C., now in private practice in New Jersey). It was three o'clock by the time we finished.

"While the defense of course must present its position as strongly as possible," I began, "I can assure you there will be no cheap bickering over trivia." I told them that Abel, for his own reasons, concurred in the concept of a dignified defense.

I also pointed out that in so complex a case, it was difficult for an individual defense attorney to cope with the limitless resources of the Federal government. I had only begun to research the case, but already was painfully aware that I was working against the resources of the Justice Department and an army of FBI agents. Meanwhile, I had the New York bar and press watching over my shoulder.

I hopefully mentioned to them the Nuremberg Trials procedure requiring pretrial disclosure of evidence, under which nothing could be introduced by the prosecution which had not been previously reviewed by the defense. For example, at Nuremberg the night before I put into evidence the movies on Nazi concentration camps we were required to have a private showing for all defense counsel.

This rule was adopted from European court procedures, and we agreed to its use in Nuremberg because we were seeking to have the international military trials accepted all over the world—and especially in Germany—as giving a fair hearing to the accused.

"I believe," Mr. Moore said, "that so general a pretrial disclosure would be an unfortunate precedent for criminal prosecutions in this country."

"Perhaps in the ordinary case," I said. "But in the Abel trial, as at Nuremberg, there are international interests at stake. We want all other countries to recognize that there is no higher justice

24

than that found in American courts. The procedures, for example, should appear to be fair to the ordinary European."

We agreed on the principle but they made clear I would get exactly what they must give me under the Federal Rules of Criminal Procedure—and nothing more.

Tompkins then said, "This is an open-and-shut case. It will be made in a simple and straightforward manner—no wiretaps or other potentially illegal evidence are needed and the prosecution will not involve any procedures upon which the Supreme Court has upset other espionage convictions."

When I asked whether the Government would demand the death penalty, he said the official position at this time was simply to report the facts to the court and make no recommendation as to sentence. "Personally," he said, "I don't believe the Government should demand the death sentence, but the picture could change overnight."

The conference was pleasant and, I felt, mutually profitable. On principle, we had consistently agreed. I liked and respected both men.

Back in the office, I found that the mail was heavy. There had been a good number of telephone callers, the greater number of them commenting favorably on my acceptance of the assignment. The letters were mostly sympathetic. They were from business friends and lawyers all over the United States, and some even from Europe. They offered encouragement, showed an understanding of the difficulties, and one of them, from an Episcopalian friend, even carried a little prayer.

Quite a few of them read like this: "I am not quite certain whether to offer congratulations or condolences." A lawyer friend in Bridgeport, Connecticut, wrote, "I hope you lose the case but that you distinguish yourself in defeat." Col. Robert Storey of Dallas, former president of the American Bar Association with whom I had served at Nuremberg, wrote a wonderfully encouraging letter. There were many which struck this note: "Defense of an unpopular cause is one of the things that make our profession a calling."

A close personal friend whom I admired for a career of patriotism and courage (Ray Murphy—former national commander of the American Legion) wrote from California, "Here's a chance to demonstrate American justice at its finest to all the world and to Abel's Russian masters. Though the demonstration will not change the Kremlin, it can have its impress on the rest of the world."

That night I went to an old-time Irish wake in Bay Ridge, one of Brooklyn's finest residential neighborhoods. A friend of my wife's family had died and now reposed in Clavin's, an institution in Brooklyn. While I was paying my respects, I was pleased to find that those present, many of whom I had not seen for a long time, were most friendly. A fair cross section of Irish Catholics from Brooklyn were present. Driving out to the wake, I had wondered how the Russian Colonel's lawyer would be received.

Straining to be polite, an elderly woman remarked, "My, those pictures in the newspapers don't do you justice, Mr. Donovan." Any references to the case followed such discreet lines. No one expressly raised the question of my representing the Colonel.

If the wake was a fair indication, and most letters and phone calls reflected the public mood, there seemed to be a growing appreciation of the difference between the accused Abel's obtaining American justice and the detested record of the Soviet government. Also, the distinction between American traitors and Russians serving their own country had apparently been accepted as valid. However, it remained vital to the defense, I reflected, that one point be hammered home: Soviet Russia would not be the defendant in the case.

Meanwhile, the trial loomed like a storm cloud on the horizon. It was set for September 16, less than a month away.

Friday, August 23

At nine in the morning I met with United States Attorney Moore to discuss what to do with Abel's property not held for use as evidence: a great bulk of tools, books, "containers" and the paintings Abel

26

was so anxious to keep safe. I stated to the Federal prosecutor that I would not accept responsibility for the paintings unless the FBI X-rayed and cleared them. I explained that for centuries spies had posed as artists and painted over concealed maps, plans and messages. I did not regard my assignment as requiring me to become a caretaker of possible espionage materials. (When I later told Abel my position, he laughed and said—which I disclosed to the FBI—that he mixed barium with his oil paints and to X-ray the paintings "would be a waste of time." The barium works to render X-rays worthless by concealing whatever might be under the oil painting.)

The United States Attorney and I agreed that Abel's property should be placed in a public storehouse with joint access by the Government and the defense. On June 29, two FBI agents had searched Abel's studio and come away with 202 items. They returned August 16 and took 126 other items from his storeroom down the hall from the studio. These things were packed in twenty pasteboard and wooden boxes.

This was some of what the FBI found, and it seemed to be a measure of my client's dual life in the United States: a one-third-horsepower generator; a Hallicrafter short-wave radio and earphones; a Speed-graphic camera and a great clutter of photographic equipment and supplies; metal dies and tools; numerous film containers and some clothing; a typewritten set of notes, "You Cannot Mix Art and Politics"; a general map of Bear Mountain-Harriman section of Palisades Interstate Park and street maps of Queens, Brooklyn, Westchester and Putnam Counties, New York; other maps, of Chicago, Baltimore and Los Angeles; loose nails, film strips, cuff-link "containers" and odds and ends packed in 13 Sucrets boxes; a schedule of international mails; a clip pad with mathematical formulas; musical scores, a phonograph and records; art sketchbooks; scientific magazines and technical pamphlets; a bankbook; an oil painting of a refinery; a box of prophylactics; and 64 artists' paintbrushes.

At 2:30 P.M. I made my first visit to Abel in the Federal house of detention, an unimposing but very efficient-looking building on

West Street in Manhattan. I was admitted through the electrically controlled jail doors and signed the register. Only one person had ever attempted to escape from here and the attempt was unsuccessful.

I met with Abel in a narrow cubicle. I immediately decided it was most difficult to have a relaxed discussion under such conditions, and thereafter, to the extent it could be arranged, I would confer with him in the Brooklyn Federal Building. Besides, Rudolf might feel "at home" if he could look out the window and see Fulton Street, Brooklyn.

At this second meeting, Abel seemed at ease with his court-assigned counsel. When he sat down I said, "I don't want to raise any false hopes but I think we've made a constructive beginning." Then I told him about the mail response and the phone calls, and the understanding coverage we had received from my first press conference.

"My conviction, Rudolf, is that you're going to benefit from the American trait of fair play. Every American likes to see an honest hearing for every man, no matter what he represents." He said, "I know. After all, I've lived among them a long time. But my worry has been the yellow press."

I then launched into a discussion of my work to date and told him that in keeping with our concept of a dignified defense, I didn't want him to appear in court or to be photographed until he was looking his best. This meant he needed new clothes. I took all his sizes and said that I would buy him a whole new outfit, from top to bottom.

"What kind of suit would you like?" I asked.

"I'll leave it to you," he said and then, smiling, added, "Maybe I ought to look like a Wall Street lawyer. Better get me a gray flannel suit with a vest." We both laughed, but actually my own judgment had been along similar lines.

The next order of business was a list of questions concerning his interest in art. The questions had been given me by reporters and we agreed upon appropriate answers. Most questions concerned whether he believed that his artistic growth had been stunted by party discipline. These were unanswered. He did say, in response to an inquiry, that his favorite painters were Rembrandt and Hals.

Abel's paintings had never been exhibited here, but a portrait of "Emil Goldfus" hung in the National Academy of Design in 1957 for the month of February. Done by a painter friend in Brooklyn, Burt Silverman, it showed Abel (or Emil Goldfus) sitting in his studio surrounded by paints and brushes, with his short-wave radio in the background. The artist called the painting "The Amateur," using the original meaning of the word: "one with a loving interest in things." The artist said the short-wave radio showed his subject's "active intelligence." Of course, Silverman had no idea that his neighbor was a colonel in the Soviet overseas intelligence service.

Abel said he painted as a realist and told me he was not the author of the notes found in his apartment entitled "You Cannot Mix Art and Politics." He said a friend had left the notes years before.

I told Abel that I had made plans to have all his belongings, including the paintings, stored in a warehouse. He signed an authorization for me to dispose of his things as I saw fit. However, he was so sharp that he asked whether he should sign "Emil R. Goldfus," the name under which he leased his Brooklyn studio.

"Maybe," he said, "I should follow the indictment and put 'also known as Mark and Rudolf I. Abel.'"

"Forget it," I said. Actually, I had discussed this point earlier with United States Attorney Moore and we concluded that since Abel had signed the lease as Emil Goldfus it would simplify things if he continued to use that signature.

I then broached the question of whether he would want me to contact the Soviet Embassy in Washington, in the hope of getting an official declaration of his status and possibly a claim of immunity. Until now, their public attitude had been "Not interested." I told Abel I had given the matter some thought and it was my opinion we should not make such an attempt.

To begin with, I would not initiate communication with the Soviet Embassy unless I first consulted United States officials. I told

Abel I was wary of entering any area of a potential conflict of inter-est between my duty to him as defense attorney and my duty as an American citizen. I explained further that such a move might boo-merang against the defense. After reading my background in the newspapers, the Soviet Embassy probably regarded me as an FBI "plant" and would believe my communication with them on this question to be part of a United States "plot" to embarrass Russia.

"In my opinion, Rudolf, Russia has written you off its books as a secret agent," I said. "You're on your own."

"I don't agree with you," he snapped back. "I have not been 'writ-ten off the books.' Of course they can't become involved. It's a tra-ditional rule of my profession and this I understand. But I am not 'written off,' and I resent your implying it."

It was the nearest we had come to a disagreement. Nonetheless, he said he had arrived at precisely the same conclusion about the feasibility of my communicating with Soviet officials in this coun-try. I said I could probably accomplish almost the same legal result by stating at the proper time that the prosecution declared Abel to be a colonel in Russian military intelligence; that while my client stood mute, the defense for purposes of the trial would be willing to accept what the Government alleged to be the truth. Unless this would support a motion to dismiss on the ground of immunity, however, we probably should risk such a gambit only if the jury convicted him and then only if it would be to his advantage at the time of sentencing or on appeal.

He seemed satisfied with my reasoning and that is how I left him. We had been together two hours.

Outside the West Street jail, a group of reporters who were beginning to "shadow" me asked how it had gone and what Abel had said this time. There was little I could tell them. I said Abel was "maintaining his calm" and "wishes no visitors and will see none." I also mentioned that he was seeking no outside help and trusted to the papers to interpret this to mean we were steering clear of the Soviet Embassy and didn't want a bandwagon of left-wingers or bleeding hearts trailing behind us.

From the oppressive Federal Detention Headquarters, we all traveled across the river to Abel's cluttered Brooklyn studio. Reporters and photographers then got their first look at the hide-out, which had been locked and guarded since his arrest.

The room was dirty and oddly shaped, with no walls at right angles. The floor, a closet and a long table were piled with his art and photographic materials. The sink was unwashed, the windows were coated with soot, and everywhere there were paintings. The walls held sixteen; others were stacked on the floor and sticking out of boxes. I counted fifty finished canvases, ranging from a nude to street scenes, head studies and three self-portraits. Among all the clutter, standing out like a sore thumb, was an unopened can of pea soup.

The United States Attorney's office had said that the paintings appeared to have no connection with Abel's "professional" activities. That is, with the possible exception of one showing an oil refinery. This one had them nonplused.

Abel's sketches and paintings were of great interest to the reporters, principally because of their subject matter. To the layman's eye they were good enough, but they fared less well in the face of expert appraisal. "He uses the colors of a beginner who has talent but has never analyzed his tools," one of his professional painter-friends summed up. "In another five years, though, he would have been a very good painter."

(When I so reported, Abel said lightly, "I would have progressed more in my painting career if I had had more time to give to it." He was saying, of course, that demands on his time were greater from other quarters.)

As for Abel's subjects, most were sketched in run-down neighborhoods of New York City. In his sketch pad I discovered page after page of lonely, older men standing, sitting or huddled over. Some were playing chess or checkers in a small park; others talked quietly, almost sadly, on the street. Some were the Bowery-bum type, but most were not. They were forsaken loafers and loners, patiently going nowhere.

One of Abel's circle of artist-acquaintances thought he carried the scars of a man who had made a comeback from being "on the bum." He remarked, "There's something about guys like that; no matter how much their luck improves they never lose that look. And he's got it." This of course suited Abel's purposes.

After leaving the Fulton Street studio I went over to the Brooklyn Bar Association to confer with the committee of three lawyers responsible for my assignment (Lynn Goodnough, Frederick Weisbrod and Raymond Reisler), as well as the president, Louis Merrill. We all were disappointed to receive a phone call from a prominent trial lawyer whom we had hoped to enlist as assistant counsel for the defense. He had had considerable criminal trial experience as a prosecutor. He apologized by saying that his business partner (who was not a lawyer) objected to his taking the assignment, for fear public reaction would be so unfavorable that their business would be boycotted.

Saturday, Sunday, August 24–25

I worked on the case both days and also found time for several of my less publicized, but nevertheless successful, commercial clients. Some of the men in our law firm believed we would lose many conservative clients because of my defending a Russian spy. I disagreed with their predictions and told them so. However, at least one of the associates in the firm threatened to resign.

There was welcome news in the mail. We received several editorials from out-of-town newspapers which recognized the Colonel's position as that of a soldier on a dangerous mission, serving his own country. One of them—from the San Francisco *Chronicle*, sent to me by an old friend, Rollo Fay—also dealt favorably with my role as court-assigned defense counsel. The *Chronicle* said:

> Donovan will do so [defend Abel] as a "public duty." This ascription, in view of the despised nature of the defendant's alleged crimes, may at first blush appear preposterously farfetched. But on

second thought, it jibes precisely with the hallowed American principle that every malefactor—not excepting Communist spies—is entitled to a day in court and the fairest of all public hearings.

The editorial quoted my press conference remarks on Nathan Hale and the hope that our government had "similar men on similar missions," and concluded with this summation:

The odds, of course, are prohibitive against Donovan's winning this case. He doubtless knows it and so does Colonel Abel. But the appearance of such a lawyer in such a case must certainly contribute to the prestige of American justice the world around and, at the same time, temper with cold reality the American loathing for the sorry, but necessary, profession of espionage.

The most nervous of my partners immediately began to send out photostats of the *Chronicle* editorial to all important clients of the firm.

Monday, August 26

I devoted the morning to a detailed analysis of the indictment and to informal discussion of the case with a few men in the firm. The consensus was that I badly needed help, especially with the legal research and background details so necessary if the defense was to make any kind of a showing. I made clear to my partners that the court assignment was personal, not the firm's, and that I would not ask them to contribute more than my own time.

In searching for an assistant, I called upon a former United States Attorney for the Southern District of New York, who could understand my pressing need for an experienced young lawyer familiar with the new Federal rules of criminal procedure. He very kindly gave me a list of former assistant United States Attorneys with whose qualifications he was familiar. After analyzing the list, I concluded that my best hope would be to induce a large Wall Street law firm to donate the time of such a man, as a public service.

Tuesday, August 27

Abel was in good spirits when we met in the afternoon to review everything to date and look ahead. He said, not altogether in jest, I was not the only one interested in his defense.

He explained that despite the fact he was in a solitary cell and a "maximum security" prisoner, he managed to be advised on his legal rights by fellow inmates. They passed him even the exact citations to pertinent legal precedents. He showed me a carefully written outline of a "brief," smuggled to his cell. To judge by the citations and legal points made, the authors had had long experience, undoubtedly firsthand, with criminal procedures. They now were willing to give Abel free "jailhouse lawyer" advice. While most prison inmates were very patriotic and had been known to assault American Communists in prison, the Colonel apparently had won the support of the prison population.

Rudolf said the inmates were following the case closely in the New York newspapers and one man was preparing a complete "brief" on the weak points of the Government's indictment. I told Abel I would look forward to reviewing it.

We then moved to a discussion of the recent Jencks decision by the Supreme Court of the United States. Under this ruling, within certain bounds the Government must provide defense counsel with FBI and other investigation files pertinent to testimony by prosecution witnesses, so that a cross-examiner may search for prior inconsistent statements.

Abel discussed the entire subject intelligently but said he would leave to me the question of how best to handle this new legal development. I jokingly suggested that he might wish to take up the matter with my newly discovered co-counsel, the jailhouse members of his "defense staff."

Wednesday, August 28

Early in the morning, I walked down to the Wall Street offices of Dewey, Ballantine, Bushby, Palmer and Wood and by prior appointment met with Wilkie Bushby, a senior partner. The firm was large and its staff of lawyers included a number of the former assistant United States Attorneys on the list given me a few days before. I explained to Mr. Bushby my immediate need for qualified help. He listened patiently and said he would take my appeal before a meeting of all available senior partners. At 3 P.M. he phoned with the answer.

"In the interests of the bar," he said, "we've decided to lend you a young associate, Arnold Fraiman, for the duration of the entire trial. We'll continue to compensate Mr. Fraiman and will make no charge for his services." The decision, Mr. Bushby added, was made after a meeting which included former New York Governor and Presidential candidate Thomas E. Dewey. I expressed my gratitude, as well as appreciation of his firm's high sense of professional responsibility.

Fraiman, thirty-two, was a graduate of Columbia Law School and had served a three-year term in the United States Attorney's office for the Southern District of New York. We met promptly and at 5 P.M. I introduced him to the Brooklyn Bar Association committee responsible for the selection of Abel's defense. Fraiman was young and aggressive. This was what the defense needed right now.

A newspaper story, recounting the background of the case, said that I had been meeting regularly with Abel in prison; that I had "mapped out" a series of possible moves but would not disclose what these "contemplated steps" would be.

While I did not want to announce it, the first of the mysterious "contemplated steps" was to buy the Colonel a new suit of clothes. I did this chore in the afternoon, stopping at a long-established men's haberdasher on lower Broadway. I asked to see a charcoal-gray suit and gave the salesman all Rudolf's measurements. I wanted Abel to look like a banker, but in the small-loan department.

The clothing salesman, I'm sure, thought I was on an errand of Christian charity, buying clothes for a dead friend so the corpse would be presentable. I volunteered no unnecessary information. I purchased a complete outfit: suit, white shirt and a regimental-striped tie (the salesman solicitously suggesting "somber shades"). The trousers needed alteration, so I instructed the salesman to let me know when they were ready and I would send someone over. I gravely asked him to hurry the order, since "there is an urgent need." He nodded sympathetically.

Friday, August 30

At 11 o'clock Fraiman and I met with Abel in Brooklyn. We were back in the more comfortable United States Court House in a vacant hearing room. I introduced Fraiman to Abel and quickly ran through his professional background. Abel accepted him without comment.

I suggested that we review the case in detail, including what Rudolf could tell us about his betrayer, Hayhanen. I was anxious to meet Hayhanen and, if possible, throw some questions at him and take a pretrial deposition. First, however, I had to know something of his background. Then we had to locate him, or people who had known him. The newspapers were saying that he was "carefully hidden by American security agents." Abel seemed willing, even eager, to talk about this man who had ended his career and put him in jail with the threat of execution.

Hayhanen, he said, lived in the United States as Eugene Nicolo Maki and was a "low type." He had been involved in several drunken brawls which brought him to the attention of the police. In addition, he had had an automobile accident in Newark, New Jersey, the preceding fall and narrowly passed a drunkometer test. I inferred that some of this information had been gleaned from Hayhanen, some from other sources.

Abel said Maki had lived at times in lower Bay Ridge, Brooklyn, in a section known as "Finntown." Hayhanen had built up his espionage cover in Finland; his bogus passport records declared that he was born in Enaville, Idaho, but had lived most of his early life in Finland. The real Maki, Abel explained, was a native-born American whose parents had taken him to Finland on a visit just before the Russian-Finnish War in 1938. They all were subsequently killed during the fighting, he said.

I knew Bay Ridge well. Parts of it are heavily populated with Scandinavians who have their own community life: Scandinavian-American singing clubs, churches, holidays, parades, newspapers and restaurants. They form a very law-abiding community, and I had many friends among them.

With contempt written across his face, Abel told how Hayhanen had devoted most of his attention in the United States to a young blond Scandinavian woman, about twenty-five years old, whom Abel reluctantly conceded to be "fairly attractive." Hayhanen had left behind in Russia a wife and a young son to whom, he told Abel, he was "devoted."

Abel had complained that Hayhanen did not circulate enough in New York and that his English suffered because of his insular way of life. "I told him to spend more time with native-born Americans," he said, "because I wanted him to speak English that wouldn't attract attention. I repeatedly emphasized this, because he spoke with such a heavy accent."

Abel explained that Hayhanen, or Maki, had reported in December (1956) that he believed he was being shadowed; he was extremely nervous, noticeably jittery. However, when Abel had next seen him, early this year, he appeared quite self-confident. Abel said he now believed that Hayhanen had been secretly apprehended in December by the FBI and that he had met Abel thereafter on orders from Federal agents.

In April this year (1957) Abel had met Hayhanen for the last time and told him to flee the country. He had given him $200 and a false birth certificate. Abel said that if Hayhanen had sold out to the FBI, it was possible this meeting had been both photographed and recorded. When Abel said this, I thought of what prosecutor Tompkins had said of the case being "open-and-shut" with no need for wiretaps or other dubious evidence. Perhaps Tompkins was right.

I wanted now to get from Abel, in affidavit form, the complete story of his arrest. The newspapers had carried only a fragmentary outline disclosed by the government: that he was seized in a New York hotel, taken as an illegal alien to a detention camp in Texas and, based on information subsequently obtained, later indicted in Brooklyn as a spy.

As the Colonel now poured out the story of how he had been seized, I realized, for the first time, what a truly fantastic tale it was. Following his arrest at the Hotel Latham for deportation, on an Immigration and Naturalization Service warrant which need not be made public, he and all his effects had vanished for five days. He was secretly though officially flown to Texas and there held in a solitary cell, while being interrogated by FBI and INS agents. He and his belongings had disappeared from Manhattan off the face of the earth; there was no public disclosure of his arrest, his transfer to Texas 2,000 miles away, or his being held as a prisoner suspected of committing a capital crime. Since his rights as a criminal defendant were the same as those of any American citizen, something seemed to be drastically wrong.

This was his story in the draft of affidavit:

"On May 11, 1957, I registered at the Hotel Latham, 4 East 28th Street, Manhattan, New York City, under the name of Martin Collins. I rented Room 839 for $29 a week, which I paid every Saturday."

When the story of his arrest broke, reporters interviewed the manager of the Hotel Latham. He described Martin Collins as a "quiet, unobtrusive man who asked for little service." By the hotel's standards, Collins was a good tenant since he paid on time, made no demands and "was not known to have visitors." In fact, they hardly knew he was there, most of the time. This, of course, was Rudolf's forte: he was always just a face in a crowd, a name in a register, a silent figure in the majority legion who plod out their lives with uncomplaining, unobtrusive anonymity.

"Room 839 was on the eighth floor of the hotel and a small bathroom was attached. The room was approximately 10 feet wide and 13 feet deep. The furniture consisted of a double bed, a low chest of drawers, a small desk, two chairs and a folding baggage rack. A clothes closet, with a door, protruded into the room."

The room also had a small table beside the bed and, according to the FBI, it held a Hallicrafter short-wave radio. The aerial ran up the wall, across the ceiling into the bathroom and out the bathroom window.

"About 7:30 A.M. on Friday morning, June 21, there was a knock on my door which awakened me. The night had been warm and I was sleeping naked on top of the sheets.

"Without putting on any clothes, I opened the door a few inches to see who was there. Three men pushed their way in. They said they were 'agents of the FBI' and showed me identification cards in wallets. I assumed they were armed but I do not recall seeing any weapons displayed. They told me to sit down on the bed. Still naked, I sat back down on the bed.

"For the next five minutes the three men, who said their names were Phelan, Gamber and Blasco, talked to me. They said, 'We know all about you'; that they had been following me and knew all my 'agents.' They urged me to 'cooperate.' I told them I didn't know what they were talking about; I had a right not to talk and I did not wish to do so. After a while, I received permission to, and did, put on a pair of underwear shorts.

"Throughout the questioning they addressed me as 'Colonel,' although I never had used this title or any similar title in the United States."

Abel said that when they called him "Colonel" this was the tipoff that Hayhanen had turned him in, because he was the only one in the United States who knew he had that rank in Soviet secret intelligence.

The FBI agents then told Abel, "Colonel, we have received information concerning your involvement in espionage; we'd like you to cooperate. If you don't cooperate, you'll be under arrest before you leave this room." Had he "cooperated," one of the agents was to "call his immediate superior at the New York FBI office and report the degree of cooperation being exhibited by Collins." However, when Abel was most "uncooperative," they called in three Immigration Service officers who had been waiting outside the hotel room.

"By now," Abel said, "my room was overcrowded. The Immigration officers proceeded to search the premises. I assumed they had the right to do so. The search appeared to be conducted principally by the Immigration officers, but the FBI men remained throughout the search. They searched the clothes I had worn the night before which were piled on top of the bureau; they opened the clothes closet, searched the clothing hanging there and removed my suitcases, spreading their contents on the bed. All my belongings were removed, searched and then packed in my suitcases."

While his wardrobe was not new, it was adequate, and most of the unassuming clothes had been purchased in quality stores. It was part of his genius for masquerade that people should see him as "unobtrusive" or "nondescript." So, too, it was not frugality which made him a tenant of the small hotel. Money was not one of his problems. The Immigration officers were sure of it that morning when they found over $6,500 in cash in Room 839. In a brown wrapper inside a zippered briefcase, there was $4,000 in twenty-dollar bills. There was also $2,500 in fifties and twenties, a bankbook showing a balance of $1,386.22 at the East River Savings Bank, and a key to a safe-deposit box later found to hold $15,000 in cash.

Along with the money, the government agents found a birth certificate for Emil Robert Goldfus, showing he was born August 2, 1902, and one for Martin Collins, listing the date of birth as July 2, 1897. (When the FBI checked the New York City Department of Health records they learned Emil Robert Goldfus, a white male child, of 120 East 87th Street, died at the age of two months and seven days on October 9, 1903.) Among the other objects in the room were two photographs, with "Shirley and Morris" written on the back of one.

At a subsequent pretrial hearing one of the arresting Immigration officers testified, "While we were searching the alien's effects we came on a store bill in the name of Goldfus and asked who that was.

"'That's me,' Collins replied."

"After he was fully dressed," swore INS officer Farley, "I started to pack his belongings in his suitcases. The alien became displeased over the manner in which I was packing his things and asked permission to repack them himself. We gave him permission and he started to fold each item of clothing carefully and place them in his suitcases. He also placed his other belongings carefully in the suitcases.

"While he was packing, he at times would pick up objects which were lying about in the room and cast them into a wastebasket. By the time he finished packing, the wastebasket was about half filled with discarded items."

The Immigration officers said Abel left some small jars of painters' supplies on a windowsill and threw a handful of pencils, a couple of Kleenex packages, some wire, bits of paper and six books in the basket. (The books were *The Penguin Hazle, Nights of Love and Laughter, The Ribald Reader, A Time to Love and a Time to Die, Three Plays*, and *Paintings from the São Paulo Museum.*)

While Abel was repacking his things, he was being watched closely by Robert E. Schoenenberger, supervisory investigator for the Immigration Service. "At the completion of this packing," Schoenenberger testified, "he asked permission to repack one of the larger bags so he could transfer material from a camera case to this big bag.

"During the course of his repacking I saw him in the act of removing some papers from the bag and attempting to slip them inside the right sleeve of the jacket he was wearing. I reached down, pulled his hand up and took the three pieces of paper.

"Two of them were strips with but a few lines on them. They had Spanish words on them. One started out with the word 'Balmora.' The other started out with 'In.' It looked like 'In Mex.' I noticed the word 'Chihuahua' in the body of it. The other was a piece of paper like graph paper with number groups on it, five numbers in a group. I suppose there were eight lines, eight or ten lines."

When Abel resumed his story in his affidavit, he said, "At the end of about an hour, the Immigration officers told me to dress, took the packed suitcases and my other property and handcuffed me. Then they led me out of the room. Before leaving, at their request I authorized them to pay the rent through the day [June 21] and they said they would check me out of the hotel.

"We left the hotel by a rear door, entered a waiting sedan and drove to Immigration headquarters at 70 Columbus Avenue, Manhattan. I was fingerprinted, photographed and held there until approximately 4:30 P.M., when I was taken by car to an airport near Newark, New Jersey.

"At the airport I entered what appeared to be a special DC-3 in which I and two Immigration officers named Seely and Judge were the sole passengers. I asked them our destination and both stated they did not know. My handcuffs were removed while I was aboard the plane. The plane stopped once about five hours later and I believe that it was in Alabama."

(One of the Immigration investigators later told a reporter that when the plane began its descent, Abel looked out his window and asked, "What are we doing in Alabama?" They were about to land at Mobile and Abel explained he knew they were over Alabama because from the sun's position he had calculated the direction they were flying, time in the air and their probable speed.)

"At approximately 4:30 A.M. the next morning [Saturday, June 22] we arrived at what I learned to be Brownsville, Texas. Here I was rehandcuffed; we entered a waiting car which was accompanied by another car and we drove 60 miles to McAllen, Texas. There I was placed in solitary confinement in a cell within a Federal detention camp for aliens.

"After two hours' sleep I was given breakfast and at about 9 A.M. I was led to a room where I was questioned until mid-afternoon (with a break for lunch) by Seely and Judge. At the outset of this questioning I requested a lawyer but was told that this would be appropriate only at a later 'formal' proceeding."

Abel told us that the following day, Sunday, June 23, he was questioned all day. "FBI agents Gamber and Blasco questioned me," he said, "and, as a separate team, Immigration investigators Seely and Judge. The questioners worked in relays. I refused to say anything. I received lunch but except for the intermission, I was questioned steadily from approximately 10 A.M. until 4 P.M. [The government version differed only in minor details.]

"This same procedure was repeated on Monday, June 24. On Tuesday, June 25, I decided to state that my real name was Rudolf Ivanovich Abel; that I was a Russian citizen; that I had found a large sum of American money in a ruined blockhouse in Russia; that I then bought in Denmark a forged American passport and with this passport I entered the United States from Canada in 1948. They ended the questioning then and told me that I now could see a lawyer. That afternoon I obtained a lawyer in McAllen and he visited me.

"On June 27, I went before Immigration officials at a formal hearing in the detention camp. I was accompanied by counsel, Morris Atlas, Esq., of McAllen. I stated that my true name was Rudolf Ivanovich Abel; that I entered the country illegally from Canada; that while I lived here I had used the names 'Emil Gold-fus' and 'Martin Collins' at various times and places and that I was a citizen of the U.S.S.R."

In the Texas formal hearing, Abel also stated that he had never registered as an alien and therefore had violated the registration and address report requirement of the Immigration and Nationality Act. He gave his occupation as teacher, said he had attended elementary school from 1910 to 1916 and high school in Moscow from 1916 to 1920. He gave his father's name as Ivan Abel and said he was born in Moscow. He gave no indication whether his father was dead or alive or of his "present address." His mother's name, he said, was Karneeva Lubow and she was born in December—no year given—at Saratov, Russia. For his last native country address, he gave "Nikitsky Boulevard, Moscow." He said he had left there in May, 1948—nine years before.

"I was asked to state the country to which I wished to be deported," said Abel, "and I answered, 'The U.S.S.R.'"

A transcript of the deportation proceeding showed that in the middle of the hearing, Abel and his counsel took a 32-minute recess to confer. The counsel, Mr. Atlas, had been selected by Abel from a local directory and of course thought he was handling a routine deportation case. Thereafter Abel admitted to all allegations, including the charge that he had not furnished his address because he feared that "by so doing you would disclose your illegal presence in the United States."

"I admit that, too," he said and concluded his testimony by stating, "I would say I accept deportation."

Abel, continuing his affidavit story, explained that "for approximately three weeks thereafter I was questioned daily by various FBI agents. They stated over and over again that if I would 'cooperate' they would get me good food, liquor, an air-conditioned room in a Texas hotel, and they could assure me a $10,000-a-year job with another United States government agency. I refused to discuss such matters and at the end of three weeks I was no longer questioned.

"During my sixth week in McAllen jail, I was served by agent Phelan of the FBI, and another agent, with a criminal warrant for my arrest. I was told about but was not given a copy of an indictment dated August 7, 1957. Thereafter I was brought before a United States Commissioner, and waived extradition to New York."

The Government never denied Abel was questioned every day for three weeks by FBI agents and that they offered him food, liquor and an air-conditioned hotel room as barter for his cooperation. It simply said, "From June 27 until August 7, the day petitioner was indicted and removed to New York City, he remained in custody" at the McAllen detention center. Then events moved very swiftly for Abel, a man accustomed to cautious, deliberate movement. The extradition proceeding was in Edinburg, Texas, on August 7 before United States Commissioner J. C. Hall and lasted twenty minutes.

"Where'd you get that name?" Commissioner Hall wanted to know. "Abel is a popular name down here. There are a lot of Abels in South Texas and the Valley."

Abel grinned and replied, "It's originally from the German." What Colonel Abel did not tell J. C. Hall was that the name "Abel" had been used by other Soviet agents in other countries in other times.

The following day, Abel was flown up from Texas to answer the indictment and stand trial. He landed after dark in Newark but this time it was no secret. The airport was heavily guarded; local police and Federal agents were everywhere; the New York and New Jersey press were on hand.

To some, Abel looked tense. Others thought that for a spy, he was "loquacious." It seems that on the flight from Houston, the Colonel passed the time talking with a United States marshal. They compared living conditions in their respective countries.

"Some things," he had said, "they [the Russians] are short of but some things they have plenty of." He agreed with the marshal, Neil Matthews of Houston, that conditions in the United States were indeed good. He said he was impressed by the fact almost everyone had a refrigerator. This was not yet the case in Russia, he said.

Abel agreed, too, when Marshal Matthews said conditions between the two countries were not good. He said he believed they could be improved, however, if more people in each country spoke the other's language. The Colonel said this would lead to a better understanding.

In our Federal courthouse conference to prepare the affidavit, I kept going back to that room in the Hotel Latham. After Abel had been taken into custody that morning, the FBI had returned and found letters from his family in Russian; microfilm; a partially encoded message which he was preparing to send; a hollowed-out pencil to be used to carry microfilm; and a piece of ebony which he had hollowed out and which held a complete 250-page cryptographic code in Russian. The pencil and the block of ebony had been tossed into the wastebasket.

The bits of paper included three addresses (one in Austria and two in Russia), as well as some instructions to go to Mexico City and meet an agent at a certain address.

"It's incredible," I said. "You violated most of the basic rules of espionage with all that paraphernalia lying about."

Abel's sole defense was "I tried to get rid of everything." However, he realized that I knew his disregard for basic rules had been his undoing.

Hayhanen never should have known where Abel lived and worked. Soviet intelligence agents have always been devoted to an exaggerated security and the inviolate rule that subagents remain ignorant of their superiors' names, addresses and "cover legends." Yet Abel admitted to me that Hayhanen had seen his Fulton Street studio—just once. He had taken Hayhanen up to his room to give him an "extra" short-wave radio he kept in his storeroom and some photographic supplies. He was anxious that Hayhanen open a photographer's shop in Newark, New Jersey, for a cover.

It was said of the Colonel that he lived his whole life as though his first mistake would be his last. Perhaps that is the way it happened. He said of Hayhanen, "I couldn't believe he was so stupid, such an incompetent. I kept thinking he couldn't be this bad, they never would have sent him. I was sure it was part of his 'legend,' that he was preparing to become a double agent and go to work for the FBI as a 'defector.'"

One other thing still bothered me about the case—the reference in the indictment to Salida, Colorado. Abel said Salida was believed by the Soviet to be the home of an American soldier named Rhodes who served on the American Embassy staff in Moscow from 1951 to 1953. The Russians had found Rhodes with a Russian woman, in what Abel described as a "compromising situation," and in turn for not exposing him they persuaded Rhodes to give them secret information smuggled out of the Embassy.

After Rhodes's tour of duty in Moscow was over and he was sent home, Abel was asked to locate him. Rhodes's last known address had been in Salida, so Abel sent Hayhanen to find the sergeant. Abel said that they never found him and when he asked "home" for further instructions, the query went unanswered. This, Abel said, was the only episode he knew which would relate to the charge in the indictment that read, "attempting to subvert members of the Armed Forces."

The Colonel also declared that he had no connection with espionage in atomic energy. He said it was his own intellectual curiosity that had led him to buy a book in a public bookstore about the "use of atomic energy in industrial power plants." He told us that his sole mission in the United States was to obtain general information—information of a non-military nature. I looked at him quizzically but did not probe.

This seemed like a good point at which to end the conference. We had been sitting and talking better than two hours. Abel was led down the hall by two deputy marshals, and his defense counsel walked out into the heat of the Brooklyn day.

Sunday, September 1

Although it was Sunday, we held a "staff" meeting. Tom Harnett of our firm, experienced in Federal litigation, consented to sit in. We discussed possible maneuvers. First and foremost, we agreed, was a motion for adjournment of the trial—until at least October 16. The trial opening had been marked down for September 16, only two weeks away. This was an impossible date, we thought, if a reasonable defense was to be prepared.

More routinely, we decided to demand a list of Government witnesses, the panel of possible jurors and a bill of particulars detailing the charges. Since the newspapers had pictured Hayhanen as the key Government witness, we would apply to interview him, once we found his name on the witness list. If we were successful, then we would ask to look at the grand jury minutes of his testimony and the FBI reports on the case. These could show prior inconsistent statements, helpful for cross-examination.

It was agreed that we should seek an early conference with the United States Attorney on these matters and try to determine whether it was definite, as we had heard, that Judge Mortimer W.

Byers would preside at the trial. The court clerk who tipped us off to this possibility had added, with a knowing look, "He's one who wouldn't hesitate to put on the black cap."

While I had never argued before him, I knew Judge Byers to be highly regarded as an independent thinker. He was eighty-one, tall, erect and quick. Byers would be best remembered by the public as the judge who had presided over the Duquesne "Nazi spy" trial in 1941, which involved an espionage ring operating a clandestine radio on Long Island. He had sentenced fourteen Nazi agents to long prison terms and taken guilty pleas from nineteen others in a mass trial.

The judge and I had never been personal friends but did meet occasionally as fellow members of one of Brooklyn's oldest societies, the Rembrandt Club. This small stag group met once each month during the winter, at the homes of members, and we had a cultural lecture followed by a light champagne supper. It was black tie and most enjoyable in a reserved way.

That night I talked about Hayhanen with a former New York City lieutenant of detectives, Ed Farrell, who lived in Bay Ridge. I explained how important it was to the defense that we build a dossier on "Maki" but that we must do it without tipping our hand to the Government. I impressed on Ed the fact that Hayhanen's cover name "Maki" was, for the moment, an official "secret" undisclosed to the defense by the prosecution.

I was told that "Finntown," where Abel had said Hayhanen used to spend a great deal of time, had many respected residents but also, late at night, could be a very tough neighborhood. Ed said, "It's popular with Finnish seamen and some of them when drunk would kill you as soon as look at you." He advised against my personally looking for the trail of "Maki" in the haunts of "Finntown." He said that he would make discreet inquiries, through local precinct detectives and the owner of a "Finntown" tavern whom he knew to be well-informed since the man was also the neighborhood bookie.

I deputized Ed as the Colonel's minister without portfolio to all of "Finntown," thinking to myself that the case was getting stranger by the hour.

I returned home to find Mary annoyed and upset. A woman at the golf club had cattily asked her whether her husband "has always been interested in left-wing causes."

From the first day of the Abel assignment, I had to put up regularly with everything from open hostility to so-called banter, some good-natured and the rest not so well-intentioned. One lower-court judge, with uncertain motivation, introduced me to strangers at a cocktail party as the "last of the Commie millionaires." I told him this was about as sound as his legal opinions. Another alleged wit joshed me for half an hour one night because I had ordered Russian dressing for my salad.

The first snide outburst had come after my initial meeting with Abel. In answer to a question, I told newsmen that he was concerned for his paintings and that I had assured him I would take care of them myself, if need be. There were more than fifty canvases and I meant to place them in the basement storeroom of our apartment building. Someone misunderstood and a newspaper story came out that I planned to hang the paintings in my living room.

The next thing I knew, Mary called from Lake Placid to say several women had asked, "Is Jim losing his mind? Why would you hang a Russian spy's paintings on your living room walls?" Stupid, but annoying.

Then there were the crackpot letters and phone calls. The letters were mostly emotional denunciations, only a couple threatening reprisals if I "went too far" in defending the Russian spy. I turned the latter over to the police. The phone calls were made by a sneakier breed. They mostly came in the middle of the night, when the house was dark and the family in bed. I would bolt up, wondering who it was and what the trouble could be. Most calls were from drunks, a few from fanatics.

At about 4 o'clock one morning the phone rang and before I was awake long enough to hang up, I was called an unusually choice selection of four-letter names and told I should take off for Russia "to join Hiss and the other Jewish traitors." That afternoon I had the telephone company disconnect the phone and put in an unlisted number until the case was over.

In a way, I was prepared for such nonsense, and I have a thick skin. But it bothered Mary, and even the children were forced to take a small dose during the trial. "My father says your father defends Communists," an eight-year-old told Mary Ellen in her parochial school. In the beginning, the children brought that sort of thing home. But I must say that after carefully explaining to them what my court assignment meant, they seemed satisfied.

One night at the Brooklyn Bar Association an elderly Catholic lawyer asked me, with deep emotion, if I didn't feel at times an "overwhelming sense of guilt." I was too shocked to make an adequate reply. If they bothered to reflect upon it, such people would realize that to become so emotionally involved in the morality of a client's cause is vanity. It is an exaggeration of the importance of an individual advocate's role. The advocate never makes a final judgment in a case. For that, our common law system of justice provides an impartial judge and jury. We advocates fight hard for our clients' causes but should have the humility to believe that it is our system of jurisprudence which produces just determinations. "Que sais-je?" said Montaigne.

These slurs, letters and phone calls may seem trivial, but I confess that sometimes I lost my patience and, more important, my sense of humor.

Monday, September 2

I devoted the morning to a further study of the indictment. It was important to remember that only the first count carried the death penalty and this would depend on proof that Abel had actually conspired to transmit information to Russia. Abel had stated they had no such proof, and perhaps the Government's case on this would be shaky. The second count charged merely a conspiracy to gather information, with no mention of transmission. If only the latter were borne out at the trial, we could move for a directed acquittal on the first count and, if successful, save the Colonel's life.

Later in the day, I read most of a new book called *Labyrinth*, by Walter Schellenberg, chief of Adolf Hitler's counterespionage service. Schellenberg, whom I knew when he testified at the Nuremberg Trials, made an interesting point. He mentioned that in his personal interrogation of an "unbreakable" (though tortured) Polish espionage agent, he found that once the man realized they were both "in the same profession" he talked quite freely to Schellenberg about espionage techniques. This was true even though the man knew he was scheduled for execution.

That was exactly what I found. The fact that I had a wartime background in espionage apparently led Abel to regard me as a sort of retired spy who could appreciate his professional predicament. However, I also believe he had satisfied himself that I honestly intended to do my best in his behalf.

Tuesday, September 3

This was a lost day. Time was precious and so it was painful to be frustrated at every turn. We had taken over a room in the Brooklyn Bar Association building on Remsen Street in downtown Brooklyn. This brought us close to the Federal courthouse and took us away from our own law offices, where too often we were interrupted.

First, we tried to have a private phone installed immediately in our Bar Association office. We failed; a long list of applicants were before us. Then we tried to reach United States Attorney Moore and Judge Abruzzo to discuss our contemplated motions. Again we failed; both men were out of town. Third, we tried to enlist another "volunteer" defense lawyer. No luck.

In most firms we were told, "With so many men still on vacation, we're shorthanded ourselves." Another favorite was "We're not certain the firm's clients would want us to lend our name to such a defense, though we have a professional sympathy with your position."

The only bright note in the whole day was Rudolf's new suit and other clothes. The alterations to the trousers had been made and I had the outfit delivered to him. He now should look as well-dressed as the warden.

I decided that my nerves needed a change of pace. In the evening I took Mary to the landmark Lundy's Restaurant in Sheepshead Bay, where I had my favorite bucket of steamed clams and a broiled lobster. We came home and watched a George Raft gangster movie on TV.

Wednesday, September 4

In the morning we met with United States Attorney Moore and told him the preliminary motions we had planned, stressing of course the importance of postponing the trial date. He agreed to an adjournment of two weeks, subject to approval in Washington. He also agreed that if in two weeks we were still not ready, he would consent to two additional weeks.

After leaving the United States Attorney's office, we met again with Abel in another part of the courthouse. He was wearing his new suit and looked entirely different in "banker's gray," a white shirt and his conservative Ivy League striped tie. He was smiling quite affably when he stood up to greet us.

We got right down to the day's business, which was Hayhanen. In answer to my questions, Abel gave us a complete physical description of the accomplice: "about thirty-five . . . five feet eight, around a hundred and seventy-five pounds . . . a husky build . . . fair-complexioned with a full head of light brown hair . . . thin lips and a square jaw . . . light grayish-blue eyes. . . ."

Abel said Hayhanen had stayed in a number of inexpensive hotels in Manhattan, lived in Brooklyn (in "Finntown") off and on, and early in 1955 moved to Newark, New Jersey, where he rented a vacant store with living quarters in the rear. Abel could not remember the address but, under our questioning, said he knew that the shop had once been a five-and-ten-cent store; that a No. 8 Newark bus passed by; and a bar which featured a Polish accordion player was around the corner. Abel also remembered that Hayhanen had belonged to a Finnish social club when he lived in Brooklyn. I made notes on this potpourri of information, hoping that one clue would help our planned investigation.

Abel felt certain Hayhanen had made a deal with the FBI and then gone to Europe, under their direction, to build the story of his "defection." He believed this because he had learned that in January or February Hayhanen had an automobile accident and was taken to a Newark hospital. He had had over $1,000 in cash in his pockets, and when police searched his home they had found a short-wave radio receiver among his things. The Colonel said someone must have put two and two together.

Abel told us that Hayhanen was always strangely short of cash and he repeatedly had to advance money to his assistant. Previously he had told us that Hayhanen was a heavy vodka drinker. Abel thought Hayhanen had realized he was making a bad job of it and had been afraid to "go home." In this regard, Abel said Hayhanen had been foolish. "He had nothing to fear," he said. "His only punishment would have been a demotion."

My own conclusion, which I thought unnecessary to express to Abel, was that whatever his other failings, Hayhanen was not a dope when it came to self-preservation. He had undoubtedly realized that when Abel urged him to go home for a "vacation" he would take his rest cure somewhere in Siberia.

Going back over ground we had previously covered, Abel again denied he had ever arranged to transmit information by radio out of the United States. This would have been, he pointed out, "dangerous and unnecessary." He also denied that he was ever instructed to steal atomic secrets. He said that in late 1954 or early 1955, he had refused an assignment having to do with Nike missile installations on the basis he did not have the background for the assignment; that he lacked the personnel with which to undertake such a mission; and that the best of the information sought was a matter of public knowledge through scientific magazines and newspapers such as *The New York Times.* He claimed he told Hayhanen of this decision.

With respect to the other paragraphs in the indictment, he denied he had ever personally received any "classified" information, explaining—with a good deal of emphasis—that his principal work in the United States was to report "general information" and to "establish contacts."

He said his trips to New Hyde Park, New York, and Hayhanen's trip to Quincy, Massachusetts, were for the purpose of determining whether "certain individuals" were in town. He and Hayhanen had visited Atlantic City one time, he said, to report on a public exhibition of objects reportedly injured by an atomic explosion.

He added that he knew of no proof the Government could have of his transmitting information to the Russians and that his sole connection to the indictment was the weblike charge of conspiracy. Hayhanen, he said, had directly transmitted some information to Russia. He declined to elaborate.

Friday, September 6

In the afternoon I met with Thomas M. Debevoise, a possible addition to our defense team. He was a graduate of Columbia Law School and served several years on the United States Attorney's staff here in Manhattan. He was from an old New York family, distinguished in the legal profession for generations.

Debevoise had an opportunity to practice in Woodstock, Vermont, his wife's home town, and was waiting to take the Vermont state bar exams. He was familiar with the details of the Abel case from the newspapers, and because of his interest was willing to work with us the next few months while drawing only enough to cover actual out-of-pocket expenses. I found Debevoise likable, willing, and possessing a great deal of common sense.

The three of us then reviewed the case at length and agreed that our newest member should immediately begin library research on the possible unconstitutionality of the arrest of Abel in Room 839 of the Hotel Latham on the morning of June 21.

Monday, September 9

I traveled to Atlantic City in the morning to lecture before an association of life insurance companies, on legal problems created by the recent development of civilian uses of atomic energy in the United States. The commitment had been made in the spring, long before the Abel assignment.

It was nearly 4 P.M. when my bus arrived back in New York and I hurried downtown to the office. I found my associates waiting for me and both were greatly excited. They were like two prosecutors who had just uncovered a cache of heroin or an eyewitness to a murder. They spoke at the same time, saying the same thing: The seizure of Abel and all his effects at the Hotel Latham unquestionably violated the United States Constitution.

If we were right, no evidence seized in the Hotel Latham or in the Fulton Street studio could be used in any criminal prosecution. Moreover, since a substantial part of this evidence had been placed before the grand jury, the indictment would have to be thrown out as based on "tainted evidence." In short, the Government's case against Abel would collapse.

We sat down and I acted as an examining magistrate, hearing each man on the law and asking questions. They held their ground. We went back over the facts and the case law many times. By now it was dark outside and from the windows of my office we could see, down below us, the lights framing the Brooklyn Bridge and the traffic moving up and down East River Drive. Across the river lay the Brooklyn Federal courthouse, the Fulton Street studio, and my home where dinner and family were growing cold.

I was finally compelled to agree with their conclusions.

Tuesday, September 10

I was up very early to rework a draft of an affadavit by Abel telling the detailed story of his arrest. I had begun it late the night before. This affidavit would be the basis of our motion to suppress all evidence seized from the Colonel.

I rewrote the story and chipped at it until it was lean and taut. The only adjectives described the weather on June 21 and the color of Abel's suitcases. The statement was based on everything Abel had told me, especially what he had had to say on Friday: "About 7:30 A.M. on Friday morning, June 21, there was a knock on my door which awakened me. The night had been warm. . . ."

When the story was put together in terse narrative, it became a Hemingway-like tale. Because the methods used by the Government trapped a suspected enemy agent, the average citizen would not become alarmed, nor be shocked. In such a case, he would feel, the end justifies the means. But under our law, the constitutional guarantees apply to every one of us as well as to a suspect like Abel.

The fact that government agents had seized in his home a person and all his property, without a criminal warrant of arrest or a public search warrant; secretly transported him to an alien detention camp in Texas and held him forty-seven days, the first five incommunicado—these facts appeared to be a classic example of the kind of thing the Fourth Amendment to the Constitution was designed to end in America.

The Fourth Amendment is the constitutional definition of a man's home as "his castle." It provides:

> The right of the people to be secure in their person, houses, papers, and effects, against unreasonable searches and seizures, shall not be violated, and no warrants shall issue, but upon probable cause, supported by oath or affirmation, and particularly describing the place to be searched and the persons or things to be seized.

Drafting Abel's affidavit and reflecting upon its intended consequences, I found myself with a mixed conscience on what had been done by the Government. Our counterintelligence must have a strong hand but without sacrificing our constitutional rights and traditional liberties.

If there were substantial grounds to believe that Abel, an alien illegally in the country, was an important Soviet spy, it would not disturb me if he were picked up on a deportation warrant; were kept incommunicado for a proper time; and if he then refused to "cooperate," were kicked across the Mexican border. However, having gone down the secret counterintelligence road without public arrest or search warrants, on the deliberate gamble that Abel would eventually "cooperate," the Government could not, after its gamble failed, ignore everything that had gone before and attempt to convict Abel of a capital crime in open court in the United States. This would be paying only lip service to our "due process of law."

The two roads—the one marked "Secret" and the other reading "Due Process"—lead in very different directions.

I believed that we had uncovered the most important point that could be raised in Abel's defense. The principle was vivid to me because of a crucial argument advanced by Maj. Gen. "Wild Bill" Donovan in early 1945. President Roosevelt had asked him then to propose a postwar plan for a central intelligence agency, to carry on after our OSS was disbanded. When General Donovan directed me, as his general counsel, to draft such a plan, he repeatedly stressed the necessary differences between secret intelligence and counterintelligence on an international level and the constitutional bounds of domestic law enforcement within the United States. He believed that any attempted unification of such powers in a single government agency would be dangerous in a democracy, since the temptation to "efficient" methods of investigation inevitably leads to creating a Gestapo.

When the draft of Abel's affidavit had been properly molded, I took it to the Federal house of detention in New York and showed it to the Colonel, asking him to test it against his memory. I explained the search-and-seizure point as a matter of law, and then impressed upon him the importance of his meticulously remembering and relating every true detail. I warned him that the Government would level its best firepower on our papers, and if they were exaggerated or false in any aspect, it could be fatal to this motion and any possible appeal on constitutional grounds.

We went over what I had written, line by line. Abel, looking his professorial best in rimless glasses, listened intently and nodded in silent assent.

The draft described how the Colonel dropped out of sight from the Hotel Latham and was held in Texas, where he was questioned nearly every day for a month and was promised a profitable "deal" by the FBI if he "cooperated." It concluded:

> My court-assigned counsel have discussed with me the search and seizure of my property on June 21 at the Hotel Latham and have explained to me what they consider to be the applicable provisions of law. I have instructed them to institute whatever legal proceedings are appropriate in this respect and to assert any rights which I may possess under the Constitution and laws of the United States.

I left Abel a copy of the affidavit, telling him to give it some hard thought while we continued to polish it.

Late that afternoon two lawyers were in my office and I read them the draft of the affidavit tentatively approved by Abel. To my amazement, one of the lawyers denounced the entire document and said that to present such "lurid" material in open court would smear the FBI.

With this opening shot, he then added in a rude way, "If I were you, I wouldn't be that interested in saving the son-of-a-bitch's life. Let him take what's coming to him."

To be sure, this touched off what lawyers call a "strenuous argument." I quickly explained I had no desire to "smear" the FBI and that I held a high regard for the Bureau's efficiency as law enforcement officers. However, having been assigned to defend Colonel Abel, it was my duty to present his strongest arguments to the court. "To deliberately pull a punch or soften the impact of this point," I said, "would be, to my way of thinking, unethical." I pointed out that Abel was about to stand trial for his life and if I should knowingly give him anything but my best efforts, it would be I who was deserving of the "son-of-a-bitch" epithet.

We broke up very late in the evening, but there was no convincing the voluble dissenter.

Wednesday, September 11

Tuesday's argument over the affidavit was still gnawing at me and I asked John Walsh, a senior member of our firm, to have lunch. An experienced lawyer of integrity, he was also known among his friends as a political conservative who regarded the late Sen. Robert Taft as "too liberal" in many respects. I thought he would be an ideal man to consult on such a matter of conscience.

Over coffee I told John my predicament, showed him Abel's affidavit and said I would appreciate his opinion.

He carefully read the draft, then said, "If this is an accurate recital of Abel's story, it's your duty to present it to the court as best you can—even if you don't personally believe that it's true. If you fail to present the point, or don't use your best efforts in presenting it, you should be disbarred. And that is how I would rule if I sat on an ethics committee and the case came before me."

This unqualified opinion of a trusted friend greatly relieved me.

Thursday, September 12

Our search-and-seizure papers were being drawn as a civil proceeding, independent of the criminal case, and since the property had been seized in Manhattan we believed that we were required to bring our suit there in the Southern District of New York. Abel was to be tried, of course, in the Eastern District of New York, which consists of Brooklyn, Staten Island and all Long Island. However, by commencing the action in Manhattan, we could gain the advantage of the right to an immediate appeal in the event the District Court ruled against us. This might avoid a trial. If we brought the action in Brooklyn as part of the criminal case, it was doubtful whether we could appeal until after a jury verdict was returned and judgment entered. Such procedural considerations are always important in litigation.

To avoid any possible suggestion that through our motion we sought to "smear" the FBI, I wrote into the final draft this sentence: "From the time of my arrest to the time of my indictment, physical violence was never used or threatened." Then I sent my associates up to the jail to get Abel to sign the affidavit. He refused.

"As it is now written," he said, "it's untrue." Then he told of a long, hot day in Texas when one of his interrogators, whom he identified, became exasperated and "lost his temper." Abel said the agent cuffed him across the face and, as he put it, "the blow knocked my glasses to the floor."

The Colonel and I had been together in conferences for over ten hours. We had talked principally of the case: his arrest, his betrayer, his conduct under questioning, his future, our defense. He had never mentioned this Texas incident, and I feel certain he had no intention of ever bringing it up. His self-respect, I suppose, would not permit him to whine over a single slap in the face, and as a professional soldier serving a totalitarian government, perhaps he expected to undergo really rough handling. Furthermore, correct as the behavior of his interrogators had been throughout his imprisonment, they were only human and the one slap seemed trivial; on a hot afternoon in Texas, maybe he deserved it.

However, his disciplined regard for absolute truth in reporting facts was such that he could not approve a single misstatement. This dedication to accuracy, I was to learn, was deeply a part of his character as well as his profession. He had, after all, earned his livelihood by writing reports, and his rewards were predicated on their precise truth. Many months later he lectured me from Atlanta Penitentiary, in a letter on the necessity for accuracy in intelligence work, saying:

> As a lawyer you know how difficult it is to obtain a true picture from evidence given even by an eyewitness to an occurrence. How much more difficult it is to evaluate political situations, when the sources are human beings with their own backgrounds and political opinions unconsciously coloring their factual reports!

So the affidavit was returned to me unsigned. I went to the jail and argued unsuccessfully that a single slap did not constitute "physical violence." The Colonel was adamant. He gave me a dictionary definition of violence: "physical force unlawfully exercised." We finally agreed that the questioned sentence be omitted, as not material to the search-and-seizure proceeding.

Friday, September 13

I worked the entire day on legal papers to support our attempt to suppress the evidence seized at the Hotel Latham and in Fulton Street. These included the final corrected draft of Abel's affidavit. Late that afternoon Abel signed it and it was notarized by a prison official.

It was nearly 10 P.M. when I finished and rushed home to Brooklyn, omitting dinner because I had scheduled a small, informal "background" press conference at my apartment. I briefed the half-dozen reporters present and carefully explained the motion papers to be filed the following morning. The reporters seemed genuinely interested, especially in Abel. They informally asked, "What makes him tick? What's he like?" They also wanted complete sets of our new papers. I declined to give them out until they were filed in court but promised, for their convenience, to have a set delivered to each newspaper office as early as possible the next day.

It had been clear all along that Abel's position, and now his story, must be fully explained to the general public. The prosecution briefed the press on its every move; all national magazines carried lengthy accounts and photographs of the Government's "proof" of the guilt of the "master spy." When this crucial motion for the defense was filed, its significance must be understood by the public as well as lawyers. It should not appear that we were making an unimportant, harassing or frivolous motion—only a "maneuver" designed to stall off the inevitable.

I served drinks to the reporters and answered questions, well past midnight.

Saturday, September 14

In the morning Tom Debevoise filed our papers in Manhattan Federal Court in Foley Square. I waited for him outside the courthouse and then we drove to the newspaper offices; in each he dropped off a set of the documents. After this, Tom and I took off a few hours for a good lunch—and to get to know each other a little better.

Sunday, September 15

At 2 P.M. "the defense" gathered in my office to plot our course and to do a post-mortem on the Sunday morning papers. We were well pleased. The story was page one in the *Times* and the *Herald Tribune*; once past the tabloid headlines (ABEL CALLS FBI ACTS ILLEGAL, RED SPY SUSPECT ACCUSES FBI), the press treatment was, in our judgment, accurate and fair. The texts of our affidavits were quoted at length. All the papers carried Abel's version of the raid, the arrest, the flight to Texas and the FBI interrogation. They pointed out that if the defense should be successful the indictment would fall.

My own affidavit, supporting Abel's sworn narrative, explained that prior to June 21 the FBI had reliable information about a Soviet spy named Abel, believed to hold the high rank of colonel, and had kept him under secret surveillance—probably for a considerable time. They also knew he was living in Room 839 at the Hotel Latham, under the name of Martin Collins. I pointed out that the FBI agents were first to "push into" his room on the morning of the 21st.

My affidavit continued:

From June 21 to August 7, Abel was treated by the Justice Department, as a matter of law, as an alien illegally in the United States. Actually, however, it is evident that the Department believed that he had committed the capital crime of Russian espionage and this was the principal interest of the government in the man.

Such undoubtedly was considered to be in our national interest. Any person familiar with counter-espionage realizes that a defecting enemy agent can be of far greater value than one of our own operating agents. Not only is there the opportunity for our government to obtain complete information on the enemy's espionage apparatus but it can lead to such specifics as the names and locations of other enemy agents, the breaking of enemy ciphers, etc. Moreover, there can be the possibility of using such a man as a "double-agent" who, although believed by his original principals to be still working on their behalf, in reality is serving the other side.

However, the Constitution and laws of the United States are clear on the procedures which must be followed in order to arrest an individual and to search and seize property in his control or possession. In the instant case, for example, absent an indictment, the FBI, having reason to believe that a Russian spy was in room 839 at the Hotel Latham, would obtain a warrant for his arrest . . . charging him with espionage.

In the event the man was arrested in room 839, the law is clear that the agents could search the room and seize anything which could be considered as the instruments or means of committing espionage, the crime charged. The prisoner would then be taken before the nearest available U.S. Commissioner or Federal Judge "without unnecessary delay," where he would be entitled to consult counsel. He would then be remanded to Federal prison. In the event the agents wished to search room 839, in the absence of its occupant, they could have obtained a search warrant by complying with equally clear and precise procedure.

Sometime prior to June 21, 1957, the Department of Justice, believing Abel to be a spy, had to make a decision with respect to him. The FBI possesses the dual functions of a law enforcement agency and of a counterespionage arm of our national intelligence forces. The decision had to be as to whether:

(a) As law enforcement officers, they should arrest Abel on charges of espionage, conduct any lawful search and seizure, and follow all other procedures established under the Constitution and other laws of the United States; or

(b) As counter-espionage agents, fulfilling a national intelligence function, they should seize Abel, conceal his detention from his co-conspirators for the longest possible time, and meanwhile seek to induce him to come over to our side.

The election between the two alternate courses of action was made. While that election may have been prospectively in the best interest of the United States, it did not succeed. The government thereafter cannot pretend that such an election was not made, or attempt to pay lip service to due process of law.

The Fourth Amendment is clear. . . . The abuses before the Revolution which led to adoption of this Amendment are well known. Based on the facts in this case, it is the belief of your deponent that the Fourth and Fifth Amendments to the Constitution, as interpreted by the Supreme Court of the United States, have been violated.

Abel is an alien charged with the capital offense of Soviet espionage. It may seem anomalous that our Constitutional guarantees protect such a man. The unthinking may view America's conscientious adherence to the principles of a free society as an altruism so scrupulous that self-destruction must result. Yet our principles are engraved in the history and the law of the land. If the free world

64

is not faithful to its own moral code, there remains no society for which others may hunger.

We asked that a court hearing on the search-and-seizure issue be held the next week on September 23.

For immediate attention, though, were our so-called preliminary motions, to be argued the following day in Brooklyn. They concerned the all-important trial date, the list of government witnesses (especially one named Hayhanen), the prospective jurors and a bill of particulars spelling out the charges in the indictment.

We spent a few hours going over these matters and then broke up. I was home in good time and had a Sunday night roast-turkey dinner with the family. It was the first occasion, since my assignment twenty-seven days before, that we were all together. I actually felt like a husband and father again. Of course I had to answer a hundred questions, with twelve-year-old John asking grave ones about communism or criminal law and the girls wanting to know whether Abel really had a family in Russia.

We gathered around the piano after dinner and, with everyone contributing a line here and there, finally put together a song "Rudolf Ivanovich Abel" to the tune of "Rudolf, the Red-Nosed Reindeer." It went:

> Rudolf Ivanovich Abel
> Was a very happy spy,
> And wherever spies would gather
> They would say, "What a guy!"
>
> Then one dark and stormy night
> Came the FBI:
> "Rudolf, in our very sight
> You did dare to spy tonight!"
>
> Now Rudolf's days are over,
> But all other spies agree

> Rudolf Ivanovich Abel
> Will go down in history.

(Many weeks later, on a Saturday morning when my son John and I visited Abel in the West Street jail, we sang our ditty for him. He laughed with the understanding of a family man, but rather quickly changed the subject.)

After the family went to bed, I spent the night catching up on my diary, further reading on the case and preparing for our coming foray in court. It would be the first plunge in what, I was sure, would be icy judicial waters.

Monday, September 16

At 10:30 A.M. we appeared before Judge Byers in the United States Court House in Brooklyn. We sat across from a phalanx of Government attorneys headed by Assistant Attorney General Tompkins and including Kevin T. Maroney, James J. Featherstone and Anthony R. Palermo, all "special attorneys" of the Justice Department brought up from Washington for the Abel case.

When the Colonel was led into the courtroom, most heads turned his way. He made a neat, trim appearance in his new conservative suit. He quickly and quietly took his seat, and then gave strict attention to the calling of the calendar and to a few routine narcotics cases which preceded ours. Hardly anyone else paid the slightest attention.

When our case was called, I argued first for a realistic trial date. Originally, the trial was to have started on this day. I pointed out that while we wished for an early trial, we must have sufficient time for adequate defense preparation. The judge curtly said lawyers always wanted more time and he was setting the case down for trial September 26. He directed me to report our progress at that time. This would be just ten days. We sincerely believed that we needed a month for investigation and preparation.

Apparently, however, I was not the only party bothered over the trial date. In an off-the-record discussion at the bench, Cornelius W. Wickersham, Jr., the new acting United States Attorney (Leonard Moore had been appointed to a judgeship on the U.S. Court of Appeals, Second Circuit), pressed Judge Byers for a definite date. He explained he wanted to spare the Federal government any unnecessary expense and did not wish to call a large jury panel unless he was certain how long they would actually serve. (Federal jurors are paid the munificent sum of $6 a day.)

Judge Byers looked patiently at Wickersham. Then he said that "over a long and undistinguished career" he found he lacked the "gift of prophecy" and could tell only each day what then should happen. He suggested the United States Attorney return on September 26 and he too might learn more. He added, "I don't want to be bothered about the government's finance problems. If you need more money for this case, maybe you can check with the Department of Agriculture for some farm surplus money."

I argued next for a list of prosecution witnesses and prospective jurors. The number of Government witnesses was still its secret under the law, but I said that undoubtedly we would need a month to conduct a proper investigation into the list. Although the Government was required to give the list only "at least three days" before trial in a capital case, Judge Byers ordered that we be immediately supplied with the names.

I agreed to the Government's request that the name and address of one witness (presumably Hayhanen) be sealed when it was handed to me. Our request was denied, however, when I asked for a picture of this "secret" witness. The Government said it would arrange for me to have a meeting with him but on the ground of "security" it could not provide us with a photograph. To no avail I argued that if the witness had been serving in the Soviet secret intelligence service, as the Government claimed, the Russians obviously had photographs of him in their files. What harm, then, could be done by giving us one, when we needed it for investigation purposes? I got nowhere.

After the arguments, I talked briefly with Abel in the detention pen, asking him what he thought of my final search-and-seizure affidavit. He said it was excellent but singled out for criticism the concluding paragraph, which ended with this sentence: "If the free world is not faithful to its own moral code, there remains no society for which others may hunger."

"Too emotional," he said. In his best schoolteacher manner he added, "I would not expect so emotional a plea to be material in a legal matter of this nature."

"Rudolf," I said, "it's fortunate for you that you're not practicing law in the United States. If that is your idea on how to present a case effectively, you'd never make a dollar."

He thought this quite funny.

There was nothing funny about my talk, a few minutes later, with prosecutor Tompkins. He stopped me outside the courtroom to tell me there was a "new line of thinking" in the Department of Justice concerning the possible punishment the prosecution should demand. He explained there was a "division of opinion." One side felt it would be more in the government's interest to have Abel imprisoned for life, in the hope that someday he might talk. The second group, however, strongly believed that the Government should ask for the death penalty—not only as a deterrent to other Soviet agents, but in the hope that Abel might "crack" under the strain of having to face the electric chair. All who had reviewed the evidence, he told me, assumed a quick conviction.

I told Tompkins that at the moment we were intent on Abel's defense, and if our efforts were successful, any sentence planned for him would become academic. However, I added, if Abel should be convicted, the decision on the sentence to be recommended should not be made solely by the Justice Department. I suggested that the State Department and the Central Intelligence Agency, our overseas intelligence force, be consulted.

"It's possible," I said, "that the punishment given Abel might have an effect on how the Russians treat some of our own people. You should find out whether Russia has captured any American secret agents."

I also expressed a hope that all Federal agencies would now cooperate more harmoniously in the national interest than they had done during my years with the government in Washington during World War II. Tompkins said, "Amen."

Thursday, September 19

The prosecution, of course, was fighting our search-and-seizure procedure with every possible argument. It claimed our suit should have been brought in Brooklyn—not Manhattan—and asked the Southern District court to decline jurisdiction. Tompkins argued that the question should be part of the criminal proceeding in Brooklyn. He said in an affidavit, "This will make for more orderly judicial administration and avoid the possibility that issues raised by this motion will be brought up again at the trial."

If the Court ruled in favor of the Government and our matter were shunted to Brooklyn, we would lose all chance of an immediate appeal of an adverse ruling and would have to proceed to trial.

In the morning the Brooklyn bar celebrated the ancient and colorful Red Mass, marking the advent of a new court year. The church service, held annually in St. Charles Borromeo on Brooklyn Heights, is attended by great numbers of non-Catholics as well as lawyers of my own faith. Virtually the entire borough judiciary and Brooklyn's numerous bar members attend to pray together for a proper administration of justice through the coming year.

I arrived early and stood outside the church before we entered. It was reassuring that among friends who spoke about the Abel case, several made a point of expressing professional satisfaction that "every proper step" was being taken by the defense.

Retired Supreme Court Justice Peter P. Smith, a delightful gentleman past eighty, said he had carefully studied the newspaper reports of our search-and-seizure proceeding and thought we should win the legal point. He told me not to become upset over unpleasant incidents, since many "otherwise intelligent" people were hostile to a lawyer who defended an unpopular cause. He said he had some understanding of what I must be going through because long ago, by court assignment, he had once defended a notorious criminal in a widely publicized case.

"The man," he said, "was a safecracker. Just like you, I moved to suppress the prosecution's most vital evidence. I won. I kept them from presenting a whole safeload of documentary evidence and the man was freed.

"Do you know what? I was a young trustee of the Bay Ridge Savings Bank at the time. Most of the senior trustees didn't speak to me for weeks. They accused me of frustrating justice and a couple of them never did get over it."

I told Judge Smith the only real trouble I had was biting my tongue so I didn't lose my temper.

The afternoon and evening were given over to research and to drafting memoranda on the two separate questions to be argued Monday: (1) whether our proceeding should remain in the Southern District; (2) whether the Government had violated Abel's constitutional rights.

Friday, September 20

I spent nearly two hours with the Colonel in the Federal house of detention, reviewing a host of matters. I presented a list of my out-of-pocket expenses to date, which he approved after first carefully reviewing them. He then signed a letter to Judge Abruzzo requesting that I be reimbursed from his impounded funds.

He said that while he wanted no proper defense expense spared, he would appreciate it if he could be left with some funds since he would need them if he got "a ten- or fifteen-year sentence." I nodded, but said nothing. In view of my last conversation with Tompkins, what was there to say?

He asked me whether he could earn money in prison, and I

assured him that under our penal system he could earn all that he should need for personal necessities.

He said some of his fellow inmates had predicted that eventually he would be traded to Russia for an American agent. But he shook his head. "I doubt this will come to pass," he said, "because I don't believe my people have captured anyone of my rank from your side."

As I rose to leave, we encountered the amiable but efficient warden Alex Krimsky in the detention room. Abel seemed quite familiar with him and immediately asked whether he could get more books. He said, "For me, Warden, cell life is very tedious." The warden said he appreciated this fact and promised he would find more literature for him. I told Abel, in front of the warden, that I thought he would be interested in the book *Labyrinth* on German wartime counterespionage, by Schellenberg of Hitler's staff.

"Schellenberg claims," I said, "that at one time during the war the Germans had captured over fifty radio transmitters belonging to Russian agents, and turned them around to feed misleading military information back to Russia."

Krimsky laughed loudly but Abel quickly countered, "Did he tell how many of theirs we grabbed and did the same thing with?" Abel was said to have worked inside Germany during World War II.

After Abel returned to his cell I asked warden Krimsky, who had been most courteous, whether I might send Abel a copy of the Schellenberg book. He hesitated, saying it sounded like an espionage text, and told me there was a Bureau of Prisons rule forbidding inmates to read anything that might encourage them to return to the criminal activity in which they had been engaged.

Now it was my turn to laugh. A Soviet military officer with thirty years' service in secret intelligence, I said, was not likely to be led "astray" by something he read. At the same time, the chances of rehabilitating Abel were virtually nil. I finally persuaded the warden to see my viewpoint. He explained that the book must arrive at the prison in a fresh copy directly from the publisher. Then he asked me with genuine curiosity whether my conscience ever bothered me because I was Abel's lawyer. He said, "I couldn't go through your experience." I told him that we all were different and that my conscience had never felt better. He shrugged.

When I returned to the office, Debevoise had left word that the Government had that day turned over to us its list of witnesses. There were sixty-nine names on the roster, thirty-two of them being FBI special agents. Hayhanen and Army Sergeant Roy A. Rhodes appeared on the list.

Saturday, September 21

The defense worked the entire day. I drew up a new supplemental affidavit on our search-and-seizure point. I had found what appeared to be valuable support for our thesis that the FBI carried on secret searches for counterintelligence purposes, inadmissible in court as evidence, in addition to their law enforcement activities in strict compliance with statutes. An admission of such FBI "clandestine" searches would lend strong support to our contention that the Constitution had been violated.

I had come upon a particular nugget the night before while carefully rereading the best-selling *FBI Story* by Don Whitehead. A footnote in the book explained that in addition to investigations designed to uncover "legal evidence admissible in court," the FBI also conducted so-called "clandestine" probes for intelligence purposes. An example of this type of work, the book said, was when it was necessary to have access to the papers of "a suspected espionage agent." Since the factual accuracy of the book was attested to by FBI Director J. Edgar Hoover in a foreword, the statements would carry a ring of authenticity.

The *Daily News* on this day featured a story about a Brooklyn newsboy who had found a hollowed-out nickel "stuffed" with microfilm containing a cipher message. This was supposed to have given the FBI its first lead in "cracking the Soviet spy ring allegedly masterminded by Rudolf Ivanovich Abel." But the boy, who by now was seventeen, had found the coin four years earlier, and the story claimed the coin discovery had been kept secret in the interim while "local and Federal authorities spun a tight web around Abel." The newsboy was to be a Government witness. I made a note to ask Abel about this, but it sounded to me as though the prosecution was also spinning a little publicity out of that web.

Sunday, September 22

I spent the morning and part of the afternoon in preparation for the next day's argument in the Southern District. I worked at home and came out of the library just long enough to eat and to make sure the youngsters did their homework. Ever-patient Mary fended off casual visitors and some well-meaning friends, headed for Manhattan, who wanted to take me away from the case "for my own good."

Monday, September 23

In the morning we argued our motions in Manhattan before United States District Judge Sylvester J. Ryan, the chief judge of that court. When we were finished, he graciously complimented the defense on the volume of legal research we had done in the short time available. I found the compliments very disturbing; when a judge compliments you, it usually means you have lost.

After directing that a further memorandum covering a technical point of law be submitted by Thursday, Judge Ryan reserved decision on both motions.

At my suggestion, both prosecution and defense met at 3:30 in the afternoon in Judge Byers' chambers, to discuss informally the future of the case. For our part, we explained to the judge that we had been working day and night and in our best judgment would need until November 1 to prepare our defense adequately. In accordance with United States Attorney Moore's earlier promise, the prosecution did not object to such an adjournment.

Judge Byers said he would not consent to any such "delay in the proceedings" and intimated he expected us to go to trial on September 30, a week away.

"While I appreciate the diligence which defense counsel are exercising," he said, "I assure you that I can dispose of all your preliminary motions in short order."

Then, in a discursive mood, he expressed frankly but forcefully his views on the trend of recent Supreme Court decisions relating to both Communists and common criminals, remarking that in his judgment "they're making law enforcement almost impossible."

We left his chambers very much disturbed. However, I held to my original view that while the judge was a man of ultraconservative convictions, we would get a fair hearing of all our contentions.

Tuesday, September 24

My defense associates called early, and were furious as only young lawyers can be. After the session in chambers the day before, they were convinced that Judge Byers would send us to trial on Monday and that we must do something to head him off. They believed that if we were forced into a trial before we were fully prepared, it would constitute "reversible error" and the appellate courts would order a new trial. None of us wanted this to happen.

I suggested we unburden ourselves before Judge Abruzzo, who by assigning us to the defense had tied this millstone around our necks. The judge had repeatedly said that if ever we needed advice we should turn to him.

We sat down with Judge Abruzzo at 4:30 P.M. and explained our predicament. "In our view," we said, "forcing us to trial now would be an arbitrary action on the part of the Court. It might possibly be a violation of due process, and if this is so, it would be reversible error. Frankly, one trial is going to be more than enough for all concerned; we surely don't need two."

Judge Abruzzo said he sympathized with us but there was "a very important Government reason" that the case should be tried as soon as possible. If we would allow a jury to be picked, he was sure the Court would then give us any reasonable adjournment. He added, as an afterthought, that he couldn't discuss the Government reason for proceeding with the trial at once. (Many months later we learned that Hayhanen had been drinking heavily and had tried to back out on his promise to testify against Abel. Without his testimony, the Government would have had no provable case.)

"If we are to select a jury and then get an adjournment," I argued, "it will be highly prejudicial to the defense. Once the jury is picked, the trial has commenced. There'll be wide publicity, and the individual jurors will personally receive considerable public attention. You can't pick a jury and then turn them loose in Brooklyn neighborhoods for a month."

The judge said that he would take up the matter with Judge Byers.

Wednesday, September 25

On this day the defense hired a private investigator and put him on the trail of Reino Hayhanen, alias Eugene Maki. I met the "private eye" and we went over all areas of the case which would require investigation. I stressed our deep interest in Hayhanen, his checkered career, sordid background and his hard-drinking lady friend. Based on what Abel had told me, I suggested "the eye" begin looking in Newark.

"All you have to do," I said, "is find a bar with a Polish accordion player."

I told the investigator that we hoped to meet Hayhanen before the week was out and then would be able to supply a sketch or drawing of our man. For the time being, he would have to work along with the physical description and background material given us by Colonel Abel.

After leaving the investigator I struggled with an affidavit detailing the work we had done up to the moment and explaining all that remained to do. This catalogue of activity, we hoped, should convince any court that the trial must be adjourned to November 1. Despite the fact that such a recital was bound to irritate Judge Byers, we were agreed that in fairness to Abel it must be stated. This was the only way to get our story into the official court records.

On this day the Russians made a claim that they had captured an American "master spy" who, they said, was trained at "an intelligence center on a farm outside Washington." *The New York Times* man in Moscow reported that the American was arrested in Latvia, along with a Latvian assistant. The Soviet State Security Committee said the American agent had complete spy equipment: firearms, a radio transmitter, a Soviet bankroll and forms for making false documents.

I could not help but feel that the publication of such a story in the controlled Soviet press somehow tied in with my client.

Thursday, September 26

Judge Byers scheduled the Abel trial to open the following Thursday. He heard us out in open court and then declared our request for a November 1 date was "unreasonable." In his best tongue-in-cheek manner he said, "I understood that the defense was pressing for an early trial. Because of this, a panel of jurors has been called. . . ."

When I explained that our motion to suppress was still pending before Judge Ryan and we therefore could not go to trial next week, Tompkins said Judge Ryan was expected to hand down his decision the following day. Judge Byers called the entire search-and-seizure argument a minor point he could "dispose of quickly."

Abel was brought over from Detention Headquarters for the

proceeding and, as the papers noted, he followed the arguments keenly. He certainly was a good listener; one might even have concluded that he had made a career of it.

He and I met for an hour after the court session, and together we reviewed the Government's answering affidavits to our search-and-seizure motion. Abel read along without comment until he came to the statement: "In addition, petitioner was orally advised at the time of his arrest that he had a right to counsel." Putting his finger on the line, he said, "This is untrue. They never said that."

I also had him look over the Government's list of witnesses, and he said that Arlene Brown—the name was unfamiliar to us—was a married sister of Sgt. Roy Rhodes. This was the woman Hayhanen had telephoned while in Colorado, he said.

"The FBI knows all about Rhodes," Abel said. "One of the agents told me that, during the questioning in Texas. He said Rhodes confessed. They wanted to impress me with all their evidence."

"Were you impressed?" I asked curiously.

"Does it matter?" he answered.

We turned next to Hayhanen. Abel said that when I cross-examined "the rat"—and he seemed to be looking forward to this moment—I should "explore" all the factors that had led to Hayhanen's defection—his drinking, his blonde, his free spending and his penchant for being debt-ridden. Abel then told me a curious story to illustrate that Hayhanen and money could not stay together.

He said that in July, 1955, he "went away on a trip" (probably home to Russia on a leave) and left $5,000 in cash with Hayhanen. The money, he explained, was earmarked for a specific use, but he would not disclose to me what this was. When he returned, Hayhanen said he had taken care of the matter, but this turned out to be a lie.

"Hayhanen," said Abel, "probably kept the money for himself."

I questioned Abel then about the *Daily News* story of the newsboy and the nickel with the microfilm. He said he did not remember losing such a nickel. I knew Rudolf well enough by now to appreciate that if he had lost a hollowed-out nickel containing microfilm, he would have recalled his loss.

I did not tell him, but when the story appeared we suspected that the Government had "leaked" it to the *News* (2,400,000 daily readers) in an effort to find additional witnesses linking other hollowed-out coins and microfilm messages to Abel and Hayhanen. Tompkins, however, not only denied this but said he thought *we* had "leaked" it.

At any rate, Abel knew nothing of the hollowed-out coin and did not believe the microfilm was in his code. He explained that every agent had an individual cipher and its only other key lay in Moscow.

Now was the time, I thought, to tell my self-assured client how confident of a conviction the prosecution was. This morning one of their staff had confided to us that there were "important new developments" and added, with a significant look, that they might not have to use any of the evidence we claimed to have been illegally seized.

I told Abel all this with an explanation of its grave consequences. "It sounds to me," I said, "as though they have a surprise witness who will corroborate Hayhanen's story; someone whose testimony will prove difficult to impeach on cross-examination.

"Is there anyone else, perhaps an American," I asked, "who knew about your real work?"

When I had asked similar questions before, he had always dismissed them with a cavalier gesture. But now he became upset. He was pale and his hand shook. He put his cigarette down, for it only drew attention to his nervousness.

"In your own interest," I pressed, "so that we can give you the strongest possible defense, you must tell me."

He made out that he was thinking, but I had the impression he was not taxing his memory, that he was only determining what he should tell me about any such person.

"I believe there is just one man they might try to implicate," he said finally. "His name is Alan Winston."

Winston, he explained, was a young pseudo-intellectual who

was supposed to be studying for a graduate degree at a New York university. He described him further as the son of a wealthy textile manufacturer who had rebelled against his parents and their "bourgeois" way of life, which he considered to be decadent. However, I gathered, he still permitted them to support him.

Abel said that Winston and he had met in Central Park one day when they both happened to be sketching. They shared common interests in art, music, good food and became fast friends. They traveled together to concerts, movies, museums and restaurants. With a girl friend of Winston's, they often had dinner at his young friend's midtown apartment, with Abel choosing the wines and doing gourmet cooking.

The Colonel said he had tried once to turn this young critic of capitalism into cooperating "to allow all nations to share all knowledge," but Winston never gave a firm answer. His initial reaction, said Abel, was negative. Apparently, Abel never forced the issue and did not go into detail with Winston about Abel's own role in the apparatus. He trusted Winston nonetheless and even borrowed the use of his safe-deposit box in which to keep $15,000 in cash.

The Colonel's whole life, his very existence, was built on the rock of self-discipline and self-denial. But such a life is so desperately lonely that one must compromise by permitting himself the dangerous luxury of a few carefully chosen friends. In Abel's case, they were all of a type: young men, all artists and all with another common trait. They were not especially astute where practical politics and international affairs were concerned.

Winston and two other young artist friends, Burt Silverman and Dave Levine, fitted the Colonel's exacting specifications. And in his own way, Abel was a good older friend: kind, considerate and constant. I discovered an example of this shortly after I became Abel's lawyer.

After Abel was arrested, he wrote Levine from Texas, giving him a power of attorney to dispose of all his property in Brooklyn. A copy of these papers became part of the trial record. The letter to Levine reads:

I am writing this to you in the hope that you will see your way to help me in the disposal of whatever remains of mine. I have no specific desires except that you go through my paintings and pre-serve those you think worth keeping, until (if ever) I may be able to get them again.

I have no objection to having you keep and use any materials you may find useful for yourself or the other friends of mine. . . . If you find it possible to sell anything I would like you to pay yourself a sum that would repay you for your trouble.

Abel made no mention of his arrest or his whereabouts, nor did he explain the curious remark about reclaiming his paintings "if ever." The power of attorney, however, showed it was notarized in Hidalgo County, Texas. It was never used.

When Abel had finished telling me about Winston and their relationship, I told him that there seemed to be nothing in their friendship that would prove especially damaging to his defense. He assured me Winston was unaware of his true identity and believed only that Abel was a somewhat disenchanted rebel against society, living in an environment alien to his philosophy.

To change the subject, I asked him about his own background and his racial origin. He replied, "Pure Georgian." With obvious relish, he added that he frequently had been accepted as a Jew by Jewish people, a German by Germans, and a Pole by Poles. It was unnecessary for him to add that he had also passed as a Brook-lynite in Brooklyn.

"That's all well and good," I told him, "but to an Irish-American you don't look like someone baptized 'Martin Collins.'"

This drew a laugh and now he was himself again, safely beyond his previous loss of composure. He picked up the conversation, referring with great interest to the newspaper story from Mos-cow about the American "master spy" seized by the Russians. He explained that this could be a "feeler," with a view toward a possible exchange of prisoners, since announcements of this nature were most unusual in his country.

I said I seriously doubted this would be possible since the story described that the "American agent" was a Latvian national and had been arrested as soon as he set foot in Latvia. He could hardly be considered valuable to anyone and it did not appear to be a fair exchange for our government.

Abel wanted to argue the point. "But I am no longer of much value to my service," he said. "I can never again be used outside my country."

"That may be so," I said, "but your experience would make you extremely valuable in the equally important job of evaluating information received from abroad. You'll probably head up the North American desk at headquarters when you get back to Moscow."

He did not disagree with this, but he was not finished with his argument. He said with a smile, "The experience of this Latvian should make him of value to the United States. It would probably be very helpful to the CIA to know the mistakes he made."

I gave him some final quip on the subject and turned then to the next item on my agenda. I had deliberately held it back. I wanted to know now whether he wanted to plead guilty in any respect.

"A court attendant," I began, "told me that after watching Judge Byers this morning, and listening to his questions, he is convinced the judge is looking for some sign of whether you might plead guilty to any of the charges."

I explained that if, for example, he wanted to plead guilty to the second count of the indictment, conspiring to gather but not to transmit information, the maximum punishment would be ten years. If he pleaded to the third, five years.

"And I'm not so sure this would embarrass your government," I said. "After all, they've disclaimed any knowledge of you; they're not involved. You could have been doing all this on your own."

We talked around the subject for several minutes, and then Abel said he wanted to think more about it. He reminded me of the severe sentence given David Greenglass after he pleaded guilty to spying for the Rosenbergs. Greenglass received a fifteen-year prison term; Julius and Ethel Rosenberg, his brother-in-law and sister, were electrocuted June 19, 1953, after testimony by Greenglass helped to convict them. Abel said other prisoners had told him of the grim life Greenglass now lived in prison; other inmates would try to spit or even urinate on his food.

The Colonel added quickly, "Of course, a Russian is in an entirely different position than American Communists." There was contempt in his voice.

We parted, with agreement that he would give serious consideration to all aspects of the possibility of a guilty plea to one count of the indictment.

Friday, September 27

The prosecution called my office and said arrangements had been completed for us to inspect the "seized evidence" at FBI headquarters the next day at 10 A.M. Our date to interview Hayhanen was set for two o'clock the same afternoon.

Frankly, I felt, I would be surprised if Hayhanen gave us the time of day at our meeting. But we needed the interview, to learn something about what he was like and to make a sketch of him which would help our private investigator.

Saturday, September 28

At exactly 10 A.M. we entered the New York FBI headquarters at 69th Street and Third Avenue, and I pointed out to my associates another of the strange ironies in the case of Colonel Abel.

On October 13, 1953, Abel had stored a supply of tools and instruments, for which he had no day-to-day need, at the Lincoln Warehouse. By coincidence, this building had now become the recently renovated FBI headquarters. Some of the materials held by the Federal agency undoubtedly were once stored in this same building, but as the innocent property of an inconspicuous painter named Emil R. Goldfus.

The evidence compiled under the present FBI roof was formidable. It spread out before us in a long, well-lighted room like some giant smorgasbord, filling twenty-five tables. A fair description would be that it included complete equipment for an important espionage operation.

The FBI agents were very polite. We took our time, wandering from table to table and turning over each piece of evidence, inspecting the tag precisely identifying it. Small objects were neatly placed in cellophane wrappers.

First, we looked at the most incriminating of the evidence. This included: (1) hollowed-out screws, pencils, and other containers—including a shaving brush—which could, of course, hold microfilm messages; (2) microfilm letters to Abel from his wife and daughter in Russia and a microfilm schedule of future radio broadcasts from Russia; (3) a hollowed-out ebony block (the one we had discussed a few days earlier) which contained a complete set of cipher tables on extremely thin paper of a very unusual quality, like very thin silver foil. I gathered that the paper could be readily destroyed by an apprehended agent, perhaps by chewing and digesting.

The hollowed-out screws were ingenious. On the outside, they were old and rusty. By twisting them, you performed a certain magic. On the inside, new brass threads were in perfect working condition, and a simple and innocent screw became a watertight container for microfilm.

The exhibit also included a lathe and a great variety of ordinary tools, which undoubtedly were used in the making of screw-containers and other devices. Abel also possessed a complete photographic laboratory, with chemicals, and a good deal of expensive camera equipment. He was so expert that he could reduce messages to the size of a pinhead. Such "microdots," virtually impossible to discover, had been devised by German intelligence services during World War II.

There was one table for his library, which included a text on thermonuclear applications of atomic energy, a copy of Einstein on relativity (Abel read Einstein the way some people read Erle Stanley Gardner: for divertissement), several books on the history of art, and textbooks on mathematics and systems of statistics. There were also a score of maps, which seemed to be ordinary United States road maps with certain vicinities circled in pencil. However, the circled parts were major national defense areas.

Among his assorted papers were two bankbooks showing deposits and withdrawals in 1954 and 1955; matchbook covers with cipher notations on the insides; and one giving the rank, serial number and address of Alan Winston during the time he was in the army. Also, a woman named Gladys had sent Abel a postcard with a friendly message in July, 1954. For some reason, he had kept it.

As we made our way through the maze of evidence, I struck up a conversation with one of the FBI agents. He was from Ticonderoga in upstate New York, and as we talked we suddenly found that we had played semipro baseball against each other years ago, when I was a counselor in a boys' camp near his home town. After reviewing the mass of damning evidence, the conversation was a relief.

At noontime we went to lunch, and around the table in a local delicatessen we talked of the cumulative weight of the Government's evidence. None of it came as a total surprise; we had read about some in the papers, we had seen Government affidavits which included lists of much of the evidence; and, of course, Abel had described his belongings. Nevertheless, when the evidence was stretched out in bulk, this was something else again.

I said to my two associates, with rather strained humor, "I don't think our client has a good lawsuit for false arrest." Neither smiled.

At 1 p.m., we returned to the FBI headquarters and met James Featherstone, a young member of the prosecution team whom we had seen in court several times. He was to conduct us to our meeting with Hayhanen. He asked us to leave our car and ride with him; he was alone and was driving an unmarked Justice Department car with official plates.

We rode across Manhattan and then headed north up the West Side Highway, along the edge of the Hudson River. I sat in the front with Featherstone but no one said much. He gave his full attention to the driving and occasionally checked the rearview mirror. Probably we were being followed by FBI agents, I thought.

I pictured Abel and Hayhanen traveling this same road, on their way to Poughkeepsie or Bear Mountain, or to keep some other rendezvous.

We crossed the city line into Westchester County and before long reached the town of Elmsford. Here we turned west and picked up signs directing us toward the Tappan Zee Bridge, which spans the Hudson to link Tarrytown on the east bank with South Nyack on the west. After traveling only a short distance in this direction, we pulled off the road and into the parking lot of the Muffin Man, a roadside restaurant.

"If you'll wait here," said Featherstone, "I'll be right out. I just want to make a phone call."

The Government was being mysterious and supercautious, but I was not surprised. I really could not blame them. Hayhanen was a marked man; the KGB surely had put a price on his head and he was the Government's key witness. Without him, their case would be in bad shape.

When the young prosecutor returned, he said there would be a wait of fifteen minutes and suggested we all have a cup of coffee in the Muffin Man. It was fairly crowded inside; defense counsel took a table to one side and ordered our coffee, while Featherstone went about his business. Several men, wearing business suits and gray fedoras, spoke with the Government lawyer. It was fairly obvious that FBI special agents had infiltrated the Muffin Man.

After we had finished our coffee, Featherstone came over to the table and announced, "We can go on now." We followed him outside, and by the time we reached the curb another black sedan had drawn up. This one was steered by a powerfully built agent who, unless I miss my guess, had had a career as a tackle or fullback throughout his undergraduate days.

The driver was decidedly uncommunicative and never bothered to look our way, or even nod, as we climbed in. He immediately sped off in the direction of the Tappan Zee Bridge at a fast clip. Before we had traveled more than half a mile, he abruptly turned into a circular drive belonging to a tree nursery and swung back in the opposite direction. This course took us straight back to our old friend Muffin Man. We raced through its parking lot, out the other end and down a side road which ran parallel to the parkway in the general direction of New York City. We flew by a motel and then, just beyond it, pulled into a gas station. Before the attendant had a chance to reach us, we turned around and started back along the same road. We were, of course, headed for the restaurant once again. Turning to our grim driver, I asked as genially as I could, "Are we trying to lose the scent of the Muffin Man?"

There was no reply. The retired fullback instead suddenly spun the car into the parking lot of a motel. We got out and were led up to a second-floor room in one of the buildings. The door stood open, and inside, pacing the middle of the room, was Lt. Col. Reino Hayhanen, alias Maki. I recognized him from Abel's description. Outside there was a balcony where several large men, presumably FBI special agents, lounged around with a sort of "at ease" military nonchalance.

The room showed no sign of prior occupancy, except for a television set, which was playing loudly. Hayhanen must have been watching TV when we arrived and now he made no move either to turn it off or to sit down. It was plain that the room had been taken for this confrontation and no one here, with the exception of defense counsel, expected the interview to last very long.

"I principal witness for Government," Hayhanen said, breaking the first silence. "You Mark's lawyers and you can talk to me. But I have right not to talk with you and I will not talk until trial."

The speech was obviously rehearsed. His English was clear enough, but slowly recited with a heavy Baltic accent. I thought of Abel's professional impatience with his subagent for not spending more time among native Americans.

I wanted time to study him, so I ignored his little speech and began asking general questions. To all he repeated his stock answer, "I not talk with you until trial."

Abel had said he was five feet, eight inches tall and weighed 175 pounds. He was now very much heavier, over 225 pounds. He certainly was at least thirty-five, as Abel had said, perhaps even forty-five. He had pale blue eyes which shifted, and his black hair, combed straight back, was thinning. His teeth were very white and even. He had a receding hairline but his hair had been darkened by heavy dye. His black mustache and jet-black eyebrows also seemed to be colored by dye. He bore a remarkable resemblance to the ousted King of Egypt, Farouk.

His body had grown soft, but unquestionably it had once been powerful. He had broad, sloping shoulders and hard, muscular hands which shook throughout the entire time we were there. It was apparent that he was going through a personal hell on earth, probably aided by vodka, and it was no wonder the Government was anxious to go to trial. If I had been the prosecutor, I certainly would have worried about getting this man into the witness chair in open court.

"When were you arrested?" I asked, and this question rankled him.

"I never been arrested," he answered. "I just guarded, but I never arrested."

In the background, the large-screen television drama droned on. An old gangster movie was being rerun, and by a weird coincidence a mobster said, "I may be a criminal, but I'm entitled to a lawyer." The door to the motel room remained open and the burly guards patrolled outside.

To all questions about his background as a Soviet agent, Hayhanen said, "Why not ask Mark that question? He knows answer better than I do."

Another time he said loudly, as though for the guards to hear, "You ask Mark, he knows. He's gotten radio messages about me. He knows everything about me these last months."

Like many before him, Hayhanen was learning that the life of most "defectors" does not suddenly cease to be hell. When he had crossed the line, his old fears were replaced by new ones. He had escaped a hated life, but he had also left his family, his country, his past. Abel and his court-assigned counsel were reminders of what Hayhanen had left behind, the things he wanted to put out of his mind: guilt, doubts, fear. I knew many World War II turncoats. Accidents, drunkenness, so-called nervous breakdowns and suicides were prevalent in their ranks. The only ones who survived well had changed sides sincerely for moral motives.

Hayhanen finally said that it would be better for him and for "the Attorney General" if he did not say anything further. "I talk no more," he said. "You wasting your time here."

"As you wish," I said—and then smilingly, as I turned to go, "We'll see you on the witness stand."

Hayhanen smiled back, showing his white teeth. As the smile crossed his face, his whole body seemed to relax and he suddenly looked younger. He was relieved to be done with this incident.

On the ride back to the city, I made a careful sketch of Hayhanen's face. I drew him first as he had looked today; then underneath that version, I did another sketch removing the mustache and making his hair and eyebrows lighter.

The only mark on Hayhanen's face was a small scar on his right cheek. Inside the man, of course, was an open wound. Despite being well guarded, he lived in constant fear. What sort of witness he would make for the Government remained to be seen.

Sunday, Monday, September 29, 30

With the possibility of being forced to trial that week, I worked Sunday on an opening statement to the jury. It was not easy; the defense obviously had not much of a case on the facts. After eight or nine hours of drafting and redrafting, the opening had become terse and was pitched in a low key. Above all, the jury should be reminded that in this proceeding Soviet Russia would not be on trial for its crimes.

My associates meanwhile were working on questions to be asked the jury panel. In our state courts, opposing counsel directly question the prospective jurors, but in Federal Court the judge has the right to do the questioning. The lawyers, however, may submit questions in advance to the trial judge, and Judge Byers had indicated that he wished to follow this procedure.

I had been working in the office Monday afternoon, struggling with my opening statement, when to my amazement—and, I am sure, that of our switchboard operator—I received an unusual telephone call.

"Mr. Donovan, this is Rudolf," the voice said.

"Rudolf who?" I asked.

"Rudolf Abel."

I thought it was a practical joker friend, but it really was the Colonel on the phone. He explained that just as I had the privilege of phoning him on ten minutes' notice to Warden Krimsky, he could call me under the same arrangement. He said he was phoning because he was anxious to see me. As he put it, there were "important new points" which he wished to discuss with me. I told him I would visit him at the jail the next day.

Late in the afternoon, our private detective turned in his first report, and this, by far, was the most significant development of the day. The report was stamped "Confidential," ran to ten pages, and the only identifying marks on it were initials: "To: JBD" and "From: FFZ."

Using our basic data and my amateurish sketches, the investigator had traced Hayhanen—or Eugene Maki, as he was locally known—to 806 Bergen Street, Newark, a dilapidated three-story frame building. Hayhanen had lived there during 1955–56. He had answered a newspaper ad for the apartment and signed a three-year lease on March 29, 1955. About a year ago, he and his "wife" had moved away suddenly and quietly, leaving behind nothing except a broken lease.

Our man's report described the Bergen Street neighborhood as "lower class," explaining it was made up of small shops and tenements—part Negro, part white. Hayhanen's building, he said, was "shabbily maintained."

There were two local bars, but no Polish accordion player; perhaps he was a gypsy and had migrated. Hayhanen, according to neighborhood intelligence, had done his drinking at home, and this was considerable. His neighbors, who knew him as a somewhat mysterious and not desirable figure in the community, told how he had drunk heavily and littered the hallways of his building with beer and whiskey bottles. Naturally, he had attracted attention.

They knew Hayhanen in Dave's Barber Shop across the street, in the bakery at 808 Bergen, in Star Credit Company where he paid cash for an electric refrigerator, and in the dry cleaning store one house down. These are some of the things they knew, and told our investigator:

He drank heavily every day; he and his "beautiful blonde" wife fought often and sometimes violently; he beat her; he never worked but always had money for whiskey and a car; the police were called often but never took any action. He never let anybody in to see his place; he had covered the front windows with Glass Wax in a way which prevented anyone on the sidewalk from seeing inside.

His neighbors were inclined to overlook his drinking, but they were bitter about the way he treated his wife, described by everyone as a woman of exceptional beauty. One man, who said he would never treat her that way if she were his wife, said Hayhanen beat her "unmercifully."

"The screams coming from that place during the night were terrible," another said. "People were always calling the police. I called them myself one night but the cops couldn't get in, so they dropped it."

One account, relating how he forced his wife to suffer "indignities," went like this: he bought a loaf of bread one morning and then hurled it to the floor of the bakery, scattering the slices. He ordered his wife to her knees, to pick up the slices of bread. She did.

Hayhanen's wife, about thirty-five and known as "Hannah," spoke no English, and this might explain why she endured such physical punishment without ever appealing to neighbors or police for help.

On May 24, 1956, she apparently had taken enough. At 8:30 A.M., somebody phoned the police and the desk officer in the Sixth Precinct put out an alarm that a "casual" at 806 Bergen Street needed assistance. Sergeant Gavarny and Patrolman Kuehl investigated and in their official report said, "Eugene Maki, 36, accidentally cut his right leg while packing and suffered from loss of blood. He was removed to Martland Medical Center and treated by Dr. Kanther."

Sergeant Gavarny told our investigator he had found Hayhanen, or Maki, lying on a bed with his leg wrapped in a rough bandage to stop the bleeding. It was a deep cut which required three stitches to close. The officer said there was a large pool of blood in the front of the apartment and it ran through to the back. Some blood had splattered the walls. He remembered that the wife had stayed behind when the ambulance took the man to the hospital.

The policeman took Hayhanen's word for it: he was packing, was using a knife and slipped. They never asked what he was packing or where he was going, but they did remember seeing some cases of photographic equipment about and noted that there seemed to be little furniture in the apartment.

Hayhanen's neighbors, however, thought they knew better. And there was something else about Hayhanen that bothered them. "What's his business?" they asked each other. "Why does he keep the windows covered over? What's he need that big police dog for?"

A young woman who worked in the cleaning store claimed that when Hayhanen had taken the shop he said he intended to open a photography studio. But after he moved in, he became a recluse with his unfortunate spouse.

His car, too, came in for neighborhood attention. It would stand in the street day after day, but then for several weeks at a time it would not be seen. Even his home state was a mystery. He had told a bus inspector, who was stationed on a corner opposite his apartment, that he was "from Illinois and Indiana."

The remainder of our investigator's report was filled with bits and ends of information which all sleuths seek out to describe a man, to evaluate his standing in the community and to tell how he lives: Hayhanen sometimes paid his rent by check . . . he had a telephone . . . his wife was with him most of the time . . . the FBI had recently been over to the neighborhood and had talked with local police . . . he insured his car with the Lincoln Mutual Casualty Company on Washington Street . . . his mailbox looked as if it had been broken into at one time.

The report made it seem preposterous that such a man should be a lieutenant colonel in Soviet military intelligence, engaged in important undercover work. In a profession where one must be most circumspect, he had done all in his power to attract unfavorable attention. No wonder, I thought, that Abel had treated him as an inferior and questioned his real purpose in this country.

Tuesday, October 1

Abel and I spent two solid hours together in the morning. He was carrying three sheets of legal arguments, prepared by his "jailhouse counsel," when he came in. These, it developed, were the "important new points" he had mentioned in his surprise phone call. Several of the statements of law were supported with precise citations of authority.

For instance, the brief said: "Can two different crimes: 1) to collect and obtain, 2) to transmit and obtain, be supported by identical overt acts? See *Peterson* v. *U.S. Circuit Court of Appeals, Alaska*, 297 F 1002. Two separate and distinct crimes cannot be charged when such crimes are the result of the same acts or omissions."

"Where in the world," I asked, "did you get all this? Who gave you these detailed legal points?"

"Other prisoners," he said. "Other prisoners in maximum security. I told you I was getting good 'inside' information."

I read the memorandum carefully and considered its arguments for several minutes. The Colonel perhaps had been prepared to walk out of the house of detention this afternoon when, in reliance on his memo, I filed motion papers and made application for bail.

Using all the tact I could muster and with great deliberation, I began to explain that these were all good points, to be sure, and defense counsel had considered each one. Then I explained our reasoning in deciding not to take advantage of them.

Point: Make a motion forcing the Government to elect whether it will prosecute on the first or second counts of the indictment, because both charge the same overt acts.

Counterpoint: We believe such a motion would result in the Government's electing the first count, punishable by death. We are hopeful that if the Government's evidence on this count proves to be weak, we can plead with the jury for an acquittal on Count Number One. Count Number Two carries a maximum penalty of 10 years' imprisonment. In effect, we're depending on the jury to make the election—and to make the right one. This is better than our removing the alternative in advance.

The other ten points, each documented with legal authority, received similar analytical treatment. As always, Abel listened intently and patiently. When I had finished, he said he would abide by our judgment, which, as he had said repeatedly, he found sound and trusted implicitly.

I told Abel of our meeting the preceding Saturday with Hayhanen. He leaned forward and cupped his hand behind his right ear. This was his best listening position. Although he never said anything to me about it, some people thought he strained to hear and must be hard of hearing. It never seemed to affect his ability to deliver quick and intelligent answers to questions, provided he wanted to make a reply.

When I described how Hayhanen trembled and fought to keep his hands still, he said, "It's from his drinking. And then drinking only tends to accentuate his fear. Every coward drinks to forget his fears."

I showed him my sketch of Hayhanen and he nodded; but then

in a kindly way he suggested that I pull the eyes closer together. "If his eyes were that far apart," he said, "finding him would be rather simple."

Abel said that he had bided his time with Hayhanen, hoping that this bumbling misfit would "work out" or that his gross inadequacy was part of a more devious Soviet design meant to lead Hayhanen to the FBI in an assigned role of a triple agent. Abel's faith in the Soviet and its intelligence service would not permit him to believe the KGB had sent him so dangerous an incompetent.

Abel and I reviewed the evidence which the FBI had displayed to defense counsel on Saturday morning. Abel denied he had any instrument which would transmit a powerful radio signal. He said his signal generator was too weak for long-distance transmission, and I had to agree with him when he said the risk of detection would be too great to attempt to send messages from downtown Brooklyn, less than a mile from the Brooklyn Navy Yard.

As for the postcard signed "Gladys," the Colonel explained she was a friendly Negro entertainer; that he had loaned her money to help her along and made arty photographs of her for use in night-club advertising. He said he did not believe she could give "relevant testimony," for she knew him only as the photographer Emil Goldfus.

With their customary thoroughness, the FBI had located and questioned Gladys, and one of the prosecution team thereafter delighted in twitting me about Rudolf's girl friend, who he reported was not especially attractive and was unworthy of my scholarly client.

Wednesday, October 2

We carried an eleventh-hour appeal to Judge Byers to hold the trial over to November 1, so that we might adequately prepare.

"Your Honor," I said, "proper preparation of this defense really requires time. However, if prior to November 1 we believe in good faith that the trial can fairly begin, we will notify the Court and the prosecution."

"Mr. Donovan, I shall insist upon impaneling the jury tomorrow," the judge replied. "Then, if the defense needs more time, I will give any reasonable adjournment."

The judge was a man of great consistency. He had said all along that he would pick the jury on October 3 and then send them home; but I never quite allowed myself to believe he would make good on the threat. However, he was a man of his word—and that, in this instance, was law.

Tompkins and I had lunch together. We agreed the Government and the defense could certainly compromise on October 15 as a reasonable date for the selection of a jury. At my suggestion, we paid one more visit to Judge Byers. We found him in his chambers and most unyielding.

I told him that under these circumstances and with his declared attitude, "I feel obligated to go to the U.S. Court of Appeals and in an emergency session apply for an order against your opening the trial."

He seemed taken aback. "The Court of Appeals?" he asked. "To delay a trial date?"

This course of action struck him as highly unusual, he said, but it was my prerogative. He repeated his assurances that if a jury was impaneled tomorrow, he would listen to a request for additional time. My answer, equally adamant and unyielding, was that it did not seem right in a capital case of such importance to select a jury and then have them go about their business and social affairs in Brooklyn for ten days or more.

At 4 P.M. the highly unusual emergency session began before Chief Judge J. Edward Lumbard in the U.S. Court of Appeals, located in the United States Court House in Foley Square. The courtroom was hushed, for it was late in the day and we were the only ones in the deep and handsome chamber.

There was little to say that had not already been pleaded over and over. Tompkins said the Government was ready to go to trial, but would not oppose our request for any reasonable adjournment.

I repeated our contention that if we were forced to trial the next day there would be a denial of due process to Abel, because we simply had not been given the time to adequately prepare our case. I elaborated on the extensive papers we had filed and the time already spent in court, and I stressed the importance of our search-and-seizure motion, which at the moment was still undecided before Chief Judge Ryan of the District Court.

Near the end of the argument, a newspaperman passed a message to Prosecutor Tompkins, who interrupted to inform the Court that Judge Ryan had just handed down his decision. "In light of this development," Judge Lumbard said, "I now believe the entire matter must be left to the trial judge. I have every confidence that Judge Byers will handle this matter so as not to unduly prejudice the rights of the defendant."

We hurried out of court to learn details of Judge Ryan's decision. His opinion stated that we had properly brought the proceeding in New York, where Abel's belongings were seized, and he further recognized this as an independent civil action, separate from the criminal case. On the other hand, he continued, considering all the circumstances, he believed the proper exercise of his discretion called for him to dismiss the proceeding, with permission to bring a similar petition in the Eastern District.

Our procedure had been scuttled. There was not time to bring a new civil proceeding in Brooklyn, and we were forced to admit to ourselves that there seemed little hope of a reversal of Judge Ryan's ruling by an appellate court.

So many other matters remained for us to prepare, it now seemed best to ask Judge Byers in the morning to consider all the search-and-seizure papers as part of the criminal proceeding in Brooklyn, thus preserving our right to argue the point should there be an appeal.

Meanwhile, we decided to work that night, all night if necessary, to plan the position of the defense at the opening of trial the following morning.

We discussed the kind of jury we should seek. I reminded my colleagues that in this case "no matter who sits in the box, we must assume that we open with at least two strikes against us." However, there were special problems presented to those defending Colonel Abel.

In Brooklyn, the overwhelming percentage of a Federal jury panel is bound to be Jewish or Catholic. Ordinarily in defending any capital case I would seek as many Jewish jurors as possible. Their own history of persecution leads them to be basically sympathetic with an accused. Further, their historical sense of the need for a rule of law, equally applicable to all, impels them to set a man free unless his guilt is proven beyond a reasonable doubt.

However, Russia's recent cynical arming of the Arabs for probable aggression against Israel had disturbed the large and influential Jewish community in Brooklyn. Under these circumstances, there logically would be few people of the Jewish faith without a currently inflamed prejudice against any representative of the Soviet government. At least, the risk was too great.

As to Catholics, we felt they would approach such a case with a deep moral condemnation of communism and all its followers. By all means we must eliminate from the jury any Catholic extremists who would regard the trial as a prosecution of Soviet communism, rather than charges against an individual defendant for a specific offense under United States law.

We also agreed that as for Negro jurors, their racial problems in recent years, especially since the 1954 Supreme Court decision on integration, had so filled Negro minds and emotions that they would want every constitutional guarantee afforded to every man, however unpopular.

On the whole, we concluded that our object must be to judge each prospective juror as an individual American; but we must get as intelligent a jury as possible, since the benefit of any confusion of issues would seem to lie with the prosecution. This would be particularly so since our principal hope appeared to be that the jury might acquit Abel under Count Number One (conspir-

97

acy to *transmit* information, the only count with a penalty of death) even if it convicted him under the other two charges in the indictment.

"We've made headway," I said to my associates, "but what I told Rudolf the first day still holds true. We'll still need a miracle to save his life."

Thursday, October 3

You can drive from our home on Prospect Park West to the United States Court House, which faces a landscaped plaza in downtown Brooklyn, within fifteen minutes. When traffic is heavy along Flatbush Avenue and the side streets, it can take an hour. On this day it took a half hour, and as I entered the old courthouse I was glad I had arrived early. There were long lines of the curious outside the courtroom, which was already jammed by spectators. Oversolicitous guards searched all for weapons, as though they expected trial by combat.

"All rise." At exactly 10:30, the door behind the bench was pulled open by a blue-coated court attendant, and the tall, erect figure of Judge Byers strode in and mounted the high wooden bench.

Before we moved to the selection of the jury, I asked the judge to permit us to transfer our search-and-seizure papers from New York, explaining that Judge Ryan's decision suggested this arrangement. Judge Byers agreed, saying, "This Court will accept the papers and will entertain the motion as though it had originally been made in the Eastern District." He said he would reserve decision, explaining, "I want to study the papers."

Then he turned to the jury box, already filled with the first twelve veniremen. After asking a few preliminary questions, he said, "I am just going to tell you briefly what kind of a case this is. I shall not go into any great detail."

I wondered how many in this crowded courtroom, especially in the jury box, were ignorant of what "kind of a case" this was.

If they truly did not know, they did not own television sets, or read newspapers or news magazines, or speak to their Brooklyn neighbors.

"The indictment charges the defendant Abel with having been a party to three separate conspiracies," the judge continued. "A conspiracy is an agreement between two or more persons, and in order to be punishable it must be an agreement to violate the law. Sometimes, roughly and inaccurately, it is called a partnership. It is a joint enterprise. . . .

"Now, does any one of you object to sitting on a jury because it is a criminal case? Do you shrink from that kind of jury duty? Has any one of you in the past been connected with any government agency, Federal, state or city?"

Juror No. 1 (lifting his hand): I am presently a reserve Army officer.

Juror No. 10: About ten years ago I was a part-time postal employee.

Judge Byers: As to those of you who have had this government service, would the fact of the service create any prejudice in your mind that would interfere with your ability to fairly and impartially reach a verdict?

Juror No. 1: It would in my case, sir.

Judge Byers: You will be excused for cause.

Colonel Abel, neatly and conservatively dressed in his charcoal-gray suit and fashionably slender striped tie, was sitting behind me. From time to time, we spoke. Once or twice he heard something which caused him to smile. The newspapers described him as "dapper," "completely at ease," and one said he "exuded confidence . . . laughed and talked animatedly with his court-appointed counsel."

Judge Byers addressed the jury panel again and said, "Now, the defendant in this case is Rudolf Ivanovich Abel—is that the way you pronounce it?"

99

Abel: Yes, sir. [Rudolf smiled as he answered.]

Judge Byers: Do any of you know him?

[There was no response.]

Judge Byers: Have any of you read about him? Will you raise your hands, those who have read about him. Number one, five, six, number eight, number nine, number eleven.

Six of the twelve prospective jurors, half of those in the box, admitted to reading of the case.

"Has your reading," the judge was asking now, "whatever you have read, created any impression in your mind concerning the guilt or innocence of the defendant?"

Juror No. 6: I have.

Judge Byers: Number six, you have formed an impression?

Juror No. 6: An opinion.

Judge Byers: And that opinion would not yield to evidence?

Juror No. 6: I believe it would, sir. Yes.

[The juror, named Randall, had told the judge that he was a clerk.]

Judge Byers: Well, it is a pretty important thing and I must rely upon you pretty much.

Let me explain that in a criminal case the defendant is presumed to be innocent, and that presumption attaches to him from the opening of the trial until the jury shall return with a verdict.

In order to overcome that presumption of innocence, the burden of proof rests on the Government to establish guilt beyond a reasonable doubt. That is the kind of case it is.

Now, you say you have an opinion. You will have to tell me whether that opinion would yield to evidence, or whether that opinion would be given up by you if the Government failed to prove its case by the required margin of proof.

Juror No. 6: I believe if the evidence is showed one way or the other, I would be able to distinguish one way or the other, but I still have an opinion.

Judge Byers: It is important to bear in mind that the evidence to support any conviction must be supplied by the Government, and that it must establish guilt beyond a reasonable doubt.

Now, if the Government failed to prove such evidence, would this opinion that you say you have stand in your way of performing your duty as a juror fairly and impartially?

Juror No. 6: Well, I believe it would, sir.

Judge Byers: You will be excused.

The clerk called another name, and a man came forward and took the No. 6 position in the jury box. The judge, while the exchange was taking place, had asked each of the other jury candidates who admitted reading of the case whether they had formed an opinion. They said they had no opinion. Then he went on, asking the routine, mechanical questions. Did the jurors know any members of the prosecution? Any of the defense? Did any of their family work or seek work with the government? Did they know any judge or employee of the court?

Judge Byers next asked, "Would you be influenced by threatening letters, phone calls or other communications which might result from any publicity that you receive from having been chosen as a juror in this case?"

The courtroom fell perfectly silent at this moment. None of the jury stirred following this dramatic query. Then a woman juror raised her hand. The judge nodded to her.

"Is a sister-in-law included in the family?" she asked. "I just remember I have one in the government."

The judge, smiling, said, "That is sort of a difficult question. Some people do and some people do not include a sister-in-law in the family. Suppose you tell me what the facts are."

The woman said her sister-in-law was a clerk for the FBI, but she believed she could serve without prejudice despite the association.

"Listen carefully to this question," said Judge Byers. "As to each of you, is there a member of your family who now resides in the countries that are described as being behind the Iron Curtain?"

The judge read the names of the countries and then looked at each of the jurors. When there was no response, he said, "I understand by your silence that as to each of you there is no member of your family that is at present residing behind the Iron Curtain."

He took the question of capital punishment next, asking, "Are any of you opposed to capital punishment?

"Would your verdict be influenced in any way by the fact that the death penalty may be imposed against the defendant if he is found guilty under Count One of the indictment?"

There was no response from the jury box.

At our request, the judge asked these two questions: "Would you give greater weight to the testimony of a witness because the witness claimed to be a former Russian spy who is now aiding the United States government?

"Would the recent war in Korea or the present world situation affect your ability to give this defendant at this time a fair trial on the question of whether he is guilty as charged in the indictment?"

Now we were ready for questioning which could be the basis for the lawyers' challenges, either peremptory or for cause. All questions, the judge had ruled, must be asked through him.

When Fraiman once jumped up and addressed a question directly to a juror, the judge cut him down sharply. "I will ask the questions, as I told you yesterday," he said.

It was obvious, too, that he was not about to excuse any jurors for cause, at least not without a scrap. When I pointed out that Juror No. 12 was an employee of the Navy and therefore should be excused for cause, he said, "He's a civilian employee. . . . No, I won't excuse him for cause."

"The charge involves national defense, Your Honor."

Judge Byers replied, "He is a civilian employee. I will not excuse him for cause."

While the judge was loath to excuse jurors, they were equally reluctant to give up their places on the panel. For the most part, they gave answers least calculated to lead to challenge by either side. Being one of the "Abel jury" would be grist for the back fence, the bridge club or the neighborhood tavern. Also it was better than serving on another jury in a stolen-car case.

One white-haired woman was noticeably, suspiciously intent upon becoming a member of the jury. She said she had never heard of Abel or the case against him. She did not even have a prejudice against Communists. We tried to guess her motives. Finally, through the judge, we asked her if she had any children.

"I had an only boy who was killed in the service, and I have a daughter," she quietly said.

Not hearing the answer, Judge Byers asked, "You say you have a boy in service?"

"He was killed," she said again. "He was an airman killed by the Communists in Korea."

At our suggestion, the judge then asked, "Would the fact that you lost your son as you stated have an effect upon your judgment in this case?"

Juror No. 2 (emphatically): No, it wouldn't have any bearing.

The insistence on her clear conscience and her incredible lack of knowledge of Abel was so vigorous that the defense agreed she should be the first to be dismissed peremptorily without cause. The poor woman saw the trial as a way of evening the score, in her life. I had compassion for her in the tragic murder of her son by the Reds, but a United States courtroom during a capital trial is no place for inflamed emotion.

New panel members took seats in the box as the challenges were made; the same questioning was repeated. When the judge again asked about relatives in government service, one juror said, "My mother works for the post office in Hoboken."

John T. Dublynn, thirty-six, took his seat as Juror No. 1; said he worked for the city Department of Public Works ("operation and

103

maintenance of the sewage treatment and disposal plant in Rock-away Park"); and when the judge asked if he had read about the defendant he coolly answered, "Just a line that he was picked up or something."

> *Judge Byers:* That his case was coming up?
> *Mr. Dublynn:* No, just a line that he was picked up.
> *Judge Byers:* Now, have you formed any opinion?
> *Mr. Dublynn:* No.

The juror stared across the courtroom at Abel for his first close look at the accused master spy. What he saw surprised him, and months after the trial he told a reporter, "Why, he could be walking down the street and he could be anybody."

There were thirty-two challenges; eight other jurors were excused for cause, and at 3:15 P.M., after three and a half hours, the panel of twelve was satisfactory to both sides. The jury had been chosen in good time, without any bitter or prolonged exchange.

Mr. Dublynn was named jury foreman.

On the whole, the defense were agreed we had a reasonably intelligent jury and should be satisfied. We were keeping our fingers crossed on two of the panel: the civilian working in the Navy Yard and a Mrs. Kathryn McTague, whose husband was a civilian doctor at the Brooklyn Army Base.

After dinner we reviewed the day, did a full post-mortem on the jury and looked ahead. Tomorrow we would select four alternate jurors.

Friday, October 4

I woke early after a good night's sleep and ate a light breakfast, with the morning papers spread across the table. Mary again accused me of giving more time to Abel than to our family. She, of course, was right. I told her that she was not "on trial" but the minute she became a defendant charged with a capital crime I would immediately reverse the division of my time. She asked me how I could do that if I were the victim of her capital crime.

One of the tabloids reported that Hayhanen might not take the stand. "Reliable sources" said he was afraid to testify for fear of reprisals against his mother, two brothers and a sister still living in Russia. Tompkins, according to the story, refused to discuss his principal witness.

The court session that morning went quickly and smoothly. In thirty minutes we had chosen four alternate jurors: three men and a woman. The judge swore them in and then granted the defense an adjournment until a week from Monday, October 14. Before dismissing the jury, he instructed them to talk to no one about the case "and that means members of your family or anybody else.

"If any person attempts to speak with you about this case, please report that fact to the Court.

"Also, I hope you will avoid reading any comment that may appear. . . . Your duties, as the jury in this case, will be to keep open minds and in order that you may do that, I am suggesting that no precaution to that end be omitted."

Because the Government had filed three new affidavits referring to our search-and-seizure motion, and they seemed to contradict our version of what had happened on June 21, we asked Judge Byers for a formal hearing. The judge told us to return Tuesday and he then would "deal with the situation as I think it exists." He said curtly, "I am not going to handle this as an additional reason for postponing the trial."

Saturday, October 5

I took the day off and after lunch played gin rummy at the Montauk Club. Ed Quigley, postmaster of Brooklyn, asked me how I liked "his" courthouse. He explained that since it was basically the United States Post Office Building he acted as the landlord. I told him we lacked a room in which to confer, keep files, etc. He made a phone call and returned to say that the defense thereafter could use his private conference room. For the remainder of the trial we enjoyed this courtesy, including fresh coffee each day.

I worked late that night at home on a new draft of an opening statement, to be delivered the next day before the "mock jury" of Debevoise and Fraiman.

Sunday, October 6

The defense met in the afternoon in its little office at the Brooklyn Bar Association building on Remsen Street. There was general agreement that my opening to the jury must be short, but we divided on how specific it should be with respect to evidence the prosecution might produce. For instance, should we describe Hayhanen's miserable background at this point?

We could state that neither the jury nor I knew what the Government would attempt to prove, and that we must wait for the production of evidence before making a final judgment. On the other hand, since we had no case of our own and would stand or fall on vigorous cross-examination, it seemed to us the jury should be warned about Hayhanen.

We would not call any witnesses, we agreed. There would be little sense in our putting on character witnesses, for these people did not know Colonel Abel of the KGB; they knew a poor, kindly painter named Emil Goldfus of Fulton Street, Brooklyn. It was clear that it would be unwise to have Abel take the witness stand, but I had told him he must make his own decision on the matter. I suggested he wait until the Government completed its case and then tell me what he wanted to do. My own feeling, I told him, was that it would be foolhardy to subject himself to cross-examination.

As for our respective courtroom roles and how best to work as a team, we agreed that while I would make the opening statement and the summation, as well as cross-examine principal witnesses, my two associates should handle technical objections to evidence during the prosecution's direct presentation of its case. In other words, while I studied the Government's witnesses and analyzed possible lines of cross-examination, comparing testimony with information given us by Abel, my associates would closely follow the lines of direct examination and object to the form of questions, etc.

Our sole concern was that Judge Byers might not allow us to carry out effectively such a joint operation.

Tuesday, Wednesday, October 8, 9

With the trial less than a week away, we went into court Tuesday morning and forced the Government into a hearing on our search-and-seizure motion. In two days we examined four Immigration officers and an FBI agent, who were in on the Hotel Latham raid. The record of the testimony already ran to 437 pages.

We placed in the record the story of what newspapers were calling "a midnight meeting and an early morning rendezvous" between the FBI and Immigration investigators. Our objective was to show that in making the arrest the Immigration officers were pawns of the FBI. Furthermore, we tried to establish that the raid and arrest, made without proper criminal warrants, were an FBI subterfuge to seize Abel and his belongings and keep the fact secret as long as possible. Had Abel "cooperated" it would have been a brilliant counterespionage coup. When the bold maneuver failed, however, and the Justice Department elected to prosecute, it forgot—and wanted us to forget—that it had already violated the man's constitutional rights if he should be tried for a criminal offense under our law.

This was the story which we pieced together from the testimony of five government agents:

Sometime during the week of June 13–20, the Justice Department's liaison officer between the FBI and the Immigration and

Naturalization Service (INS) telephoned Deputy Immigration Commissioner Mario T. Noto and told him of an alien who was in the country illegally, adding, "The FBI is interested in him because of espionage activities."

Noto said he heard from the FBI again later in the week and was informed that this alien "held some kind of rank in the Soviet espionage apparatus; that information concerning his true identity had been established; and that he was not in fact Emil Goldfus [as he pretended], that he was known as Rudolf Abel."

On June 20, Noto testified, the INS decided to arrest Abel in New York, where the FBI learned he was operating, and to bring deportation proceedings against him. At approximately 3 P.M., Noto directed Immigration officers Robert E. Schoenenberger and Lennox Kanzler to go to New York and apprehend Abel.

The two investigators, carrying with them an unsigned warrant of arrest and "show cause" order, arrived at Newark Airport at 10:30 P.M. and were met by two men from the New York office of INS. Together they drove to the local office and District Director John R. Murff signed administrative orders empowering the officers to pick up Abel. From there, the four INS men continued on to New York FBI headquarters where, immediately after midnight, they planned an early morning raid on the Hotel Latham with "six or eight" special agents of the FBI. Then they went to sleep in the FBI offices.

It was our contention the FBI actually directed the movements of the Immigration Service. Schoenenberger, from the witness stand, told us, "We asked them [the FBI] to show us where the suspect was. . . . They asked to be allowed to first contact the suspect . . . to interview, prior to our arrest."

At 6:30 A.M. the two groups of Federal agents started out for the Hotel Latham. Other agents, it developed, were already "staked out" in the hotel, down the hall from the unsuspecting Soviet Colonel who was sleeping naked on top of the sheets.

Edward J. Farley, an investigator from the New York Immigration office, told us of meeting the FBI agents.

Q. So that there were approximately six agents of the FBI whom you met?

A. I would say approximately that number, sir.

Q. Where did you meet them?

A. I met them in the hall or the corridor on the eighth floor and also in an adjoining room to where Martin Collins was residing, which was a room a short distance down the hall.

Q. Mr. Collins, as we understand, was in Room 839 and you met these agents in the hallway and a room adjoining 839?

A. 841, I believe the other number was.

At this point, Farley engaged in a little sport, and I'm sure, believed it was at my expense.

Q. Was that an unoccupied room?

A. It was occupied, sir.

Q. Occupied by whom?

A. By the FBI.

Q. There weren't any paying guests in the room?

A. No, sir. Not to my knowledge.

Judge Byers was obviously irritated that the hearings should continue two days and grew impatient with our detailed questioning. He wanted to know what "our theory" was.

"What we are seeking to bring home through this hearing," I said, "is that the man was suspected of two crimes: illegal entry into the United States and espionage. . . . The ordinary legal process that would be followed in pursuit of a person suspected of either one of those two crimes was not followed . . . the dominant motivation of the Department of Justice was to keep this entire proceeding as secret as possible. . . .

"This civil warrant which was served on the man at the time of his arrest is issued within the Department of Justice and no return is made before a United States commissioner or United States judge. . . .

[The so-called administrative warrant was a simple two-paragraph form titled "Warrant for Arrest of Alien" and made out "To any officer in the service of the United States Immigration and Naturalization Service." In vague and legalistic language, it stated that it appeared the alien was in violation of the immigration laws.]

"Despite the fact that two crimes were suspected, they adopted these extraordinary measures in order to serve the dominant counterespionage objective of the Department of Justice . . . the civil warrant of arrest and these Immigration officers were in effect simply used as pawns. . . .

"So we will be clear on this, Your Honor, we are not in any way saying that to do this was reprehensible. Our only point is that, having gone down that road, the road of counter-espionage in which you keep it as secret as possible . . . and having taken that gamble down in Texas for weeks and lost, then you cannot come back up the other road as though you had issued a criminal warrant.

"That in substance is the object of our hearing today, because we believe . . . that this was not conducted in what the Supreme Court calls 'good faith' and accordingly . . . the search and seizure was illegal.

"Furthermore, in the event that the Hotel Latham evidence falls, we would move to dismiss the indictment on the ground that tainted evidence was presented to the grand jury."

The judge said, "Thank you for explaining your views to me. I should be very reluctant to tell the FBI how to perform its function. I think it is the job of the FBI to bring to light information concerning violations of the law, and I don't think it is part of the Court's duty to tell them how to function."

"Even if we show," I asked, "that they were proceeding in a way that violates the Constitution of the United States?"

"I am not deciding the motion," Judge Byers said. "I am just telling you that that is an extreme attitude that you want the Court to take."

The hearing confirmed Abel's entire story of how he was seized, searched, taken to Texas, held incommunicado for five days and questioned for three weeks beyond that. The simple fact was that the Colonel and all his belongings were made to disappear from the face of the earth while FBI agents, in a counterintelligence function, carried out their plan.

Our great difficulty, of course, was that the case did not concern an ordinary citizen seized in his home. It involved Col. Rudolf Ivanovich Abel of Soviet secret intelligence. Yet the legal question was precisely the same: his constitutional rights were no less than my own.

At the end of the second day of hearings, Judge Byers said, "Now, gentlemen, I expect to dispose of this motion tomorrow. If there is anything that you want me to see, it must be in my chambers by 11 A.M. tomorrow.

"Decision reserved."

Thursday, October 10

On this day the Government reported to us they had learned an FBI agent was friendly with the family of Mrs. McTague, Juror No. 5. She was the woman whose husband was a doctor at the army base. On the strength of this information, I wrote to Judge Byers asking that she be excused. I explained that if we had known the facts during the questioning, we would have challenged the woman.

We filed what must be our final affidavit on the motion to suppress the Hotel Latham evidence; it was based on a *Herald Tribune* story which appeared before we came into the case but had just been called to our attention. It bore out what we had said all along about Abel's arrest and quoted Lt. Gen. Joseph M. Swing, Commissioner of Immigration, as saying; "We were well aware of what he [Abel] was when we picked him up. Our idea at the time was to hold him as long as we could . . . and of course, we were holding him in the hope that sufficient evidence could be gathered to indict him."

The article explained that the Commissioner "indicated" Abel would not have been arrested if our "counterintelligence" hadn't requested it; he was finally picked up when "several government agencies" asked he be apprehended.

The story continued: "Conceivably, the Immigration officials were called in as a device to arrest Abel while preserving as much secrecy as possible. . . . The agencies [probably the FBI and CIA] had followed Abel for a year and undoubtedly knew whether he planned to skip the country. They might have wanted a chance to search his effects thoroughly without tipping their hand."

Friday, October 11

Judge Byers denied our search-and-seizure motion. In a twelve-page decision, he said he saw no good reason why two branches of the United States government should not cooperate in a case of this kind.

"It is not apparent to this Court," he said, "that there is anything to be criticized in that procedure. The Department of Justice owes its first allegiance to the United States and it is not perceived that an alien unlawfully in this country has suffered any deprivation of his constitutional rights in any respect."

He said the articles seized—the false birth certificates, bankbooks and other papers—were "instrumentalities" used by Abel to continue his illegal residence here.

The decision, at least, was simple and lucid. We also thought it was wrong, under established law. However, I had concluded the week before, and so informed Abel, that our best chance of success on the legal issue would lie with the appellate courts, not on the trial level.

I gave in to growing demands of my family and turned the day into an outing. As eight-year-old daughter Mary Ellen, a classic phrasemaker, succinctly said, "It's long overdue. Remember, you can be replaced." We took a ferryboat to Staten Island and spent the day visiting with Ed Gross and his family in their new home, a white house on Emerson Hill which overlooks the Narrows and New York harbor. We cooked steaks over a grill and relaxed in sport shirts.

"As the trial is about to start," I told Ed, "it's only fair we spend the day with you. After all, it was your phone call which not only broke up our Lake Placid vacation but put me in the middle of this assignment."

Around four o'clock, I called Abel at the House of Detention and brought him up to date. I told him about the affidavit, quoting Commissioner Swing, to which Judge Byers had given such short shrift, and about the juror we had asked the judge to excuse.

We had informed Rudolf of every move we might make. He was appreciative and, as one might expect, keenly interested in each development. When I then asked him if he needed anything, he said he was resigned to his "present situation" but occasionally would like "a good steak." I reminded him of a Syrian proverb which goes, "I had no shoes and I was sad; but then I met a man who had no feet." He said curtly, "This is no time to quote proverbs."

I gave him the good news that Tom Debevoise had passed the Vermont bar examinations. He seemed genuinely pleased and asked me to extend personal congratulations.

When I returned home at night there was a letter from a highly placed London solicitor, Sir Edwin Herbert, regarding my assignment to defend Abel. I had written Sir Edwin on a confidential basis to learn how such an espionage case would fare in Great Britain, from which our American common law is derived.

Sir Edwin wrote that there was no capital punishment in England for espionage by a foreign agent in peacetime. Espionage was not even a crime in Great Britain until 1868. He also informed me that generally British courts had dealt less severely with an alien spying for his own country than with a British subject betraying the Crown.

Sunday, October 13

The day got off poorly. Late in the morning a bumptious client, or perhaps at that point a former client, called and with splashing wit wished me "sincere bad luck" in the trial the next day. My conclusion was that he had been working all morning on whiskey sours.

The majority of our most valued clients had made it clear that they regarded the court assignment as a gracious tribute by fellow lawyers. Lord Middleton, chairman of the Yorkshire Insurance Group in England, had written a chivalrous note to congratulate me on being "briefed in the Abel defense." To Lord Middleton, a great gentleman, the tradition of advocacy in the common law meant that being "briefed" in an important though unpopular cause represented a high honor.

It was obvious from correspondence with other British friends that a lawyer in their Isles would run little risk of public disfavor by undertaking an unpopular defense, either voluntarily or by court assignment. This probably was due in great part to their distinction between barristers, who try the cases in court, and solicitors, who normally are office lawyers. Under British customs, some barristers never meet their clients before trial. The public does not associate an advocate with the views of the accused whom he may defend. It is a sound system.

Monday, October 14

Morning in our apartment came early, to bring a sense of inadequacy. There had been so little time to prepare.

United States District Court
Eastern District of New York

UNITED STATES OF AMERICA

vs.

RUDOLF IVANOVICH ABEL,
*also known as "Mark" and also known
as Martin Collins and Emil R. Goldfus,
et al.*

} *Criminal*
No. 45094

TRIAL

UNITED STATES COURTHOUSE
Eastern District of New York,
Brooklyn, New York,
Monday October 14, 1957

PRESIDING: Mortimer W. Byers, D.J.

Appearances

FOR THE GOVERNMENT: William F. Tompkins, *Asst. Atty.
Gen., Washington, D.C.*; (Cornelius
W. Wickersham, Jr., *U.S. Atty.,
E.D.N.Y.*; Kevin T. Maroney,
Anthony R. Palermo, James T.
Featherstone, *Attys. Dept. of
Justice, Washington, D.C.*)

FOR THE DEFENSE: James B. Donovan, *Brooklyn, N.Y.*;
(*of counsel*, Arnold G. Fraiman,
New York City; Thomas M. Debevoise II, *Woodstock, Vt.*)

Preparation is the only way to get ready for a hard test, whether a court trial, race, boxing match, Broadway appearance or death. You can fake readiness, falling back on past experience and bravado. But without backbreaking preparation for a main event, you know inside that you aren't really ready.

For four months the Department of Justice had been preparing the Abel prosecution in depth. This was currently its most important criminal case. Every potential witness had been endlessly examined, cross-examined and re-examined by probers seeking strengths and flaws in possible testimony. Every document had been analyzed by experts. Trial tactics had been weighed; plans were made, then discarded for sounder ones. Legal memoranda had been drafted, on substance and procedure.

For trial purposes, the Government's case was also ours. There could be no defense as such. Abel could not take the stand, to face cross-examination, and the nature of the charges would prevent our having either witnesses or documents to aid the defense. Meanwhile, discovery demands on our behalf had been either summarily rejected or reduced to a bare minimum by Judge Byers. Our independent investigation of the facts had necessarily been sketchy, and there had been no time for the research on legal points which any good firm of lawyers would desire.

That morning, a second cup of coffee helped. After all, I reasoned, anything can happen at a trial. Perhaps Hayhanen would refuse to testify; perhaps Rhodes would plead self-incrimination; perhaps a mistrial would be declared, on any one of twenty grounds. Perhaps. Meanwhile, I thought, we always have our search-and-seizure point for appeal. This would be no sickly technicality. It was an issue that would trouble any student of constitutional law.

All we could do was our best. Furthermore, there was the delectable anticipation of a good scrap.

It was an Indian-summer day. Air hung limply about the old Eastern District courthouse, built in 1889. Its Gothic towers stared across to 252 Fulton Street where Abel had painted his most successful portrait, that of an inconspicuous artist living off modest savings.

When I reached Judge Byers' courtroom on the third floor, an overflow crowd waited outside. In the days of great courtroom orators, like Clarence Darrow, a popular trial would run on for weeks before a packed courthouse. But it was rare in this day to see more than a handful of spectators in a New York courtroom, unless it was an unusual murder trial or the prosecution of a leading racketeer.

Trial lawyers no longer have personal followings, and public respect for the role of a criminal defense lawyer is deplorably low in our country. Some criminal courtrooms in New York City have regular spectator buffs, retired civil servants and pensioners with a better than average understanding of the law. All are people with time on their hands. Their female counterparts sit in television show audiences five mornings a week.

Like most civil trial lawyers I had grown accustomed to arguing before a handful of fellow barristers, but I was not surprised to see the courtroom packed that morning. Accounts of Abel's arrest had been carried in newspapers from Tokyo to Johannesburg, and now this same worldwide attention was focused on the American trial. Only the Soviet press chose to ignore the Colonel and his difficulties. "As God is my witness," said Khrushchev, "we have no spies."

Outside the courtroom door, and stationed inside from where they could watch the court audience, stood United States marshals. Metal shields were fixed over their lapel pockets, identifying them as armed government officers. A delegation of FBI agents was seated somewhere in the crowd.

In the courtroom was the unmistakable air of tension. Tension is a part of every trial. A lawyer learns to live with it, to control it and make it work for him. But tension is not the same for any two men, or for any two experiences. There is tension in wartime, tension between rounds of a prizefight and tension in a boardroom while directors crowd around a table and plot corporate strategy to strangle a competitor. It was clear to me that the Abel trial would have a tension all its own.

Looking clean-shaven and fresh in his banker's suit, Abel was led in and took his place behind us at the defense table. The jury was next, and finally, with the stage set, Judge Byers, the white-haired old campaigner, appeared. All rose at the stentorian call of the clerk, and the judge slipped quietly into his high-backed leather throne. Twenty-eight years before, President Hoover had appointed Mortimer Byers to the Federal bench and it had become his lifetime dedication.

The judge peered over his glasses. "Both sides ready?"

"Government ready," Assistant Attorney General Tompkins said.

"Defense is ready, Your Honor."

Quietly the drama had begun.

"There is a little matter that I think should be dealt with before the taking of testimony and before counsel open," the judge was saying. He went on to explain to the jury that it had become known to the Government that an FBI agent and a daughter of Juror No. 5 were friendly.

"Please understand," he said to the juror, "there is no question of qualification involved. You will, therefore, be excused and alternate No. 1 will take your place."

Juror No. 5 said, "Thank you very much."

Tompkins then rose to make his opening. He was a slight, dark-haired man, only forty-four years old but with a public service career behind him. He had been a military prosecutor of war crimes in Singapore at the end of World War II and then served for a year as United States Attorney for New Jersey, his home state. Under his direction, the Justice Department's Internal Security division had a hand in cases resulting in over one hundred indictments.

"May it please the Court, ladies and gentlemen of the jury . . . it is our duty to present the evidence that has been assembled by the investigative agencies of the Government and to prove the truth of the charges set forth by the grand jury. . . .

"My colleagues and myself are conscious of our obligation to represent the Government of the United States and the people of the United States, and conscious of the obligation to protect the rights of the individual defendant as well as the rights of all American citizens, by proceeding diligently against those who have transgressed our laws and who, perhaps, have dedicated themselves to the destruction of our country.

"Now I want to make this very clear. The interest of the Government is not that we shall win a case—but that justice shall be done. In other words, that innocence shall not suffer nor guilt escape. In accordance with that, I want to pledge to you on behalf of my colleagues and myself that we will conduct ourselves in such a fashion that this defendant will be insured a fair trial."

To the right of the judge, the jury and the alternates sat in round-backed wooden swivel chairs with armrests. A clock high over their heads silently marked the passage of time and reminded the judge when to adjourn.

To the left of the judge, directly opposite the jury and backed against the windows, sat the press. They looked like a much more difficult jury, from New York newspapers, radio and TV stations, and at least half a dozen representing foreign papers. There was a French journalist, a German magazine writer, a court specialist from a London paper and even a barrister from England's famous trial court, Old Bailey.

The question on everyone's mind was "Can Abel receive a fair trial?"

The Senator McCarthy era was drawing to a close. Soviet Russia was arming the Arab states against Israel. Just ten days earlier, the Soviets had successfully launched the first manmade satellite, Sputnik I. This amazing feat had stunned the American public; it served to accentuate the cold war and its concomitant arms race, a race which now found the United States apparently in second place. As our trial began, Sputnik I, a 184-pound sphere, was circling the earth every hour and a half.

"The nature of the charge is one of unusual significance," said Tompkins, "and it takes on added significance when you consider that it occurred during critical years of our history. However, the seriousness of the charge does not make it a difficult one. The grand jury indictment is simple, and I just want to talk to you about that for a few minutes. I first of all say this: The indictment is a charge; it is not proof of anything.

"Now in Count One, the grand jury has charged the defendant with conspiracy to commit espionage and with conspiring with other conspirators . . . to transmit information relating to our national defense. . . ."

The prosecutor then summarized the indictment, referring to Abel as "the defendant." He never called him by name. He included in his summary all the spy paraphernalia which, of course, would impress the jury—the short-wave radio, the hollowed-out containers, the "drops" in the city parks, great sums of money, birth certificates and passports.

Then he said, "And it was also charged by the grand jury that in the event of war between the United States and Russia, the conspirators would set up clandestine radio transmitters and receiving posts for the purpose of continuing to furnish information to Russia."

Referring to the overt acts listed in support of the indictment, Tompkins said, "I am going to talk very generally about these because I feel it is far more preferable that you hear the testimony from the mouths of witnesses rather than lawyers.

"As you know, you are the sole judges of the truth and the facts and the Court is the sole judge of the law. . . .

"The evidence and the corroboration will come from various witnesses. It will be direct evidence. The Government will present circumstantial evidence, and one of the witnesses will be a member of this conspiracy, a co-conspirator who was selected by the other conspirators to participate.

"Invariable experience, I may as well say to you, shows that the defense will attack him. However, I think you should remember this: The co-conspirator has now left the conspiracy. He is no longer adding to his past sins and he is telling the truth. His testimony will be corroborated and by corroboration I mean confirmation—confirmation by the testimony of other witnesses and by documentary evidence and by admissions of the defendant. It is evidence which the Government feels cannot be contradicted because it is the truth, and it will prove beyond any doubt the guilt of the defendant.

"We shall prove that the defendant, a colonel in the Soviet State Security Service, together with other high-ranking Russian officials, put into operation a most elaborate apparatus of Soviet intelligence and espionage in an endeavor to secure our most important secrets—secrets of great importance to this country as well as the free world."

The prosecutor told how Abel had been in the United States since 1948 ("he concealed his presence here deliberately") and was later joined by an assistant; "their clandestine and secret activities, assisted by Russian diplomatic and United Nations officials, were directed at our most important secrets."

But in May, 1957, the conspiracy collapsed. Tompkins explained, "One of the co-conspirators defected, and he related his story to American officials abroad. The FBI, in their very vigilant and efficient manner, conducted an investigation, a very intensive investigation, which resulted in the uncovering of overwhelming and devastating corroboration of the defendant's guilt. . . .

"Now, in conclusion, let me say this to you: the Government feels that the evidence we will adduce before this jury will prove to you not only beyond a reasonable doubt, but beyond any possible doubt, the guilt of the defendant. In other words, the evidence will clearly point to one and only one possible verdict—that of guilty as charged by the grand jury."

My opening for the defense ran some nine hundred words and was planned for delivery in twenty minutes. The prosecution opening had taken twice this long. I had worked on the brief address a total of ten hours.

"May it please the Court, ladies and gentlemen of the jury.

"This is a case which you, the jury, after hearing the evidence presented and under instructions of the judge, are to decide whether or not the defendant has been proven guilty beyond a reasonable doubt of a crime for which he could be sentenced to death.

"The prosecutor has outlined to you the nature of the charges and has described the evidence which he contends will prove these charges. It is important to remember with respect to the three counts in this indictment that it is only under Count Number One, that is the conspiracy to *transmit* information to Russia, that the defendant could be sentenced to death.

"Now, I am the attorney for the defendant. I was assigned this task by the Court, and under our system of American justice it will be my duty throughout this proceeding to represent the interests of the defendant in every respect. This is done, under our law, so that you may know the truth and render a just verdict.

"This case is not only extraordinary; it is unique. For the first time in American history a man is being threatened with death as a sentence on the charge that he acted as a spy for a foreign nation with which we are legally at peace.

"The defendant is a man named Abel. It is most important that you keep that fact uppermost in your mind throughout the days ahead. This is not a case against communism. It is not a case against Soviet Russia. Our grievances against Russia have been voiced and are being voiced every day in the United Nations and in various other forums. But the sole issues in this case, on which you are going to render the verdict, deal with whether or not this man Abel has been proved guilty beyond a reasonable doubt of the specific crimes with which he is now charged.

"The prosecution has just told you that among the principal witnesses against the defendant will be a man, whose name is Hayhanen, who claims that he helped the defendant to spy against the United States.

"This means that within a very short while, this man will take the stand and testify before you. Observe his demeanor very carefully. Bear in mind that if what the Government says is true, it means that this man has been here for some years living among

122

us, spying on behalf of Soviet Russia. In order to do this it means, and it is so charged in the indictment, that he entered the United States on false papers, that he swore falsely in order to obtain these papers, that he has lived here every day only by lying about his true identity, about his background, about every fact of his everyday life. Furthermore, if what the Government says is true, he was being paid to do this by Soviet Russia and we can assume that if Russia properly trains her spies, he was trained abroad in what his 'cover' should be here, meaning that he was trained in the art of deception. He was trained to lie. In short, assuming that what the Government says is true, this man is literally a professional liar.

"Now, bear this in mind as you hear his testimony. Bear also in mind that if what the Government has told you is true, it means that this man has committed many crimes against our laws, including the capital offense of conspiring to transmit information to Russia. He has not yet been indicted for any of these crimes, and bear in mind that the man's sole hope of clemency presumably is not only that he implicate as many as he can in his crimes, but that he make as important as possible the information which he says he has to give to our government.

"Simply bear these facts in mind when you consider what motivation the witness has to tell the truth; and what justification or motivation he would have to do again what he has been doing for some years, and that is lying. Observe the demeanor of all these witnesses carefully.

"Remember at all times that the only evidence that can be presented in this case, the only evidence which you can consider, must come from the witness stand. The indictment is not evidence; what the prosecution counsel may say or I may say is not evidence."

I looked into the jury box and saw a cross section of Brooklyn, U.S.A. They were a clerk, an accountant, two insurance company executives, the owner of a gas station, two housewives, a woman investigator for the City Welfare Department, a civilian worker for the Navy, a mail room superintendent, a staff assistant for a utility and a city sewage engineer who was their foreman. Some big business, some small business; some on the public payroll, some engaged in private enterprise.

They were, I judged, reasonable, sincere men and women and intensely serious about their assignment, as though they were first-time jurors. I moved close to the jury box.

"Remember at all times," I said, "that a man's life can depend on your conscientious performance of your duty.

"Throughout this trial you will hear the judge and us lawyers refer to the prosecution as 'the Government.' Now, that is precisely correct. But remember that in a larger sense, His Honor the judge, all counsel and especially *you* represent the Government of the United States. We all have precisely the same aim: a just verdict under the law.

"I know this jury will do its conscientious duty and render a just verdict, in the tradition of a fair American trial."

The courtroom fell silent as I took my seat. The only noise came from outside, from the street below. The windows along the right-hand side of the courtroom were all open. They are old-fashioned panel windows with crank handles. Faded yellow-brown shades were pulled halfway down. Below us, on Washington and Fulton Streets, which run parallel to the building, the big Transit Authority buses roared and sputtered. The park area around the courthouse serves as their terminus point.

"The Government," Tompkins said in a loud voice, "will call Reino Hayhanen, Your Honor."

The portly witness, wearing a light two-button suit with long lapels, was ushered into the courtroom at the rear and quickly walked to the front. The courtroom was about sixty feet long. As he strode forward all eyes, except for those of the defendant, followed him. He took the oath and then climbed two steps into the carpeted witness stand. Behind him was the American flag, the brightest object in this bare, functional chamber.

Debevoise and I thought we noticed the Colonel tense up at this moment. He, like most of us in the room, had no idea of what this man Hayhanen was to say—or how far he would go. Abel busied

124

himself by making ready to take notes on lined yellow pads, nine by five and a half inches in size.

Tompkins eased into the direct examination: "Will you speak up, so that your voice is heard all the way back here to the last juryman, please?"

> *Q.* Now, what was your last permanent address in the United States?
> *A.* Peekskill, New York State.
> *Q.* You are a citizen of Russia, is that correct?
> *A.* Yes, I am.
> *Q.* And from 1939 roughly until 1957 you were employed by the Soviet Union?

Fraiman jumped to his feet, objecting. We immediately ran into trouble. Fraiman said, "If Your Honor please, at this stage I object to Mr. Tompkins' leading the witness."

> *Judge Byers:* Who is going to conduct the trial for the defense, please?
> *Tompkins:* I would like to know that too, please.
> *Judge Byers:* I understood that Mr. Donovan is chief counsel.
> *Fraiman:* Yes.
> *Judge Byers:* Are you going to conduct the trial, Mr. Donovan?
> *Donovan:* I intend to; on the other hand Mr. Fraiman was also assigned . . .
> *Judge Byers:* You make the objections. What is the objection?
> *Fraiman:* The objection is—
> *Judge Byers:* Will you allow Mr. Donovan to do the talking, please?
> *Donovan:* I believe, Your Honor, that Mr. Fraiman's objection was that Mr. Tompkins was leading the witness.

Judge Byers: Now, what is your objection?

Donovan: I make the same objection.

Judge Byers: I don't think it is harmful leading thus far. Overruled.

Our carefully planned trial strategy, under which Fraiman and Debevoise would make routine objections to questions, was gone. Tompkins had his question to Hayhanen repeated and then picked up his line of thought.

Q. I am getting at, what agency in the government of the U.S.S.R. were you employed by?

A. The last time I was employed with the KGB. It means espionage work. That is Committee of State Security.

Q. Mr. Hayhanen, when did you first enter the United States?

A. In October, 1952.

Q. And did you have a passport?

A. Yes, I did.

Q. What was the name on that passport?

A. Eugene Nicoli Maki.

The Government produced the passport, Hayhanen identified it and it was offered as evidence, Exhibit No. 1. Hayhanen said, "This is my first passport, what I got in Finland, what I was using to come to this country."

Q. Did you enter the United States in 1952 in connection with your employment by the government of the U.S.S.R.?

A. That is right, I did.

Q. What were your duties in behalf of the Russian government in this country?

A. I was sent to this country to be resident assistant in espionage work.

We were building up to the confrontation. The whole court-room could feel it. In the press gallery there was shuffling and jock-eying. On his notepad, Abel had just written, "Exhibit 1—passport which he got in Helsinki, Finland; used to enter U.S."

Hayhanen had made no mention of Helsinki; he merely said Finland. Apparently, Abel knew the story intimately.

Q. Now, do you know the name of the resident officer?
A. I know him just by the nickname Mark.
Q. Do you know him by any other name?
A. No, I don't. I didn't know him by any other name. I know him just for security reasons by his nickname.

Hayhanen sat stiffly in the witness chair. His pudgy body was rigid. He stared at Tompkins through dark horn-rimmed glasses. His thick mustache moved up and down as he spoke.

Q. Now, do you see him in the courtroom here?
A. Yes, I do.
Q. Would you please point him out?
A. Yes. He is sitting there at the end of that table.
Q. The end of the table?
A. That is right.

They would never be closer than this again, twenty feet apart. Hayhanen seemed surprisingly steady and sure of himself. It is possible, of course, that he was held together by tranquilizing drugs.

Tompkins: Will the defendant stand up, please?
Q. Is that the gentleman? (Tompkins pointed down at Abel.)
A. Yes.

There was a marked physical contrast between the two men who held center stage. As he stood looking like a professor at his accuser, Abel was thin and even anemic-looking. Hayhanen was obese and ruddy-faced. His suit jacket buckled across his thick middle. Their real-life roles were now reversed. Hayhanen could play the militant taskmaster of an uneasy, silent Abel.

All Abel then wrote in his pad to describe this dramatic scene was "Sent to be resident's assistant by name of MARK. Knew him only by that name."

Tompkins continued: "Now, do you know what his occupation is?"

A. He told me that he worked as a photographer, that he had somewhere a photo studio.

Q. Do you know whether he was an employee of the Russian government?

A. Yes, he was—or he was up to this time.

Q. And what agency of the government, if you know, was he employed by?

A. Yes. He was employed by the KGB.

Q. Did he have any rank?

A. Yes, he had the rank of colonel.

Q. Now, when did you first meet Mark?

A. I met him in 1954, the first time.

Q. And you saw him—did you see him subsequently?

A. Yes, then I was meeting him mostly once or twice a week.

Q. When did you last see him before today?

A. The last I saw this year, February, middle of February.

Q. Now, Mr. Hayhanen, I want to ask you to answer some specific questions more in detail.

The prosecutor then drew from the witness his pedigree. It was an undistinguished autobiography in espionage. Hayhanen said he was born May 14, 1920, in the village of Kaskisarri, about twenty-five miles from Leningrad. He attended elementary and secondary schools and when nineteen he was graduated from teachers' college. After three months as a schoolteacher, he was drafted into the NKVD.

Q. Now, at that time was the NKVD a part of the Army?
A. No, it was like secret police . . .
Q. When you were drafted in November, 1939, what branch of the NKVD were you assigned to?
A. I was assigned as interpreter to operations group on Finnish territory, what was occupied by Russian troops after Finnish-Russian War . . .
Q. Do you speak Finnish?
A. I do.

Hayhanen explained that when he was drafted he received a ten-day training course which consisted of lectures on how to interrogate war prisoners and "how to find anti-Soviet people or some espionage agents from some other countries on Russian territory."

When the war ended (the Russo-Finnish peace treaty was signed in Moscow, March 12, 1940), he was sent to Karelia where he continued to serve as an interpreter and "I was working as NKVD official, too." Then, in May, 1943, after a year's candidacy, Hayhanen became a member of the Communist party and five years later he was recalled to Moscow for reassignment. During all this time, the NKVD had undergone reorganization and Hayhanen was now a KGB agent with a lieutenant's rank.

"In Moscow," Hayhanen said, "my bosses explained to me that now they need me, instead of counter-espionage work, on espionage work."

Throughout his testimony, he insisted on referring to his "bosses." It was like a parody of the Moscow Trials in the 1930s. In reading the trial transcript later, I was struck by this awkward reference. I had visions of KGB officers in the Kremlin nodding as they read this testimony and I was certain that if this had been Moscow instead of Brooklyn some witness would have been saying "my Washington bosses."

Hayhanen said that in 1948 he spent two and a half days in Moscow, met with certain Soviet espionage officials (his "bosses") and learned that he was to be transferred to Estonia. After a year in Estonia, during which time he received espionage training, including photography instruction, English lessons and training in the driving and repairing of automobiles, he was promoted to major and told that his future assignment was to be the United States.

To prepare him for this move, he was recalled to Moscow again and given his cover name, Eugene Nicoli Maki. According to Hayhanen, Maki was an American citizen born in Idaho who traveled to Finland with his parents in 1927. Nothing further was learned about the unfortunate Maki family, either during the trial or thereafter. The FBI stated, "What became of the Maki family, we do not know."

Hayhanen was then directed by his "bosses" to go to Finland and build up his "legend," his new identity. He testified that he traveled to the Russo-Finnish border and was smuggled across in the trunk of a car driven by accredited Soviet officials serving in Finland. One of these men was an intelligence officer working in the office of Tass, the Soviet news agency.

It was Hayhanen's assignment to establish that as Eugene Maki he had been living in Finland since 1943. This took money. In Lapland, where he lived and worked with a blacksmith for three months ("for a while, just to show some kind of connection that I really was working in Lapland"), he found two false witnesses. He paid the one 15,000 Finnish marks and the other 20,000.

Tompkins asked him:

Q. Was that your own money?
A. No.
Q. Whose was it?
A. I got that money from Moscow . . .

Hayhanen moved to southern Finland in 1950 and for the next two and a half years he lived as Eugene Maki in the cities of Tampere and Turku. He worked in a factory at Tampere, building safes and doing auto body repairs. On July 3, 1951, he applied at the American Embassy in Helsinki for a passport to the United States as a native-born citizen.

He told the American authorities he was born May 30, 1919, at Enaville, Idaho, and produced a birth certificate. He wrote on his application that his mother, Lillian Luoma Maki, was American-born (New York) and his father, August, was a naturalized American who had been born in Oulu, Finland. On a separate affidavit, required to explain any "protracted foreign residence," he said that when he was eight years old he and his brother, Allen August, traveled with their mother to Valga, in southern Estonia, and lived with her until her death in 1941. His father had died in March of 1933, he said.

The following November, Hayhanen, still adding to his legend as Eugene Maki, married a twenty-seven-year-old Finnish girl from Siilinjarvi. This, of course, was Hannah, the beautiful blond woman. Then, on July 28, 1952, his American passport was issued and he returned to Moscow, traveling across the border again in an automobile trunk. He spent three weeks in Moscow this trip and at a private home. ("It was some private address, but I don't know that address.") He received additional training in code, in the ciphering and deciphering of secret messages, and in the advanced photography techniques a spy must possess: the reduction of a text to a microdot the size of a pinhead, and the treatment of film so that it becomes soft and will fold and bend and fit into a hollowed-out container, such as a coin or pencil.

Q. Now, did you go to Estonia upon orders from the KGB?

A. Yes, from Moscow.

Donovan: Your Honor, haven't we reached a point where we are entitled to instructions that the Government can't lead the witness?

Judge Byers: I don't think that is harmful leading. That is simply saving time.

Tompkins: This is really just background.

Our original objection against the Government's leading the witness had been overruled as "not harmful leading." Now we were told they were merely saving time and this was just background. Despite Tompkins' assurance, the prosecution had already made its first move to establish the formation of a conspiracy traceable to the Kremlin. This was a vital part of their case and hardly "background." As one will understand, an examiner "leading" a witness tends to shape his testimony.

Tompkins asked:

Q. Before you were transferred to Estonia ... did you meet Colonel Korotkov?
A. Yes, I met.
Q. Will you tell us the circumstances ... ?
A. Korotkov was the assistant boss of PGU.

The PGU, Hayhanen testified, was the Ministry of State Security's First Division of espionage. This almost casual reference, carefully and calculatingly extracted from a not overly bright witness, was to stand throughout the trial as the only mention of Col. Alekssandr Mikhailovich Korotkov, one of the four accused co-conspirators.

The prosecutor moved now to draw in the others, Vitali G. Pavlov and Mikhail N. Svirin, first secretary of the Soviet United Nations delegation in New York from August, 1952, to April, 1954. The witness told how he had been given a new code name, Vic, and "I met my bosses and I got new instructions, written instructions, what I have to do in the United States."

Q. Now, on this trip to Moscow did you meet Pavlov?
A. Yes, I did.
Q. Will you tell us about that, please?
A. Pavlov—
Q. First of all, I beg your pardon. Excuse me. Will you tell us first of all who he is?

A. Pavlov was in 1952 assistant boss to American Section of espionage work . . .

Q. Did you see in Moscow that trip Mikhail Svirin?

A. Yes, I did.

Q. Would you tell us about him? Was he assigned—

A. They explained to me that Svirin came for vacation to Moscow and he is assigned to Soviet official work in the United States and I have to meet him and have contact with him when I will come to New York.

I objected to this on the ground that it was hearsay. The Court allowed the fact that Hayhanen was instructed to meet with Svirin; the remainder of the answer was to be stricken.

The witness continued to explain his instructions. He said he was informed he was to be the assistant resident agent in New York and would be expected to recruit illegal agents and "I have to get some espionage information from those agents."

Q. Where were you to get these illegal agents, did the instructions say?

A. Yes, those instructions said that those illegal agents I will get from Soviet official people.

Q. By Soviet official people, what do you mean?

A. I mean Soviet officials who are coming to the United States or some other country by Soviet passports.

Tompkins asked next about Hayhanen's salary as a spy.

Q. Did your instructions contain anything relative to money?

A. Pardon?

Q. To money?

A. Yes. In the same instructions there was that I will get five thousand dollars money for cover work and that I will get salary four hundred a month plus one hundred for trip expenses. That's—will be salary what I am getting in the United States and then another salary what I was getting in Russian currency, it was different but I left to my relatives.

Q. Did your instructions contain anything concerning communications or codes?

I considered this a patently leading question and I stood to object, mindful of the Court's previous rulings about saving time.

Donovan: Your Honor, at what point can I properly object under Your Honor's previous rulings with respect to the witness being asked a leading question?

Judge Byers: If you are objecting to its being a leading question, I agree with you.

Donovan: Thank you.

The prosecutor rephrased the question, asking if there were anything the witness had not told us about his written instructions.

Hayhanen: Let me see, written instructions, that is what I told. That is about written instructions.

Q. That is all you remember about the written instructions?

A. Yes.

My objection, and the interruption, seemed to throw him off balance. Whatever he had been about to testify to, concerning codes and communications, had slipped his mind. Tompkins then asked him about his oral instructions.

Hayhanen: Pavlov explained me that on espionage work we are all the time in war, but if real war will be . . . that I don't have to move . . . even if they don't have any connections with me, so still I have to do my espionage work in the country where I was assigned. And he explained that after war our country or our officials will ask everyone what he did to win this war.

134

The beginning of a trial is like the opening of a play. The curtain goes up and under ideal conditions a story is unfolded which the Court and the jury are hearing for the first time. The tale is told and retold; confirmed or corroborated and denied. Piece by piece, the story is built; first one side, then the other side constructs it. Each witness is a new player when he enters.

Hayhanen had been on the stand for over an hour. He had been asked, and he answered, 212 questions. His Baltic accent and clumsy speech were now familiar, and the jury, careful not to show any sign of emotion, seemed to accept these burdens. Perhaps this awkwardness added to the picture of the foreign-born secret intelligence agent. Would he be easier to believe if he spoke English clearly and well? I doubted it. Nevertheless, even the prosecution and at times the Court seemed to grow impatient with this witness.

Q. During this conversation or during the receipt of these oral instructions from Pavlov, did he give you any directions as to the type of information?

A. Yes, he did. He told that it depends what kind of illegal agents I will have, so it depends then what kind of information they can give, where they work or whom they have as friends and such and such things.

He told that I have to consider with their help in every different occasion or with every different agent.

Tompkins, stern now, bore in:

Q. Now, let me ask you this directly: what type of information were you seeking?

A. Espionage information.

Q. Would you describe that, what you mean by espionage information?

A. By espionage information I mean all information what you can look to get from newspapers or official way, by asking from, I suppose, legally from some office, and I mean

135

espionage information that kind of information what you have to get illegal way. That is, it is secret information for—

The Judge broke in, cutting off Hayhanen in the middle of the sentence.

Judge Byers: Concerning what? What kind of information?
Hayhanen: Concerning national security or—
Judge Byers (impatiently): What do you mean by that?
The witness (floundering): In this case, the United States of America.
Judge Byers (in a resigned tone): What do you mean by national security?
Hayhanen: I mean it—that some military information or atomic secrets.

This answer was virtually the legal definition of espionage as a capital offense. Satisfied that this conclusion was on the record, the judge turned the witness back to the prosecutor, but Hayhanen said he could remember nothing more about his oral instructions. Tompkins quickly shifted the scene and tried to put the witness in New York.

Q. Did you receive any instructions at this time or at any subsequent date on communicating with people in the United States when you arrived here?
Donovan: Objected to as leading.
Judge Byers: I suppose it is leading, Mr. Tompkins. Ask him if the subject was broached, what was said.
Tompkins: I might say this, Your Honor. The only reason I use that type of question is certainly not to suggest the tenor of the answer but merely a topic. We have a witness who is not as conversant in the English language as the rest of us.

The question was nevertheless withdrawn and the witness was asked what he was expected to do after he reached the United

States. He answered that he was instructed to find a place to live first and then, after making certain he was not being followed, to report he was ready for assignment.

Hayhanen: When I noticed that nobody followed me I went to Central Park close to Tavern-on-the-Green where is that horse path and put a white thumbtack to that sign warning "Be Careful, Horse Riding" or something like that. It means that nobody is following me, there is no danger for me.

For the remainder of the day, Hayhanen delivered a halting but fascinating recital of his complicated life as a Soviet espionage agent in New York City. It was an admixture of the bizarre, the startling and sometimes the ludicrous as he told of drops, signal areas, visual meetings, soft film, magnetic containers and secret messages in hollowed-out flashlight batteries.

(The newsmen seized these details to weave into their stories and one of the tabloids carried a page-one headline: LIFE OF RED SPY BARED AT ABEL TRIAL. Another tabloid, in a headline bigger and blacker, said, ABEL FINGERED AS SOVIET SPY.

One graphic résumé of Hayhanen's testimony began, "The life and times of a Russian spy in the United States—making chalk marks in Central Park, leaving messages in hollowed-out coins, picking up $3000 at a lamp post hideaway, standing in a subway station wearing a red-striped tie and smoking a pipe—were told in Brooklyn Federal Court by a man who was one. The story, with the cloak and dagger trappings of a Hollywood thriller . . .")

Hayhanen testified his Moscow bosses assigned him three drops where he was to leave messages and to look for assignments ("By drop I mean a secret place which only you or several people just know, where you can hide some container . . . and another person will pick up that container . . ."). One of these was in Central Park, another was in the base of a lamppost in Fort Tryon Park near the tip of Manhattan, and a third was a hole between the sidewalk and a wall along Jerome Avenue, between 165th and 167th Streets, in the Bronx.

In addition, he said he was given signal areas: a streetlight in Brooklyn and an area in a railroad station in Newark, New Jersey. He was to leave significant chalk signs at these locations. A horizontal line meant he had a message for one of his superiors, and a vertical line confirmed that he had received a message at one of his drops.

By this testimony, largely a chronicle of Hayhanen's professional routines, the Government not only revealed a spy apparatus in our midst, but intimated that if these were Hayhanen's rounds, surely the master spy Abel's comings and goings were undoubtedly more dangerous to our national security.

At only one point in his testimony did the witness actually describe Abel ("Mark") as a partner in the routines. He told of a time when he left a magnetic container in a drop (a lamppost near a bus stop at the end of Seventh Avenue, near Macombs Dam Bridge) while Abel stood by as a lookout.

Hayhanen: I put that magnetic container into that drop and Mark was close to that drop and he of course was looking around that nobody can notice us.

Q. By Mark you mean the defendant?

A. I mean defendant, yes.

Our only defense against this testimony was to stay on top of Hayhanen and force him, wherever possible, to be explicit so that we could test his explanations on cross-examination. The greatest number of his statements were vague and unsupported by hard fact: dates, times, exact locations and identifications.

He testified, for instance, that shortly after he came to the United States he reported he was ready to establish his "cover" operations and asked for money. He was told in reply that it was too early to discuss "that kind of matters." (Later, he received $3,000 in the Fort Tryon Park drop.)

Donovan: Your Honor, could we have some testimony with respect to when he got such an answer, how he got it and so on, rather than leave it in the record in this shape?

Judge Byers: Don't you think you and I could both be patient and let Mr. Tompkins try his case? I know he will be patient and let you conduct your cross-examination.

Donovan: I am trying to be very patient, Your Honor.

Tompkins: Now, would you fix a date, to the best of your recollection, when you sent this message?

A. I sent that message in the end of November or first part of December, 1952.

Q. Was this through the Fort Tryon drop or Jerome Avenue?

A. It was through Fort Tryon Park, from my best recollection.

Tompkins: My recollection had been you said Jerome— drop Number Three at Jerome Avenue. Drop Number Three is actually in Fort Tryon Park, isn't it?

Hayhanen: Yes, drop Number Three is Fort Tryon Park, not Jerome Avenue.

Tompkins: Jerome Avenue was drop Number One?

Judge Byers (interrupting): Which drop did you use for that first message? I think you have already testified on the subject.

Hayhanen: Let me see now, Your Honor.

Donovan: He has testified both ways, Your Honor . . .

Hayhanen: I can—

Tompkins: Wait a minute.

Judge Byers: It is so hard to hear more than two people.

Hayhanen: After all, five years passed and—almost five years passed and I cannot remember exactly in which drop I put some certain message. It could be drop Number One, Jerome Avenue, or drop Number Three, Fort Tryon Park. I am not so certain through which drop I sent that message, but the main thing is that I sent that message through drops.

Donovan: Objection, Your Honor, to the testimony or any

testimony as to the contents of the message unless the witness can identify in which drop he left it.

Just then a Transit Authority bus roared past the Brooklyn court, passing directly under the opened windows.

Judge Byers: You know, that bus is a little bit louder than your voice, Mr. Donovan. I didn't hear you.

Donovan: I said, Your Honor, that I object to the admission of the contents of any such message he has testified to, under these circumstances where he cannot identify where he put such a message.

Judge Byers: He said it was either one or the other. The jury will know how to treat the testimony. If there is an objection, it will be overruled.

Throughout, Hayhanen repeatedly testified that he met with "Soviet officials," he was in communication with these "Soviet officials" and when the old drops were no longer convenient he was given new locations by the "Russian officials." When I complained that we were entitled to know who these people were, the judge again suggested that if I were patient the prosecution would "get around to these facts."

Judge Byers: Let's not interfere with Mr. Tompkins. He may ask that question. All I am saying is that if you will give Mr. Tompkins a chance, it is possible that he will develop it.

The Government took the hint.

Q. Mr. Hayhanen, will you describe who these Soviet officials that you have referred to in your testimony are?

A. I know just about one Soviet official who was connected, who had conversations, several conversations, with me and would be talking about these espionage work.

140

The Court: Who is the one you know? What is his name?

Hayhanen: Svirin.

The prosecutor, not satisfied to have it appear he knew only one official, plunged forward.

Q. Now, when you speak of communicating with Soviet officials, receiving communications through drops and sending them, who are you referring to? You called them Soviet official people, I believe?

A. Yes.

Q. What do you mean by that term?

A. I mean like I explained already, I mean that kind of people who came to this country with Soviet passports, Soviet citizens.

Donovan: Your Honor, I respectfully object that instead of simply defining "what you mean by such a word," he should tell who are these specific Soviet officials.

Judge Byers: He has told us that there was only one that he knew.

Donovan: But then, Your Honor, he dealt with Soviet officials, as I understand his testimony, and yet he cannot apparently pinpoint his testimony . . .

Tompkins: Your Honor, he was instructed in Moscow who to communicate with.

Judge Byers: You know, these arguments are diverting, but they also interfere with the trial. If you have an objection, Mr. Donovan, if you will state your objection, I will try to rule on it.

Donovan: I object, Your Honor, to the last question and ask that the answer be stricken from the record.

The judge asked the court reporter to read the question again and then instructed the prosecutor to ask the witness, instead, whether he had met any of the people he was talking about.

Tompkins: If I can develop it this way, I would rather.

Judge Byers: All right; you do it your way.

Q. As I understand your testimony, you were given the location of three drops in Moscow in your instructions?

A. That is right.

Q. And the purpose of locating those drops was to enable you to communicate with Soviet officials, is that correct?

A. That is right.

Q. Did you ever meet any of those Soviet officials?

A. I met only Svirin, like I mentioned before, and by Soviet officials, I meant Soviet people, like I told . . .

Donovan: Your Honor, I respectfully suggest that all of this testimony is highly prejudicial and is properly objectionable.

Judge Byers: I don't think it is prejudicial, I agree that it is quite vague and indefinite; but I can't see that it is prejudicial. I think specifically he has said that he deposited in the drops information intended for certain people whom he never met, isn't that so?

Hayhanen: That is right.

Tompkins: Pursuant to his instructions in Moscow.

Judge Byers: Yes. I guess that is as far as he can testify, except that he dealt with this man Svirin.

Hayhanen testified further that on the twenty-first of each month he would stand near the Lincoln Road exit of the BMT Prospect Park subway station in Brooklyn, for what he described as visual meeting. For identification purposes he would be smoking a pipe and wearing a colored tie. His testimony on this subject provided a touch of comic relief.

Q. What did you wear, if you remember, at these meetings?

A. I had to wear a blue tie with red strips, and I had to smoke a pipe.

Judge Byers: Blue tie with red what?

Hayhanen: Stripes or strips, how it is.

Tompkins: Stripes.

Judge Byers: Stripes?

Hayhanen: Yes, with red stripes.

Judge Byers: You say you also smoked a pipe?

Hayhanen: Yes, but I do not smoke myself, but I had to smoke that time.

It was at this rendezvous that Hayhanen and Svirin met. The Soviet UN official gave the secret agent a package of photographed letters from his family in Russia and a message which Hayhanen explained was a May Day greeting with a note that his family was well and "hoped me success." There were two such meetings.

Hayhanen: I met him at least twice, what I remember. It was fall because it was raining, and I believe it was fall. It was raining that night, and I believe it was fall, 1953. Or maybe it was in—could be even spring, 1954, because in springtime, there is raining, too. But only thing what I remember about that night, that it was raining.

Q. Can you fix the date this way, to the best of your recollection: How many months after the first meeting? You say the first meeting was in the spring of 1953. How many months after that meeting, roughly, would you say you met Svirin the second time?

A. I cannot remember, for my best recollection.

The prosecutor turned then from Svirin to a Finnish sailor (code name Asko) who served as a courier between Moscow and New York. Hayhanen and the sailor had drops and signal areas. One of their drops was a phone booth in a Manhattan bar. At this point the judge stirred and at 3:50 P.M. motioned to Tompkins.

"Take a recess, Mr. Tompkins, until tomorrow morning at 10:30."

Tuesday, October 15

The setting and the players could be the same, but each day was different. Everyone appeared in exactly the same position: the judge behind the long, chest-high bench designed for a three-member Federal court; the sober jury, as before; the lawyers with their papers and pads at their long smooth-topped tables and, in a moment, the now familiar figure on the witness stand.

"United States versus Abel," the clerk called.

Tompkins: May we have the witness, please.

Walking quickly over the faded and dusty floor tiles, Reino Hayhanen came on for his second full day of testimony.

Outside the court, Hayhanen wore large dark glasses. These, his brush mustache and perhaps the extra weight he carried, all were part of his disguise. Before long, he might begin a new life in the United States and already he was trying to create a new identity for himself—or so it seemed.

The prosecutor began with a recap of yesterday's closing moments.

Tompkins: Now, Mr. Hayhanen, at the close of yesterday's session, I had commenced asking you some questions about Asko. I believe you said you knew him. I believe you testified you had drops with Asko . . .

Hayhanen proceeded to tell of the drops he and Asko used ("in Riverside Park around Eightieth Street, and under lamp-post Number 8113.") and then, in a curious piece of testimony, said he was ordered by Mark to test Asko's trustworthiness.

We had not been under way five minutes, but I was determined not to permit a continuation of yesterday's leading of the witness by the prosecution. I got to my feet slowly.

Donovan: Your Honor, I ask that the answer be stricken unless it is identified with respect to this conversation as to when and where it took place.

Tompkins (obviously annoyed): If I could only try my own case, Your Honor. I would develop that. I think I am entitled to develop it my own way and not Mr. Donovan's way.

Donovan: Your Honor, I have been extremely patient in accordance with your request yesterday. He is not only trying his own case, he is his own witness—

Tompkins (sharply): That is ridiculous.

Donovan: I have not objected to questions as to form, I have been very careful in objecting to those that are leading; on the other hand with respect to vague testimony, at this time with respect to whether he had a conversation, we don't know when it was, where it was. I simply want the record to note that.

Judge Byers: Your objection is noted. I think the conversation he had with Mark is admissible in evidence.

Repeated defense objections became part of the pattern of this second trial day. We naturally ran the risk of alienating the jury, but we were now convinced this risk was necessary to keep the trial record from becoming overlarded with irrelevant, unsupported and prejudicial testimony.

Abel, who properly exercised a voice in the defense, threw his full support behind our tactics. I had heard him on the subject the evening before, after we had adjourned, and I was reminded of what he had told Judge Abruzzo in August when he first asked for assigned defense counsel. He had said he wanted a lawyer who would fight for him but would not turn the trial into a public spectacle. The Colonel was surprisingly familiar with recent American trials, especially those of American Communists. He called some "side shows" and was critical of the defense lawyers.

As I stood to be heard each time, to put forth an objection on behalf of Abel, one could feel the hostility of almost all in the courtroom. I was trying to prevent "the Government" from establishing the truth about this Russian spy. The resentment was like a chain reaction, triggered by my slightest movement. If I sat still, all was calm. If I climbed up out of my chair, it was touched off.

(Long after the trial was ended, I had a quiet drink and a long talk with an FBI agent who had worked on the case and sat through the trial as an observer.

"We used to sit there in the back," he said, "and you were the enemy. We began by hating you, wondering what it would be like to be on the stand against you. But after a while we liked the way you fought for your man. Some of us even got to like you a little.")

Tompkins began again by asking about Hayhanen's first meeting with Abel. The witness told how they came together in the smoking room of the movie theater in Flushing.

> *Q.* At this first meeting, did Mark tell you where he lived?
> *A.* No.
> *Q.* Did he tell you where he—whether he worked or not?
> *A.* Not in the first meeting. Then, later, in later meetings he told that he has some small shop somewhere in Brooklyn.
> *Donovan:* Objection.
> *Judge Byers:* Did he say what kind of shop?
> *Hayhanen:* He told that small shop, but he didn't explain it more carefully or in more detail. Then, later, he told that he has storage place in Brooklyn, storage room for his equipment and what he has, and other things.
> *Donovan:* Do I understand it to be this witness's testimony that all of this was told at this meeting? This first meeting?
> *Judge Byers:* No. He said that it was at a later meeting, Mr. Donovan.
> *Donovan:* He has never identified the time or place of those meetings.
> *Judge Byers:* You know what cross-examination is, don't you? You are an experienced lawyer.

Donovan: Your Honor, I also know when objections should be made to incompetent testimony.

Judge Byers: All right. Your objection is noted, and it is overruled.

A second new pattern also began to take form. Whereas the Government had been content the day before to establish that Hayhanen was a Soviet agent and have him tell something of his routines, they were now ready to forge the link between Hayhanen and Abel. They were intent on showing the authority Abel held over this witness.

It was May of 1955, Hayhanen said, and Mark had told him of his Fulton Street storage room.

Q. Did you ever visit the storage room?
A. Yes, I did once . . . one evening Mark told me that he has some photo equipment to give me and let's go and take them from storage room. So we came to Fulton Street, 252, on fourth or fifth floor, it was located that his storage room . . . but Mark already brought downstairs some photo equipment, some more photo equipment, and I took it to Newark, New Jersey.

The jury did not realize it, perhaps, but they had just heard how Abel's career had come crashing down about him. If Abel had not committed the unthinkable espionage error of allowing subagent Hayhanen to learn the whereabouts of his superior's studio, things might have been different. This error of judgment had led to Abel's arrest and, in time, the jury trial for his life.

(Despite Hayhanen's testimony that he remembered the precise address of the storage studio on Fulton Street, the FBI was to tell a slightly different story three years later. In a signed article, "The Case of the Faceless Spy," which appeared in a newspaper Sunday supplement on October 23, 1960, FBI Director J. Edgar Hoover wrote: "On just one occasion Abel had incautiously exposed himself to discovery. Hayhanen had been short of photographic material and Abel took him to a storage room in Brooklyn where he kept supplies. Hayhanen could not remember the address, but the room was on the fourth or fifth floor, and he knew the building was somewhere around Fulton and Clark Streets. Agents swarmed over the area . . . a surveillance was set up. . . .")

Tompkins continued: Now, in addition to the photograph supplies that you said you picked up, did you pick up anything else at 252 Fulton Street from Mark?

> A. Yes, I picked up also radio.
> Q. What kind of a radio?
> A. A short-wave radio.

Hayhanen and Abel drove into Westchester County, he said, and they tested the radio near the Croton Reservoir. Abel had explained he needed a place where he could safely pick up radio messages. The radio, however, failed to work ("maybe fuse was burned out or something happened"), so Abel gave it to Hayhanen, saying he had another one back in Brooklyn.

In fixing a time for this incident, Hayhanen said it took place in late May or early June in 1955, "before Mark went to Moscow." Throughout the day, he repeatedly dated a conversation, a meeting, a message as happening either before or after "Mark went to Moscow." Just as often, I objected. There was nothing in the record, I urged, to show Abel ever went to Moscow.

> Tompkins: Mr. Hayhanen, in your testimony you have referred on a couple of occasions, in attempting to fix a date— you have used the phrase "before Mark went to Moscow." Do you know whether Mark did go to Moscow? Did you ever have a conversation with him about it, let's put it that way?
>
> A. Yes. We had several conversations about his trip to Moscow, and he went for Moscow, from my best recollection, tenth of June, 1955.

Q. Do you know how he went to Moscow? Boat or train or what method of conveyance?

Donovan: Objection.

Judge Byers: Well, if the witness saw Mark off, he could say that he saw him leave by a certain method of transportation. I don't know that he isn't going to.

Donovan: Unless he saw Mark on a nonstop flight to Moscow, I don't know how he could testify that Mark went to Moscow.

Tompkins: I will withdraw the question.

Q. Did Mark tell you he was going to Moscow?

A. Yes, he did. He told me that he has to go through Austria, and then when he came back from Moscow and we met he explained to me first he took a plane to Paris; from Paris by train he went to Austria and from Austria—then I cannot remember exactly how he went from Austria.

But this did not end the vague questions and answers. They occurred again, and again.

Donovan: Pardon me, Your Honor, couldn't we have references to the normal calendar years and months, rather than repeating over and over again an identification prior to a trip to Moscow which has not been proven?

Judge Byers: Does it make any difference to you if we refer to June, 1955, or the trip to Moscow? Does it make any difference to you?

Tompkins: I can't see any great difference.

Donovan: It makes a great difference to me.

Tompkins: If Mr. Donovan will tell me what difference it makes to him, I will be glad to do it.

Judge Byers: I would rather not do that, I am afraid he will make a speech.

Tompkins: All right.

My objections were meeting with less and less success. This time I did not sit down, I was sat down.

The prosecution went back now, to the early meetings between Abel and Hayhanen. Tompkins asked if he knew the locations of Abel's drops, and Hayhanen said he could identify Nos. 2, 4, 6 and 7. The Symphony Theater at 2537 Broadway he described as both a meeting place and drop No. 2: under a carpet in the balcony.

"I know he had drop Number Six on Riverside Drive around 104th Street, I believe . . . it was for thumbtacks on the bench. There are benches for public and underneath . . . middle bolt [slat] of bench, under that Mark put thumbtack . . . Once he put message over there, and he showed me how he is using it."

For Abel, this testimony must have been particularly humiliating. Here he was being exposed, stripped of his professional veneer, by this bungler sent to be his protégé and in whom he had had to place a certain trust and confidence. There was a pathetic quality to this last scene: the old master spy sitting on a park bench and feeling underneath to leave a message, while a short distance away the young man watched to see how it was done. Now the incompetent apprentice turned on the prideful old master.

Unlike yesterday, their eyes never met. During this second day in the witness box, propped up before the entire court, Hayhanen never looked down at Abel. The Colonel, in turn, rarely looked up from his note taking. He was conscious that he was the central figure in the drama that filled the deep, high-ceilinged courtroom.

Newsmen and others who sat in the courtroom day after day, watching Abel take notes, sketch and talk easily with defense counsel during recesses, believed that he was ice-cold, a dispassionate calculator unconcerned over the outcome of the trial. They couldn't have been more wrong. It was his iron self-discipline that allowed him to sit there calmly and silently, showing no sign that he was living through a physical and emotional ordeal. Unknown to all of us, he was not a well man. He suffered from a serious stomach disorder but never complained of it, or anything else for that matter.

A government officer later told me of Abel's wife's concern for his health. She had once written to him in the Atlanta penitentiary:

> I know and want to trust that you can adapt yourself to any circumstances, but still I worry much of your health. I read somewhere in one of the papers that, as somebody said it then, thanks to that too modest life you used to have, you have now acquired a pain in your stomach. What kind of pain is it, my dear? Is it what you used to have when we were together, that now came back to you again? Do you remember it? How painful it was for you then! You could not swallow even liquid food. How sad if it is so! I know that you would not tell me that your health is bad, only when it would be quite evident that it is really bad, but please, do tell me the truth.

From the subject of Abel's drops and signal areas, Tompkins opened up the question of Hayhanen's assignments—assignments in espionage given him by Abel.

Under close questioning, Hayhanen told of five such ventures, all of which had a common result. They were undistinguished and, in the main, unsuccessful. In one, he said he had traveled to Quincy, Massachusetts (he could not remember the town, only that it was near Boston), to locate a Swedish ship engineer named Olaf Carlson. He believed he had found the right man but could not be sure, for he was instructed only to locate him, not to talk with him.

Hayhanen said he and Abel had also traveled in New York, New Jersey and Pennsylvania ("just to—we been taking some few photos") and then described two trips out of town in search of a good location for sending radio messages. One trip took them to Hopewell Junction, New York; the second to a New Jersey site, near Route 17. Abel rejected the Jersey property because of its price: $15,000. He said this was too much money. He turned down the Hopewell Junction location, too—but never explained why to Hayhanen.

Tompkins asked the witness if Abel had discussed with him the reason for these last two trips.

> *Hayhanen:* Yes, he explained that this illegal radio station should be for transmitting messages to Moscow for officials.
>
> *Q.* Mark ever tell you that he was sending messages?
>
> *A.* He was telling only about sending messages through drops, but not by radio transmitting; but he told that he was receiving by radio messages.
>
> *Q.* Did he tell you how he received the messages? What method?
>
> *A.* Yes, he did . . . He told that he is taking that radio message on tape recording and from tape recording then he is taking it to paper and deciphering it.
>
> *Q.* Do you know whether the defendant had any sending equipment?
>
> *A.* He mentioned couple of times about key, Morse code key.

From the Government's point of view, the most important of Hayhanen's assignments was the locating of Roy Rhodes, code name "Quebec." The orders from Moscow were to proceed to Red Bank, New Jersey, where the agent's family was said to operate three garages. Before Hayhanen plunged into this account, however, we became caught up in intracourt repartee typical of every few minutes of the trial. Innocently enough, I began it.

> *Donovan:* Could we know, Your Honor, when he is supposed to have received these instructions?
>
> *Judge Byers:* You mean, must we know it now or may we know it when you cross-examine him?
>
> *Donovan:* I think we should know it now, Your Honor, in order to enable us to—
>
> *Tompkins:* I submit, Your Honor, I asked the witness a question whether or not he had an assignment, and he starts

telling me about an assignment, and I immediately get an objection on a date.

Judge Byers: Yes. You know what lawyers are, Mr. Tompkins.

Donovan: Your Honor, yesterday he testified that he knew it was the springtime because of the rain, and then he said it might have been fall because it rains in the fall, too.

Tompkins: Is Mr. Donovan summing up?

Judge Byers: No. This is just a little aside, that's all.

Roy Rhodes, of course, was the American soldier Abel had said was tied to the Russians after he compromised himself during a military tour of duty in Moscow at our Embassy. Hayhanen explained that he and Mark failed to locate Rhodes or his family in Red Bank, and at Mark's direction he messaged Moscow for additional information. Word came back that "Quebec" had relatives in Colorado. This time Hayhanen went alone; he made a phone call from Salida, Colorado, to Rhodes's family in nearby Howard and learned from a sister that the soldier was now stationed in Tucson, Arizona.

Q. Now, as I understand, you reported to Mark when you came back that you located Rhodes in Tucson, Arizona?

A. That's right.

Q. Did you discuss Quebec further?

A. Yes. We been discussing that it is, after all, too far to meet him each and to have some meeting place over there, that it will take long time. And Mark told that because he has some other agents and he cannot go for so long trip that I have to locate Quebec. [This was the sole reference during the trial to "other agents" and they never were identified.]

Q. Now, did Mark tell you in any conversation the reason for locating Quebec?

A. Yes. Then, before going to that Colorado trip he gave me a message on film where was more information about

153

Quebec. There was his nickname, his real name, then when he was born and where he was working, and who his parents and relatives are.

Q. What kind of film?

A. It was ordinary thirty-five-millimeter film, but later then I made soft film from it.

Q. What did Mark, if Mark discussed the purpose of locating Rhodes, what did he say to you?

A. He said that Quebec could be good agent because he is—some of his relatives and he are working on military lands. He meant Quebec's brother who was working somewhere, I cannot remember exactly, but in some atomic plant.

Hayhanen then identified a photostat of a film strip which, he said, he had kept hidden in a hollowed-out bolt in his Peekskill home. The prosecution did not offer it as evidence; presumably, they were holding it out for an appropriately dramatic moment.

The witness closed out his testimony on Rhodes with the information that Abel later told him not to bother about Quebec, that on his way to Moscow he would make the contact himself. Moscow apparently changed its mind, for when Abel returned he told Hayhanen he had neither seen nor talked to Rhodes. That was the end of it.

A new development began when Tompkins asked Hayhanen about his trips with Abel outside the city.

Q. On one of these trips did you have occasion to go to Bear Mountain Park?

A. Yes, we did.

Q. And what was the purpose of your trip to Bear Mountain Park?

Donovan: Objection.

Judge Byers: Did you have any conversation about or with Mark concerning the trip to Bear Mountain?

A. Yes.

Judge Byers: What did he say?

A. He said that we have to find couple places to hide some money.

Tompkins: How much money?

A. Five thousand dollars.

Q. Now, will you tell us what else he said?

A. And he said that five thousand dollars we have to give to agent Stone's wife.

Q. Agent Stone's wife?

A. Yes.

Q. Was Stone a code name?

A. Yes, code name.

Q. Will you tell us the name of Stone's wife?

A. His wife is Helen Sobell.

Tompkins (spelling slowly): S-O-B-E-L-L?

A. That is right.

It came quickly and without warning. But it was out, it was on the record. Abel was tied to the Rosenbergs, for Morton Sobell was a convicted member of the Rosenberg apparatus. Julius and Ethel Rosenberg had been convicted of providing the Russians during World War II with vital information on United States atomic weapons. They had been executed in 1953.

Q. What were you to do with the money in Bear Mountain Park?

A. Mark told that we have to locate Stone's wife and ask her to come to Bear Mountain Park where we can talk with her and give her that money.

Q. Did you actually bury the money in Bear Mountain Park?

A. Yes, we did.

Q. All right. Did you at any time in the future bring Helen Sobell to Bear Mountain Park?

A. No, we did not.

Q. Now, after you buried the money, what did you do? Did you leave Bear Mountain Park?

A. Yes, we had . . . Mark told me that I got instructions to give these money to Helen Sobell.

Q. Did he say from whom he had gotten the instructions?

A. From Moscow.

Hayhanen said this was June of 1955 and because Abel was busy preparing for his trip to Moscow, the assignment of getting the money to Mrs. Sobell fell to him. Abel told him that he had tried to approach the woman several times before this but "there was almost all the time a policeman" stationed on a corner near her Manhattan apartment. Hayhanen explained he would identify himself with a letter sent to Abel by the man who recruited "Stone" as an agent.

Q. How was the money buried, all together or how?

A. No, in two different places; three thousand and two thousand dollars.

Judge Byers: Why not gratify our curiosity about it? Were the bills encased in anything? Were they wrapped in anything?

Hayhanen: Yes, they been wrapped in cellophane bag and in paper.

Judge Byers: Who did the wrapping?

Hayhanen: Mark did.

Judge Byers: Did you see him do it?

Hayhanen: No, I didn't see him doing it, but I saw those two packages.

Judge Byers: In his possession?

Hayhanen: Yes, and then we buried them together at Bear Mountain Park.

Tompkins: Did you follow Mark's instructions and give Mrs. Sobell the five thousand dollars?

Hayhanen: No, I did not.

Q. Did you report what you had done in connection with Mrs. Sobell?

A. Yes, I did.

Q. And how did you report your action?

A. I reported that I located Helen Sobell and I gave money and told her to spend them carefully.

At the defense table Abel wrote on his pad, "H reported later that he had located Sobell and given her money, telling her to be careful in spending it." Then he underlined the sentence. It was the only time he was to call attention in this way to any portion of the testimony of any witness. His professional expression, however, never changed.

Hayhanen said he made his report to Moscow through a drop. The reply message called on him to go back to Mrs. Sobell, talk with her and judge whether it was possible to use her as an agent. Prosecutor Tompkins asked the witness if he knew whether Mrs. Sobell previously had been a Soviet agent.

Hayhanen: When Mark explained to me that money should be given to Stone's wife, he explained that usually in Soviet espionage practice they recruit husband and wife together as agents.

Q. So it is your understanding from Mark that both husband and wife had been agents for the Soviet Union?

A. Yes.

The next development in this subplot, said Hayhanen, came after Abel returned from Moscow. Abel reported that he had been instructed to pay Mrs. Sobell an additional $5,000. On this basis, he ordered Hayhanen to arrange a meeting with the woman.

Q. Did you have a meeting with Helen Sobell?

A. No.

Q. Did you have any communication with her?

A. No, but Mark explained that he got those five thousand dollars in the bank.

Q. Now, this is not the same five thousand dollars that you buried?

A. No.

Q. Did you have any other conversation with the defendant Mark concerning Helen Sobell thereafter?

A. No.

The prosecutor now started to ask the witness about his life in Newark but after several minutes of this he broke off and said to the Court, "Your Honor, could I suggest a recess at this point? The witness has been on without interruption. I don't know whether his voice or my legs are giving out."

Without comment, Judge Byers recessed the trial for lunch until two o'clock.

A lot of "little towns" make Brooklyn a metropolis but at noontime in downtown Brooklyn, where the courts are centralized around the Civic Center, it is very much a county seat. Court Street lawyers take their current cases to the curbfront, and during this hour "everybody knows everybody." We left the courthouse this day and crossed the plaza to Joe's Restaurant on Fulton Street. During the trial, there never was any question where we would take lunch. It was local custom that you ate in the hub's most popular restaurant, a throwback to old Brooklyn. It was big, crowded, noisy and there was sawdust on the floor; the service and the food, especially the bean soup, were always good.

When our hour was up, we made our way back to court, stopping to look at the headlines on the newsstands. The trial was still page-one and the latest headline was LINK ABEL TO ROSENBERGS. Meanwhile, in Manhattan, Mrs. Sobell was denying that she or her husband ever committed espionage. She said Hayhanen's "meaningless testimony is just a way of smearing me . . ." All she asked was visitation rights with her husband, for the stated purpose of breeding.

Back on the witness stand Hayhanen was like a sad-faced clown

158

in the circus. By his own recital he was so clumsy and unsuccessful that it had become increasingly difficult to think of him as an enemy agent dangerous to our government. In the corridor outside the courtroom a Federal agent was saying to a magazine writer, "That guy couldn't get a job as a spy in a Marx Brothers movie."

The prosecutor wanted to know when and where Hayhanen had met with Abel after the Colonel returned. The two agents had not been together from June, 1955, until July the following year. Where was this reunion?

Hayhanen: There was some misunderstanding. When I got that message there was just that "I like to meet you in the same place as before."

The last time Abel and Hayhanen had been together, they were in the Symphony Theater on Broadway. Abel, who sent the message, wanted Hayhanen to meet him in the theater in Flushing, where they first joined up.

Hayhanen: I remembered that I met Mark last time in movie theater, Symphony movie theater, so I went over there and looks to me Mark was looking for me in RKO Keith Theater. So then I sent a message that I will go and wait for meeting with you in the same place where I met first time Mark.

When they finally held their meeting, Abel told Hayhanen that his work was unsatisfactory and he should return home to visit his family.

Q. Now, Mark . . . was dissatisfied because of your failing to set up the photographic shop in Newark?
A. That's right.
Q. And he suggested that you might go home on leave to Moscow; is that correct?
A. That's right . . . Mark explained that he sent the message

to Moscow which said that because I didn't open the photo shop, I may as well go—or, there is time for me to go for a vacation.

Q. Did you receive any communication granting you leave?

A. Yes. I got a message from Moscow where it was said that my vacation is permitted and as soon as possible I have to apply for United States passport and go as a tourist to Europe. [This same message also promoted Hayhanen to lieutenant colonel.]

On April 24, 1957, Hayhanen sailed for Le Havre aboard the French liner *Liberté*. In Paris, he followed Abel's instructions. He called the special number (KLE-3341) and asked, "Can I send through your office two parcels to the U.S.S.R. without Mori Company?"

Tompkins: And you got a reply to that statement?
Hayhanen: Yes, I got the reply.

Q. After receiving the reply what did you do?

A. Then I went to meeting place and I met one Russian official. I was wearing the same blue tie and was smoking a pipe . . . We been walking several blocks and then we went to one bar where we been drinking cognac and had a cup of coffee.

Q. What happened after that?

A. Then he gave me some money in French francs and in American dollars, two hundred dollars.

The following night Hayhanen and the Soviet official held a visual meeting. Neither one spoke. By prearrangement, Hayhanen was wearing no hat and carried a newspaper. This meant he would leave the next day for West Berlin and then on to Moscow.

Q. Now, the next day, where did you go?

A. The next day I went then to American Legation in Paris.

Q. After you went to the Embassy what did you do?

A. I explained that I am Russian espionage officer in rank of lieutenant colonel and I have some information what I like to give to American officials to help.

Hayhanen never went any further than this. He gave no reason for his defection and, in fact, never used the word. He was supposed to have told the FBI he was "fed up" with the whole business and had grown disenchanted when he had not been given a "safe" post in an embassy—in the world of "legal" espionage.

Q. At the time that you went in the American Embassy and conferred with these officials, did you give them anything?

A. Yes, I gave as proof Finnish five marks coin which I explained is a container, that is made from two coins.

The Government then introduced into evidence the coin which Hayhanen said he had turned in at the American Embassy in Paris. He explained that it could be identified by a tiny hole which, "if you punch it with needle you can open this container." He then demonstrated for the jury.

I objected to the introduction of the coin on the ground that Hayhanen, the minute he walked into the Embassy, had left the conspiracy ("if he ever was in one") and therefore could not give testimony about what happened after this time in a manner binding upon the accused defendant Abel. I also added a second objection to the coin.

Donovan: Your Honor, will the Government stipulate that similar devices are readily obtainable in magician supply shops and various similar stores?

Tompkins: Your Honor, I have never seen anything like this in my life.

Donovan: That isn't what I asked, Your Honor.

Tompkins: I honestly don't—I don't think they are obtainable anyplace.

Judge Byers: I don't think that Mr. Donovan's request is germane to the present state of the examination. You have asked the witness to demonstrate how this exhibit can be opened . . . and he demonstrated. Now, I suggest that you reassemble it and let the jury look at it, perhaps they would like to experiment with it. In the meantime, you find out if Mr. Donovan is well informed as to his source of supply. I don't think it is important.

It was ten minutes to four. The courtroom was close and warm. The prosecution put another exhibit before the Court—some notes Abel had given Hayhanen—and we haggled on a minor point. Was Hayhanen competent to identify Abel's handwriting?

The judge looked over at the jury; they were passing the split coin down the row.

Judge Byers: It is within three minutes of closing time, Mr. Tompkins. Do you want to use the three minutes screwing and unscrewing that?

Tompkins: No. I think, if we are that close, sir, that we are just going to start a new subject, and that will be the close of our direct examination.

With the monotonously familiar warning ("Members of the jury, I have to repeat, I do not do it because I like to, you are not . . .") that they must not discuss the case or talk to anyone about it, the judge sent the jury on its way. We moved slowly out of the courtroom; Hayhanen was almost finished and cross-examination was at hand.

"The Government wants a long trial—three weeks, maybe a month. It wants to show, once and for all, how the Russians spy on the free world."

This was the rumor. I had heard it before the trial, read it in one of the papers and even now it circulated in the court corridors. The prosecution staff assured us it was only a rumor. I hoped so.

As this third trial day began, I had a feeling that I'd been inside the courtroom listening to Hayhanen for days on end. It seemed too that we had been here, all of us, without interruption and there had been no recess Monday night or Tuesday night. There was a sameness to everything and a staleness to the room, the cast of characters and especially to the hulking witness.

For eight and a half hours Hayhanen had sat up there in front. Meanwhile, each night we had studied every scrap of information we had about him and his fantastic career; last evening we had raced around Manhattan looking for hollowed-out coins and, between taxis, reading a typed transcript of the preceding day's testimony.

In this atmosphere, we welcomed the diversion produced by the battle of the coins. Despite the fact the judge had told us he didn't regard it as important, we threw ourselves into this side-bar controversy as if the outcome of the trial was to be balanced by this single Finnish five-mark piece.

The coin was hollow and so was our dispute, but neither side wanted to recognize it in this moment.

Tompkins: If Your Honor please, at the close of yesterday or pretty close to it, I think you had asked Mr. Donovan and me if we would check on whether devices similar to the coin were readily available. I can only give the Court the benefit of information on a similar type coin that was machined the same way—it was a nickel in this case. Inquiries were made, and the coin exhibited, and the owner of a novelty business who had been in the business for twenty-eight years, and who said he was thoroughly familiar with every known trick coin, examined it and said he did not believe it was a trick coin made for novelty purposes.

In other words, he pointed out the coin could not be used for any other coin and said the hole in the head side of the coin was something he had never seen before.

Donovan: Your Honor, none of these statements is made on the basis of expert testimony. It is improper to introduce them in evidence.

Tompkins: Just bearing on the fact Mr. Donovan said that these were readily available, sir.

Judge Byers: You are not stating something you believe to be in evidence?

Tompkins: Not evidence, no, sir.

Judge Byers: You are answering a comment made by Mr. Donovan to the effect that these articles were currently on sale by those who sell devices that are used by sleight of hand—

Tompkins: Magicians.

Judge Byers:—performers and other magicians, and you are just answering that comment now.

Tompkins: That is right.

Judge Byers: And what Mr. Donovan said is not evidence and what you say is not evidence.

Tompkins: That is correct, sir.

Donovan: Your Honor, with all respect to whoever is the owner of the novelty shop, last night I saw several hollowed-out American pennies. I am prepared to produce some hollowed-out foreign coins, which I made arrangements to have delivered to me, and I am also prepared, even with very little practice last night, at some appropriate point to perform several coin tricks which are based on the hollowed-out coin principle; and I even have the tricks with me now. I suggest until I have the hollowed-out—

Judge Byers: What would that tend to prove?

Donovan: I can show, Your Honor, I am sure, that hollowed-out coins have not only been known for many years, but are commonly sold in magic circles. I saw one last night, Your Honor.

Judge Byers: We have the statement of counsel in the record, and I repeat, it is not evidence before the jury.

Tompkins: Your Honor, may I ask Mr. Donovan one question? Do his hollowed-out coins have a hole you can put a needle in?

Donovan: I have one that has a hollow you can put a needle in. In fact, I have it in my pocket.

The argument was dropped here and I never did have the opportunity to display my hollowed-out coins to the jury. I later gave them to my children.

Tompkins began now by cleaning up odds and scraps left over from yesterday. Top item on the agenda was the $5,000 buried in Bear Mountain Park. Some people, including one of the newspapers, which reported the United States government had found the money, were unsure of what Hayhanen had done with the $5,000.

Q. Mr. Hayhanen, yesterday you testified that you and the defendant buried five thousand dollars in Bear Mountain Park and that the purpose was to transmit the five thousand dollars eventually to Mrs. Sobell. Is that correct?

A. That's right.

Q. And you also testified you did not transmit that money, isn't that correct?

A. I did.

Q. Will you tell us what you did with it?

A. I kept it myself.

Q. Now, after the defendant returned from Moscow—

The Judge wasn't satisfied. He interrupted to ask:

Q. Let me see. Didn't he testify that he had buried it?
Tompkins: They buried it together, Your Honor.
Judge Byers: Yes. How could he both keep it and bury it?
Tompkins: He was instructed, as I recall, to turn over the money to Mrs. Sobell by the defendant when the defendant left this country.
Judge Byers: Yes.
Tompkins: And the witness says he did not do so.
Q. Did you dig up the money?
A. Yes, I digged them out and I kept them myself.

The dark red walls of the Kremlin, dating from the fifteenth century, were more than 4,600 miles from this Brooklyn courthouse. Hayhanen took courage from this fact. Calmly and deliberately, he was testifying—for the second time—how he double-crossed the KGB and stole the $5,000. Just as coolly, he now explained that he lied to Abel when he told him a story of three men following him. This had been his excuse for not leaving the United States when so ordered by Abel.

Q. Now, was that true or not? Were you followed?
A. No, it is not.

Tompkins wanted to know next about his experience with secret messages sent as microdots. Hayhanen said that in November or December, 1954, Abel had given him written instructions on the preparation of microdots and told him to practice.

Q. Did you transmit microdots on any occasion yourself?
A. I got the instructions from Mark to practice on making those microdots the way he showed me and I was practicing in 1954–55 winter.
Q. Did you ever show him the results of your practicing?

A. Yes, I did . . . he explained to me that I didn't get good enough results, that he was getting better and more contrasting microdots, so I was practicing more, later.

Q. Do you know whether the defendant transmitted microdots?

A. Yes, he did.

Q. Do you know whether he mailed any of these microdots?

A. Yes, I know by his own words.

Q. What did he tell you?

A. He told me that he is sending microdots by mail to Paris, France.

Q. Was he sending them by letter?

A. No, he was sending them inside of magazines.

Q. Will you explain what he told you, how he sent them, if you know?

A. Without magazine it is difficult for me to explain. But he put those microdots, he glued them inside where magazine is. How you call them—

Q. Stapled?

A. Stapled, yes, he just wrote where staple was . . . then he stapled it back again and nobody could recognize because nobody would look in between stapling.

Q. Do you know what kind of or type of magazine he used?

A. He was using *Better Homes* [*Better Homes and Gardens*] and *American Home*. There is two types he mentioned to me.

Despite this ingenious method and despite what Hayhanen said about nobody looking along the stapled edges, the respectable middle-class magazines and their hidden messages were not received. Abel was finally told "by Moscow" to discontinue sending them and "they did not find what happened to those magazines."

Tompkins sat down then and assistant prosecutor Kevin Maroney questioned Hayhanen on the messages he had received and the code in which the messages were written. The witness said he sent about twenty-five messages and received thirty in the four and a half years he was resident assistant. All these messages were in his individual code.

Q. In other words, no other agent had that particular code, is that correct?
A. No. That is right.

The Government introduced what it called a hypothetical message, written in Russian in Hayhanen's personal code. He proceeded to give a detailed explanation of how the code worked, deciphering one of the Government's hypothetical messages.

I objected on the ground that the message, as explained by Hayhanen, was incomprehensible, meaningless as an exhibit and therefore irrelevant.

Judge Byers disallowed the objection, commenting caustically, "Perhaps the jury will understand what isn't clear to you and me."

During Hayhanen's lengthy code explanation, which I still regard as unintelligible, people left the courtroom for a smoke and a juror looked at his watch. Several others in the jury rows stared across the court and out the twelve windows—four banks of three. I had counted them a thousand times since 10:30 Monday morning.

When the witness finished, Maroney asked him whether Abel had a similar code.

Hayhanen: Mark told me that he had the code but he was using—he was ciphering and deciphering different way; that he was using special small books with numbers what makes ciphering easier than by this method.

After two and a half days—it seemed sometimes like two and a half light years—the direct examination was done. Even the judge was skeptical.

Judge Byers: Does that mean that the direct examination is closed?

Maroney: Yes, sir.

We promptly made a motion to have the Government turn over to us all the statements Hayhanen had made to the FBI, including the "substantially verbatim" notes taken by agents during the interrogations. Under a new Federal Court rule, an outgrowth of the Supreme Court's famous Jencks decision, the defense had a right to inspect certain statements made to the FBI by Government witnesses. The Supreme Court declared that these were "relevant to the cross-examining process of testing the credibility of a witness' trial testimony."

At our insistence, and only after considerable tugging and pulling, Judge Byers agreed to inspect the FBI file in the Abel case and rule on what constituted "notes" and to which materials we were entitled. There was no argument about the fact that we should get all of Hayhanen's signed statements; three of these, along with a diagram he drew, were immediately turned over by the prosecution. The judge said he would begin his review at 2 P.M. and then turned to the subject of my cross-examination.

Judge Byers: Couldn't you begin your cross-examination now? Get the reports, study them, and then continue your cross-examination?

Donovan: No, Your Honor. This man now has been testifying for two and a half days. I assure you from the reading of the transcript that at times when I think I am in 1951 in Moscow, I find him at New Utrecht Avenue and Fifty-sixth Street, Brooklyn.

It simply is going to take time. We worked last night trying to do this, but I respectfully ask that since Your Honor had told me at the very commencement of the case that you would give us sufficient time to prepare his cross-examination, I ask that I have until tomorrow morning to go over what the man has spent two and a half days testifying to.

Tompkins said he had no objection to the continuance, explaining he did not want to "bind Mr. Donovan." The judge looked to the jury. "Members of the jury, apparently it is necessary for us to take a recess until tomorrow morning, say ten-forty in the morning . . ."

As the courtroom cleared, we began to make plans. There were 325 pages of Hayhanen's direct testimony; we had to pick up later the transcript of the morning's session; and there were the FBI notes Judge Byers would permit us to see. We also had to confer with Abel. Debevoise offered to visit him now, down in the court detention pen.

Tom reported back later that Abel seemed relieved that this part of the trial was behind him. He also told a curious story. Abel smilingly said Hayhanen had forgotten to tell of the time they were driving across the George Washington Bridge and Abel volunteered that one bomb probably could take care of it.

"Abel laughed and made out it was a joke," said Tom. "At least I hope it was a joke."

Thursday, October 17

On this day, for the first time, the defense would control the action. This would be our show. It was opening day all over again: a crowded courtroom, excitement, tension, people talking in the lobby, in the elevators, the corridors.

I felt very strongly that we must not "overtry" our case. Every defense lawyer in a criminal action risks alienating the judge and jury when he moves to the offensive. If he attacks blindly, without reason or motive, asking questions without reasonable assurance of the answers, he shows himself to be a desperate fool. This is always the temptation of a young trial lawyer.

Hayhanen today took the stand mechanically, and the judge, ready to get on with the day's work, said only, "Cross-examination."

Donovan: Mr. Hayhanen, to your knowledge have you ever been indicted in the United States?

A. I couldn't understand your question.

Tompkins (immediately objecting): If Your Honor please, if counsel can show any conviction I have no objection, but the indictment—

Judge Byers: I do not understand that the question is competent as to an indictment. You know, any person is presumed to be innocent.

Donovan: Your Honor, he has been named in this indictment as a co-conspirator. He has been testifying for three days that he has committed a wide variety of offenses against the United States.

Tompkins: If Your Honor please, I think this is highly prejudicial.

Donovan: It has the additional advantage of being true, Your Honor.

Tompkins: As to his being named as a co-conspirator, I concede that.

Judge Byers: I am against interruptions. Let Mr. Donovan finish, please.

Donovan: I submit, Your Honor, that it is very relevant and competent to ask this witness whether he has, up to this time, either been indicted with respect to any of these matters, or has been accused by any Federal officials of having committed these crimes.

Judge Byers: I didn't understand that to be your question.

Donovan: That is the sole question that I had, Your Honor.

Judge Byers: If your question is: Have you been indicted with respect to any matters concerning which you have testified in this trial, I will allow the question.

Donovan (facing the witness): With respect to these matters concerning which you have testified in this trial, to your knowledge, Mr. Hayhanen, have you ever been indicted in the United States?

A. I cannot understand the word "indicted."

Q. Have you been formally charged with any crime, with respect to these matters concerning which you have been testifying?

A. For my best knowledge, no.

Q. Now, prior to May 6, 1957, did you ever have any conversation with any American officials, police or otherwise, concerning your activities in the United States or Russia?

A. No.

I then introduced as Exhibit A for identification, a 37-page statement in Hayhanen's handwriting which he had drawn up in May and June for the FBI and which we had read for the first time the night before. It was in Russian and our translation into English was added to the statement and became Exhibit B. The witness gave this explanation of the paper: "FBI agents asked me to write about my life, so I did. I wrote this in my hotel room. I didn't write in the same day because FBI agents been questioning me, and when I had time I was writing this letter."

The judge and then Tompkins, when he caught the drift, requested me to name the translator of the statement written in Russian by Hayhanen. I was extremely reluctant. The translator, of course, was the defendant Abel, whom we had pressed into service late yesterday.

Tompkins: I beg your pardon. Will counsel tell the witness? I can't see any objection to telling the witness who translated this document.

Donovan: Your Honor, I believe the witness is ready to answer my question ["Is the translation accurate?"].

Judge Byers: Mr. Donovan doesn't want to do it, so let's yield to his reluctance.

Donovan: I can assure you that I didn't do it.

Following this, I introduced two additional exhibits which bore the signature of Eugene Nicoli Maki. One was his passport application file from Helsinki, and the other his lease for the store at 806 Bergen Street, Newark. Hayhanen admitted the signatures were his.

Q. I believe, Mr. Hayhanen, that you have testified that in February, 1953, your wife joined you in the United States, is that correct?

A. That is right.

Q. And I believe that you have testified that you were married in 1951? [It was part of the passport application.]

A. That is right.

Q. Isn't it a fact, Mr. Hayhanen, that at the time you say that you married in 1951, you already had a wife and child?

A. It is.

Q. That is true?

A. Yes.

Donovan: And I read to you [from his 37-page life history] the following, which purports to be your own statement to the FBI:

"During the summer of 1948 I was called to Moscow . . . for personal interview with some fellow workers and superiors of PGU [intelligence]. I was in Moscow during several days. . . . A former chief of the operative section who held the rank of major general and was chief of PGU section interviewed me [Hayhanen gave his name as Barishnikov]. . . . After, I gave formal consent to do intelligence work with a condition that I can leave with my wife and son."

Q. Is that correct?

A. Yes, it is, and correct translation, too.

Q. So as I understand your testimony, you are testifying that you have been a bigamist?

Tompkins (jumping up): Now, if Your Honor please, I think his testimony speaks for itself.

Judge Byers (calmly): I don't think he needs to characterize the legal effect of his testimony.

Tompkins: Mr. Donovan is quoting from a document concerning the year 1948?

Judge Byers: Yes.

Hayhanen: I was married in 1951.

Donovan: He has already testified that in 1951—

Judge Byers: I have sustained the objection, Mr. Donovan.

I backed off, paused, then came back at Hayhanen from a different angle.

Q. Is it legal in Russia to have two wives at once?

Tompkins had no more than sat down when he was up again: "I object to that."

Donovan: I think he knows, Your Honor.

Judge Byers: Maybe he knows, but perhaps the jury doesn't care. I will sustain the objection.

I looked at the jury—Dublynn, Burke, Hughes, Farace, Ellman, Kerwin, Marshall, Clair, Smith, McGrath, Werbell and Scheinin.

Donovan: I think the jury would be very interested.

Tompkins: Well, now—

No prosecutor could afford to be on the side of an argument which defended or was indifferent to polygamy. Especially in Brooklyn, the Borough of Churches.

Judge Byers: Perhaps I misapprehended their attitude. I may be wrong.

Donovan: And referring, Mr. Hayhanen, to Exhibit C, consisting of these certified copies of passport documents, is it not a fact that in this passport application upon which your passport was issued December 4, 1956, and signed by you, that in response to the question of present legal spouse you wrote, "Hannah Maki" and gave the date of your marriage as November 25, 1951?

A. That is right.

Q. And yet you admit that on November 25, 1951, you had a wife and son in Russia; is that right?

Hayhanen (suffering now): It was part of my "legend" because—that is why I wrote—answered this way questions.

Q. I asked you a simple question. On November 25, 1951, is it not a fact you had a wife and son in Russia?

A. It is.

Q. To the best of your knowledge, do you still have a wife and son in Russia?

A. I don't know.

Q. Now, with respect to your testimony that in 1953 you were joined here by a woman, who is that woman who joined you?

Again, the prosecutor objected. The judge directed that I ask only: "Who joined you in the United States in 1953?"

Hayhanen: My wife by church marriage.

Q. What is her name?

A. Hannah Maki.

Q. And is this the Mrs. Maki who signed the lease with you on the Bergen Street premises?

A. Yes, she is.

Q. Now, your testimony, as I understand it, Mr. Hayhanen, is that you leased these premises on Bergen Street to serve as a cover for espionage work. Is that correct?

A. It is . . . I was planning to open both a studio and the same—at the same time to sell some photo equipment as film, photo paper, or some cameras.

Q. And this was supposed to be your cover?

A. That's right.

Q. Did you ever open up any such shop—

A. No.

Q. Is it not a fact you boarded up the front windows so as to completely close out any light?

A. I didn't board it.

Q. What did you do with respect to the front windows?

A. I put Glass Wax on front windows because they have been dirty and I left that Glass Wax on those windows up to opening of that business. And because I didn't open, I didn't wash those—that Glass Wax off.

Q. How long were you there?

A. About one year.

Q. During that time, when you had this espionage cover, you had this photographic shop that never opened and had Glass Wax covering the front windows, is that right?

A. That's right.

Q. Now, I want you to think very carefully, Mr. Hayhanen. While you were living at that address with wife number two—

The prosecutor (impatiently): Oh, now, if Your Honor please, I don't think that is fair, to characterize.

Judge Byers (in an even voice): I suppose that numerically he is correct, isn't he?

No answer. Objection overruled, quietly. The prosecutor takes his seat.

Q. I want you to think very carefully—search your recollection on this. While you were living there, was an ambulance ever called to attend you?

A. Yes.

Q. Did the police call that ambulance?

A. No.

Q. Would you kindly explain how the ambulance was called?

Late the night before, our private detective had phoned from Newark. He had finally found, and interviewed, the landlord of the Bergen Street building. The man said he did not "want to become involved" because he had relatives in Russia and pleaded not to become a witness. However, he confirmed everything we had previously learned about Hayhanen. The landlord said he went to the Maki apartment to collect overdue rent and called for an ambulance when he saw Hayhanen's blood condition and blood splattered about the rooms.

A. Landlord came to see us, and he called an ambulance.

Q. Why, if you know?

Tompkins: If Your Honor please. Just a minute. I would like to know what the materiality of this questioning is, Your Honor.

Donovan: The materiality, Your Honor, is this, if you need any—

Judge Byers: You don't have to make a speech every time Mr. Tompkins says he would like to know something. We would all like to know. We will make progress if you continue with your questioning.

Q. If you know, what was the reason why the ambulance arrived?

A. Yes, I know.

Q. Well, tell us.

A. We been packing everything what was ours to move out from that storage; and when I was cutting rope from one package my hand with knife just went around and I cut my leg.

Q. How severe was this wound?

A. It was maybe one and a half inch.

Q. (more quickly now, and raising my voice): Isn't it a fact that the reason the landlord called the ambulance was that blood was all over the premises?

Hayhanen (taken aback): Yes. Not all over, but in a couple rooms.

Donovan: Yes [emphasizing his answer: "Yes."], and isn't it a fact that, I ask you, wife number two had stabbed you in a drunken brawl? Isn't that true?

A. No, it is not. I can answer more if you like about that whole situation.

Q. If you deny that she stabbed you, there is nothing more I can do at this time.

A. She did not. She did not.

Q. Isn't it true that the police on various occasions visited your premises?

A. On various occasions, no.

Q. On several?

A. Just only one.

Q. Would you explain the circumstances?

A. Like I explained already, that when they called an ambulance, with ambulance came some police.

Q. I am not referring to that occasion. I am asking you whether or not the Newark police came to your premises at any other time, to your knowledge, while you were living there.

A. They never been in our premises when we been living over there.

Q. Did they try to get in one night?

A. I don't know but—I believe that nobody tried to, otherwise I would open the door, and ask who is over there, if I was inside.

It was like holding a mirror up to Hayhanen and asking him only to tell what he saw. The mirror, of course, was our private investigator's report. His vision was deliberately distorted. Obviously, he did not know just how much we knew about him and so his answers were a heavy blend: part lie, part truth, part double-talk and all of it poorly translated from his slow Baltic mind into English.

Q. Is it true that on any of these occasions you had been beating your wife?

A. No, it is not.

Judge Byers: Just a minute. You will have to reframe your question. I don't know what you mean by "any of these occasions." He told you the police were there once, to his knowledge. So, please change the form of the question. Were the police there more than once?

Hayhanen: No. Just only once with that ambulance, like I explained.

Again, I stepped back, paused to let the jury reflect on the last question and then began my approach from another direction, never losing sight of my objective.

Q. Do you remember the bakery store next to 806 Bergen Street?

A. Yes, I remember.

Q. Is it not true that one day you entered the store with your wife, bought a loaf of bread, threw it on the floor and ordered the woman to pick it up? Is that true or false?

I wanted a simple one-word answer. Instead, there was an objection.

Tompkins: I don't see what the materiality—

Hayhanen (breaking in): When?

Tompkins (continuing):—of throwing a loaf of bread on the floor is in an espionage case.

Donovan: Your Honor, he has answered, I believe.

Hayhanen: No. I asked you a question, when it was? I cannot recall that kind of thing right now.

After three days on the witness stand, even as stolid a man as Hayhanen learns to protect himself. He had acquired some courtroom clichés but he garbled them, saying, "For my best recollection."

Donovan (incredulously): You mean this is an ordinary incident and you just wouldn't recall it?

Hayhanen: No, it isn't ordinary, but because it is extraordinary, that way, that I believe that it didn't happen. Maybe you can recall to me when it happened.

Q. Do you deny that this ever happened?

A. I just asked, will you please tell me when it happened?

Q. If you can't even recall such an incident—

A. No. Maybe I will recall at that time I was even in different city. That is what I would like to know.

We went round three times and he did not deny that it ever happened. That was good enough. Now to turn the vise still tighter.

Q. At the time you lived in Bergen Street, did you drink?

A. (straightforward) Yes, I was drinking.

Q. How much?

A. (double-talk) In different ways, different weeks, different way.

Q. What is the most you ever drank in one night while you were living at that address?

A. About one pint.

Q. A pint?

A. Yes.

Judge Byers (evincing interest): Of what?

Hayhanen: A pint of vodka.

Q. Isn't it a fact that while you were living there, in Bergen Street, you used to put out in the trash large quantities of liquor bottles? Isn't that true?

Tompkins: What—I would like to know what Mr. Donovan calls large quantities of liquor bottles.

Donovan: A pint of vodka would be good enough for me, but I am just asking the question, Your Honor.

Tompkins: What is a large quantity to Mr. Donovan? A pint?

Judge Byers: I think that the witness is entitled to a rather definite suggestion. A large quantity of bottles over a long period of time would be one thing; a large quantity of bottles over a day or two would be another. Now, he is entitled to know what you are asking him about.

Q. Didn't you at least once a week put out into your trash four or five whiskey bottles or other liquor bottles?

A. Sometimes I put them once a week. Sometimes I put them once in three weeks. Because there are four rooms and big storeroom, there is enough hiding place where I could put those empty bottles.

The answer was a classic confession of a confirmed alcoholic. It conjured up the image of a four-room flat where a man had more than ample room to hide his very own vodka and whiskey bottles: "Because there are four rooms and big storeroom, there is enough hiding place where I could put those empty bottles."

Q. All the time, as we understand your testimony, while you are living there with the windows covered with Glass Wax and throwing out these liquor bottles and having—

Judge Byers (sharply): There is no testimony about windows being covered or his throwing out anything. If you are quoting him, please do it accurately. He said the windows were lined. That is number one. He has not testified that he threw out a large number of liquor bottles. That is number two. Now, please start over again and be accurate.

Hayhanen had covered his storefront with Glass Wax, and he had testified he threw out his hidden empty liquor bottles once a week or once every three weeks. I felt the judge was wrong but my battle was with the witness. He was not in a good position and I wanted to keep him there.

Q. (disregarding the judge) And with an ambulance being called, attended by the police because of this wound on your leg, at this time we are to believe that you are a lieutenant colonel in the Soviet Secret Intelligence and that you were there to conduct a secret espionage cover operation; is that right?

Tompkins: Wait a minute. Is there any proof that the ambulance was attended by a policeman?

Donovan: Yes. I believe that he has so stated.

Judge Byers: I don't think he says the ambulance was attended by the police. I think he said the police were sent with the ambulance.

Donovan: No, Your Honor. The landlord sent for the ambulance. And because of the nature of the injury, a policeman was present.

Q. (to Hayhanen) Isn't that true?

Tompkins: Wait just a minute. Secondly, I think the question is argumentative.

Judge Byers: It certainly is argumentative and recitative. If he answered a plain question: What was your position in the year 1953? That would save time and trouble. Do you wish that?

Donovan: No, Your Honor.

Donovan (shifting fronts): Now, returning to the subject of drink, Mr. Hayhanen, do you still drink?

A. Yes.

Q. How much did you drink yesterday?

A. The whole day?

Again, perfect for our side. Hayhanen thinks like an alcoholic. He is ready, and quick, to rationalize. I could imagine him telling a Big Brother in Alcoholics Anonymous, "I had ten or twelve drinks—but that was all day. We started a little early . . ."

Q. The whole day and the evening.

A. About four drinks as they serve in bars.

Q. Have you had anything to drink this morning?

A. (flatly and guilelessly) I drink this morning coffee and had my breakfast.

Q. [I had nothing to lose here] Any alcohol this morning?

A. No.

Tompkins: I still, Your Honor, don't see the materiality of this line of questioning in a conspiracy to commit espionage.

Judge Byers: It may go to the credibility of the witness.

And that ended that.

I now wound up the cross-examination. Picking up Hayhanen's 37-page written statement to the FBI, I offered it in evidence and then slowly read one portion to the jury, reminding the witness that he had written in his own handwriting:

"I resided and worked in Finland from July 1949 to October of 1952. There I received my American passport and arrived to New York in October of 1952. *I did not engage in espionage activity and did not receive any espionage or secret information from anyone during my stay abroad, neither in Finland nor in the United States of America.*"

Donovan: No further questions, Your Honor.

Tompkins never explained or attacked this curious and contradictory confession of Hayhanen's. He met it with only one quick question—the only one on redirect examination.

Q. Mr. Hayhanen, what were you sent to the United States for?

A. I was sent to the United States as Mark's assistant for espionage work.

Hayhanen left the witness stand; four years later he would be dead, killed in a mysterious automobile crash on the Pennsylvania Turnpike.

Like a pendulum, the case now swung back to the prosecution. For the remainder of that morning and through the afternoon the prosecution continued to strengthen its chain of evidence, adding detail and building background to what already was on the record. Five minor witnesses took the stand: four FBI agents and Mrs. Arlene Brown of Radium, Colorado, sister to Sgt. Roy Rhodes. Mrs. Brown told how in the spring of 1955 she received a phone call from a man—"He had a very heavy accent"—who asked for her brother Roy.

Late in the day, just before we adjourned, there was another piece of testimony on Rhodes, this enigmatic figure. It was dramatic, "surprise" testimony which drew the American soldier closer to this courtroom and catapulted his name into the headlines of the trial which he soon would dominate.

Two days before, Hayhanen had described his search for Rhodes and explained how Moscow had sent a microfilmed message, with a dossier on the GI. FBI agents shuttled to the stand now, to testify in their exact, flat language that the film was found in a bolt wrapped in a Dugan Brothers bread wrapping in Hayhanen's Peekskill home. Special agent Frederick E. Webb, an expert in handwriting and typewriter comparisons, came up from the Bureau's Washington laboratory, to show to the jury photo enlargements of the bolt and to read the message on Rhodes allegedly received by Abel and delivered by him to Hayhanen:

Quebec. Roy A. Rhodes, born 1917 in Oilton, Oklahoma, U.S. Senior Sergeant of the War Ministry, former employee of the U.S. Military Attaché in our country. He was a chief of the garage of the Embassy.

He was recruited to our service in January, 1952, in our country which he left in June, 1953. Recruited on the basis of compromising materials but he is tied up to us with his receipts and information he had given in his own handwriting.

He had been trained in code work at the Ministry before he went to work at the Embassy but as a code worker he was not used by the Embassy.

After he left our country he was to be sent to the School of Communications of the Army C.I. Service which is at the City of San Luis, California. He was to be trained there as a mechanic of the coding machines. He fully agreed to continue to cooperate with us in the States or any other country. It was agreed that he was to have written to our Embassy here special letters, but we had received none during the last year.

It has recently been learned that Quebec is living in Red Bank, N. J., where he owns three garages. The garage job is being done by his wife. His own occupation at present is not known. His father, Mr. W. A. Rhodes, resides in the U.S. His brother is also in the States where he works as an engineer at an Atomic Plant in a Camp in Georgia, together with his brother-in-law and his father.

The judge had explained to both Tompkins and myself that a prior commitment would keep him from the bench the following morning. It was agreed therefore to recess until Monday morning, and he made this announcement to the jury.

We left the courtroom with pluses and minuses. Judge Byers had opened the session in the morning by denying us general access to the FBI notes (he examined the notes of four agents, six packets in all, describing between 75 and 100 interviews, he said). However, we believed that the defense had, to a large degree, discredited Hayhanen as a trustworthy witness.

One news account said, "Mr. Donovan's cross-examination disclosed that whatever the reason for his [Hayhanen's] illegal entry to this country in 1952, he was never of the slightest help to the Soviet government."

Our job now was to prepare to meet M/Sgt. Roy Rhodes, U.S.

Army, as a witness. Outside court the prosecution announced that "early next week" the sergeant would testify. Meanwhile, adding to the mystery which already surrounded the man, public reports circulated that he actually was an American counterspy.

"While there is nothing to substantiate the idea," one news story said, "it is generally believed by observers at the trial that Sergeant Rhodes will be revealed as a counterspy who deliberately led the Russians on."

Monday, October 21

The fifth day, the second week.

Through the first week the shadow of the bulky Reino Hayhanen had lain across the trial and the crowded courtroom in which it was held. Would we go faster, now that we were past Hayhanen's confessional? The prosecution said it had more than fifty witnesses prepared to testify.

The procedures which govern a trial and carry it forward have little regard for dramatic unity, for orderly transition or sequence. A witness is often left over from the day before; a prime witness with revelatory testimony waits in the wings until adjournment and interruption threaten; and after we have faced one witness four successive days, suddenly there are fourteen witnesses to fill the record with only 158 pages of testimony.

The first witness that Monday was Burton Silverman, an artist who had been a friend to "Emil Goldfus" in Brooklyn. Whenever Abel, in his role as Goldfus or Martin Collins, filled in a hotel blotter, he had put Silverman's name in the space left for: "Notify in Case of Emergency."

Silverman was the first person Abel had asked to write him after his capture and imprisonment. The young artist's poignant reply was addressed to me: "After long and painful deliberation I have come to the conclusion that correspondence . . . will not be possible. I trust you understand what motivates this decision, and that it goes counter to my feelings of sympathy for Colonel Abel's isolation and loneliness."

The Government lawyer now was assistant prosecutor Maroney.

> Q. Do you know one Emil R. Goldfus?
> A. Yes.
> Q. Do you see him in the courtroom?
> A. Yes.
> Q. Would you indicate where you see him?

The witness pointed at Abel. Now he was positively identified as the impostor. But the Government called Silverman not to point out Goldfus-Abel, the man with the multiple identities, but to identify his typewriter, found by the FBI in the Fulton Street studio.

"This apparently is a machine that I borrowed from Mr. Goldfus. I think it was toward the end of April or around that time."

When Maroney had put the typewriter (Remington portable, serial number N 1128064) in evidence, he was finished with the witness. We conducted a brief cross-examination and turned the witness around to our side.

> Q. In the course of your acquaintance with the defendant did you visit him on a number of occasions?
> A. Yes.
> Q. Did you converse with him frequently?
> A. Yes.
> Q. And you were friends with the defendant—you and your wife were on friendly terms with the defendant throughout this period, were you not?
> A. Yes.
> Q. And what was the defendant's reputation in the community for honesty and integrity?

There was an objection and the judge stepped in.

Judge Byers: Oh, I think I will allow it. Did you ever discuss his reputation—with other people?

Silverman: Yes. Very definitely.

Judge Byers: For truth telling?

Silverman: Yes. It was beyond reproach.

Q. (repeating) Beyond reproach?

A. Yes.

Q. Did you ever hear anything bad about the defendant in any way?

A. No.

Judge Byers: And these discussions had to do with a man by the name of Goldfus?

Silverman: Yes.

Then there was Harry McMullen, for twelve years the superintendent at the Ovington Studios of 252 Fulton Street. He crossed the street to the courthouse and became a witness. He pointed out Abel as the tenant who had No. 505 and also took storage space in 509 down the hall.

Q. Did you know whether he conducted any business?

A. No. I never saw anybody there.

Q. You never saw anybody there. What do you mean by that?

A. He just painted.

It was Mr. McMullen's purpose as a Government witness to tell the jury that in the middle of 1955 Abel left on a vacation and was gone five or six months. Then, in April of 1957 he paid cash for the months of May and June, explaining he had a sinus infection and was going out of town on a vacation.

"I never saw him no more," the superintendent said, concluding the direct examination.

This was our cross:

Q. Have you ever had occasion to discuss the defendant's reputation with any of these people [in the building]?

A. You mean of late?

[After Abel had been indicted and brought back from Texas to stand trial, one of the weekly news magazines had interviewed and taken pictures of the Colonel's neighbors. McMullen, shown standing in front of his building in an open-necked sport shirt with short sleeves, had said Abel paid his rent on time and once helped him fix the elevator.]

Q. At any time.

A. No, not that I know of. I mean that he was a tenant there, a good tenant.

Q. He was a good tenant?

A. Yes.

In quick succession, four witnesses were called and then went, each telling of his part in the discovery and identification four years ago of the mysterious nickel which split apart and revealed a Soviet coded message.

It was James Bozart, a thirteen-year-old newsboy making his collections one day in the summer of 1953, who had found the coin and began the story.

"And the change slipped from my hand and it dropped on the staircase; and when I picked it up, one of the nickels was split in half. One of them—half of the nickel had a piece of microfilm in it."

The coin and film were turned in to the local police precinct, where a detective called the FBI. The New York office sent them to their Washington laboratory, where the microfilm message lay undeciphered for four years until Hayhanen supplied his personal code. Only then was the message decoded and translated. It now was read to the Court:

We congratulate you on a safe arrival. We confirm receipt of your letter to the address 'V' repeat 'V' and the reading of letter Number 1.

For organization of cover, we gave instructions to transmit to you three thousand in local [currency]. Consult with us prior to investing it in any kind of business, advising the character of this business.

According to your request, we will transmit the formula for the preparation of soft film and news separately, together with [your] mother's letter.

It is too early to send you the Gammas . . .

[The FBI was unsure of what this last meant. The translator had written in the margin, "Meaning here unknown, literally musical exercises."]

Encipher short letters, but the longer ones make with insertions. All the data about yourself, place of work, address, etc., must not be transmitted in one cipher message. Transmit insertions separately.

The packages were delivered to your wife personally. Everything is all right with the family. We wish you success. Greetings from the comrades. Number 1, 3rd of December.

The message clearly—"Number 1"—was the first sent to Hayhanen. The nickel probably was dropped or spent by the frequently drunken and absent-minded agent.

Equally as fascinating and ironical as the story of this misplaced spy coin was the tale which the prosecution now unfolded. Again it began with Hayhanen's defection and disclosure to the FBI that his Prospect Park drop, a hole in a flight of cement steps, had been sealed up with mortar. Apparently, the repairs were the routine work of a conscientious Parks Department crew.

The FBI cracked open the cement step and found a hollowed-out bolt secreting a message. The witness, FBI agent Webb who was recalled to the stand, read the message:

Nobody came to meeting either 8th or 9th at 203. 2030 as I was advised he should. Why? Should he be inside or outside? Is time wrong? Place seems right. Please check.

Webb further testified the typed message had been written on Abel's typewriter, found in the Fulton Street studio, and explained how this note matched other specimens from the same machine. He used, for demonstration purposes, a letter from Emil Goldfus to his landlord and some pamphlets given Hayhanen by Abel on "Use of Vacuum for Making Matrices" and "Color Photography, Separation Negatives."

We took a recess for lunch, then back again at two o'clock for more testimony on the typewriter—"the typewriter sitting right here, Exhibit Number 52." Like most expert testimony, it seemed endless, repetitious and, at times, needless: "The small letter M, which shows next along the top line, the serif to the right—the outside part of the serif is partially missing, as also can be seen. . . . The letter S strikes heavy to the right. . . . The letter P is tilted to the right in so far as the top is concerned, which is a characteristic previously pointed out."

Then the Government called a doctor. There was milling about behind us and some of the back benches emptied. People drifted outside for a smoke, or a breath of cool air, in the long, wide and high-ceilinged corridors. Newsmen headed for the pressroom phones to "check the desk."

Tompkins explained, "If Your Honor please, we are going to put on Dr. Groopman. He will be a little bit out of order, but it is because of his profession. It will be short, Your Honor."

Dr. Samuel F. Groopman said he had offices in the Hotel Latham and on May 21, 1957, the defendant (calling himself Martin Collins) came in for a vaccination.

> Q. Did you so vaccinate him, Dr. Groopman?
> A. Yes, I did.
> Q. At that time did you have any conversation with the defendant concerning foreign travel?
> A. Yes, sir, I did. I asked him where he was going.
> Q. And what did he say?
> A. He said he was going to the north countries to paint.

Two minor witnesses followed the doctor. An FBI agent said he went to Brand's Bar, 58th Street and Fourth Avenue, Brooklyn, and found a thumbtack the alleged courier (Asko) had left for Hay-hanen. The men's room in the bar was a signal area for two agents. Then a State Department records chief testified that Abel never filed as the agent of a foreign government—testimony technically required but almost ludicrous under the circumstances. The State Department man was the prosecution's thirteenth witness.

Tompkins then stood dramatically to make an announcement. "The prosecution is going to call Roy A. Rhodes, Your Honor—Sergeant Rhodes."

He came on, tall and lean, a big-eared fellow. He was a Gary Cooper type but dissolute-looking and could easily have played the deputy marshal in camp shows. He was wearing civilian clothes: a suit too big for him; a broad, colored tie; white shirt with a wide soft collar.

By the time he was on the stand and sworn, the courtroom had filled up again. Tompkins, who had questioned only one witness all day, stood in front of the witness and we were under way.

Q. Sergeant, your full name is Roy A. Rhodes?

A. Yes, sir.

Q. You are a member of the armed forces of the United States?

A. I am, sir.

Q. What branch?

A. Signal Corps, sir.

Q. And what is your rank?

A. Master sergeant, sir.

Q. And how long have you been a member of the armed forces?

A. A little over fifteen years.

Tompkins then drew from the witness a series of answers which established that he was the man whom Moscow called "Quebec," the subject of the microfilmed message to Abel read to the Court last Thursday. Rhodes said he was born March 11, 1917, at Royalton, Oklahoma; his father's name was W. A. Rhodes and in 1955 he lived in Howard, Colorado, just outside Salida. He added that he had three sisters and one of them was Mrs. Arlene Brown of Radium, Colorado, formerly of Howard. His brother was Franklin S. Rhodes.

The Regular Army sergeant testified that he had served at Fort Monmouth, New Jersey (post office address: Eatontown, a neighbor to Red Bank) and his permanent post was Fort Huachuca, Arizona. While stationed there he had lived in Tucson.

Q. Now, during the course of your military service, Sergeant, were you assigned to duty in the Soviet Union?
A. I was.
Q. And what date did you arrive in the Soviet Union?
A. May 22, 1951.

The prosecutor was moving slowly, spreading the facts on the record. Rhodes was showing that a career army man almost never forgets a date on which his duty station was changed and almost always says "sir." He was in Moscow until June of 1953 and during these two years he was motor sergeant for the American Embassy, having charge of the Embassy's fleet of cars maintained in a garage a mile and a half away.

He said he was married, the father of an eight-year-old girl, and that his family joined him in Moscow in February, 1952, ten months after his own arrival. He remembered that his application to bring his wife and daughter to Russia was approved in December of 1951.

Q. Now, Sergeant, directing your attention to the day just prior to Christmas, on which you were advised that your family was going to be permitted to join you—would you tell us what happened, just briefly, on that day? Where did you receive the news?
A. This day in question, as I can recall, I had worked in the

garage in the morning, and came down to the Embassy for lunch, and on arriving in the Embassy I was notified by the State Department that the Russian foreign office had approved my wife's visa and that she would be joining me shortly.

Q. Did you have lunch?

A. I had lunch.

Q. And what did you do after lunch?

A. Well, during lunch—I had a few drinks. That is what you want me to bring out?

Long, deep lines ran along both sides of his broad mouth. When he held his thin lips together tightly, the face was hard and cold and he looked older than the forty years he carried. Yet oddly enough, an almost silly grin slipped across his face at times—as if this were all part of the game for a Regular Army "noncom."

Tompkins: Well, whatever happened.

Judge Byers: I think he is going to leave this to your judgment.

Rhodes: All right, sir.

Q. Whatever happened after lunch.

A. Well, during lunch—I went down to the Marines. There had been a few drinks. In fact, several drinks, before I got around to going back to the garage. On arriving back to the garage, two Russian nationals, mechanics that worked for me there in the garage . . . [their names were Vassily and Ivan, he said] decided that they should have a drink with me, and so one drink led to another, and apparently it went on all afternoon. At three-thirty or four o'clock in the afternoon, I suppose, something like that, the youngest mechanic's girl friend had his car that day, and she came up to the garage to pick him up, and there was still some of the vodka left that we had been drinking that afternoon, so I said, "Why don't you bring your girl in for a drink?" And when she came in there was a girl with her, and I had never seen the girl before.

So we had a few more drinks from whatever was left of the vodka, as I can recall it, and I don't know who suggested it, that maybe we should have dinner that night, but possibly I did. I just can't recall exactly how it got started, but we left the garage in his car with the two girls, and I know we made a trip to, I guess it was, his apartment. I never was inside of it. I don't know what was on the inside of this building.

But anyway he was gone fifteen or twenty minutes. He cleaned up and changed his clothes, and came back to the car, and the four of us went to one of the hotels in Moscow, and the party just rolled on through the night, and I know that I was dancing, drinking and eating with these people, and I have no recollection of leaving the hotel in any way, shape or form. I don't know—possibly I passed out there and they had to carry me out.

I know I woke up the next morning in bed with this girl in what I had taken to be her room.

When he stopped the narrative, I stood up.

Donovan: The defense respectfully moves, Your Honor, that all this recital be stricken from the record on the ground that it is not binding on this defendant.

Judge Byers: Not at the present time. I don't know how much of this is material. I have no way of telling at the moment.

Rhodes now testified that it was five or seven weeks "after the party" when he received a phone call from the young woman with whom he had spent the night.

Q. As a result of that phone call, or following that phone call, did you see the young lady?
A. I did. I agreed to meet her and did meet her.
Q. Was she alone or was somebody with her?

A. At the time that I met her she was by herself.

Q. All right. What did you do?

A. I rode the subway to the appointed place where I agreed to meet this girl. So we were walking on the street, and she was telling me that she has trouble—

Donovan: I object.

Judge Byers: Don't tell us what she said.

Rhodes: All right. We walked up the street, and we were accosted by two men, two Russians. I had taken them to be nationals.

Q. Did one of the men speak English?

A. One of the men spoke English.

Q. Do you know the names of either of these two men?

A. One of them was introduced as the girl's brother. I have no idea what his name was. The other was introduced—the girl introduced him, I think, by a Russian name and he said, "Just call me Bob Day."

Q. Bob Day?

A. Bob Smith or Bob Day. I am not positive which name was used, but I believe it was Bob Day.

Q. All right. Now, after you met these two men, what did you do? Don't tell us anything about any conversation, but just exactly what did you do?

A. We went back into what I had taken to be the room I woke up in prior to this meeting, where I had been after this party.

Q. Did the three of you enter the room?

A. The two men and myself, yes, sir. The girl did not go in.

Q. What happened to the girl, do you know?

A. She walked on down the hall after we went upstairs.

Q. Did you ever see her after that?

A. I have never seen her again.

It seemed incredible that Rhodes, fifteen years in the Army and a master sergeant, should be duped by this hackneyed, transparent "blackmail" scheme. Even harder for me to accept was the fact that he had not been warned that in Moscow every Russian national who works in the American Embassy—and this includes the Embassy garage—is an intelligence agent. Vassily and Ivan, whom Rhodes said he "knew well," had obviously found his weakness and then set him up for a fall.

Q. Now, Bob Smith, or the man that you think is Bob Smith, and another man and yourself were in the room. Could you tell us what happened? Did you have a conversation?

A. We had a conversation.

Q. How long did it last?

A. Two hours, approximately, the best that I can figure it out. Maybe a little longer.

Q. Did you thereafter depart?

A. I did.

Q. And where did you go?

A. I don't know, but I think I walked back to the Embassy that night.

To us at the defense table it seemed blatantly obvious that Mr. Prosecutor and Mr. Witness were playing cat-and-mouse. What was to be left unsaid, I was sure, would be far more damaging to Rhodes than what he would be called on to admit.

Q. Now, did you see any of these two individuals at a later date?

A. I did. There was only one of them, the one I called Bob Day, and he met me three days later—about three days later.

Q. Can you tell us what you did with Bob Smith?

A. At this meeting? I don't know. At this meeting, I ate, drank and got drunk, and as to what actually happened at this meeting, I don't actually know.

Q. Do you remember where it took place?

A. This was in a hotel. The name I don't know.

Q. When did you next see Bob Smith, or Bob Day?

A. It would have been two or three months after that.

Q. And where did you see him?

A. That was in an apartment.

Q. And did you see him alone?

A. No. At this meeting there was, I recall, five other Russians. I had taken them to be Russians. There was two in civilian clothes and three in military uniform.

Q. You said that they were in military uniform. And military uniform of what nation?

A. Of Russia.

Q. All right. Will you go on and tell us what happened in that room?

A. We had a meeting. I don't recall, I believe I drank a little. There was eats there if I wanted to use them.

Q. And how long did that meeting last?

A. It would have been about the same time, anywhere from an hour and a half to two hours.

Rhodes said that he attended a total of fifteen meetings. Almost all of these meetings were with Bob Day; the uniformed Russians sat in on only two or three sessions. There was one meeting nearly every month.

Q. Now, at these meetings, did you furnish any information?

A. Yes, sir.

Q. Did you at any time receive money from these individuals?

A. Yes, sir.

Q. Would you tell us the total amount, over the period that you were in Moscow?

A. Somewhere between twenty-five hundred and three thousand dollars.

Q. Do you recall the number of times the money was given to you?

A. Five or six times, I believe.

Q. Do you recall the first payment or the first sum, excuse me, that was given to you, Sergeant?

A. I do. The first money I had from them, I discovered it in my clothing . . .

The day after his first meeting with Bob Day, Rhodes had left for Germany to meet his wife and daughter who were coming on to join him in Moscow. He was gone twelve or fifteen days, and when he returned, he suddenly discovered two thousand rubles he could not account for.

Q. What is two thousand rubles in American money?

A. Five hundred dollars.

Q. And then, it is your testimony that maybe on five or six other occasions you received money from the Russians?

A. Yes, sir.

Q. Now, Sergeant, did you give any receipts for this money?

A. I did.

Q. Were the receipts signed by you?

A. They were.

Q. If you recall, Sergeant, did you give these people any written statements?

A. I just don't know, sir.

Rhodes was not a legal prisoner but now was confined to his military post and told to wear civilian clothes in court. The Army was waiting its turn and it was only a matter of time until the court-martial.

Tompkins: Now, you stated that you did give information to these people?

Rhodes: Yes, sir.

Q. Was your information truthful or untruthful?

A. Some of both.

Q. Did you furnish them with information with relation to your duties in the Embassy?

A. Yes, sir.

Q. Did you furnish them with information that you had been trained in code work?

A. Yes, sir.

Q. Now, do you recall whether you furnished them information relative to the habits of military personnel assigned to the Embassy?

A. Yes, sir.

Q. And relative to the habits of State Department personnel?

A. Yes, sir.

Rhodes testified he had been stationed during his army career at Aberdeen, Maryland; Fort Belvoir, Virginia; and the Pentagon, where he received his code room training. The career soldier admitted giving the Russians information about all his duties and the posts at which he served.

Q. Now, Sergeant, after you returned to the United States [to San Luis Obispo] did you have a method of communicating—by that I mean, getting in touch with the Russian Embassy in the United States?

A. I did, yes, sir.

For three consecutive weeks, he was to send an article clipped from *The New York Times* which was critical of Russia. The articles were to have a red question mark on them. On the fourth week, on the same day the news clippings were mailed to the Russian Embassy in Washington, Rhodes was to stand in front of a theater in Mexico City. He would be met there by a Soviet agent.

Q. Did you have any knowledge of how you were to be dressed?

A. There was no particular dress, but I was to be carrying or smoking a pipe they furnished me.

Q. Now, after you came back to the United States, getting back to your instructions for a minute, did you try and communicate with the Russian Embassy?

A. No, sir.

Q. Did you try and communicate with anybody in this country?

A. No, sir.

This ended the Government's examination of Rhodes.

Donovan: I move to strike the entire line of testimony and ask that the jury be instructed to disregard it as incompetent and immaterial and not binding on this defendant.

Because it was past four o'clock Judge Byers dismissed the jury, and defense counsel argued why we believed Rhodes's testimony was unfair and did not belong on the record.

Donovan: Your Honor, ninety-nine per cent of this man's testimony this afternoon is with respect to a conspiracy, if it existed, totally unrelated to that charged in this indictment. There is no testimony, Your Honor, that this man ever knew the defendant, and no testimony that this man ever knew Hayhanen. There is no testimony that he ever knew anyone named as a co-conspirator in this indictment.

Judge Byers: In this kind of conspiracy, Mr. Donovan, it wouldn't be any surprise to you that several of the conspirators do not know several of the other conspirators. This is not the kind of a little two per cent conspiracy entered into to burn down a building. This is a pretty widespread conspiracy.

Donovan: Your Honor, the conspiracy in this case is supposed to be one planned by Soviet military intelligence. The other conspiracy that we heard about this afternoon would seem to be the misfortunes of a man who got drunk in Moscow and did these various things, but I respectfully submit that there is no link that makes this evidence competent in this case.

Judge Byers: Well, I am not prepared to say yes and I am not prepared to say no. I would like to reserve decision on your motion.

Donovan: Thank you.

Tuesday, October 22

It was hard to remember just when Tuesday slipped over Monday and what filled each hour. We treated all time alike as we worked most of Monday night in our preparation to face Roy Rhodes. The Government had complied with our request for statements Rhodes made to the several investigatory agencies. We read through all the notes and listened to the tape-recorded interrogations conducted by Army counter-intelligence agents.

As each tape recording spun smaller, I realized why Tompkins had only begun to extract from this man the full story of his crime against his country. Rhodes had given the Russians information on national security matters, and the Government simply could not ask him to disclose in open court the secrets he had sold to the Russians: if Rhodes were to tell "all," his testimony could rock the American diplomatic representation in Moscow and other foreign capitals.

To compound the problem this witness presented, we also learned from the tapes that he had given conflicting testimony on vital points, telling one story to the FBI and another to Army investigators. The jury was entitled to this knowledge of his duplicity, but how were we to demolish Rhodes's testimony without making public the secret intelligence information?

It was almost three o'clock when I got to bed. I slept until nine, then quickly shaved and showered and read the morning headlines over breakfast of black coffee, ice water and a cigarette: GI SAYS WOMEN AND VODKA LED HIM TO SPY, GI TELLS OF SALE OF DATA TO SOVIET, GI ADMITS HE SPIED FOR RUSSIANS WHILE ON DUTY IN MOSCOW. One paper carried a picture of a smirking Roy Rhodes leaving the courthouse.

Judge Byers began the court day with a brief statement. He denied our motion to strike Rhodes's direct testimony. Tompkins and I then approached the bench, and, out of hearing of the jury, I explained the conflict in Sergeant Rhodes's out-of-court testimony. He agreed to my request that there should be a conference in his chambers and excused the jury, saying, "We will take a recess, members of the jury, for thirty minutes. I guess you had better wait in the jury room."

A special assistant from the Army judge advocate general's office and an Air Force colonel sat in on our conference. I began by telling Judge Byers that parts of the confessions Rhodes made to the military were still "classified" for security reasons and their disclosure would be against the best national interests of the United States.

"They concern this man's activities in Moscow," I continued, "and specifically show that he was informing on our own attempts to obtain intelligence there. Disclosure would publicly show that our own attachés in the Embassy were carrying out intelligence operations in Moscow."

I went on to say that the prosecution had elected to put Rhodes on the stand. Now I was expected to cross-examine him. The prosecution, I said, had placed me in an outrageous predicament. As court-assigned counsel I was bound to do everything I could for my client; but I was also a United States citizen, still held a commission as a commander in Naval Intelligence, and had worked for three years in the OSS during World War II to help establish a permanent central intelligence system in this country. The last thing I wanted to see happen, I added, would be to have our intelligence apparatus hampered. Yet in my duty as defense counsel for Abel,

I was compelled to bring before the jury the contradictory statements of Rhodes. I argued that for this reason, as well as the others I had voiced the day before, the entire testimony of Rhodes should be stricken from the court record.

The judge listened attentively, then agreed that the jury, in deciding whether they would believe anything that Rhodes said in court, should know that he had told more than one story about his activities in Moscow.

"I am also troubled," I said, "by the fact that this man's statements, plus the transcriptions, show a shocking account of his life in Moscow. But I honestly believe the jury thinks of him as a fellow who got drunk to celebrate the arrival of his family and wound up in a pickle.

"I respectfully submit that a full reading of these transcriptions show this man was in the black market over there, and that this was primarily a money transaction with him. I believe the picture of this man, as presented to the jury, as a loving husband and father who happened to stray just is absurd, and I think that I am entitled to demolish that story and show he was passing out information for which the Russians paid him well."

Judge Byers said, "I would like to provide Mr. Donovan with all the ammunition he is entitled to as a trial lawyer, in order to discredit this witness in the eyes of the jury."

I repeated my contention that since the witness was linked to this specific case against Abel by so thin a thread, the proper solution was that Rhodes's testimony be stricken from the record.

The judge would not grant my motion. The best I could obtain was a decision (unique in a capital trial, so far as I know) that His Honor would address the jury on the subject.

The jury filed back in, looking a little confused by the recess, which they had used to send out for coffee. When all were seated, Judge Byers faced them and read from his notes.

Judge Byers: Members of the jury, as you probably realize, when we took a recess it was for the purpose of a consultation . . . As a result of that conference, it was brought to light that the witness Rhodes gave certain statements to the Army and to the FBI during the month of June, 1957, and, I think, July and perhaps later.

Those statements were the basis of the consultation. At the end of the discussion, which was quite informal, the United States conceded that with respect to one item referred to in those statements this witness has made conflicting statements.

The subject matter involved was not brought out on his direct testimony because, in the opinion of the Government, it would not have been in the interests of national security for that subject to have been inquired into.

The conflict pertained to his version of his activities in Moscow, and an important incident which there occurred.

Both counsel have agreed that since this concession is before the jury—namely, the concession that the witness has made conflicting statements—*the witness has been to this extent discredited.* Such is the purpose of cross-examination.

Counsel for both sides have agreed that no useful purpose would be served by pursuing the subject further.

M/Sgt. Roy A. Rhodes, U.S. Army, was wearing the same cheap two-button suit, bright tie and soft shirt. The flickering grin was missing today and the angular face was set and hard.

I walked near the witness stand, looked quickly at Rhodes, and made a half turn.

Donovan: May it please the Court: would the defendant rise? [Abel rose.]

Q. Sergeant Rhodes, have you ever seen this man before?

A. No, sir.

Q. Do you recognize him as anyone you have ever known under any name?

A. No, sir.

Q. Do you know a man named Rudolf Abel?

A. No, sir.

Q. Do you know a man named Emil Goldfus?

A. No, sir.

Q. Do you know a man named Martin Collins?

A. No, sir.

Q. Do you know a man named Reino Hayhanen, also known as Vic?

A. No, sir.

Q. Do you know a man named Eugene Maki?

A. No, sir.

Q. Do you know a man named Mikhail Svirin?

A. No, sir.

Q. Do you know a man named Vitali G. Pavlov?

A. I don't think so. No, sir.

Q. Do you know a man named Alekssandr M. Korotkov?

A. No, sir.

Q. Have you ever had any representative of Soviet Russia communicate personally with you in the United States?

A. No, sir, not to my knowledge.

Q. In the United States did you ever transmit to any Russian information concerning the national defense of the United States?

A. No, sir.

Q. Did you in the United States ever receive any such information for any Russian?

A. No, sir.

Donovan: Your Honor, I respectfully renew my motion to strike the man's entire testimony.

Judge Byers: The same ruling.

Thirteen questions with but one thought and one expected answer. Despite the ruling (a foregone conclusion) our point of the irrelevance of Rhodes's testimony had been made to the jury and recorded for review by an appellate court.

Q. Now, Sergeant, you testified yesterday concerning information you transmitted to Russian officials while you were stationed in Moscow. Is that correct?

A. Yes, sir.

Q. Did you at the time make any report on these treasonable activities to your superiors, to your superior officers?

A. No, sir.

Q. Did you make any report on these activities to any American official?

A. No, sir.

Q. What was the first time when you admitted these activities to any official of the United States?

A. To the FBI in last of June, I believe, of this year.

When Rhodes's name had first been introduced the week before, his wife had denied he had been involved with the Russians. The Army transcriptions showed Mrs. Rhodes had known exactly what her husband was doing with his nights out in Moscow, but at her Eatontown, New Jersey, home she told newsmen, "It's all a big lie. It's the biggest frame-up I've ever seen." She gave the stock answer to the stock question: she was "sticking by" her innocent husband. I didn't see her in court.

Q. Now, yesterday, Sergeant, you testified that your first meeting with that Russian girl occurred after you were celebrating the expected arrival of your wife and daughter in Russia; is that correct?

A. That is the way I can recall it, yes, sir.

Q. Now, is it not true that long *after* your family arrived in Moscow, you attended a party in a hotel in Moscow at which uniformed Russians were present?

A. I did, yes, sir.

Q. Is it not a fact, sir, that subsequently that same evening you found yourself in bed with a girl?

Rhodes (hedging now): I found myself alone with her, yes, sir. I don't recall myself in bed with her, no, sir.

Donovan (paper in hand): Would it help to refresh your recollection if I read to you a statement signed by you on July 2, 1957, and given to the FBI, which says, in part: "At this party in the hotel room we also ate and drank, and I proceeded to get drunk. I remember that someone in the party had a girl brought in, and I was talking to her. I am very hazy on what took place, but recall at one time in the evening everybody had evidently left the room and I found myself alone on the bed with this girl."

A. That is true, I believe.

Q. Now, this is after your wife—

A. That's right.

Q.—and daughter had arrived in Moscow?

A. That's right.

Judge Byers: Just a moment. Is it correct to say that Mr. Donovan has been reading from a report furnished to him by the United States Attorney?

Tompkins: That is correct, Your Honor. It is a report we furnished Mr. Donovan yesterday pursuant to his motion.

Q. While you were in Moscow attached to the American Embassy, did you use any intoxicating liquors?

A. I did, yes, sir.

Q. What liquor?

A. Whiskey, vodka, almost anything you want to name.

Judge Byers: You mean anything you could get?

Rhodes: Yes, sir.

The testimony had a familiar ring. It was the story of Reino Hayhanen all over again. Even the judge's interruptions were alike.

Q. In what quantities would you drink these liquors?

A. (bluntly) They weren't moderate.

Q. (sternly) Isn't the truth, Sergeant, that while you were in the American Embassy in Moscow—

Judge Byers: Just a minute. You don't mean that.

Q. While attached to the American Embassy in Moscow, is it not true that for the last two months of your stay in Moscow you were drunk every day?

A. (calmly) I believe that is right, yes, sir.

Q. Now, you testified yesterday, Sergeant, that during the period of time you were selling information to the Russians you received in return between twenty-five hundred and three thousand dollars.

A. The best I can recall it, that's about what it figured out.

Q. Isn't it a fact that over the same period you deposited in your personal bank account approximately nineteen thousand dollars?

A. No, sir.

Q. How much did you deposit, to the best of your recollection?

A. That—I—can I explain that?

Q. No. I want the answer to the question. I want to know how much you deposited while you were in Moscow.

A. All right—

Judge Byers: Are you speaking now of the entire period?

Donovan: I was speaking, Your Honor, of the period during which he says that he received only twenty-five hundred to three thousand dollars from the Russians.

Rhodes: That is right. But my wages all went home.

Q. Again, is it not true that over the last year and a half you were in Moscow you deposited around nineteen thousand dollars in your bank account?

A. No, sir. I was in Moscow over two years, and my total wages went home, which would have run around fifteen thousand, maybe more, I don't know. I never figured it up. Pay and allowance there would have run to eight or nine hundred dollars a month.

Q. Are you denying under oath that you deposited any such amounts of money in your bank account?

A. No. I said it went.

Q. You are not suggesting that all this was your salary as a sergeant?

A. That's right.

Q. Do you deny making statements to Army interrogation officers in which you not only admitted that the nineteen thousand dollars was approximately right, but attempted to explain it on the ground that you were dealing in a black market in Russian rubles?

A. No.

Q. Don't you remember making that statement?

A. Certainly, I made that statement.

Q. In October, 1952, for example, didn't you write a check on your personal account in the amount of eleven hundred dollars to a Dr. Backerhock?

A. I did.

Q. What was it for?

A. I . . . I can't recall what it was for.

Q. (impatiently) You are a sergeant in the Army. You mean you write so many eleven-hundred-dollar checks that you can't recall why you made one out to a Russian doctor?

A. I have no idea that it was a Russian doctor. This check came up before.

Q. You just made them out to anyone?

A. As well as I can explain that one, because I have no recollection of the check.

Sergeant Rhodes had been a dutiful barracks-room soldier, by his own lights. His brass would be shined, his shoes polished and his uniform would have a sharp crease. World War II GIs had an expression to throw up to the likes of Roy Rhodes. They'd cynically say, "Man, you found a home in the Army." But Roy Rhodes had betrayed the uniform he took such good care of, and sold out his Army home.

Q. Now, are you still a master sergeant in the United States Army?

A. I am still a master sergeant in the United States Army.

Q. Are you still drawing regular pay?

A. I am still drawing regular pay.

Q. What is the amount of that pay?

A. It would figure out, pay and allowance, about three hundred and fifty a month.

Q. You are still drawing this regularly?

A. That's right, yes, sir.

Q. Now, with respect to this treason to which you have confessed—

Judge Byers: I think you ought to change the form of the question to "With respect to the activities which you say you conducted in Moscow." I don't think you should brand them. Treason is only possible in time of war.

Donovan: Would it be satisfactory to the Court if I rephrased it to ask him about his betrayal of his own country?

This brought the first objection from the prosecutor.

Tompkins: If Your Honor please, I think just the facts speak for themselves. We don't have to characterize them.

Judge Byers: I think if you phrase the question so as to make it clear that you refer to the activities that he says he conducted in Moscow and for which he was paid, you will make your point, Mr. Donovan.

Q. With respect to your activities in Moscow with these Russians, and for which you received money from them, have you ever been court-martialed in—

A. I have not.

Q.—in connection with these activities?

A. No, sir.

Q. Have you ever been arrested?

A. No, sir.

211

Q. Have you ever been indicted?

A. No, sir.

Q. And you are still on duty drawing pay?

A. As far as I know, yes, sir.

By now the true character of Roy A. Rhodes, master sergeant, U.S. Army, was apparent and it was difficult to conceal disgust.

Q. Sergeant, I think you testified that you are a native-born American?

A. Yes, sir.

Q. Were you educated in this country?

A. I was.

Q. Did you ever hear of a man named Benedict Arnold?

A. Yes, sir.

Q. How does he stay in your mind as a figure in American history?

A. Not so good.

Q. I didn't hear your answer.

A. I said, not so good.

Q. I asked you, how you would think of him?

A. I answered that. I said, not so good.

Q. Why?

A. I—

Q. Isn't it because he betrayed his country?

A. I think so.

Q. Do you know enough history to know that even Benedict Arnold didn't do it for money?

A. I know it.

Donovan: Sergeant, Benedict Arnold may have been the greatest traitor in American military history, but it was only until today.

I turned my back on the witness stand and walked away to the defense table. The courtroom was still. Then, the judge broke in.

Judge Byers: Is that a question?

Donovan: It is an attempted statement of fact.

Tompkins asked two questions on redirect.

Q. Sergeant, you are in arrest of quarters, aren't you?

A. That is right, yes, sir.

Q. One more question. What do you mean by arrest of quarters?

A. I mean I can't leave the post.

The prosecutor then suggested that my last statement in cross-examination be stricken from the record, saying, "It wasn't a question. I think Mr. Donovan made the statement—"

Donovan: I didn't want to make it on the record, Your Honor. I just wanted to make it.

Judge Byers: You had the satisfaction of making it. Now, are you willing that it be stricken from the record?

Donovan: Very well.

M/Sgt. Roy A. Rhodes was excused. In a subsequent colloquy at the bench, Judge Byers could not resist saying tersely to Tompkins and me, "Please notify me if the sergeant is proposed for a commendation."

The remainder of the day was given over to the story of Abel's arrest. We had gone through all this in our pretrial hearing with one exception—the FBI surveillance that led them to the Hotel Latham. This testimony became fascinating. The first witness was special agent Neil D. Heiner. It was the night of May 23, 1957, and he was watching Abel's room on the fifth floor of 252 Fulton Street through binoculars—"Ten-fifties. That means they have a power of ten magnification and the fifty designates the millimeter width across the front of the lens."

Q. Will you tell the Court and jury where you were?

A. I was in a position where I could observe the windows of studio or suite 505 at 252 Fulton Street. I was on the twelfth floor of the Hotel Touraine.

Q. Will you tell us what you saw, if anything.

A. Well . . . at about ten-forty-five P.M. I was watching the studio and I saw the lights go on—rather one light was turned on in the studio. I could see a male figure moving around in the room. From time to time it would pass in back of this light. There was a light suspended on a cord from the ceiling with a shield around it.

I could see that this man, he was unidentified, was middle-aged and was bald-headed. He had a fringe of gray hair around the edges. He was wearing glasses. And as I said before, he showed himself only momentarily. My view was—my view of the entire room was obstructed, except when he stood in front of the window. The lights remained on, and at about one minute before midnight I saw this man, in back of the light, put on a dark brown or dark gray summer straw hat, and it had a very bright white band. The band stood out. About a minute later, the light went out—the single light went out.

Q. Could you describe his clothing at all?

A. Yes, I could see that he had on a short-sleeved shirt. It hit him about, oh, an inch above the elbow. It seemed to be light-colored blue. He was wearing a tie. It was darker than—darker-colored. I couldn't distinguish which color. And, as I said before, he was wearing glasses. I couldn't see his entire face because his head was down. In other words, he wasn't looking out the window so I could have a full front view of his face.

Q. What did you do after the light went out?

A. I had radio communications with other agent personnel who were on the street in the area surrounding the studio. When the light went out, I alerted the agents in the street . . .

The other agents were opposite 252 Fulton Street in the park plaza, sitting on benches under the trees or moving about in deep shadows. All were waiting. They could not see the windows of the studio but had a clear front view of the doorway.

Agent Joseph C. McDonald was one of those waiting.

Q. From where you were sitting in the park, could you see that front entrance?

A. Yes, sir.

Q. Now, will you tell us what you saw, if anything?

A. Shortly after midnight, it was twelve-two A.M., and at that time a man unknown to me, a white male, left 252 Fulton Street, and he had on a dark summer-type hat with about a two-inch white band, real white, and he had on a light tan-colored coat and dark-colored pants, and he was carrying a coat over his arm.

Q. Following your radio communication were you watching this doorway for any specific purpose?

A. Yes, sir. I was waiting to follow anyone that came out that door. He came out of the door and I followed him. He made a right turn and walked up Fulton Street to Clinton, walked up Clinton Street to Montague, turned the corner of Montague and entered the BMT subway. BMT Borough Hall subway station. [At this station, an elevator carries passengers from the street level to the subway platform.] The man had entered an elevator, and I entered the elevator with him.

Q. Now, at any time up to this present point while you were on the elevator with this unidentified individual, did you get a look at his face?

A. On the elevator, I did, sir.

Q. Would you recognize that individual?

A. Yes, sir.

Q. And is he present in court?

A. Yes, sir.

Q. Would you point him out, please?

A. He is sitting at the end of this table right here.

Maybe Abel recognized the FBI agent as a "tail" and maybe he didn't, but they rode the elevator to the station level and then both walked to the end of the platform, standing about ten yards apart.

"There were quite a few people up at that end," agent McDonald said, "so I stood in with the people. And he turned around and walked past me. Then the train came in."

Abel got in the second last car. The agent took a seat in the end car but he was unable to see the suspect, so he changed his seat at the next stop. They rode to the City Hall station in Manhattan, where Abel caught a Broadway bus which took him to within walking distance of the Hotel Latham.

On June 13, Abel showed up at the Brooklyn studio again and the FBI agents were there to watch him. This time there were agents staked out in the Brooklyn General Post Office, which houses the Federal courthouse in which our trial was being held. Ronald B. Carlson was one of these agents.

Q. Now, about midnight, or shortly before, what did you see?

A. I saw an individual leave that address [252 Fulton Street]. He could be described best by his hat. He was wearing a dark gray hat with a white or light band. He was wearing a light sport coat and he left that address and went east on Fulton Street.

Every one of the agents mentioned Abel's distinctive hat. I had not thought to buy him a new one. He was still wearing it to court—or one just like it. In fact, the dark hat with the white band showed up clearly in all news photographs of the Colonel, on his way to trial or leaving the courthouse at the end of the day.

The judge interrupted at this point to say to the jurors, "It may help you understand the testimony. When court adjourns today

216

you can look out the windows that face you and you will be able to see the premises at 252 Fulton Street and also the Hotel Touraine."

Another agent took the stand and testified that he followed Abel ("who was wearing a dark hat with a prominent white band") into the same BMT subway. This time he took the train all the way to 28th Street, Manhattan, and walked west, and "I observed him enter the Hotel Latham."

One week later came the knock on the door of Room 839 and a quiet voice calling, "Martin Collins?"

Wednesday, October 23

On this day, what was not said was more important than what was said; the big news came outside the courtroom and newspaper headlines told of a story that would not be. I met the press in the corridor during the afternoon and issued the following statement:

"We have reviewed with Mr. Abel all the Government evidence and pointed out to him the advantages and disadvantages of taking the stand as a witness in his own behalf. He is perfectly willing to let the case go to the jury on the Government's evidence. It is his own decision, made after a careful examination of all the testimony, that it would not be to his advantage to take the stand.

"We shall not call Mr. Abel and we do not plan to call any other witnesses."

During the morning, the trial had carried slowly forward on necessary but drab details. An FBI agent told how he searched Abel's rooms after the arrest; Dave Levine identified Abel's tools and paraphernalia from the storage room they shared and on cross-examination said, "He was generally accepted as an honest man among us."

FBI laboratory expert Webb took the stand for a third time, to talk of a hollowed-out pencil found in Abel's hotel wastebasket. Inside the tip of the pencil were microfilms. One of these was a broadcast schedule giving dates, times and radio call letters for

217

short-wave broadcasts. Using this schedule and the listed frequencies, the Government on July 15 and August 4 had conducted a radio monitoring operation. Tompkins introduced an exhibit showing the results of the monitoring and "the receipt of messages in five-digit blocks."

I objected to all this evidence on the ground that the exhibits were the fruits of an illegal search and seizure and there was no connection between these undeciphered messages and the defendant. In a July message, for instance, the sender used call letters different from those on the alleged schedule.

Donovan: This shows no consistency. This demonstrably shows a complete inconsistency. If you are looking for a man named John, you don't go around calling for Thomas. That is what happened here.

Judge Byers: It depends on whether John was also known as Thomas. Then you might do it.

Donovan: These have been undeciphered; so far as we know, it might be a commercial from Bulgaria.

Tompkins: I haven't seen a commercial from Bulgaria in five-digit figures.

The prosecutor than launched into a long explanation to show how the coded radio messages heard by the Government monitor were related to the microfilmed broadcast schedule. While he was talking, Abel wrote a note to Tom Debevoise pointing out technical errors in his explanation.

When Tompkins finished, the judge said this was all something about which he was ignorant and asked, "Is it your position that this exhibit tends to prove anything?"

Tompkins: Your Honor, all it does is corroborate the schedule that was found on the defendant and show that messages were being sent in accordance with that schedule.

Donovan: I respectfully submit, Your Honor, if it shows

anything it shows that such messages were not being sent in accordance with the schedule. The fact that they tuned in on the same frequency is no corroboration of anything. Every day, every hour, every minute, an amateur radio operator can pick up any number of messages in code that are being transmitted . . .

Judge Byers: It is for the jury to say whether or not they consider it of any weight as a matter of evidence.

Six of the microfilms hidden in the pencil were letters to Abel from his wife and daughter. The Government chose to read one paragraph of one letter—purporting to show the Colonel had been home in the fall of 1955—and this opened the door to our reading all of them. The prosecution opposed their being read to the jury because "they are personal letters which have nothing whatever to do with the issues charged in the indictment." Their objection was overruled by Judge Byers.

The letters were warm and told far better than we could that the man "Rudolf Abel" was a devoted husband and father. They were sentimental and typically Russian in their earthiness. All but one of daughter Evelyn's letters were in English. Abel's wife, Elya (or Hellen, as she later signed her letters), wrote in Russian. At our request, the FBI provided English translations.

The first paragraph of the following letter from daughter Evelyn was the one the prosecution read to the jury:

Dear Dad,

It's almost three months since you went away. Although it's not so much as compared with eternity, still it is a long time and the more so as there is a great quantity of news to tell you.

First of all, I am going to marry. Please don't be astounded. I am much surprised myself, and still it is a fact to be taken for granted.

My future husband seems to be a good guy. He is thirty-four and a radio engineer. Mother likes him very much. We met at the birthday of our friend who lives in our bungalow. On February 25 we shall celebrate our wedding. I hope you will like him when you come back. I think you will have much to talk about.

News number two: we are to get a new flat of two rooms. It is not what we supposed to get but it is a flat for ourselves and it is much better than what we have now.

News number three: I have found a job, engineer referent in aviation, so that now I shall be somewhat closer to you. The job seems to be a decent one. They promised to pay well, and my future boss seems to be intellectual and polite guy. I did some odd jobs there and received a pretty sum of money.

My future husband and I are both deeply interested in photography, especially in color photography. He has an Olympia car and we both enjoy meddling with it.

We received both your letters and the key from the suitcase, but the latter is still wandering somewhere.

Our aunt, the one we took home with us, still lives here. Our childhood friend writes regularly and sends you his and his family's best regards and wishes.

All our friends wish you health and happiness and a happy and quick way home.

Well, this is all I have to say.

Yours, Evelyn
(February 20, 1956)

We read to the jury all of the other letters. Some were dated, others were not. This was Evelyn's shortest letter; it was barely a note:

Dear Papa,

I am very lonesome and await a letter from you. I married. My husband is an engineer in communication, the same as you he likes to fool around with the radio. He likes photography.

Now we are getting ready to make an electronic exposure meter for the automatic determination of exposure while printing. Write what you think of this.

My husband sends a big greeting and the best wishes. He wants very much to meet you as soon as he can. I also very much want that you will come. I await your letter and your arrival. Our maid sends her greetings. I kiss you firmly,

                                        Your Evelyn.

Some of the newsmen said Abel flushed during the reading of the family letters, which apparently had meant so much to him that he could not destroy them. One of the magazine writers who covered the trial wrote, "As the attorneys droned through the letters, Abel's steel cage of self-discipline almost cracked. His face grew red and his sharp, deep-set eyes filled with tears."

There were others, however, who believed the letters were in code and refused to accept them as genuine. Years later, the FBI said that after exhaustive examination they were convinced the letters were bona fide and carried no coded or secret instructions.

Debevoise read to the jury the last two letters from Abel's daughter. He said afterward that he thought one or two of the women jurors had tears in their eyes and he added dryly, "Just as I had in my voice."

Dear Dad:

I was very glad to receive your letter and know that you have at least received our letter, though only the first one. We got our parcel in May, and thank you very much for it. We liked your presents very much. We planted the hyacinths that have survived and by now three of them have sprouted. You say that you want to have some more particulars about my husband.

I shall try now to give you a better picture of him. He is short, green-eyed, dark-haired and rather handsome. He is rather gay and talkative when the conversation considers cars or football. He seems to be a good specialist (an engineer in communications) though he has no higher education. He is capable though rather lazy. My first task is to make him study. I am afraid that it would be a difficult one.

Well, I must say that he is a nice chap, that he loves me, and loves Mother, though he is not very warm toward his own parents. He has an Opel Olympia and spends most of his spare time repairing it.

You asked me whether I am happy with him. As one of our greatest poets once said, there is no happiness in life but there is peace and free will. As regards my freedom and will, they are not hampered in any respect. But as regards peace, I seem to possess an immense ability to find or invent troubles.

My husband is liable to all sorts of fantastic ideas, such as to build a bar of brick in the pond that is in our forest. Thank the Lord, he has forgotten about it. I am very glad that he likes Mother and the whole of our family. The only thing that troubles me is that I find him boring sometimes.

Now about my in-laws. They are awful. The mother is anxious to persuade me that she loves me dearly, but somehow I don't believe her. The father likes to make the great man of himself and to poke his nose in other people's business. I have had a couple of warm conversations with him.

I do wish you were here with us. Everything would be much easier for me then. I am missing you very much. I thought at first that my husband could substitute for you more or less in some respects, but I now see that I was mistaken.

My health is okay. Sometimes when I am overtired I have headaches but it is not very often. I work much and with pleasure. All our friends send you their regards. My husband hopes you will like him when you come home.

With all my love,
Evelyn

P.S. I have started writing poetry in this language. Next time I shall send you a sample.

The last of the daughter's letters was a birthday greeting to her father who, on July 2, 1956, was then fifty-four years old. The letter also shows she now had serious doubts about her marriage—a marriage which was to fail two years later. In 1958 Evelyn was to write, "I have given the boot to my husband and so far do not feel like marrying again." But, for now, it was:

Dear Dad,

I wish you many happy returns. Many thanks for the parcel and all you sent us. It all came in very handy. Daddy, dear, I am missing you so much. You cannot imagine how much I need you.

It is about four months since I have married and to me it seems it is eternity. So dull it sometimes is. In general he is a good chap, but he isn't you, or even like you. I have already got used to the fact that all people must remind me of you somehow but in this case it isn't so.

I have got a job, and a very interesting one. I work as an engineer referent in aviation. My boss is a very good man, and we like each other. We often talk about all sorts of things. He is a bit like you, though not so broadminded and not a very great erudite, though very clever. Good-bye. Forgive me please for the awful letter. I am in a great hurry as I have to go to work.

> With all my love,
> Evelyn.

The first letter from Abel's wife, though undated, was obviously written shortly after they were separated and is mainly about a woman who longs for her husband.

My dear,

See again has begun our endless correspondence. I do not like it so much, it would be better to sit down and talk. From the letter of Ev you know about our luck during your short absence.

After your departure, I certainly was ill. There was hardening of the arteries of the heart, or hypertension crisis. I was in bed a month and a half. Now I go and do a little but my nerves are not fully recovered. I sleep poorly and do not go out on the street. I walk on the balcony.

Sometimes I approach your instrument [Abel's classical guitar] and look at it and want to again hear you play and I become sad. [When Abel was in prison in Atlanta his wife wrote how she would look at his paintings and recall the past. "I look at these things, and I am always waiting and waiting, and I trust that we must be together again, trust that you should never again want to abandon us."]

Daughter and I have everything except you. And she after getting married always says there are no such men as her papa and therefore she is not too much in love with her husband. You are the best of all for us. And don't frown, everyone says this who knows you.

The little daughter is working. She got the job through her niece and her husband. She is very pleased with her work, which pays well. Already she grieves that you are not here. Maybe tomorrow I will receive a letter from you. When I think about this my heart dies. I kiss you firmly and congratulate you. Try to arrange everything so that you do not delay the period of our meeting. Years and age will not wait for us.

Your Elya kisses you. Son and daughter and all your friends congratulate you and send you the best of everything. Now the move to the new apartment will bring trouble and care. I asked for three rooms but didn't get them. It would be necessary to discuss this matter with you. Such is the news with us. How are you there? How is your stomach? I think much about everything, that even Evunya's [Evelyn's] happiness does not make me happy. Take care of yourself. I want to live together with you for ourselves. I kiss you and ask you to take care of yourself.

Elya

Elya Abel's letters followed a pattern. She was a housewife and a mother and she wrote of her world: her health and her husband's health, her summer home, the trees and flowers, her daughter, friends and family, the pets. She did not burden her husband, but she spared him no detail either. And no part of the family life was too small or insignificant for Elya Abel to take note of; her letters were tender and full of love. This is her letter of April 6:

My dear,

I am writing a second letter. Up till now I only heard from you from the trip. I want very much to find out how are you? How is your health?

I am gradually beginning to come to myself. I am able to do some things around the house and am thinking about the summer home. I could go for a rest but I am afraid to move alone, so that I have not yet decided although I passed the medical board. How necessary you would be to me now. And how good it is that you do not feel the need of being with me.

Everything is the same with us. The children meanwhile live in friendship, and move around one after the other, when they are together. Evelyn does not work steady yet, it takes a long time to process, but is doing translations at home and has a pupil.

Spring here will again be late. Up till now, it has been cold, damp and snow. The winter was simply horrible, and I am worried about my flowers. Evunya says the plum trees froze and it's hard to get to the pears.

Your father-in-law arrived long ago, he is well-established, and they are very pleased. He is now waiting your earliest return and I, although I know it is silly, I am counting off the days of the known period.

Your gift, the dog, feels very well and is fully accustomed to us. A childhood friend visited us: he was here on business for a week and every day when he was free he visited us. We talked a lot, reminisced, and most of all daydreamed. Don't let us down.

It is not clear yet about the apartment. We are waiting. And in general, our whole life, constant waiting. That's the way it is, my dear. My servant is leaving. I am seeking a new one, and I'm not especially sorry. Write often as possible. The children, there are two now, send greetings and all the best for you. "Son" is very disturbed, what kind of an impression he will make on you; he might not appeal to you at once. I kiss you firmly. I wish you luck, health, and most of all a speedy return.

Elya

The family made a special day of Abel's birthday, even though he was away. "There was the traditional pie and tea under the trees on your birthday," Elya Abel wrote one year. But in another year she made no mention of the celebration and the Colonel wrote to ask how his family had spent July 2. The wife obliged: "You would like to know how we celebrated your birthday. I baked a blackberry pie with cream, as you like. Lydia [Evelyn] brought a bottle of good Riesling and we drank to your health and our reunion. All my thoughts were with you that day."

The June 21 letter from Elya Abel was her birthday greeting. She could never know that it would become part of the court record at her husband's trial and would be shared by thousands of American newspaper readers:

My dear,

At last we received your small package. Everything pleased us very much and as usual, whatever you do you do successfully with care and attention.

Thank you, my good one. We were also very glad to have received a letter from you and to learn that everything is fine with you. It is a pity that you have not had letters from us in such a long time. I sent you several. [It took longer for the letters to reach Abel, for obvious reasons. They had to be microfilmed and passed from courier to courier until they reached a "drop" in Prospect Park, a crack in the cement somewhere in the Bronx.]

We congratulate you on your birthday. Remember, on this day we will drink a toast for your well-being and your early promised return.

We are at the summer place. In this raw year, our garden has suffered. On the best apple trees, from which last year you culled a plentiful harvest, only now have the leaves started to appear. The pears, plums also barely coming to life. In this year I do very little in the garden and house. I feel very bad, I have no strength. How sad the hyacinths traveled so long and dried out very much. Nevertheless, I planted them and am waiting to find out if they died or not.

226

Everyone very much wants to see you soon and to even kiss you a lot. Herman, the husband of Ev, sits beside me and is drying my ink blotches. The television works. Our whole family sits around and watches, but I seldom look at it. I become very tired and my head starts to hurt.

I am now without a house servant, she left for a vacation. Still the same one. Although she does not satisfy me—she is very rude, but you can't find another.

The dog, Carrie, who was given to you by the husband of my sister is with us. [The Abel were fond of animals. Over the years that Abel was imprisoned, the letters from his family made frequent mention of dogs and cats. One time the wife wrote, "Our house always is full of animals. They make life more pleasant, and besides we continue your tradition."] She is a wonderful creature with thoughtful eyes. She behaves very well and resembles our Spotty in character. She too awaits her master, and I also wait. It is desirable to have a husband at home. At the present time I feel your absence much more, especially since I have been with you, remember what you promised before your departure. [Abel may have promised his wife he would ask for an assignment in Russia or perhaps a post in overt "legal" intelligence, in an Embassy where he could live with his wife. Elya and Rudolf Abel were separated through a large part of their middle age. "If we told some stranger," she once wrote, "that a wife and a husband could live apart for so many years and still love each other and wait for their reunion, he would not believe us. It is natural only for novels."]

I kiss you firmly and all of our friends and relatives also do so. I wish you success and health. Our new chef is wonderful, attentive and tactful so that you can be calm. I kiss you.

Elya

The Colonel's wife wrote of her television, her servant problem, the summer home in the country and her gardens. This led one of the tabloids to write of her "luxury existence." The headline read SPY'S WIFE LIVES IT UP IN MOSCOW.

The last letter was dated August 20:

My dear:

How glad I was to learn that you finally received one of my letters. In the congratulations I wrote little, certainly because it was inconvenient and not because I would not write in general, you are making this up.

Once more I thank you for the package. It is a shame the hyacinths traveled long and two of them perished altogether. The rest are planted and already have rooted. Further, leaves are in pairs, firm, and I go to them to talk with you. You know this is a live greeting from you. Next year they will bloom . . .

I just now arrived from a northern resort where I was once before. I went with my people. Evunya couldn't because she is working, and I was afraid to go alone. Now I feel all right, so that don't worry about me. Take care of yourself and come soon, we count every month that passes and you remember this. Now we have a guest from the city from where you left. All remember you, especially the niece with the wife of your brother. They grieve that there is no one to play with and to set out solitaire with.

With the reading of the Abel family letters ended, the courtroom fell quiet. There was a moment of stillness, as though a heavy curtain had dropped on a stage. Then Tompkins faced the bench. "Your Honor, at this time the prosecution rests."

Donovan (rising): May it please the Court, the defense has a variety of motions which it would like to make at this time, and I would respectfully suggest that they be made out of the presence of the jury. Following these motions, the defense will rest.

The jury filed out and then we moved for acquittal. We also moved to have portions of the testimony and the indictment stricken. All motions were denied. Abel sat there impassively, his

228

eyes steady behind his rimless glasses. When the arguments were finished, he handed me four lined sheets entitled "Notes on Case by R. I. Abel."

Hayhanen, he wrote, had created the picture of a bigamist, thief, liar and drunk and was "in the company of his spiritual brother, Sergeant Rhodes." He criticized the prosecution for linking him to Rhodes, saying this had been done by the "spoke" (spokes of a wheel) theory of "conspiracy." Applying this logic, Abel wrote, he undoubtedly could also be tied to the Rosenbergs and Alger Hiss— or anyone believed to have been directed by any espionage "hub" in Moscow.

The evidence showed only that he and Hayhanen were to "locate" Rhodes, and Abel suggested that some other person, or group, might have been called on to contact Rhodes:

"The aims of espionage are broad. In one case it may be directed specifically to military information; in another to nuclear problems; in still others to economic and to technological information, and also to questions of public reactions to political situations. It is reasonable to assume that separate groups are assigned to separate fields because of the variety of qualifications necessary for their fulfillment."

He ridiculed Hayhanen's testimony, telling how Abel had described Rhodes as good agent-potential because he was a soldier with relatives in atomic work. He said this was hypothetical "and would apply equally to anybody—J. Edgar Hoover or the Secretary of Defense, for instance, and with even more force."

Abel stressed throughout his written summary that there was no evidence of any information of military significance, collected or transmitted, that had been put before the Court in this trial. "It exists only in surmise which is not supported and is not *evidence*."

I was sure that he had written this thesis to guide me in my summation. "Dealing with the case as a whole," he wrote, "it seems preferable to adopt 'objective, common sense' attitude—no emotional pleas. Regarding H and Rh (he always wrote "H," never Hayhanen), some emotion seems in order. H has by his own words

229

been exposed as incompetent, a drunkard, liar and thief. Further, has shown complete disregard for his family in USSR. No ideological basis for defection shown, only cowardly conduct of person of no moral fiber. No patriotism, no strength of character—just a craven. Same for Rhodes.

"In advocating 'common sense' approach it might be advisable to indicate in some manner that that is the only reasonable attitude for the jury to assume since they are not legally trained."

Thursday, October 24

The courtroom was crowded and it was a hot day. I was pleased in this case that under the rules I would sum up first. My appeal now would be solely to the jury, so I moved up close before them.

Donovan: May it please the Court, ladies and gentlemen of the jury.

This trial has been an experience, I know for me and I feel sure for you as well. Like all experiences, they are meaningful when we can look at them with the benefit of hindsight.

You will remember that when this trial commenced, I spoke briefly to you about what was your conscientious duty as a juror. I explained that your duty is to conscientiously determine the facts and find whether or not this man named Abel has been proved guilty by evidence produced in this court, before you, of the specific charges made against him.

I explained to you that this is not a trial of communism, and it is not a trial of Soviet Russia. The issue I have just stated is the sole one before you.

Now, having understood that situation, you and I have been waiting to see what evidence was produced against this man. We have now seen all that evidence; we have seen and heard all the witnesses. We had an opportunity to evaluate them: to see whether or not each one of them was telling the truth; what his motives were on the one hand to tell the truth, or what his motives were on the other hand to try to tell whatever story would be best designed to save his own skin.

It is terribly important in this particular trial that you have a clear concept of the function of the jury in America. We believe that our trial-by-jury system is the best system ever devised for arriving at the truth.

Why is your function so important?

You might say to yourselves, "His Honor, the judge, knows all the law applicable to the case; he has been trained for many years to evaluate evidence. Why, then, shouldn't cases such as this simply be left to the lawyers and the judges?"

The answer is that from the time of Aristotle many centuries ago, ordinary citizens are not content to leave these questions to the lawyers and judges, with their legalisms and their legal niceties.

In the United States, at the time of the American Revolution, our country was welded together among the intellectuals by a series of papers called "The Federalist," written by a group of men that included the best legal minds in the nation. But the cause of the American Revolution was best sold to the ordinary people not by "The Federalist," but by a pamphlet written by a man named Thomas Paine and called "Common Sense."

All that I am going to ask you to do in this particular case, because of certain legal niceties and so on, is that while you receive your instructions as to the law from the judge, I ask simply that you use common sense in considering this case.

You have the right, and you are the only people that have the right in this courtroom, to come back with a verdict of guilty or not guilty on each specific count. That right, for you to come back with that verdict after hearing the judge, was established for you back in 1735 in this very city in the trial of a man named Peter Zenger. In that trial, a great lawyer named Andrew Hamilton, defending Peter Zenger, won for you the right to come back with a verdict of guilty or not guilty on the entire case, after you consider the law and the evidence. Now, all that I am going to ask you to do is to review what we have listened to for the last couple of weeks, and simply ask you to use common sense in reaching your verdict.

First of all, what was charged? Count One of the indictment, which is the only capital count, charges in summary a conspiracy to *transmit* national defense information and atomic energy information.

Now, I ask you this question, and I am going to be asking it of you repeatedly as I go through this case: What evidence of national defense information or atomic information has been put before you in this case?

When you and I commenced this case, certainly we expected evidence that this man would be shown to have stolen great military secrets, secrets of atomic energy, and so on. I ask you, looking back over the past couple of weeks, what evidence of such information was ever produced before you?

The only reason why this particular conspiracy is punishable by death, if the Court so decided, is because it is a conspiracy to *transmit* military information or information affecting the national defense. This is what has been charged here. I am simply asking you to keep in mind what evidence of that has ever been produced in this case.

Now, before I do review this evidence with you, I want briefly to ask you one common-sense question, and that is, would you just briefly compare in your own minds the evidence that you have about this man Abel, what kind of man he is, and compare that evidence with what you know, by now, of his two principal accusers whom you saw testify in this case.

In the first place, let's assume for the moment—let's assume—that the man is what the Government says he is. Let's assume that. It means that such a man was serving his country on an extraordinarily dangerous mission. We in our armed forces only send on such missions the bravest, the most intelligent men that we can find. Every American who took the witness stand in this case, who personally knew the man while he was living here, while put on the stand for another purpose, became a character witness for this defendant. You heard these men, one after the other, testify.

Meanwhile, yesterday afternoon, you had read to you these letters from the man's family. You could judge those letters. I won't bother you by repeating them again. Obviously, they painted the picture of a devoted husband, a loving father. In short, an outstanding type of family man such as we have in the United States.

So, on the one hand, assuming that all this is true, you have a very brave patriotic man serving his country on an extraordinarily hazardous military mission and who lived among us in peace during these years. On the other hand, you have the two people that you heard testify as his principal accusers.

Hayhanen, a renegade by any measure. Originally, there had been talk about Hayhanen being a man who, and I quote, "defected to the West." You might have the picture of some high-minded individual who finally "chose freedom" and so on. You saw what he was. A bum. A renegade. A liar. A thief.

He was succeeded by, so far as my knowledge would go, the only soldier in American history who has ever confessed to selling out his country for money.

These are the two principal witnesses against this man.

Now, let's turn in more detail to this man who said that his name was Reino Hayhanen. You will remember that in my opening statement I asked you to watch that man carefully, observe him. I pointed out to you that if what the Government says is true, the man was trained to live a life of deception; so he is a trained liar, who was being paid by Russia to live that life. He is a professional liar. And now, as you know, and as he testified, he is being paid by *our* government at the present time.

The prosecutor will tell you that in order to convict such people it is necessary to use such witnesses. However, I ask you, in evaluating that man's testimony, constantly keep this question in mind: Is he telling the truth, or is he telling not only lies but lies important enough that they may save his own skin?

From the evidence before you I say that you should conclude that Hayhanen is a liar, a thief, a bigamist and who, while he says he was on an undercover espionage operation—

Judge Byers: I will have to interrupt you, Mr. Donovan. I don't like to do this. Whether the man you are talking about is a bigamist or not depends upon the laws of Russia concerning the dissolution of marriage, and there is no evidence in the case on that subject.

Donovan: I attempted to ask the man about it, Your Honor, and I was overruled.

Judge Byers: There is no evidence in the case as to whether he is a bigamist, if you please.

Donovan: The man is living, presumably at the present time, with this Finnish lady whom His Honor permitted me to refer to, as being numerically correct, wife number two.

Now, with respect to what this man did while he was here, our cross-examination consisted of what a physician would call a biopsy, which is to simply remove a small piece of tissue to see whether it contains indications of a disease that would affect all related tissues. To do this, we took a segment of his life among us, in Newark, New Jersey, between the dates of August, 1953, and December, 1954. I investigated his life over there and then on the stand I questioned him about it.

Surely we can agree that from the account which was finally forced from the man's lips—surely you can conclude that if the man was supposed to be over there on an undercover espionage operation, he made every mistake that could possibly be made.

An undercover espionage operation to be successful must be done in such a way that you become faceless in a crowd. You avoid attention. This man did everything possible to attract attention.

His testimony was that he leased that shop for a photographic studio. He stayed there a year, never opened such a studio and, instead, he spread Glass Wax over the windows. You heard him testify that he was living there with this Finnish lady, drinking vodka by the pint, and at least once the police and an ambulance were called because "only two" of the rooms were splattered with blood.

Now, with respect to the Finnish lady, you heard me ask him whether he recalled an incident in the bakery next door wherein he bought a loaf of bread, then threw it on the floor and ordered the woman to pick it up. You heard his answers to that. He couldn't recall such an incident.

I specifically asked him, "Do you deny that it occurred?"

He never denied it. Never denied it.

I say to you, you have to conclude from that cross-examination of the witness that the incident did occur, and that either the man was lying and trying to be evasive before you on this stand, or else when it happened he was so drunk that he doesn't remember to this day whether it ever did happen. Those are the only conclusions you could arrive at.

While this kind of a life was going on, you and I are being asked to believe the man was a lieutenant colonel in Russian military intelligence.

At one point, with respect to the Finnish lady, although he admits that he left his wife and son in Russia, he seemed to refer to the Finnish lady as part of his "legend." When the case began, I thought that he was simply afraid to go back to Russia. By the time he finished his testimony, I think he was more afraid to go back to his wife.

Now let's assume not only the miserable character of this man; let's assume the sordid life that he led here. Nevertheless, you are left with the basic question: Assuming all that, is the man's basic story true?

He was here for some reason. We know that. Furthermore, he used all of these fantastic methods of communicating with someone. At times he said he used these drops and hollowed-out bolts and so on to communicate with the defendant. One minute after he testified to that, he was telling you he met him every week and they used to go for drives for an hour. If he met him every week and went for drives by the hour, what would be the object of communication with him through this melodramatic, boyish device?

Now, except for communicating with Abel, he used all of these devices he testified to, to communicate with a group of nameless, faceless people whom he would only describe as "Soviet officials." They were never identified by name, rank or any other description.

As you know, the man was led through, and I mean led through, hundreds of pages of testimony concerning his activities. He told what I think could fairly be characterized as a well-rehearsed story. In two places he was asked, "Why did you come to America?" "I came to America to help Mark in espionage." In another place he is asked, "What kind of information were you trying to get?" And his answer, virtually out of the law book on the statute involved, was that it was for "affecting the national security of the United States."

Except for those two tiny threads, spoken out of as miserable a witness as you ever would put on the stand, except for those two tiny threads, there is no evidence in the case of information pertaining to the national defense or atomic energy secrets. There is no such evidence in the case. Yet it is on that kind of evidence that you are being asked to send a man possibly to his death. You would only kill a dog on evidence that he had bitten.

Let's review a few of the things this man Hayhanen says that he did in the furtherance of this conspiracy.

He went out to Colorado to find a man, whom he never met to this day; he went down to Atlantic City to find another man, but he never met up with him; he went up to Quincy, Massachusetts, to locate another man, and to date, to this day, he is not sure that he found the right man; he was told, he says, that he should open a photographic shop as a cover, but he never opened the shop; he was told to learn the Morse code but he never learned the Morse code.

By the time that man got through telling his story—including the fact that he was given money to take to a woman, Mrs. Sobell, but he never met up with her and pocketed the five thousand dollars for himself—all that I could think of was that best-selling book about children *Where Did You Go? Out. What Did You Do? Nothing*.

If that man was a spy, history will certainly record he is the most bumbling, self-defeating, inefficient spy that any country ever sent on any conceivable mission. It is virtually an incredible story and we are to believe it, that this is a lieutenant colonel in Russian military intelligence, sent here to obtain our highest defense secrets.

That bum wouldn't have private-first-class stripes in the American Army.

However, rather than dwell on that man's testimony, which I say to you proved absolutely nothing on this point, I want to recall to your minds what is the most significant evidence that the man did give. He has told the truth—and he has told it within the last six months to the FBI.

You will recall that at the conclusion of his cross-examination, I asked him whether or not he had given this statement to the FBI in late May and in early June of 1957. He said he did. He said he gave it in a hotel room here in New York.

Now, let me read this again to you very carefully, and remember this is the Government's own document. Let me read to you what the man told the FBI:

> "I resided and worked in Finland from July 1949 to October of 1952. There I received my American passport and arrived in New York in October of 1952. I did not engage in espionage activity and did not receive any espionage or secret information from anyone during my stay abroad, neither in Finland nor in the United States of America."

This is the man's own statement to the FBI. And it is on this man's testimony that you are supposed to convict a man of a capital offense.

It is ridiculous. That statement, did you notice, was never cleared away on any redirect examination. To this day, that statement remains in this case as the man's own testimony. It is a complete exculpation of this defendant, and no explanation of it has ever been offered to you.

Now, what about the rest of the evidence?

Sergeant Rhodes appeared. You all had an opportunity to see the type he was: dissolute, a drunkard, betraying his own country. Words can hardly describe the depths to which that man has fallen.

Remember that Rhodes testified he never met Hayhanen, he never heard of him. He never met this man [pointing] the defendant; he never heard of him. He never heard of any of the conspirators named in the indictment. Meanwhile, he told in detail of his own life in Moscow, of selling us out for money. And how is this related to this defendant? Those events in Moscow occurred two years before Hayhanen says Abel sent him to locate a man named Rhodes. How did these relate to this man? The answer is, they don't relate in any way.

It is on evidence of that kind that you are being asked to convict this man. This is the kind of evidence that is before you to send this man possibly to his death.

Where is the evidence of information relating to the national defense and of atomic energy? The answer is that if there is any such evidence it has not been produced before you. If they had a case on it, it hasn't been made before you, and you have to pass on this specific case and on the evidence which has been introduced in this case.

In this case, if you find the man guilty it would be guilt by non-association. This defendant never met any of these people.

It is very important that you realize that you are not serving your country and you are not fighting communism, to convict a man on insufficient evidence. You are only serving your country, and you are only fighting communism, if you bring in a just verdict based upon the individual conscience of each one of you.

I say to you that if after this case is over and you want to live with your neighbors and with yourselves, you must exercise your own consciences to reach a just verdict.

Now, it may seem strange to you that the United States provides this kind of defense for a man like this. In an affidavit that I submitted in an earlier proceeding in this case, in connection with the search and seizure in the Hotel Latham, I said at the end:

"Abel is an alien charged with the capital offense of Soviet espionage. It may seem anomalous that our constitutional guarantees protect such a man. The unthinking may view America's conscientious adherence to the principles of a free society as altruism so scrupulous that self-destruction must result. Yet our principles are engraved in the history and the law of this land. If the free world is not faithful to its own moral code, there remains no society for which others may hunger."

I ask you to remember that, as you weigh your verdict; and I ask you to exercise your individual consciences as to whether or not this man was proved by evidence in this court guilty beyond a reasonable doubt of the specific crimes charged. I ask you always as you listen to the prosecutor, as you hear the charge from His Honor the judge, and then as you deliberate this question, to ask yourselves one final question: Where was the information affecting the national defense of the United States?

Ladies and gentlemen of the jury, if you will resolve this case on that higher level, so that you can leave it with a clear conscience, I have no question but that certainly on Counts One and Two in this indictment, you must bring in a verdict of not guilty.

Thank you.

We at the defense table could never have known what a writer later uncovered, that throughout the trial one juror meticulously noted on a pad black marks when the prosecutor scored a point and red marks when there was created a reasonable doubt. And how could we have guessed that some of them were displeased with Abel's sketching? "He seemed like a man apart, as though he were in a world of his own," a juryman said.

Tompkins: May it please the Court, ladies and gentlemen of the jury. Before I get into my summation I certainly want to thank you for your patience and the courtesy that you have shown to counsel for both sides. There have been some trying days, but you have been more than patient and I am most appreciative.

Now, in my opening I think I made a solemn promise to you that the Government would do everything to afford the defendant a fair trial, and I believe we have conducted ourselves that way; and I further pointed out that it wasn't the Government's aim to simply win a case but of far greater importance was that justice be done.

You are going to hear me use the term "undisputed" and "uncontradicted" many times during my summation because I can think of no substantial fact that the Government has presented to you for your consideration that has been or was attempted to be contradicted.

Penalty was brought up briefly before, and you were asked about that prior to your being sworn. Each and every one of you said that you could decide the case on the evidence without consideration of penalty. The penalty is not a matter for the defendant nor for the Government. That is entirely up to His Honor.

I just want to talk very briefly about conspiracy. In my opening I said simply that it was an agreement—a partnership in crime, if you will—and that the accomplishment of one overt act completes it; that it need not be successful nor that the overt act in itself need be a crime.

In other words, we don't have to stand idly by and permit an individual to commit espionage to get our secrets. We are not powerless in that case. We may intervene. We may prevent the consummation of the crime.

Now I want to talk briefly about Reino Hayhanen, who was referred to before as a trained liar. In my opening I think I told you that you could expect an attack, and you got it. "A trained liar; a professional liar. Trained liar." The same training as the defendant, but less time in the NKVD.

Hayhanen "a trained liar"; the defendant a brave, patriotic man serving his country on a hazardous mission. And, believe me, we intend to make that type of mission very hazardous. He is a good family man and he is living well. His family is living very well in Moscow with, and you heard the letters from the wife, a summer home and servants.

Now, Reino Hayhanen appeared and testified and was subject to cross-examination—four days on direct and cross. Counsel suggested that you watch his demeanor, and I certainly hope you did. I certainly hope you watched how readily he answered the questions, whether they were personal questions that reflected on him, on his personal habits. He admitted very readily that he drank. He admitted very readily that he took Mrs. Sobell's five thousand dollars, and nobody condones that.

I don't recall him admitting, however, that very important item that certainly must have affected his credibility: throwing a loaf of bread on a bakery floor.

Hayhanen testified on direct that the purpose of his coming to the United States was to procure secret information, military or atomic. Now, a statement was read here before, that he had said— and he signed it and it was written by himself, there is no doubt about it—that he had not committed espionage in Finland or in the United States, and it was further represented that that was unchallenged.

After that statement was read, the record shows this:

"Q. Mr. Hayhanen, what were you sent to the United States for?"

Then there is about two or three dollars' worth of vigorous objection, but finally the witness is permitted to answer:

"A. I was sent to the United States as Mark's assistant for espionage work."

Now, we had in Hayhanen, when he arrived here in 1952, a trained, skilled espionage agent. Thirteen years of experience in the use of weapons, surveillance, all of the techniques, microdot training, the use of devices, trained in the English language, trained in the use of radio, containers, false documents.

In 1954, he testified, he met the defendant and subsequently he

241

performed certain assignments for the defendant. He talked about the first one in an endeavor to locate a soldier, Roy Rhodes, in Red Bank. It was stated that Roy Rhodes was an accuser. Roy Rhodes was nothing of the sort. Roy Rhodes testified that he did not know Hayhanen. He testified that he did not know Abel. And I believe that to be true. However, let's look at it in reverse. Abel knew about Roy Rhodes and so did Hayhanen.

Now, the Government has an obligation to prove the truth of the charge of the grand jury. We are not proud of Roy Rhodes. Nobody could be.

You heard his testimony. He is an admitted espionage agent. We simply presented Roy Rhodes as he was, to corroborate the Quebec message. His testimony, I might say, coincided with items contained in the Quebec message which the defendant had given to Hayhanen—items that Roy Rhodes admitted he had given to Russian officials in Moscow.

The Government brought out on direct examination that Roy Rhodes had furnished the Russian government with information while he was there. The Government brought out that he had been paid for that information, and I think cross-examination only served to emphasize that.

In other words, I think the defense discredited an already discredited witness, if that were possible after hearing his direct testimony. But the important thing about it is, the facts contained in his testimony about the type of information that he furnished the Russians were not contradicted at any time.

What I am saying to you is that Roy Rhodes was presented to tie in an individual, to show that that person was living with the Quebec message, and this fact should not escape. Now, if he wasn't a weakling who sold out his country and was susceptible to use by this conspiracy by the Soviet government, this conspiracy would not have sought him out. Abel wasn't seeking decent citizens. He was seeking the Roy Rhodeses—because the decent citizens can be of no help to a Soviet conspiracy, but a compromised army sergeant who has previously furnished information to the Soviets can be a very big help. When you consider that he testified, and it is unchallenged, that he furnished information to the Soviets on Army personnel, on State Department personnel, you can consider the gravity of his offense and at the same time you can consider his potential value to the Soviets back here in the United States.

You give any Soviet agent an opportunity to get the habits, the training and the background and the connections of any individual in the military, whether he be a private or a general, and you have given him a lot to start from, believe me. I can't think of anything stronger than the seeking out of Quebec in an endeavor to get military information—information relating to our national defense. Quebec had been trained in code work, and he had so advised the Russians. And remember this: In the Quebec message, the Russians thought he had a brother working in an atomic plant.

I would like to talk a little bit about the Prospect Park bolt, because I think it is strong corroboration of the testimony of Reino Hayhanen. You will recall how the FBI went to that Prospect Park drop and found it sealed up, then chipping away the cement and finding the bolt. You heard the FBI agent from the laboratory in Washington testify that when he opened the bolt there was a message in it, a typed message.

And that brings me to one of the most important items of proof in the case, this typewriter. Who placed a typewriter definitely in Abel's possession? Who was the person who testified that it was Abel's typewriter? I do not even think the defense would complain about this. Of all people, one of the defendant's character witnesses. He testified that he got this typewriter—he gave you the serial number—from Abel and he turned it over to the FBI.

And you heard Mr. Webb, special agent Webb, testify to the typewriter examination.

I think the drops were referred to as "silly drops." Who do you think was using the "silly drops" in Prospect Park for a message? The defendant! You heard Webb testify that the message contained in that Prospect Park bolt had been typed on this typewriter, which belonged to the defendant.

Now, you will recall that a little newsboy, a little seventeen-year-old newsboy, a little kid with red hair and freckles, and he testified to getting a nickel in change, that he dropped it, that it came open.

One of those trick nickels that you can buy most any place, except that the ones that you buy most any place don't have microfilm in them. And the boy immediately turned it over—after it opened and he saw what was in it—very alertly to a Brooklyn police detective, who turned it over to the FBI. Remember, that was found by Jimmy in June of 1953. The message was dated December, and contained congratulations on a safe arrival. Just remember that Hayhanen arrived here in October, 1952. This nickel had nothing whatsoever to do with Hayhanen, was never in his possession, but I say that it is very strong corroboration of the truth of his story . . .

I just would like to discuss, because Hayhanen has been such an issue, some of the independent corroboration which we promised you—independent corroboration of Hayhanen's testimony.

I don't find the substance of his testimony contradicted, disputed or challenged. The cross-examination was directed to the man's personal habits. He wasn't questioned on a drop. He wasn't questioned on a conversation with the defendant. He wasn't questioned on any of his assignments. And that, to me, is very important.

Now, what about items that Hayhanen didn't know anything about, could have absolutely no connection, that could inculpate this defendant? Look at them. These are out of the storeroom over at 252 Fulton Street: a bolt, cuff link, hollow cuff link, and Hayhanen never saw this, never knew of its existence. This was in the defendant's storeroom: tie clasp, hollowed-out tie clasp. Another bolt, hollowed-out battery, not the type used by Boy Scouts. I doubt if that is readily available. And I think it is safe to say, there isn't a man on this jury who ever saw a tie clasp like that. I am sure that no woman has ever bought one for her husband, not that kind that comes open. These items have been referred to as toys, as were the coins. Toys. I don't believe anybody would call these toys for amusement. They are not toys for amusement. Ladies and gentlemen, they are tools for destruction, destruction of our country; that is the purpose of this conspiracy. These toys? Tools for destruction, believe me!

Let's talk a little bit now about the conduct of the defendant. There isn't anybody that I know who knew him as Rudolf Abel. He was known as Goldfus, known as Mark, and he was known as Martin Collins, and the tenants, not one of his character witnesses, knew him as Rudolf Abel. I think his conduct can best be described as secret, as conduct intended to deceive, conduct showing the cunning of a professional, a highly trained espionage agent. The conduct of a master spy, a real pro. Now, just remember this, this was the man's chosen career. He knows the rules of this game and so do his family, including his mature daughter. He is entitled to no sympathy.

Now, it is hot and I am sure that this jury in their very wise judgment and with the use of their very good common sense can readily arrive at a result. I can simply say this to you: Never in my experience have I seen the definite stating and overwhelming corroboration that has been presented to you in this case.

I simply say this—this is a serious case. This is a serious offense. This is an offense directed at our very existence and through us at the free world and civilization itself, particularly in light of the times. I say this, and I don't believe I have ever said anything more heartily or more seriously: I am convinced the Government has proven its case and not only beyond a reasonable doubt as required, but beyond all possible doubt. I am convinced that you people in your wisdom and judgment will be able to evaluate the truth of the statements of the various witnesses that the Government has presented. I am sure that you will be able to evaluate the facts in this case as results of the crime of conspiracy and with the direction, the charge by the judge, you will arrive at a correct result. I can't stress too much, too strongly, that you don't have to succeed to be guilty. I think that society, and the Government, is entitled to protect itself when they find people conspiring to commit an offense. We are not helpless. We don't have to wait for a corpse before we look for a criminal. We can move in as soon as the crime has been established and that is the partnership, the agreement, confederation, plus the commission of one overt act.

Now, again, in closing I just want to say this to you. We are appreciative of your courtesy, for the attention that you have paid to this very important case. I am absolutely convinced, it is my very strong conviction, that after you have deliberated and considered everything, you will find this defendant guilty, guilty as charged by the grand jury, guilty by the overwhelming weight of evidence, by the overwhelming corroboration that the Government has presented to you.

Thank you.

The Government summation lasted fifty-one minutes. Tompkins, responding to pressure from Washington in their most important pending case, had put great effort and time into his summation. His remarks were complete and forcefully delivered.

The case now became the property of the presiding judge.

Judge Byers: Members of the jury, partly to spare your having to listen to a very hoarse charge this afternoon, and partly to enable the Court to study the record more carefully, the charge will be delivered tomorrow morning at ten-thirty. Good night.

In the Brooklyn park alongside the court, it was still a warm, sunny afternoon and the benches were busy. Over at 252 Fulton, the names Silverman and Levine were gone from the shabby lobby register. The publicity had driven away the guiltless artists. And Abel was in the back of a prison van, bouncing toward the Federal Detention Headquarters in West Street, where he would wait out his eleventh and last night before hearing the verdict.

Meanwhile, a juror sat in a subway and looked across the aisle, catching the headlines on an unknown neighbor's newspaper. "I think both lawyers did the best they could with what they had to work with," he would say later of this session to a reporter. "But it's not like Perry Mason. I can't remember a word that was said, but it's only natural, isn't it? It's said and then it's gone and you carry away an impression. Guilt or innocence."

Friday, October 25

UNITED STATES OF AMERICA VS. RUDOLF IVANOVICH ABEL, ET AL.
BYERS, D. J.
CRIMINAL.

The small black-and-white bulletin board on the courtroom door told the whole story. It was a criminal case tried before Judge Byers. At no time was it anything other than this, and at no point did the participants lose sight of this fact.

The uniqueness of the trial, the international importance of the Soviet spy-defendant, the urgency of the world situation and the pressure of zealous, self-appointed guardians of United States freedom, exerted no influence on the proceedings behind the heavy oak doors of the courtroom.

"The calm of the courtroom and the absence of passionate behavior were remarkable, when one considers the potential explosiveness of the case," wrote a French newsman. And a foreign-born reporter for the *Christian Science Monitor* said, "To one not reared under the Anglo-American system of 'due process,' the trial was proof of the maturity of that system and of its capacity to deal on its own terms with representatives of the very system that seeks to destroy it."

The courtroom of stern, magisterial Mortimer W. Byers was a forum for justice. He set the pace for this trial. All eyes were on him, and the jury was turned to look up at him.

Judge Byers: Members of the jury, the time has now come for you to take over your deliberations in this case. Doubtless, you feel that you know a great deal about it and perhaps you prefer not to have to listen to anything from the Court on the subject. If that is your point of view, it is also mine, but we cannot yield to our preferences. It is my duty to give a charge and it is your duty to listen to it.

You realize that underlying this case there are three provisions of the law concerning which you should be advised, because the indictment contains the charge of three different conspiracies.

> *The judge's clerks said he lived in Brooklyn three miles from the court; he walked to the courthouse every morning and walked home at night. He was eighty years old and was the oldest man on the bench in the Eastern District, but he stood upright to deliver his charge to the jury. This was a tradition, all but dead, which went back hundreds of years to the courts of England. It was a point of pride with Judge Byers, just as his notes were. He did not read a prepared statement, he delivered the charge—with only a few handwritten notes before him.*
>
> *The judge read to the jury from the United States Code, read portions of the indictment and the overt acts, then turned to the interpretation of his readings.*

Judge Byers: A conspiracy is said to have its origin in the minds of those who become parties to the conspiracy, to become the conspirators. A conspiracy thus is essentially an agreement, but that doesn't mean that it is a formal kind of an agreement such as you will find in an ordinary business transaction.

I have never known of a conspiracy to involve a written agreement. Necessarily, it is a secret and clandestine thing. Now, since that is its nature, about the only way that you can prove the existence of a conspiracy is to prove the conduct of those to whom you impute the conspiracy. As you know, we haven't yet devised any instrument that will enable us to peer into the workings of the human mind.

The only way that we can determine what goes on within the mind is to observe the conduct, and sometimes the word, of the given individual who is under examination. So that in order to ascertain whether a conspiracy exists as the result of a common purpose or an agreement, we examine into the conduct of those who act together and who are thought to act together by reason of the agreement that they have entered into between themselves.

The mere agreement does not impose criminal responsibility, for the reason that people might conspire to violate the law but then they might be discouraged. They might change their minds; they might abandon their original plan. So that the law, in order to punish a conspiracy, requires proof not only of the existence of the conspiracy but the doing of one or more things by one or more of the conspirators to carry the plan or purpose into operation.

I should say in this connection that the doing of one or more things to carry the plan into operation is that branch of the case which is comprehended in the overt acts. It is not necessary that every one of the overt acts be proven. At least one and perhaps more, as alleged, must be proven but not the entire scheme, not the entire list of overt acts need necessarily be proven.

Now, there is another thing that should be explained in connection with this particular kind of criminal offense. The offense is complete upon the demonstration by the required measure of proof of the agreement, the parties to it, and the doing of one or more things to carry the agreement into effect. That constitutes the crime. The conspiracy may fail in its purpose and yet the offense which the law denounces is established once these requirements that I have just referred to have been demonstrated.

To illustrate this point, the judge used a simple example which he said had no reference to the testimony in the case before the jury. He said three men planned to blow up the court building. One buys dynamite, a second goes after a steel drill and a third buys a battery. But the dynamite is wet, the battery doesn't work properly and the other partner breaks a leg.

Judge Byers: But the original agreement having been shown, and each man having undertaken to do a specific thing to carry the plan into effect with the evidence showing that he has tried each to do his part, the offense under the law is made out. The fact that it comes to nothing has no bearing whatever upon the question of whether the crime has been committed.

The crime was complete when the agreement was made and when one or more things were undertaken to carry the plan into effect. I hope I have made the law reasonably clear on that subject.

Now, we move to the next step, which is the presumption of innocence which attaches to this defendant and to any other defendant in a criminal case. It pertains to him from the outset of the case until the jury shall return with its verdict. In order to overcome that presumption, the burden of proof rests upon the Government to prove guilt beyond a reasonable doubt as to every essential element of the crime as charged in the indictment. What does a reasonable doubt mean?

Well, just as the words indicate. It means a doubt which is present in your minds as the result of the exercise of your reasoning faculties, as you apply those faculties to every element of the testimony in the case. The emphasis is upon your reasoning faculties, and that necessarily excludes your emotions. You know that two of our favorite emotions are sympathy and prejudice. You may not rely upon either of those or any other emotion and call the result the creation of a reasonable doubt.

The emotions, you know—and this is true of every one of us—sometimes fly in the face of our reasoning processes, and that is why it seems necessary to warn you particularly against the exercise of emotion, prejudice, sympathy; and by reason of the nature of this case, I am going to venture to say something which I hope and believe is entirely unnecessary.

Do not for the slightest instant of time as you go over the evidence in this case allow yourselves to dwell upon the reflection of what might happen if the conditions were reversed; namely, if an American citizen unlawfully within the U.S.S.R. were to be charged before a tribunal of that country with the equivalent of what this defendant is charged with in this case.

In the first place, you don't know what would happen, and therefore, it is an entirely idle speculation. In the second place, no matter what that speculation might lead you to conclude, it would be of no value whatever to you in the performance of your duties. We are concerned, you and the Court, with the enforcement of our standards of law. We are not interested in the standards which prevail in any other parts of the world. We are responsible only for the way in which we discharge our duties as American citizens.

I will observe that while the defendant is a visible person in this courtroom, there is also an invisible presence at this trial: namely, our spirit of fair play, our spirit of administering justice according to our own standards which are in the keeping of the Court, the jury and the counsel.

Turning somewhat to the testimony: In the first place, you are relieved of the ordinary task of a criminal jury in choosing between conflicting versions of a given alleged occurrence. You are confronted with no conflict in testimony whatever.

That does not mean that you must not examine the testimony, even though it be uncontested, with the greatest of care. The contrary is the fact.

Now, with reference to the conspiracy itself: namely, its membership, its purpose, its aims and objects, you have the testimony of Hayhanen. That is the only testimony in the case on that subject. Of course, he is an accomplice by his own recital. He is one of the conspirators. The testimony of an accomplice is entirely admissible in the administration of our system of law, but in weighing what such a person says you are required to apply to it the most careful and exacting scrutiny, considering what personal object or benefit an accomplice may have in giving his testimony at all, and how far you can believe what he says in view of the fact that he is an accomplice.

As to every witness who has testified before you, if you find that he has testified falsely with respect to a material issue in the case,

251

you have the right to disregard his entire testimony because of the false element. Equally, you have the right to accept that which you find to be credible. That is entirely and exclusively a question for the jury to determine for itself.

In examining Hayhanen's testimony and in deciding whether you will accept it in whole or part, you will naturally turn to the other testimony in the case which has been offered on the theory that it tends to corroborate that which he has stated on the witness stand.

The judge told the jury it had listened to twenty-seven witnesses. Then he named each one and identified the person. Sometimes he even connected the witness to a piece of evidence. His notes were good, his memory sharp.

Judge Byers: I will comment on the witness Rhodes. The only purpose in that connection is this: There was a motion to strike his entire testimony, largely based on Rhodes's testimony that he never knew either the defendant or Hayhanen. That motion was denied, and the reason for the denial was this:

Rhodes testified concerning his career in Moscow. Hayhanen testified that, at the direction of the defendant, he, Hayhanen, had tried to locate Rhodes and that in that effort he had gone to Colorado—and I think his testimony was that the defendant paid his expenses. Having reached Colorado, he telephoned to what was thought to be the residence of Rhodes and I think that Mrs. Brown, Rhodes's sister, testified that at some time in the spring of 1955 she received a telephone inquiry from a person who spoke with a foreign accent.

Now, the purpose of retaining that testimony was to enable you to reach a conclusion as to whether in that respect Hayhanen had been corroborated and, perhaps, to enable you to form an opinion as to whether Rhodes struck you as being the kind of person that an unfriendly power would seek out in the effort to employ him as an agent for that power. That is the reason the testimony was

252

received and retained in the record; and I may still say that I think it was a correct ruling.

In denying that motion and, indeed, in deciding all other motions and ruling upon objections, the Court did not intend to convey or express an opinion as to the guilt or innocence of the defendant. Those rulings were rulings upon questions of law, and if the jury thinks it has observed an opinion on the part of the Court I urge you very strongly to disregard it because the question is solely for your determination.

Something has been said about character testimony. In the first place, that is a misnomer. The correct expression is reputation testimony, and the reason that the distinction is called to your attention is this: There is a very evident difference between reputation and character. Reputation is what people think about you; character is what you really are. Now, two or three of the witnesses were asked, somewhat casually, if the defendant's reputation was good and they said it was. Reputation testimony is regarded as important. In that connection let me say to you that if you believe the testimony, then the burden of proof resting upon the Government may be somewhat added to. It may be made heavier than would be the case if such testimony were not in the record.

You know there are a number of exhibits—I think there is an even one hundred offered by the Government and four or five offered by the defendant. Among those exhibits offered by the defendant are what both sides have argued to you are letters passing between the defendant and a member of his family. You may have been impressed by that argument. I am not saying whether you should have been or not, but I am calling your attention to the fact there is no evidence in this record as to the identity of a person who wrote any one of those letters or the person to whom any letter was addressed. So much of the argument, I think, was purely speculative.

After the trial was long over and just another page in the history of the court, this is what one of the panel of twelve jurors said of the

253

letters: "*Perhaps I did believe them because the Government didn't go after them. On the other hand they had so much evidence maybe they didn't care about the letters. I tried to put myself in his position. I mean, the father of children and all. I think they had an effect on the jury and if they weren't real, somebody did a good job with them.*"

Judge Byers: Now, your verdict will be unanimous: guilty or not guilty on Count One; guilty or not guilty on Count Two; guilty or not guilty on Count Three. I think I have now covered the subject as required by law.

The judge excused the alternate jurors with the thanks of the Court. He announced that the jury would now undertake its deliberations, and the court clerk called out, "Everybody keep their seats until the jury retires."

It was 12:15 P.M.

When the jury had gone, we gave the press what would be Abel's only comment on the trial. We had been asked repeatedly if he would say whether he had been "given a fair trial." I was reluctant to touch this subject, fearing we would prejudice any possible appeal. At the Rosenberg espionage trial, defense counsel had made a mistake which plagued him at every step of his appeals, by thanking the trial judge for the "fair" manner in which he had presided.

Requested to comment upon his defense, Abel wrote out a statement at this time, saying, "I would like to take this opportunity of expressing my appreciation of the way in which my court-appointed attorneys conducted my defense. I wish to express my thanks to them for the tremendous amount of work they put into their efforts on my behalf, for the skill and ability they have shown in doing so. R. I. Abel." He permitted reporters to copy it, in the courtroom.

Then we sat back to wait upon the jury, who now took over the ultimate responsibility. We learned later that the foreman immediately called for a vote, and to put everyone at ease he made it a secret paper ballot. Eleven slips came back marked guilty. One man voted not guilty (on Count One) and so the deliberations began. An hour went by and it was time for lunch. The marshals led them across Fulton Street to Joe's Restaurant and they had a hot meal in a room of their own, upstairs.

It was 1:15 when they went to lunch and this was our first sign. It told us they would be "out" for some time, that there was no unanimity—at least for now. It was safe for us to eat. We followed them across Fulton Street and into the same restaurant. We ate downstairs talking of the trial, while upstairs the jurors strained not to think of the afternoon ahead of them.

Court officers, meanwhile, took Abel to the detention pen for his lunch. There were no court facilities in the Eastern District to feed the prisoners, so each morning when he was checked out of his Manhattan Federal cell the Colonel was handed a bag of sandwiches with a piece of fruit for dessert. During the noonday recess, he would eat in the court lockup.

At 2:30 P.M., after an hour and five minutes, the jury returned from lunch and resumed its deliberations. The first thing they did was send a note to the judge, asking for three of the exhibits. They wanted to have Hayhanen's statement to the FBI that he never committed espionage; the "Quebec" message, and the decoded message found in the split nickel.

When we were told of this, the news touched off a round of speculation. Then we sat back to wait some more. Alan Robinson, president of the Yorkshire Insurance Companies, joined me and asked what would happen if the verdict were "not guilty." I said we must face one problem at a time.

All through the trial Abel had kept busy; his hands and his mind were constantly active. When he wasn't taking notes, he sketched. He drew Hayhanen, the jury, Judge Byers, the court attendants and his prosecutor. (He misspelled "Tomkins," leaving out the letter "p.") But now, with the court all but empty and the action taking place outside our arena, there was little to do, and the time seemed to weigh heavily upon him.

All his life had been filled with waiting—some of it so pointless. He had waited to keep secret meetings, waited to pick up a message at a drop, waited for the right moment to recruit an agent, waited for letters from his family, and waited and feared for the moment when he might be found out. Abel sometimes felt as though everyone he passed on the street was looking at him and knew who he was. He once told me he had enjoyed reading the autobiography of bank robber Willie Sutton, a celebrated fugitive who had suffered nightmares in which hundreds of people pointed at him and screamed, "You're Willie Sutton."

Abel explained that any undercover fugitive must constantly fight against the feeling that the whole world is on the verge of guessing his secret. The Colonel, who generally was given to underplaying his role, managed to control his phobia for nine years.

An hour passed, then two. Someone sent out for coffee and the latest editions of the afternoon papers. One of the reporters came up behind me and, pretending to read over my shoulder, whispered, "Jim, you better get ready to run. Maybe you did too good a job."

Waiting for a jury is like keeping a death watch, and this was the worst watch I ever kept. When the clock over the empty jury box showed 4:30 P.M., our little band grew restless but suddenly hopeful in a professional sense. Could the jury be deadlocked? The thought of a new trial, of having to go through this all over again, was discouraging. What would my partners think?

"Why were you out so long?" a reporter later would ask them.

"Do you think it was long? I don't think it was so long," said the juror. "We wanted to be careful, to take our time and give it a lot of thought. We didn't want any repercussions afterward.

"There were no big arguments. Nobody rolled up his sleeves or anything like that. You know, you get more arguments on some accident cases than on a big one like this. There was plenty of evidence and the FBI were impressive. But I think the biggest single thing was Hayhanen's testimony."

A door slammed somewhere and then I heard someone call out,

"Here they come." It was 4:50 P.M., and they had been out three and a half hours, with another hour for their lunch. The courtroom quickly filled up; there was a bewildering swiftness to everything that took place now. It was mechanical, official and efficient.

The clerk, John Scott, was standing. For this moment, he was the central figure. "In the case of the United States of America against Rudolf I. Abel," he asked the jury, "how do you find the defendant, guilty or not guilty, on Count One?"

"Guilty."

Three times the clerk called for an answer and three times jury foreman Dublynn pronounced Abel "guilty."

At my request, the jury then was polled individually, and twelve more times the word "guilty" filled the courtroom. It was like an echo: guilty, guilty, guilty . . .

Abel, through it all, sat perfectly still. His face remained set and his eyes were steady.

I made a motion to set aside the verdict as "against the weight of evidence," and Judge Byers denied it. He ordered Abel remanded and set November 15 for sentencing. The judge then addressed the jury for the last time:

"The jury is discharged with the thanks of the Court for your good and careful attention that you have given to this case. And while you may not be interested, I would like to say that if I were a member of the jury I would have reached the same verdict.

"Good night and good luck to you all."

Outside the court, Tompkins declared to the press that "the trial was conducted in accordance with the highest traditions of American justice." He said the verdict was warranted in light of the overwhelming evidence, and that with this case the United States had struck "a severe blow at Soviet espionage in this country."

The final statement of the day came in Washington, where the Army announced that M/Sgt. Roy Adair Rhodes had been confined to the criminal stockade at Fort Belvoir, Virginia. Five days later it charged Rhodes with committing espionage and with "failure to disclose prior association with Soviet agents" in a sworn statement made to military investigators.

Thursday, November 14

The calculating Soviets chose this day—the day before the sentencing—to break their silence on the Abel case. They knew, of course, that their denunciation would be carried in American and other Western newspapers the following day, when Abel was to be sentenced.

The story appeared in Moscow in the *Literary Gazette*, which is written and edited for writers and others of the Soviet intelligentsia.

The article described the Abel case as "lowbrow crime fiction," a "hoax concocted by J. Edgar Hoover and the FBI to make the American people forget the dirty side of the Bureau's business." It told how the "American authors of the crime fiction" had made Abel, a photographer, "into the brains of a spy ring which quite naturally existed on Moscow gold."

While Moscow's artists' and writers' colony was reading the local version of the case in Brooklyn, I had been drafting a letter to Judge Byers, setting forth my views as to why I believed Abel's life should be spared.

In the three months since I had first entered the case, I had come to know Mortimer Byers as a stern judge, a man with strong convictions (he had once held that an arms embargo by President Franklin D. Roosevelt was unconstitutional), and as a proud patriot by his own standards.

I knew, for instance, that during the depression he had voluntarily turned back 15 per cent of his paycheck after a government order slashing all Federal wages but exempting judges from the 15 per cent salary cut. I also knew that he had sentenced two young World War II draft dodgers to five years in jail and then jolted observers by recommending they serve the time at hard labor. I had once heard him suggest that if aliens who declined to become citizens carried a mark, or a brand, on their hands, the government would have no trouble keeping track of them.

The Eastern District Court had a proclivity for sending difficult and controversial trials to Byers, for it knew he was unflinching and tough-minded. Over his twenty-eight years on the Federal bench he had sentenced hundreds of prisoners; the question in my mind now was "Would this tough old Brooklyn judge try to impose his iron will on the Kremlin and sentence Abel to die?"

I had become convinced Abel's death would serve no purpose and was actually against the best interest of my country. When I had finished my letter about the sentencing of Abel, I sent it over to Judge Byers' chambers by messenger. I wanted him to have it and study it a full twenty-four hours in advance of the formal sentencing. I was satisfied then that I had done all in my power to save the Colonel's life.

Friday, November 15

At 10:30 A.M. the courtroom was filled and we were all ready, waiting to get on with the sentencing procedure. We lacked only one thing: the prisoner. Abel had not arrived from Detention Headquarters in Manhattan; the attendants and uniformed court officers looked worried. The big room fell perfectly silent as we waited ten minutes, fifteen, then twenty. Finally, just before 11 A.M., Judge Byers strode in and the bailiff called the court into session.

From another door at the front of the court Abel was led in. When he took his seat beside us he whispered, with a sheepish grin on his face, that the prison van had broken down and this was the cause of the delay.

I began the proceedings by reading in open court, and for the record, the letter I had addressed to Judge Byers, which first stated that my plea assumed the correctness of the jury's verdict under our law:

It is my contention that the interest of justice and the national interests of the United States dictate that the death penalty should not be considered, because:

(1) No evidence was introduced by the Government to show that the defendant actually gathered or transmitted any information pertaining to the national defense;

(2) Normal justification of the death penalty is its possible effect as a deterrent; it is absurd to believe that the execution of this man would deter the Russian military;

(3) The effect of imposing the death penalty upon a foreign national, for a peacetime conspiracy to commit espionage, should be weighed by the government with respect to the activities of our own citizens abroad;

(4) To date the government has not received from the defendant what it would regard as "cooperation"; however, it of course remains possible that in the event of various contingencies this situation would be altered in the future, and accordingly it would appear to be in the national interest to keep the man available for a reasonable period of time;

(5) It is possible that in the foreseeable future an American of equivalent rank will be captured by Soviet Russia or an ally; at such time an exchange of prisoners through diplomatic channels could be considered to be in the best interest of the United States.

[Most of the newspapers made mention of this last point, but several ignored it. Undoubtedly, they felt it could never happen; it was just a defense attorney covering all contingencies.]

With respect to an appropriate term of years, the following facts are submitted because this problem is novel in American jurisprudence:

(1) During the 1920s, when France was the strongest power on the European continent and hence a primary objective of Soviet espionage, the average sentence given by the French courts to Soviet agents

convicted of actually acquiring defense information, was three years imprisonment. (*Soviet Espionage*, Dallin, Yale University Press.)

(2) The sole British statute applicable to a similar case, of peacetime espionage by an alien, is the Official Secrets Act, first passed in 1889 with a maximum penalty of life imprisonment; repealed and re-enacted in 1911 with a maximum penalty of seven years; increased to fourteen years in 1920.

Before writing this letter I sought and obtained the opportunity to discuss the matter in Washington with various interested government departments and agencies, including the Department of Justice. This does not mean that any one of such parties necessarily concurs in the foregoing.

I then added these few concluding extemporaneous remarks in open court:

"The defendant Abel is a man fifty-five years old. He has faithfully served his country. Whether right or wrong, it is his country, and I ask only that the Court consider that we are legally at peace with that country.

"I ask that the judgment of the Court be based on logic, and justice tempered with mercy."

Judge Byers: Does the defendant wish to be heard in his own behalf?

Abel: No, I have nothing to say, Your Honor.

Judge Byers: Mr. Tompkins, has the Government anything to say?

Tompkins: If Your Honor pleases, the imposition of sentence is, of course, wholly a matter within Your Honor's discretion. However, it may be of some aid and assistance to the Court in reaching its determination to have the benefit of the Government's observations and comments.

First, just a word or two about the defendant himself. He is not a novice in the field of espionage. By training and by profession, for a period of over thirty years, he has been an agent for espionage.

During his residence in the United States, he is known to have communicated directly and indirectly with Moscow, and to have received instructions and to have activated agents and built an espionage apparatus.

The extent of Abel's activities is well-known to the Court from the evidence presented at the trial.

There are, of course, many approaches to sentencing: The deterrent effect which the sentence will have on others, rehabilitation and retribution. The concepts of rehabilitation or retribution would appear to have little application in this case, and I certainly think it would be naïve to assume that a substantial sentence would deter the Soviets from continuing their espionage operations directed at this country and at the free world. But it would certainly serve notice upon the men in the Soviet Union, in the Kremlin, and those who carry out their assignments, that the commission of espionage in the United States is a hazardous undertaking.

The prosecutor then said my references to espionage laws in France in the 1920s and in England in 1911 and 1920 were not valid because present-day espionage is a far more serious crime than it has ever been before.

Tompkins: Espionage in 1957, I think, is completely different. The threat against civilization, the threat against this country and the whole free world, is inherent in this crime. In other words, it is an offense against the whole American people, rather than a few individuals. So the punishment should be commensurate with the magnitude of the offense.

The present dangers which this country faces from the country whose leaders tell us they will bury us, must also be considered. While no shooting war exists, as Mr. Donovan points out, no shooting war exists with the Soviets, we are engaged in a cold war with that country, the outcome of which could well decide who would be victorious in a hot war. In such circumstances, this government must deal drastically with agents of foreign powers who cross our borders by subterfuge for the purpose of seeking out our vital national secrets.

Now, in light of all these factors and considerations, the Government has certainly no hesitation in commending—and indeed, it seems to me, has a duty of requesting—the imposition of a substantial and very strong sentence in this case.

Judge Byers: The question of the sentence in this case presents no particular problem concerning the defendant as an individual. The Court knows next to nothing about his personal life or his true character, nor about the motives that may have caused him to enter this country illegally in 1948 and here conduct himself ever since as an undercover agent of the U.S.S.R. for the purposes described in the testimony of his assistant and accomplice.

Lacking this insight into the man known as Abel, the evidence requires that he be dealt with as one who chose this career with knowledge of its hazards and the price that he would have to pay in the event of detection and conviction of the violation of the laws of the United States, enacted by Congress for the protection of the American people and our way of life.

Thus the problem will be seen to present the single question of how the defendant should be dealt with so that the interests of the United States in the present, and in the foreseeable future, are to be best served, so far as those interests can be reasonably forecast.

Many considerations have been involved in that study. It would not be the part of wisdom to recite them in this record, but suffice it to say that in the measured judgment of this Court the following sentence, based upon the jury's verdict of guilty as to each count of the indictment, is believed to meet the test which has been stated.

Pursuant to the verdict of guilty as to Count One, the defendant is committed to the custody of the Attorney General of the United States for imprisonment in a Federal institution to be selected by him for the period of thirty years.

Pursuant to the same verdict as to Count Two, the defendant is . . .

The judge recited the legal liturgy, sentencing Abel to thirty, ten and five years and imposing fines of $2,000 and $1,000. The sentences were to run concurrently; the fines were consecutive. This meant his total fine was $3,000 and his prison term was thirty years, less time off for good behavior.

The sentencing had taken just sixteen minutes. Now it was done and Abel was led from the courtroom. I watched him go, thinking that we had succeeded in saving his life but that for a fifty-five-year-old man the thirty-year sentence was equivalent to life imprisonment.

When I reached the prisoner detention cells in the basement, suddenly very tired, Abel was waiting for me. Casually slouched in a big wooden chair, one leg crossed over the other, he was puffing on a cigarette. His suit was no longer new, it badly needed a press, but to look at him now he seemed to have no care in the world.

"That wasn't bad," he said finally. "What you said up there was quite well done. But you are correct in your law points and I have only one question. When your appeal succeeds and the indictment is dismissed, what happens to me then?"

My shirt was damp and heavy against my sides with perspiration. I was emotionally drained, and now he had the gall to tell me, "Not bad." This cool professional's self-control was too much for me just then.

"Rudolf," I said, looking him directly in the face, "if all my work is successful, I may have to shoot you myself. Don't forget, I still am a commander in Naval Intelligence."

He puffed once, exhaled and then said quietly, "You know, I think you would."

The tension was broken. He offered me one of his cigarettes and then we got down to business. I told him we had ten days in which to decide whether to appeal the verdict. We agreed that I would visit him two days later and come to a decision then.

He offered his hand and I took it, saying goodbye. For a man about to begin serving thirty years in a foreign prison, Colonel Abel possessed an uncanny calm.

Jury foreman Dublynn bought a paper on his way home that day, looking for the story of the sentencing by Judge Byers. "I thought," he later told a journalist, "they were going to make an example of the case and that Abel would be killed. Then I read where his lawyer brought out how he could be used in a trade for an American and I saw there was no sense in killing him.

"I have a brother in the Air Force and I could see the possibility of a trade. I mean, suppose one of our fliers was shot down?"

Monday, November 18

On this day, three days after the sentencing, I visited the Colonel and found him in good humor, with a complete set of blueprints for the West Street Federal house of detention (his local habitat) tucked under his arm.

"What," I asked, "do you have in mind? A mass breakout at midnight?"

Rudolf laughed. "Nothing quite so dramatic. I have a few ideas on how the government might better utilize floor space here. The warden likes my ideas, so he gave me these architectural plans, which I'm redrafting to incorporate my ideas. He'll send them on to the Bureau of Prisons in Washington."

"If I were Warden Krinsky," I said, "I would worry that some moonless night, when the guards were looking east, you might go down a newly designed laundry chute and out into the west. Does the warden know you read Willie Sutton's book?"

"Yes, but he also knows I'll not make my break until you successfully argue your appeal," said Abel, smiling.

The appeal, of course, was the reason for my visit. If we were to challenge the District Court's rulings, we had only ten days in which to file our notice of appeal. Following this, we had forty days to prepare our full petition to the Circuit Court.

There was never any doubt in my mind that we should test the constitutionality of Abel's search and seizure, in the higher courts. However, we ran one risk when we appealed. If we were successful and a new trial was ordered, Abel could be found guilty a second time and resentenced, by a different judge—perhaps to death.

"I'll take my chances," Abel said.

The Colonel meanwhile had returned to his varied routines. He went back to drawing cartoons for the West Street prison's weekly mimeographed newspaper and turned his analytical mind to the physical problems of the overcrowded building which sits hard by the Hudson River at the foot of West 12th Street, in the shadow of the elevated West Side Highway.

He completed what he called a set of "practical drawings," which mapped out a relocation of the prison's industrial laundry and provided more storage space. The warden told him the plans were "very good" and this opinion later was confirmed by the U.S. Bureau of Prisons. But there was no money available for such improvements at the time, so the Soviet Colonel's plans for the prison were put on file.

As for Rudolf's efforts to improve the Federal detention building on West Street, this is what a senior official in the Bureau of Prisons once wrote me: "He was genuinely interested and accepted the project as a challenge. . . . He approaches all his duties with interest and a determination to do well whatever he undertakes." This, of course, had long been Abel's forte.

1958

The hollow nickel that was used by Colonel Abel to deliver messages
and gave rise to the name by which his trial became known.
(Courtesy of Dereu & Sons Mfg. Co.)

Thursday, January 16, 1958

With the tension and strain of the trial behind us, the Colonel and I were more relaxed again, and in the first weeks of the new year our meetings were both frequent and pleasant. It was during this time that we shared most completely our mutual interest in art, in intelligence and espionage, in books and in people. While we spoke of his case a good deal, Rudolf seemed less and less like a client, or a convicted defendant.

He was lonely for intellectual companionship and conversation. I found his company fascinating and stimulating, especially because of the intellectual honesty with which he addressed himself to any subject. In addition, I never lost sight of the fact that whatever the outcome, Colonel Abel would always carry with him an opinion of how he was defended by his American lawyer.

"The American public," I said to him now, "is well pleased at the outcome of your trial. They're satisfied you were afforded a full and fair hearing, but are relieved you were dealt a stiff sentence."

"It does my heart good," Abel would caustically say, "to know I have given such a sense of satisfaction to the American people."

Many of our meetings over this period were held on Saturdays and holidays. On such days, the warden would give us the privacy of his office and we would spend two and three hours, just talking easily. I often took my John along with me (he was thirteen at the time) and the Colonel was especially kind and patient with him.

Rudolf spoke of being a parent but seldom discussed his twenty-seven-year-old daughter. It was clear, however, that there were close bonds between them, whereas he never mentioned his wife. Most detailed information about the daughter Evelyn came from her letters to the Colonel. For instance, she wrote:

> I have not dropped smoking yet, but Mother stopped about a year ago. As regards my personal affairs there is nothing new. I indulge in freedom. Still I do not lose hope of making a home of my own. . . .
>
> Now I am "studying" novels by Mickey Spillane. I have read three of them (*I, The Jury; The Big Kill; The Long Wait*). Have you happened to read any of them? I must admit they do not test you very high, though they are thrilling and fast. The language is all slang and the plot is rather primitive. What I like least of all is that his sense of humor is poor. A good sense of humor is a lot, to my point of view.

On the subject of art, she was equally voluble:

> Of course, modernism as a new thing could arouse much talk, but as for me, I prefer pictures and not puzzles. . . . I hold to realism, though I am only to [*sic*] sure that every good artist ought to learn (if only a bit) from impressionists. Their knowledge of those elusive effects as light, as you write, would add to every good picture. I like Claude Manet, Cezanne and Degas and I do not like Picasso.

Evelyn adored and imitated her father, with whom I had several lengthy discussions on art. Rudolf was highly knowledgeable and strongly opinionated on the subject. He was both brilliant and acid in his antimodernism. Abel knew that I was a governor of the Brooklyn Museum and a member of the New York City Art Commission, a nonsalaried group of citizens charged with responsibility to maintain high standards in the design and decoration of all city property, including the public schools.

I explained to Rudolf that the Art Commission met regularly in City Hall (as it had done since 1898) and must approve or reject proposed building designs, sculpture, murals, etc., whenever the expenditure of public funds was required. I also told him of the heated debates we occasionally would have, over the expenditure of public funds for extremely abstract art. Was the proposal true art or was the so-called artist's effort merely a confusing substitute for talent and disciplined study? Should we spend public funds for subjective art, which might have meant self-expression to the creator but would not generally edify the viewing public? Was some of it not art but merely pleasing decoration?

Rudolf told me one day that he sympathized with my problems on such matters and would like to give them some thought. Shortly thereafter he presented me at the prison with a handwritten lecture on the subject, entitled "Art Today."

In part, he had written:

Art movements within "modern art" change nearly every year. Favorites of one or two years lose their "appeal" and the artists have to learn new tricks to keep abreast of the demands of the intelligentsia.

Modern art has reached a point in craftsmanship and content where two inmates of zoological gardens (one in the United States, the other in England) can successfully compete with the products of humans for the money of sophisticated collectors. It does seem that if a sufficient number of educated chimpanzees with a taste for art were available, they could replace the art teachers at present occupying chairs in universities. At least they would not burden their students with metaphysics and psychoanalysis.

Modern art is now a snobbish profession. People who do not understand it are classified as being on a lower scale of intellect. They have to "learn" to understand it; it is "above" them.

271

The modern artist is only interested in finding a soulmate (with money to buy his paintings) and the more restricted his public, the higher the apparent value of his work as art.

When it came to education, apprenticeship and craftsmanship, Abel was severe and "European." For this reason, perhaps, he spoke well of the Germans, for they were certainly disciplinarians and discipline was a pillar of his philosophy. So much so that he once told a prison official that he was unwisely spending the meager funds available for vocational training in prison—that the bulk of the money should go to the more intelligent and more adaptable inmates, rather than those with lower IQs and less able to absorb training. The official said to me, "A part of his philosophy was being expressed here; he always seemed to show a disregard and mild scorn for people who were not self-reliant and who had to depend on direct supervision and guidance."

This is what Abel wrote of skill and craft and learning in art:

. . . Prior to "modern art" an artist had to study for many years to learn the rudiments of his craft. For that purpose art schools and academies were established with curriculums specially adapted to the needs of the artist. The emphasis was on actual painting, etching, etc. Since modern art is not interested in form, studying the rudiments of the craft was less necessary. The art teacher became something of a psychologist in the new university courses. He attempted to teach the student to "express himself." The need for technical training became less important than the psychological approach to art.

Modern art has "benefited" from the popularity of psychoanalysis as a means of curing neuroses, both imaginary and real. People with "time on their hands" and "psychoses on the brain" were recommended to study art as a means of self-expression and emotional catharsis. The de-emphasis of technique and craftsmanship in modern art has enabled people who would have been weeded out by traditional training methods, to swell the ranks of artists.

Any neurotic could learn to squeeze paint out of a tube (and often without the benefit of palette and brush), apply it in gobs onto a piece of canvas, or anything else that suited his fancy. . . .

Whether "modern" art will have any value for future generations is a dangerous subject for discussion. Certainly some of it deserves preservation, if only as a reflection of the mental confusion of our times. How to separate what is "good" from what is "bad" is probably even more difficult to decide.

I told the Colonel I would submit his paper at the Art Commission's meeting at City Hall—if only to start another argument.

Wednesday, February 12

At our last several conferences the Colonel had mentioned how anxious he was, now that he had been sentenced, to write to and receive letters from his family. He had been permitted no foreign correspondence, a regulation which he denounced as "barbaric." He felt that it might be best now for me to try to contact his people through the Soviet Embassy here.

I decided that these problems, and others which I anticipated, could conceivably put me in an awkward if not down-right unpleasant posture and I therefore should present some practical proposals to the proper government agencies. If I were to have any dealings with the Soviets, I wanted to clear exactly the steps I proposed to take in Colonel Abel's name. I told Abel that I planned to go to Washington in due course to talk over my dilemma with friends and counselors at the Central Intelligence Agency: Allen Dulles, the director, and his general counsel, Larry Houston.

The Colonel said, sincerely, "I wish you'd give my best to Director Dulles. I have a high regard for his ability."

He also asked that I broach the subject of a possible trade with the CIA chief. He seemed to think that India or another neutral country might be willing, in the interest of lessening world tensions, to mediate his exchange for Americans imprisoned in Red China.

"You know," I said, "it's quite fitting that we should speak of how to go about freeing you on this day. It's Lincoln's Birthday, a legal holiday in the city—in honor of our Great Emancipator."

"If he is your Great Emancipator," said Abel, "why don't they celebrate the holiday in the South?"

"There are no perfect human institutions," I told him, "but at least in this country even our imperfections are in the open for the whole world to see. Why did Soviet Russia jam every day the Voice of America broadcasts reporting your trial? And why is it that we publicize the extent of drug addiction in the United States, whereas the Soviet tries to conceal such statistics as though pretending to itself that the problem can't exist in a so-called 'model Socialist state'?"

Abel replied that while many social problems are world-wide in scope, including narcotics addiction, it is not always in the public interest to publicize such facts. "The government must determine what is best for the people," he said. I replied that I could not understand how the truth could vary with political changes, such as Stalin's death.

So it went at each session, by the hour.

Saturday, February 15

This was the day we filed our appeal with the United States Court of Appeals for the Second Circuit. Much of the ground had been covered before in pretrial procedures, but I felt this was a much stronger, more lucid presentation. We based the appeal on four contentions, with principal emphasis on the search-and-seizure issue. The remaining points dealt with the conduct of the trial, including the prosecution's continually leading its witnesses, the trial judge's overruling almost all defense objections, etc.

I frankly told Abel, however, that in my opinion our best chance for a reversal on constitutional grounds would come if we could obtain a final review by the Supreme Court of the United States.

Friday, February 21

After a general court-martial before a ten-officer court, Sgt. Roy Adair Rhodes was convicted in Fort Meyers, Virginia, on this day of conspiring to commit espionage. He was given a dishonorable discharge and sentenced to five years at hard labor. Rhodes was the first American military man ever court-martialed for espionage against his own country and could have received a sentence of life imprisonment. According to the news accounts, the defendant stood at attention in uniform to hear the verdict. His wife, a spectator at the trial, wept at the pronouncement of sentence.

The principal prosecution witness had been Reino Hayhanen.

Abel's reaction to the sentence was that it was entirely too light. The Colonel believed that if it were just for him to receive a thirty-year sentence from a civilian court, surely an American military tribunal would deal equally severely with one of its own who had betrayed his country and military uniform. He said very little—he shook his head several times, in what I took to be disgust—but we both were probably thinking the same thing for different reasons: "If this were the Soviet Union . . ."

Saturday, February 22

It was again a holiday. The Soviet Colonel and his American lawyer celebrated the birthday of General and President George Washington in the warden's office at the Manhattan Federal prison with coffee, cigarettes and a marathon discussion that went on for three hours, ranging over many subjects. (I jotted down the topic headings in my desk calendar later in the day.)

We began with a review of my Circuit Court of Appeals brief,

275

which seemed to satisfy Rudolf and even his "jailhouse lawyer" friends in the prison, my severest critics. He told me that all were confident we would win.

He complained that his current "teeth" were growing loose and he feared he might lose them some night in a choice cut of prison liver. He said prison humor would not let go of an incident of this nature and he would prefer to avoid becoming an "inmate celebrity."

Contrary to my recommendation that he transfer to a United States penitentiary to begin serving (and getting credit for) his sentence, the Colonel said he had decided to stay on here in New York as a "detention inmate" where we could meet easily and talk privately. He explained that he would rather remain nearby until I had a chance, sometime within the next few weeks, to talk with Allen Dulles in Washington about his corresponding with his family and his possible exchange.

I reminded him again that I was keeping a diary on the case, which I suspected was nowhere near its conclusion. I explained I thought that in the interests of American justice I might someday write a book about the case, and about him. His attitude was "Why not? Somebody surely will and I'd rather it was you." He asked only that I treat him fairly and accurately, remembering that he was "just a soldier."

This took us into a discussion on strategic intelligence and espionage. He began by deploring the fact that fiction writers exaggerated and distorted the true role of the twentieth-century spy, who often was merely a fact gatherer.

"The popular impression created by these writers," he said, "is unfortunate. People are always disappointed when there is no element of Mata Hari, whenever espionage is written about or discussed."

I could have, if I had chosen, reminded Rudolf that there was an "element of Mata Hari" in the example of Roy Rhodes and his Moscow lady friend from the KGB. However, I agreed with him in principle. Spies would always be used and at times did score brilliant individual successes, I told him, but painstaking research and analysis of readily available information would continue to provide the bulk of intelligence materials. Contrary to popular understanding, the overwhelming amount of most important intelligence is not a result of secret espionage but is obtained by overt means. It is for this reason that a democracy (with freedom of speech and of the press) is a vulnerable target for overt intelligence by every foreign power.

Abel agreed with this and confirmed for me the fact that every Defense Department report to Congress on military strength, every scientific and technical publication in the United States, every issue of our best newspapers, were carefully collected by Russia, either directly or through intermediaries, and disseminated to proper authorities within the Soviet.

"Do you then agree with me," I asked, "that with due recognition to the individual brilliance of certain Soviet scientists, a highly developed system of overt intelligence was responsible more than any other single factor for the Soviet Union launching the first Sputnik?"

He was silent for a moment and then said, "I won't disagree, but I will point out that in the past there have been many instances of Russian scientists making discoveries, or pursuing and writing about research, that predated similar work in the United States but went unnoticed here, simply because scientists in the United States were not alert to these activities.

"Knowledge and ability are not the monopoly of any one country, and lack of interest in foreign scientific work does not condone statements such as you just made."

"I in turn won't disagree with you," I said. "We do not have nearly enough people who are fluent in the Russian or Chinese languages, and surely we do not have, or claim to have, a monopoly on knowledge. On the other hand, I'll not retreat from my position that the Soviet Union for many years, by taking full advantage of the latest scientific developments in the United States and Europe—few of which remain truly secret for a great length of time—has achieved undeserved propaganda and international prestige. The Sputnik I regard as a classic example of this. While we have been unwitting teachers, you have been apt pupils."

I told Abel that based on my wartime experiences in OSS and work in helping to plan a permanent postwar intelligence system for the United States, I had written a brief analysis of the subject. I had frequently used it over the years in talks before civic groups, in which I espoused as in our national interest what I had learned under the sage tutelage of the late Maj. Gen. William J. "Wild Bill" Donovan, director of OSS.

Abel said he would be most interested in studying my lecture and I brought him a copy. In characteristic fashion he delivered to me a week later his written analysis, which included the following trenchant observations:

> I think you did a good job considering space limitations; I might quibble that some aspects were emphasized more than they need have been (i.e., Soviet lead in rocketry being due to overt intelligence . . .).
>
> The aspect that seems to me to be least developed relative to the others is that of evaluation. As a lawyer you know how difficult it is to obtain a true picture from evidence given by eyewitnesses to an occurrence. How much more difficult must it be to evaluate political situations when the sources are human beings, with their own political opinions coloring their statements. One of the dangers in the assessment of information lies in the possibility that the men responsible will themselves slant the evaluation in response to their own opinions and prejudices. This demand for objectiveness in evaluation, i.e., restraining the evaluation to the question of the factual correctness of the information, is paramount.
>
> The determination of policy is not the function of intelligence, although some—particularly the Germans during World Wars I and II—may try to influence policy-making by biasing their information. This is one of the greatest mistakes an intelligence organization can make.

For the Colonel's court-assigned lawyer, the long hours were more than compensated by the fascination of the case. Part of this was the nature of the legal issues and their challenge, but most of it was the man Abel.

When I entered West Street this afternoon, Warden Krinsky greeted me with a solemn expression. He said that he had received a formal complaint from the attorney for an inmate whom Krinsky had been compelled to make Abel's cellmate, because of a shortage of maximum-security cells. "It's cruel and unusual punishment, and downright un-American," the lawyer had said, "to compel my client to share a cell with a convicted Russian spy. People might say my client is a Commie."

"Who is the inmate?" I asked. "Vincent J. Squillante," replied Krinsky gloomily. I could not resist a hearty laugh, in which the warden finally joined.

Vincent J. "Jimmy" Squillante was reputed to be the extortion "king" of the multimillion-dollar garbage hauling rackets in metropolitan New York. Squillante, according to newspaper accounts, claimed prestige among mobsters on the ground he was the godson of the infamous Albert Anastasia, onetime Murder, Inc. chief executioner. When Anastasia was shot to death in a barber's chair in October, 1957, things had begun to go from bad to worse for Jimmy Squillante, now incarcerated in West Street for parole violation.

I convinced Krinsky that he should shrug off the complaint. A moment later, Abel was led in and I opened the conversation by saying, "I hear you have a cellmate."

"Yes," said Abel, "an unfortunate hoodlum."

"How are you getting along?"

"Quite well," said the Colonel, lighting a cigarette. "I am teaching him French.

"You see, Squillante is very unhappy about being returned to prison and the first few days he was like a caged beast. I paid no attention to his ranting, but finally he was disturbing my work in some mathematical problems with which I have been passing the time. So I had a thought.

"I have noticed, both in his case and other strong-arm types, that physical exertion helps to quiet their emotions. This was difficult for me to plan in a small, maximum-security cell. But I commented on the unclean condition of the walls, ceiling and floor and asked whether he would like to keep in good physical shape by scrubbing them. I told him that through a friendly guard I could get us a brush and extra scrubbing powder.

"He finally said he would like it. Ever since, he scrubs several hours every day and he's keeping the place immaculate. I thought about what I could do in return, offered to teach him French, and he was delighted. With a little patience on my part, because of a lack of texts, we are making fine progress."

"Rudolf," I said with genuine astonishment, "what in heaven's name would a gorilla like Squillante do with a knowledge of French?"

The Colonel adjusted his rimless glasses and then slowly replied, "Frankly, I don't know, Mr. Donovan, but what else could I do with the fellow? After all, what do I have in common with a garbage collector?"

Some time later, when Squillante was transferred to Lewisburg Penitentiary in Pennsylvania, *The New York Times* reported the bizarre relationship in a witty article and said that other inmates described Abel as disappointed about the transfer because he had been able to get Squillante only through the active French verbs. (In September, 1963, Attorney General Robert F. Kennedy announced that after his release from Federal prisons, Squillante had been tortured and murdered in Connecticut by rival gangsters. His limited French presumably was of no aid.)

Thursday, March 6

I traveled to Washington today to keep my appointment with Director Allen Dulles of the Central Intelligence Agency. I first paid a courtesy call at the Department of Justice, having lunch with Assistant Attorney General Tompkins, and at 2:30 P.M. I met for over an hour in CIA headquarters with Allen Dulles and his counsel, Larry Houston. I had known both in OSS and had always admired Dulles' monumental contributions to the nation over forty years.

I began by explaining that at this stage of the proceedings I had mixed emotions over my court assignment: under no circumstances would I do anything not in the best interests of my client, but I also was an American lawyer holding a commission as a commander in Naval Intelligence.

"While I admire Rudolf as an individual," I said, "I don't forget that he's KGB. Bars and prison are not going to change his allegiance."

"I wish," Dulles said, puffing at his inevitable pipe, "we had three or four just like him inside Moscow, right now. I will add that when you were first assigned to his defense, a friend in the Department of Justice asked me, a little nervously, what you were like. I told him that in my judgment they would have a scrap on their hands and would be lucky to convict Abel."

I told the Director that the Soviet Colonel had asked me to undertake certain moves which I felt required United States approval, and that I was coming to him with Abel's knowledge. I mentioned that Rudolf was eager to write his family and wanted to send the letters through the Soviet Embassy. I said that I planned to write to the Embassy in his behalf and it was my thought to include a copy of our appeal brief, together with a complete transcript of the trial.

The Director said he saw no reason why Abel should not be permitted to write to his family, and he liked the idea of my sending the Russians copies of the defense brief with the record of the trial. But when I mentioned the question of a prisoner exchange, he said quickly that he knew of no such proposal being discussed in Washington, and further, he knew of no Americans held by the Russians for whom we could trade.

I then advanced the Colonel's proposal that I might trade with Russia for Americans held captive in China—through a neutral third nation like India acting as intermediary. The neutral nation, I said, could grant "political asylum" to all the prisoners. This would not involve, I commented, any official Soviet recognition of Abel. Dulles said he was intrigued by the suggestion but would want to check with State (his brother, the late John Foster Dulles, was then Secretary of State).

Just before I left, the Director tactfully cautioned me about any dealings with Soviet officials and suggested that if I "thought it advisable," I might send carbons of all correspondence to the Justice Department and to the CIA, through Larry Houston. I replied that this had been my intention.

Earlier in the day, over lunch, Tompkins had told me he shared my human respect for Abel and would urge that the Colonel be sent to a prison where his native talents could be utilized. He said he saw no point, at this stage of the proceedings, in trying to get information from the prisoner by making him miserable. I agreed wholeheartedly, both as Abel's advocate and as an American. If Abel ever changed his mind about talking, it would not be accomplished by such methods.

Several weeks after my meeting with Allen Dulles, I was informed that the Secretary of State was opposed to any trade for Abel which would not involve Russian recognition of him. If they wished to propose such a matter, I was told, they should take it up "in proper channels" with our State Department.

"I have been requested by the defendant in the case of United States vs. Abel," I wrote to Soviet Ambassador Mikhail A. Menshikov, "to inquire whether it is feasible for him to have written communication with members of his immediate family who reside in the U.S.S.R. Permission for this will be sought from the United States prison authorities, if there is no objection from the Soviet government."

I stated that it was also my client's wish—I had the Colonel initial a carbon copy for my files—that I transmit to them a copy of our defense brief and a complete record of all related proceedings "as a matter of possible interest."

Over the next three months, letters would shuttle between the Soviet Embassy in Washington and my office at 161 William Street, with the United States government looking on, as we all played cat-and-mouse over Rudolf's correspondence privileges. If this had been a private transaction it might have been resolved in a matter of minutes; but this was maneuvering between two opposing world powers with extremely cold international relations. As a result, it would be July of this year before Rudolf wrote his wife, September before his letter was "cleared," and December before Hellen Abel received her husband's first letter since he had been arrested a year and a half earlier.

The Russians replied to my first letter a week later. It was a pious note from their Consular Division saying that "according to their files" Abel was not registered as a Soviet citizen. They returned the trial transcript and brief, as of "no interest." (I had deliberately sent them immaculate, crisply bound copies; when returned, they were in such thumbed, loose shape that they obviously had been not only studied but reproduced.) Nonetheless, the letter suggested that in order "to clear up this matter" a meeting be arranged between Abel and one of their consular staff.

At the suggestion of the Justice Department, I informed S. Veschunov, chief of the Soviet Consular Division and my correspondent, that with regard to any meeting with Abel he should communicate through "proper channels" in the State Department. I further explained that as long as there was a possibility of meeting with a Soviet consular official, Abel would remain on West Street, where he was receiving no credit on his sentence and of course no word from his family.

In conclusion, I wrote, "I set forth these facts so that the advisability of an early disposition of this matter is evident."

Wednesday, April 16

In the morning I argued our appeal before the United States Court of Appeals for the Second Circuit. Tom Debevoise was with me; Fraiman had been relieved of his assignment at the end of the trial in District Court. The three-member bench comprised Chief Judge Charles E. Clark and Circuit Judges J. Edward Lumbard and Sterry R. Waterman. There was little to add to what we had already said in our printed papers, but the Court was attentive and asked a number of questions. Everyone seemed to be aware that having gone this far, we would if necessary carry the case to the Supreme Court of the United States.

Thursday, April 24

S. Veschunov dropped his official U.S.S.R. title and put aside his government stationery for a letter I received this day. It was a crudely obvious invitation for me to deal with the Soviets in a *sub rosa* manner.

The letter was on plain white paper and came in an equally plain envelope, with no return address and no markings of any kind on the outside. Unlike its predecessor, it carried a New York City postmark. Veschunov signed it, but did not further identify himself. The letter read:

We would like once again to draw your attention to the fact . . . we do not possess any data which would confirm Abel's Soviet citizenship. For this reason we have no legal basis for raising before the State Department the matter concerning a meeting between your defendant and our consular official. Our representative is prepared to meet your defendant Abel, if such a meeting can be arranged by you in the capacity of Abel's defender. In this case we would appreciate being advised of the date and place of the meeting. . . .

I was mystified. Did they believe, because I had provided Abel with an honest defense, that I would try to sneak their man into West Street as my "assistant"? Or was this standard procedure, tried in all cases and worth the small risk?

I promptly sent the letter to the Justice Department. I was instructed by phone to let them "stew a while" and then repeat my earlier letter stating they must do business through the State Department or not at all. I subsequently did precisely this, but added my own reminder that "regardless of Abel's citizenship, there remains the fact that he states his immediate family lives in the U.S.S.R. and if his sentence to a long term of years is upheld, he would wish to communicate with them. I accordingly ask that this question be considered, wholly apart from his citizenship."

When I reported the entire incident to Abel, he gave me a quizzical smile and said, "You can't blame them for trying, can you?"

Saturday, May 24

This would be our last meeting for some time. The Colonel had finally sent word to the Bureau of Prisons that he wanted to begin serving his sentence. He was notified that early next week he would be transferred to the United States Penitentiary at Atlanta.

It was a Saturday morning and we let the hours slip by, talking of Atlanta and the South, of art—his favorite New York galleries, the artists of Brooklyn Heights for whom he had a genuine affection—

and how he would occupy the interminable days which stretched ahead of him in Atlanta. He said, in his matter-of-fact manner, that his lifelong love and talent for higher mathematics would help him retain his sanity. I volunteered to get him any textbooks he needed, since a limited prison library would be a mere bagatelle for Rudolf.

"As it will be difficult for us to confer in person from now on," he said, "I want you to draw me a simple will."

Following his instructions, I drafted his last will and testament, which stipulated that if he should die in prison his body was to be cremated and his ashes with all his possessions should be sent to his family. I had it typed on the spot, had two friendly guards witness it, and gave him a copy.

Nothing about the life of a spy, I thought, is too rewarding to the ordinary man. If he is most successful in his profession, his work is unknown; if he is a failure, he becomes notorious. Once a prisoner, any permitted mail will be censored, a stranger will write his last will, and he must prepare to die in a hostile land.

Abel had several other requests. He asked that I continue to pursue the matter of his writing to his family, and also would I please write him on any subject, whenever I found time? He said that it might not be "politic" for an American lawyer to correspond too freely with an imprisoned Soviet intelligence officer, and so he added, "Just write on cultural subjects."

Thursday, June 5

"I am now in Atlanta, Georgia," Rudolf wrote.

The Colonel had arrived and the return address was: "Box PMB, Atlanta 15, Ga. Official Business." It was his first letter and it announced that he was "settled" in prison. He enclosed a bureaucratic form which instructed me to register with the warden as his attorney of record, in order to be able to write him as an "authorized correspondent."

"I am feeling well and am in reasonably good shape, getting

more exercise than previously," he wrote. "Not having heard from you as to the result of our appeal I hope that does not mean anything bad—just a delay. Hoping you are in good health. . . ."

Like all fifty-eight others that would follow (not counting four Christmas cards printed personally by him), the letter was on schoolboy-type lined paper. He wrote in pencil or pen and signed them, depending upon his mood, "Rudolf," "Rudolf I. Abel" or "R. I. Abel." Under every signature, regardless of his mood, was his USP Atlanta mark: "#80016." His parole officer, W. E. Bush, or some other censor, read and stamped each letter in the upper right-hand corner. A few of the Colonel's letters were even read and postmarked in Washington, D.C. Obviously the latter had been forwarded "for clearance."

As I read over the form Rudolf had sent me, I could see there were abundant regulations for a letter-writing inmate. He could receive up to seven "social letters" a week, but they were limited to two sheets in longhand and must be in English. (I subsequently learned that the prison, with 2,600 inmates, handled half a million pieces of mail a year.) I was advised not to mention "criminal happenings, court cases, arrests or other matters which may be detrimental to the welfare of the inmate."

Abel said very little and complained not at all in his letter. He mentioned that he had been placed in quarantine but gave no further explanation. From the prison quarterly, a surprisingly well-edited magazine, I later learned about "Quarantine":

> You are delivered through the prison entrance and led down a long hall, out a side door, down a walk and into the basement of the Quarantine Unit. You are made to strip, asked where you want your personal property sent, and in the event you die who should be notified. You shower and then you're led upstairs and delivered to a guard and a prison official. They tell you many of the things you *don't do* if you want to "make it" here.
>
> Three times a day you and the rest of the unit are taken to the Main Mess Hall to eat, while hundreds of eyes stare at you. For

thirty days you're lectured, examined by doctors, tested by more doctors, interviewed by parole officers, told when to go to bed, when to get up and when to go to bed again.

You're confused; but you know one thing, you're an inmate in prison. If you're wise, you don't like it. If you have any common sense you can see that the choice here is between opportunity and, perhaps, disaster. It's easy to get "in jail" in jail because there is a whole lot of frustration inside the walls of Atlanta.

There followed a story of the four hundred to six hundred men—about 20 per cent of the prison census—who are classified "adjustment problems" during quarantine.

I was glad, then, to receive the Colonel's second letter, which brought the news that he had been moved out of quarantine to the general prison population and was already at work:

I have been given a job in the Commercial Art Department which, of course, is very satisfactory from my point of view. My work is concerned with silk-screen processing and since I have never done any work with it, and there does not seem to be anybody who knows much about it, I am having some interesting times experimenting with it. I have several books on the subject and will be able to get more. It is a very versatile process and should give me plenty of work.

There will be a lot of work in November because we shall have to make 6,000 Christmas cards for the inmates and most of them will be silk-screened. I have several designs in mind and will send you and Tom [Debevoise] some.

Abel's correspondence followed a pattern. He was interested in seeing all news stories and magazine articles about his case, inquired frequently about his meager finances, and he continually questioned me about his belongings until we finally were able to ship them to his "wife" at an address in East Germany. He wrote sparingly of prison routines—mainly about his art work—but he

288

held forth in detail and with a sense of outrage on the matter of his corresponding with his family. This problem dogged us much of the time he was imprisoned. However, he was mainly preoccupied with his case and the appeal; his opinions, hopes and thoughts on the subject were in at least half the letters.

Finally, all his letters were communications from a cultivated gentleman. He neither complained of his lot nor criticized his jailers. He always included a warm greeting for my family, my staff— which sometimes ran his errands (buying a book, renewing his *New York Times* or *Scientific American* subscriptions, shipping his belongings, fetching an extra set of false teeth from storage, etc.)—and also my young associate counsel, Tom Debevoise. I had written him that Tom now was a Republican candidate for district attorney in Windsor County, Vermont, and he commented:

> Give Tom my best regards. I am somewhat undecided whether to wish him luck in his election campaign or not. I am probably biased [against prosecutors] and shall refrain. . . .

From his letters I judged the Colonel had made proper adjustment in Atlanta, just as he had on West Street. Prison officials at the penitentiary described him to me as "a most cooperative prisoner" who gave them no difficulty. He was accepted by the prison population but so long as he was an inmate the administration there had one fear for his welfare—that some young tough, looking for cheap publicity and thinking he would become a national "anti-Commie" hero, might attempt to murder him.

The Colonel shared a cell with eight others, one of whom had already served twenty-three years of a life sentence for kidnapping and had a grudge against the world, especially minorities. Abel told me he had been advised to avoid the man as much as possible.

On this day Chief S. Veschunov of the Soviet Consular Division capitulated. He explained, for the third time, that Abel was not registered as a Soviet citizen but in view of the fact he had asked to write to his family "which is supposed to live or to have lived on the U.S.S.R. territory, we request the sending of your defendant's letters to the Consular Division of the Embassy. The Consular Division will try to take measures to locate his family for the purpose of transferring them the letters."

I immediately wrote Rudolf, saying I considered this "a major concession on their part and substantial compliance with your request."

The Justice Department then added its approval, informing me that Abel was to write to his family (in English) under customary prison regulations and to deliver the letters to the warden. They would be "appropriately reviewed" by the Department of Justice, sent on to me, and I was to mail them to the Soviet consul. All this, of course, took weeks to straighten out.

Abel's first letter was addressed to "Ellen," an anglicized version of "Elya." She signed her subsequent letters "Hellen" and the spelling sometimes varied (Helen, Hellene).

Dear Ellen,

This is the first opportunity I have had for a very long time to write to you and our daughter Lydia. I sincerely trust that this letter will reach you and that you will be able to reply.

Presumably the person who delivers this will tell you the circumstances in which I am at present. However, it would be better for me to give you this information here: I am in prison, having been sentenced to thirty years for espionage, and at present am being held in the federal penitentiary in Atlanta, Georgia.

I am in good health and am occupying my time with mathematics and art. Music is out now, but later, maybe, I can start again.

Please, do not worry too much about what has happened; after all, it is just so much spilt milk! Better to take care of yourselves and hope for an early reunion.

The question of taking care of your health is important. Please tell me how you and Lydia are in this respect. I know from what I heard earlier (over three years?) that your condition was not too good. Please try and do all you can to improve it. I know this is not easy but you must try.

Write and tell me how Lydia and her husband are getting on. Have I become a grandfather?

If my letter may seem short and uninformative—that is partly a result of the circumstances. However, I shall try and write as much as possible and hope that you will be able to do so on your part. Give my regards to all our friends; and, again, please take care of yourselves. With all my love,

> Your husband and father
> Rudolf

In the bottom left-hand corner was his prison signature, "R.I. Abel #80016." He had written "P.S." but then thought better of it and crossed it out.

On December 18, Mrs. Abel wrote back, explaining she had just received Rudolf's letter and that it was delivered through the Red Cross. She said, "You understand that it took them long enough to locate us."

As for her husband's predicament, she wrote that the newspapers had carried the story "but we did not believe it. . . . We are deeply convinced that all that happened to you is merely a misunderstanding, that you are certainly innocent and that your sad story must have a good ending."

Friday, July 11

Abel's conviction and thirty-year sentence were on this day unanimously upheld by the Court of Appeals.

The Court declared that while there was an occasional error by the District judge, "the alleged errors were not so prejudicial as to require a new trial in this case, where the record fairly shrieks the guilt of the accused. . . ." In a trial lasting two weeks, the Court wrote, "It would be somewhat surprising not to find minor errors." The errors it found did the defendant no harm, the Court stated. The opinion, which filled thirty-three printed pages, was written by Judge Sterry Waterman. Chief Judge Clark and Judge Lumbard concurred.

As to the principal issue, the search and seizure of Abel and his possessions, the judges held there was no basis for distinguishing between a lawful arrest for a crime and a deportation proceeding. If a search was legal in the first case when incidental to the arrest, then it must be legal in the second instance.

("In my opinion," subsequently wrote Abel, "the Circuit Court decision, though proliferous, actually does not meet the points we brought up in the appeal. There are some arguments which seem to contradict each other and others which invert the arguments we used. I still think that the essential points have not been answered so much as they have been avoided.")

The Circuit Court answered our argument that the Government had failed to prove actual transmission of military secrets with this remark: "Men intent upon gathering and transmitting only such information as is available to the general public do not ordinarily find it necessary to employ secret codes, hollowed-out coins, pencils and matchbooks."

Judge Waterman closed his opinion by graciously stating that court-assigned defense counsel "represented the appellant with rare ability and in the highest tradition of their profession. We are truly grateful to them for the services which they have rendered."

The Colonel wasted no time in reminding me of my pledge to carry his appeal to the Supreme Court of the United States. "Regarding the Supreme Court appeal," he wrote promptly, "I presume that in accordance with our agreement, you are taking the necessary steps."

Rudolf, I concluded, must have been a hard man to please when "on the job." To have been a second lieutenant under Colonel Abel in his heyday must have required self-discipline and meticulous attention to every detail. Hayhanen had never made the grade.

Other than this pointed reminder, he reported, "Things are going normally with me—nothing untoward has happened."

Tuesday, August 5

A few days earlier I had received a call from Frank Gibney, a senior editor of *Life*, who had written a major article on the Abel trial. Gibney said he was in close contact with a trusted informant named Deroubian, a defected KGB counterintelligence chief in Vienna now working with United States intelligence. Gibney was planning a series of *Life* articles and a book with Deroubian, on the subject of Soviet intelligence. The ex-Soviet officer was married and needed money, Gibney explained.

Deroubian told Gibney that he could demonstrate to my satisfaction that the "family" letters introduced in evidence at the trial were written in an Aesopian code and actually contained information about the political status of the executed Beria of KGB, etc. Gibney said they would like to have lunch with me.

On this afternoon special agent Bender of the FBI delivered to me the latest letter from Abel to his wife, for my transmittal abroad. I told Bender of Gibney's call and said I would hold the letter until my meeting with Deroubian, a report to the FBI and further clearance.

I subsequently lunched with Deroubian and Gibney, was dissatisfied with the defector's explanation, reported this to Bender and continued to forward Abel's correspondence with government approval.

A year ago, I had abruptly abandoned my vacation to become Colonel Abel's court-assigned defense lawyer. Now, in Lake Placid again, I was interrupting this year's vacation to work on our appeal to the Supreme Court. Tom Debevoise kindly came over from Vermont and together we drafted a petition for certiorari, calling on the Court to hear our case and review the work of the lower tribunals.

"We have no absolute right to be heard," I had explained in a letter to Abel from Lake Placid, "and will be heard only if four of the nine justices vote to listen to us. . . . I have high hopes, but then I had similar hopes—though not as high—in the Circuit Court. If the Supreme Court grants our petition for certiorari, it of course would be most encouraging. . . .

"I am sure that you realize that our case (especially our contention regarding the proper rule on espionage proof) is inevitably affected by the flow of international events. Yours simply is not a case involving a Frenchman or a Brazilian and arising in the 1930s. However, I shall do my best under all the circumstances."

Turning to lighter subjects, I had asked the Colonel to put some of his idle hours to good use by devising a mathematical formula for my winning at gin rummy, so that I might recoup a fraction of the countless dollars I had lost to my wife during our friendly, low-stakes tournaments.

I also explained that I felt called upon to comment on his assignment to the commercial art department in the prison at Atlanta: "It has its amusing aspects, as you no doubt recognize. It would be interesting to know how news of the assignment would be received by the American public—a small and unthinking segment of which believes, I'm sure, you should be hanging by your thumbs in solitary, on the premise that such would be the fate of one of our own in Russia under similar circumstances."

His letter in reply was one of his lightest and an excellent sample of his best low-key humor. First he dealt with my gin rummy problems.

"I would believe that working out the odds of combination, melds, etc., is right up your life insurance-actuarial alley. I remember reading some reviews of books dealing with gin rummy (written, as I recollect, by bridge experts) and they seemed to show that you can win. I am not in any way a card player. My proficiency begins and ends with a few varieties of solitaire."

(The lonely spy, sitting alone in his cheap room at the Hotel Latham, playing solitaire. Now he was alone, though surrounded by 2,600 men, still playing solitaire.)

"Cards are permitted here and recently a bridge tournament was held. I have been promised lessons and sooner or later will get around to this game. Meanwhile, I am playing the Italian game of 'bocci' which resembles bowling as played on a bowling green. It is somewhat less sophisticated but is nevertheless a game requiring some skill."

I knew Abel was a sports fan, in fact a Dodger fan. ("I hope you have a good time in Los Angeles," he wrote on learning I was headed for an American Bar Association meeting on the West Coast. "Will you go to a ball game and see the Bums?") But to have him turn up in the prison yard learning to play *boccie* was a testimonial to the fifty-six-year-old scholar's versatility and his ability to adapt to every given situation.

"My life here," the letter continued, "is proceeding without incident. I have made some drawings and reproduced them by silk-screening and I think that I am making good progress. Soon I hope to initiate some experiments in color—so far I have done monochromes, something in the style of woodcuts. The medium has many possibilities but possesses many problems."

Tom Debevoise had been defeated by a narrow margin in his bid for the Republican nomination as district attorney in his home county in Vermont, and I had duly reported this to his Georgia fan. The Colonel viewed the outcome philosophically: "Although I hesitate to congratulate or condole Tom on his loss at the polls, I am glad to hear that his popularity was sufficient to keep the margin of loss to a low level. It certainly shows that he has made quite an impact on Vermont."

Monday, October 13

The telegram was judiciously and sparsely worded, but its impact nonetheless powerful: PETITION FOR CERTIORARI ABEL AGAINST UNITED STATES GRANTED TODAY. LETTER FOLLOWS.

In agreeing to review our case, the Supreme Court limited its review to two specific questions dealing with the constitutional prohibition against illegal search and seizure:

"1) Is search without a search warrant permissible in connection with arrests involving immigration law, as distinguished from criminal law? 2) May seized items be admitted as evidence when they are unrelated to the Immigration Service writ or warrant of arrest?"

These questions went to the very heart of our case.

Abel was concerned, though, because the Court had chosen to review only the search-and-seizure point. "It seems to me," he said in a letter, "that there is merit and substance in the other points."

I tried to assuage him, explaining that the "limited questions on appeal enable us to develop the search and seizure issue more thoroughly than we ever have done. It always has been the principal point in the case.

"As to the other points made in our appeal, do not be disturbed about their not being argued. They were read by the Court, are in the case and I am sure that although unmentioned they were a factor in the Court's decision to review the matter."

There was almost no public reaction to the decision granting our petition. Only one New York newspaper commented editorially. The *Herald Tribune* said there was no doubt as to Abel's guilt but it applauded the Court, "which once again demonstrated its concern for the protection of individual liberties, no matter whose.

"The questions raised are procedural," the editorial said, "yet due process is at the very heart of law. Whatever the outcome (and we don't prejudge the merits of Abel's appeal), the Court's review will serve as a reminder that the freedom of all of us is secure only so long as the freedom of each is protected."

Friday, November 21

Tom Debevoise had come down from Vermont and we had spent several days and nights preparing a first draft of a brief for the Supreme Court. Probably as a result, I had fallen victim to a virus and spent ten days at home, much of the time in bed reworking our brief.

On this day I sent a copy of the brief to Atlanta, with a note to the effect that this should be our most effective presentation to date. I explained that the Government would have thirty days to answer and then we would have twenty days in which to reply. I said we would be called to Washington for oral argument sometime in February and should have the Court's decision by spring.

"Meanwhile, you are the sole beneficiary of my infirmity," I jokingly told the Colonel in a letter to Atlanta. "My eldest daughter, Jan, is the big loser. Tonight I was to have attended a father-daughter square dance at Marymount High School, where she is a senior. In preparation, I have been sneaking away from the law firm in the late afternoons to take dancing lessons. I'm therefore crestfallen to be denied this opportunity to put my new-found agility to practice."

Thursday, December 4

When I had agreed to defend Colonel Rudolf, I had had no idea I also would play Santa Claus to him. But I did.

At this time of the year, all inmates at Atlanta were handed "gift forms" which they hopefully filled out and sent to their families or whomever they selected to serve as "Santa" for them. As the Colonel's legal representative and only correspondent in the United States, I was it. The gift form arrived on this day. Rudolf asked for books. He wanted the four-volume *Social History of Art*, and four pounds of plain milk chocolate (which, he explained, he enjoyed and also could trade in his cell).

He also wrote, "I have been very busy making up a number of Christmas cards for the inmate population. I believe that by the time I am through, I will have printed somewhere like 2,500 of them. Believe me, I will be glad to see the last of them! Since several are in five colors this means that I have looked at each design anywhere from 500 to 2,500 times—and that is enough to make any design awful!"

(Later he wrote me that the cards were "apparently well received by the inmates, as very few remain after distribution. So I got some satisfaction in that.")

He made seven different cards, including one in Spanish and one in Hebrew. He was limited, though, by prison rules to sending me a single card. It was a winter scene in black and white with a red border. The scene could have been New England or Siberia. A snow-covered cabin was in the center, against a background of dark pines. A clump of white birches was in the foreground.

"All good wishes for the holidays" was the printed greeting inside. At the bottom, inconspicuous except to one carefully seeking it, was the artist's engraved signature: RIA.

1959

Abel's self-portrait, done in the Atlanta penitentiary and given to James B. Donovan. (Courtesy of the author's estate)

Thursday, January 8

The Colonel's first letter in the new year was filled with hope. He had received word from his wife and daughter; they had written in answer to his letter of last summer which finally was delivered, allegedly through the International Red Cross.

"Needless to say, I am very happy about this and the prospect of future letters," he declared.

Hellen Abel had written, "We are trying to do our best to set you free and to have you back with us. Everybody that knows you personally, and our friends when they hear from me your story, say that you are innocent and they also believe that you will be back with us."

Perhaps Mrs. Abel believed this but I am inclined to think this was included for the government censor's consumption. More significantly, she asked, "Do you need any money? If so, we can mail it to you, only find out from your lawyer how to do it."

Following his wife's lead, Rudolf asked me for a statement of his finances—expenses to date and an estimate ("not binding," he facetiously added) of possible expenses. He also asked that I advise him on how his wife should send money, saying, "Presumably they will arrange the transfer of *Soviet* funds into foreign currency."

(The italics are mine.) The Colonel never made any pretense with me as to where he was from, where his family was living and whom he expected to underwrite his expenses. His wife's letter, however, had been mailed from Leipzig, in East Germany.

At the time of his arrest, it was rumored the Colonel had money buried all over New York City. One such report said he had buried $1,000,000 in Prospect Park. As far as the FBI was able to determine, his assets amounted to $21,000, and our legal expenses, chiefly for printing and stenographic records, had now totaled $13,227.20. With Abel's consent and the approval of the District Court, my firm had been reimbursed in full for its advances. The Court fine of $3,000 was still unpaid, pending appeal, and my agreed-upon fee of $10,000 for the entire case was outstanding.

As for future expenses, it was difficult to judge. If for any reason the case were reversed, there would be a substantial bill of costs returnable to Abel's account. However, the original defense expenses would be largely duplicated in the event of retrial.

I reported all this to Rudolf and concluded that while there was every likelihood that further funds would be necessary, I could not give him even an approximate figure as to how much he would need.

There were two other business matters on the Colonel's mind, voiced in his letter. I had neglected, apparently, to renew his subscription to *The New York Times* and he had gone five days without the crossword puzzle, the bridge game and the international news report. He brought me up short on this matter. Secondly, he said, "I would like to burden you with one more problem. That is the disposal of my 'goods and chattels.'" He now wanted to send to his family all his belongings, including paintings, cameras, books, sheet music, musical instruments, tools—everything the government would release.

Friday, February 13

It was a simple letter which began, "I am taking this liberty to write you after having learned from the newspapers about your most humane attitude towards my husband, Rudolf Abel."

Of itself, the letter was trivial. The significant fact was that it had been written at all. It was the first link in a chain of communication between the United States government (by now they must have realized I would show the letter to Washington) and someone behind the Iron Curtain, someone who cared about the welfare of KGB Col. Rudolf Ivanovich Abel.

The letter was typewritten on heavy white stationery which bore no letterhead but a distinct German watermark. It was signed "E. Abel" and the return address was c/o Frau E. Forester ("She is my good friend"), Leipzig N 22, Eisenacherstr. 24, Germany.

Mrs. Abel said she was grateful for my attempts to "alleviate the fate of our dear husband and a father." She said four weeks had gone by since she had heard from her husband and I was the only one who could inform her of "Rudolf's health and tell me if he needs help, and whether he has received our letters."

I took this last ("if he needs any help") as my cue, telephoning the Justice Department to report that I had heard from a certain Mrs. Abel of Leipzig. Previously, I had asked the Department to advise on whether there was any objection to Abel's receiving money or to shipping his belongings to his family. I had not received any answers, but this new letter seemed to demand action and a prompt reply.

After several hours my call was returned, and a government official explained that there was no objection to the Colonel's receiving money from his family and he was free to send his belongings to his wife.

With these assurances, I wrote Frau Abel that her husband was quite well, was working in the prison's commercial art department and "he produced some very lovely Christmas cards for use by his fellow inmates.

"The prison," I added, "is conducted on a very humane basis and you should have no concern about his physical welfare. We in this country approve only of the most humane prison methods."

I told "Mrs. Abel" (I doubted that she was his real wife) there was only one item which needed her present attention and that was the fee for her husband's lawyer. Lest she misinterpret, I explained, "When assigned by the court, I announced that any fee which I received would be donated to charity. I thereafter agreed with your husband upon a token fee of $10,000 for my entire efforts through the appeal to the Supreme Court. I personally shall receive no compensation for representing your husband."

(Tom Debevoise worked for out-of-pocket expenses; Fraiman's salary was continued by his law firm during the period of his service.)

I pressed for payment of the $10,000 because I reasoned that if the money were sent to me by his family and turned over to charity, it could not help but have a healthy effect upon public opinion and reflect credit upon the bar. Should the Supreme Court upset the conviction, the defense could use a little insulation from slings and arrows: "Those lawyers, always finding loopholes," etc.

Mrs. Abel's letter in reply did not exactly exude a spirit of cooperation. "I shall try to do my best to cover my husband's financial obligations," she said, "although I foresee considerable difficulties."

This second letter was equally as bland as its predecessor, but the correspondence was becoming progressively more sentimental. She wrote, "I am very glad to know that Rudolf is at least physically well and I would like to hope that he will be able to come and join his dear ones and family. It is difficult for me to judge his alleged crime, but I may tell you as his wife that Rudolf is honest and pure, a man with kind heart, and he does not deserve to be punished. You know that he is in his sixties [This probably was the truth; Abel may have shaved a few years when he became Emil Goldfus] and therefore he needs peace and calm and a family life."

After the Abel case was closed, an FBI agent who had seen all the letters from Leipzig, as well as the early ones read at the trial, discussed with me the marked difference in language and style between the letters I received from "Mrs. Abel" and those Rudolf had from his wife before his arrest.

I frankly felt that the KGB official in Moscow who wrote the line "It is difficult for me to judge his *alleged crime*" was seriously miscast. This was not the same Elya Abel who also wrote her husband in Atlanta, "The weather here is fine. The apple trees were blossoming wonderfully. Now lilacs and tulips are in full blossom and roses soon will be covered with flowers too."

Wednesday, February 25

"The Supreme Court today will tackle one of its most difficult cases, the conviction of Rudolf Ivanovich Abel as a Soviet spy."

We were in Washington, and Tom Debevoise was reading out of the morning paper. "Although the case is heavy with overtones of Communist conspiracy and espionage," he read further, "the central issue before the Court is a question of fair criminal procedure having nothing to do with communism. It is whether evidence seized . . ."

We had come on from New York by train the night before, and over grapefruit and coffee in the Hay Adams we took turns reading to each other the New York and Washington papers. It was designed to kill time and buoy confidence in the last hours before the argument. This was our second Washington call within a month. Last January 22 we had arrived in the courthouse, prepared to argue, when the case was unexpectedly put over. This did not add to my tranquility.

To argue before the Supreme Court of the United States is, each time, an exhilarating experience for any lawyer. The building is magnificent; the dignity of the courtroom is powerfully impressive; the justices are astute and a formidable challenge. But when you argue in this Court, you are arguing before nine experienced men. Naturally, there is more tension here than in the District Courthouse in Brooklyn, or Montpelier, Vermont.

Inside, people were lined up in the corridor waiting for the spectators' doors to open. By a rule of the Court, each person had already reserved a seat. Washington friends told me that the case had created a certain excitement along what is known as Embassy Row. Mrs. John Foster Dulles and members of the British Embassy staff would be in the courtroom when argument began.

My argument, which I presented wearing the traditional morning dress, was before Chief Justice Warren and Associate Justices Black, Frankfurter, Douglas, Clark, Harlan, Brennan, Whittaker and the newly appointed Stewart. The very able Solicitor General of the United States, J. Lee Rankin, was my adversary. So I began:

Since the issues before the Court have been thoroughly briefed, it appears that it might be most helpful to the Court if I commence my argument by explaining briefly what the case does not involve.

In the first place, the issues before the Court render quite irrelevant whether or not petitioner Abel is a Soviet spy. At a time when he believed in Texas that he was to be deported, he stated that he was a Russian citizen and that he had been illegally in the United States for nine years, where he lived under various aliases. The searches and seizures concerned in this case disclosed short-wave radio equipment, maps of defense areas in the United States and hollowed-out coins and other containers with microfilms in Russian. He has sought help from the Soviet government, which denied knowing of his existence. Accordingly, it is a fair statement that a jury of reasonable men and women could well conclude that the man was a Russian spy.

This is an entirely separate question from whether he was proven guilty beyond a reasonable doubt of the specific crimes charged in the indictment and upon competent evidence. In short, the question is whether or not petitioner Abel has received due process of law.

Over the Christmas holidays I had written a rough draft of my oral argument. I had reworked it several times, practiced parts of it once or twice before lawyer friends, and then put it away. Now, I argued from our brief:

Secondly, this is not a case in which counsel for the petitioner believes it essential to argue that the FBI and their sister law enforcement agency, the Immigration and Naturalization Service, have committed outrageous violations of the civil liberties of an individual. It is quite true that many in the United States, and perhaps some on this Court, could be very disturbed about the facts in this case and also about the statements in *The FBI Story*, as quoted in my brief ("Often clandestine methods are necessary to uncover clandestine operations, as for example, obtaining an espionage agent's diary or secret papers. The evidence in the diary may be inadmissible in Federal Court, but it may contain information . . ."), apparently stating that illegal searches and seizures are being regularly made by the FBI.

However, what I wish to make clear is that the reversal of judgment which I urge upon the Court is not necessarily predicated upon an argument that this man's civil liberties have been violated. In other words, the argument I put to the Court would be equally valid even if we made what to me would be the unwarranted assumption that the FBI in some extraordinary manner may lawfully conduct searches and seizures which violate the Fourth Amendment.

I then launched into my thesis as to how in mid-June of 1957 the Justice Department had been on the horns of a dilemma: arrest Abel and charge him with foreign espionage in the manner prescribed by Federal statutes; or apprehend him secretly and try to induce him to come over to our side:

A choice had to be made and it was made. Accordingly, I contend that even if the Department of Justice had this extraordinary authority to conduct illegal searches and seizures, they cannot go down that road of secret, star chamber proceedings—take their gamble, and lose when Abel refused to cooperate—and then seek to come back to the other road of normal law enforcement and attempt to pay lip service to due process of law.

Additionally, what this case does not involve is the mere seizure of a few items of property, subsequently used as evidence in bringing about a criminal conviction. There is no way to avoid the simple fact that this man and all his effects were made to disappear in the United States for several days.

By the use of the evidence obtained in this manner, through this illegal search and seizure—illegal because no search warrant had been issued—this man has been convicted of a capital crime. The only place criminal proceedings, based on such practices, occur is in police states like Nazi Germany and Soviet Russia.

In my argument and reply to the Government's argument, I spoke for an hour and a half. The last statement was the one point on which the press saw fit to quote me:

> Rather than any of the foregoing, our argument rests on the simple and clear test of the Fourth Amendment to the Constitution, part of the Bill of Rights, enacted at the specific demand of state after state fearful of too strong a centralized government and which withheld ratification of the Constitution until such safeguards were incorporated in it.
>
> The conviction of this man of a capital crime, on evidence so obtained, need only be set against the simple but binding admonition of the Fourth Amendment: "The right of the people to be secure in their persons, houses, papers and effects, against unreasonable searches and seizures, shall not be violated . . ."

From the outset, the Government maintained the arrest on the morning of June 21 was legal and therefore the search was legal, saying, "There is no rational basis for distinguishing between arrests for deportation and arrests for crimes . . . some authority to search must exist in connection with an arrest on an Immigration warrant." So argued Solicitor General Rankin.

I sent Abel copies of all the Government briefs. He was mildly critical of them all, and when he had read the Supreme Court argument he wrote, "There seems to be the same idea in the government's presentation here as in their previous briefs—perhaps on the theory that what has succeeded before will continue to do so."

In his insistence that the search was legal, the Solicitor General now stated, "When a legal arrest occurs, it is not unconstitutional to make an appropriate search—without a warrant—of the persons and immediate surroundings as an incident of arrest and also to seize articles which could be seized if the search were made pursuant to a warrant."

Chief Justice Warren posed a question to the Solicitor General: Did the Government believe at the time of arrest it would get enough evidence by the search to support prosecution on espionage charges?

"It was considered very remote," said Solicitor General Rankin, "that this could happen with such a skilled operator as Abel. Anyone so skilled was not expected to leave items of evidence around."

I wondered. Had not Hayhanen told them what they might expect to find? And was it not conceivable that the agents in the room next to Abel's in the Hotel Latham had slipped into Room 859 while the Colonel was over on Brooklyn Heights, with other FBI men watching his movements through binoculars?

In my argument I told the Court how the FBI had pushed into his room, addressed him as "Colonel" and tried to get his "cooperation." I explained that if he had agreed to "cooperate" with them, there would have been no arrest and the Immigration officers would still be out in the hall waiting, while Abel was happily working for the United States government.

Justice Frankfurter at this point asked me if I did not think it the duty of every citizen, as well as Abel, to cooperate with law enforcement officers, such as the FBI. "What would you have done?" he asked.

"Mr. Justice," I said, "if someone pushed into my home without a warrant at seven o'clock on a hot summer's morning, when I had been sleeping naked on top of the bed, I don't know what would happen, but let me put it this way: they would know they had been in a scrap."

Observed Frankfurter dryly, "I am sure of that."

This drew a laugh up and down the bench and out in the spectators' rows.

In his argument the Solicitor General laid stress upon the national defense aspects of the case. Accordingly, in my reply I addressed myself to this:

> I ask the Court to consider, what is our national defense, in an age of intercontinental missiles, hydrogen bombs and man-made satellites?
>
> Someday in our generation, when we, our allies and perhaps Soviet Russia are facing Red China (which perhaps by then has acquired India), what then will we know—with the benefit of hindsight—to have been our strongest defensive weapon? Will it be our stockpile of atomic bombs? Our development of poison gas or lethal rays? Or will it be that with quiet courage we have maintained a firm belief in the truths of freedom that led our ancestors to migrate to this land?

At the close of the arguments, the Court took the appeal under advisement. The Chief Justice then warmly thanked the defense on behalf of the entire Court. He said:

> I think I can say that in my time on this Court no man has undertaken a more arduous, more self-sacrificing task. We feel indebted to you and your associate counsel. It gives us great comfort to know that members of our bar associations are willing to undertake this sort of public service in this type case, which normally would be offensive to them.

By 6 P.M. I was back in Brooklyn at a business meeting of bankers and lawyers.

Monday, March 23

I had sent a letter to Abel:

> Each Monday is decision day in the Supreme Court.
>
> Each Monday I now have lunch at the Lawyers Club at 115 Broadway, where there is a teletype which carries Associated Press news reports. The steward has been instructed to watch for our decision.
>
> However, my personal belief is that you should be optimistic about the outcome of the case. As to what the government then does, I cannot predict. You, of course, realize that you could be re-tried. . . ."

Today my wait was over. The Supreme Court, I learned by Lawyers Club teletype, had just ordered the case re-argued on October 12, seven months away. The Solicitor General and I had already argued before the Court for three hours; now they were calling for two additional hours. To say the least, this was highly unusual.

The Court again specified we should take up the questions of the constitutionality and validity of the Immigration warrant, the arrest under the warrant, and the question whether the warrant provided grounds for the searches and seizures of Abel's person, luggage and hotel room.

"It is an extraordinary decision," I said, in a letter to Rudolf. "I find it hard to believe the Court was inclined to uphold the conviction and believe that while they wished to reverse, upon fundamental issues, they did not want to take so drastic a step at this time. As you know, the Supreme Court has been under heavy public attack in recent months. I feel though, that time is on our side since any move which would ease international tensions (such as the contemplated summit meeting) could have a favorable repercussion.

"Meanwhile, we have no alternative but to carry on."

In something of an understatement, one of the New York newspapers commented that the Court's reargument order "indicated that the justices remained troubled by the legal issue it had agreed to review."

It remained, however, for Rudolf in a letter to sum up and interpret the inscrutable high tribunal's order: "As you know, I have never professed to understand the workings of the legal process and, wishful thinking apart, try to look at its operation as objectively as possible. The decision to hold supplemental arguments does seem to augur well for our side. It looks though as if the Court were saying to the government—'We are giving you an extra inning.'

"I sincerely hope that our position will prevail."

Monday, March 30

Abel had an uncanny ability to reconcile himself to situations and events. He also had the faculty for directing his attention to all manner of detail, even in prison when presumably inconvenienced, disconsolate and frustrated.

For instance, it was only a week after the Supreme Court order, which meant he would sit it out in prison for the next seven months until the second argument, and then several months beyond that for a final decision. Yet this was his paramount concern:

> About my belongings, I think that the total volume crated would occupy a maximum of 120 cubic feet with a weight of not more than 500 pounds. I have in mind clothing, cameras, lenses, books, music, paintings. Although I would like to have some of the small tools also, I think it would be impossible to ask somebody to go

through them to make a selection, so we will not include them at all. However, there is a densitometer, some electric measuring instruments . . .

He had not forgotten for one moment that the government had granted permission to send these belongings to his family, and so came the gentle reminder to me.

Any other small photo equipment could very well be packed with the cameras. . . . Silverman has my guitar and two slide projectors, one of which he may keep, but I would like the guitar and one projector. A friend of his has a KineExakta 35 millimeter camera which I would also like to have back. . . . There is no need for rapid delivery of these goods to my family's address in Leipzig. . . .

Would it be an imposition if I asked you to get rough estimates on probable costs of packing and freight from some shipping companies?

Incidentally, among the articles "discarded" in the Hotel Latham room were some books . . . a book on math and perhaps a book on painting. These I would like to have, together with the two small radios. The big one they took in my studio is in bad shape and could be sold. . . ."

The Colonel was a great bargain hunter and I suspect this was how he had come by most of his tools and other belongings. He said he believed it would prove "simpler" to sell whatever was not shipped home, but he was willing to listen to alternate suggestions. He allowed me wide latitude, writing, "If you have any other suggestions, such as donating them to some institution, I don't think we would lose much."

His sense of charity, however, did not extend to members of the government's prosecution staff, who had asked me to get them a few souvenirs of the case, preferably a sketch or a painting done by the Colonel. He wrote:

As to paintings I promised you and Tom, you are free to choose among my things held by the Immigration Service as you please. As I recollect, there are four oil sketches and may be two or three watercolors. The latter are in my opinion no good; the oils are better. I will be happy whatever your choice.

The government attorneys, however, are in a different category. I see no great reason to indulge their desires, but should you think it proper I think it would be more appropriate to donate them some of the silk-screen prints I have done here in Atlanta, rather than the paintings and sketches I did prior to arrest. Should they desire these silk-screen prints, they will have to obtain permission from the Warden, Mr. Fred T. Wilkinson.

That was the end of that.

I reported to Colonel Abel that the reaction to the Supreme Court reargument order among members of the bar was unanimous in regarding it as a partial victory for us. But with this rather gratifying response came increased pressure upon me to bow out of the case after the reargument, before I was caught up in a second trial and, quite possibly, a complete repetition of all the appeals work. The pressure, understandably, came from my family and the long-suffering partners in my law firm.

My wife Mary said to me one night, "Ever since I met you twenty years ago, it's been one thing like this after another. Can't you write wills, form corporations and convey property like other lawyers?"

I mentioned a bit of this in a letter to Abel, assuring him that "whether or not it is possible for me personally to participate in the case, I shall do my best at all times to see that you are represented by competent counsel and receive due process of law. After all my efforts, I would not want the case to fall into the wrong hands if it proves impossible for me to continue."

He replied, "As to your continuation in the case, should there be a reversal and retrial, I would be very pleased if you could see your

314

way to carry on. I have every confidence in your integrity and abilities and am very grateful to you for your efforts.

"However, I would not like to cause you further inconvenience. . . . Unfortunately, I have no means to hire a lawyer. It is quite a problem."

Friday, May 15

Along with other details, we continued to push forward with the job of gathering and packing Abel's belongings for shipment to East Germany. I was not the least bit pleased with this aspect of my court assignment and had insisted with United States Attorney Wickersham that I would participate only after my conscience was satisfied that I was not cooperating in the furtherance of espionage.

I pointed out by letter to the Justice Department that I did not regard my court assignment as requiring me to act as a shipping agent, that I was nevertheless willing to cooperate in an otherwise awkward situation, but I must insist upon a thorough government search of all Abel's belongings before they were shipped behind the Iron Curtain.

"In my estimation," I added, "no such search has as yet been made."

We were now ready for an inspection by the FBI of the Colonel's property delivered to us by the Immigration Service, which had held it since the search and seizure. When the crate arrived in my office, I gave strict instructions that it was not to be opened. My fears were these: 1) Important espionage evidence had been overlooked; 2) the government would discover something and accuse Abel or me of trying to dispose of potential evidence; 3) should there be a second trial, the Government would claim that evidence it now wanted had been sent to East Germany.

At 4 P.M. two FBI agents arrived and broke open the sealed crate. James Neylon of my firm attended as an observer. They began a most minute examination of the belongings. With a high degree of skill, and obvious relish, they began ripping, tearing, pulling, shaking, tugging and splitting. After about ten minutes of this, one of the pair picked up Abel's wallet. A tiny pocket in the wallet, possibly sealed by some adhesive substance, opened when the agent's fingernail sliced through it.

"Oh, no," he said.

The agent took out a small black film, tissue-thin, and held it up for us to see. There were five rows of numbers, each consisting of five digits.

"This must be in Hayhanen's cipher," said the first agent, familiar with all phases of the case. After a study of it through a magnifying glass, I agreed. And it was.

At this point, there were two nervous FBI agents and one anxious attorney in the room. We decided to report the finding to the New York FBI headquarters by phone, and meantime I drafted a memorandum describing what had taken place. All parties initialed it, and it became part of my case file.

When the FBI agents finished with the examination, I wrote a rather acid letter to the Justice Department:

> Under the circumstances, I will not ship any of these articles anywhere, until I have a letter from your Department stating that after a proper examination the government has no objections to Abel's proposal. If I do not receive such a letter within the next sixty days I believe it will be my duty under my court assignment to move in open court for an order permitting the shipment under such conditions as the court may prescribe.

The reply was prompt and polite. The Justice spokesman said my "interest in this matter" was very much appreciated and that they were certain we would be able to arrive at a "mutually satisfactory arrangement."

Nevertheless, seven months were to pass before the Abel properties were sent into East Germany.

There has never been a satisfactory explanation of why the most incriminating evidence against Abel was not discovered after his arrest and introduced in evidence at the trial. Rather obviously, if a microfilm message in Hayhanen's code was secreted in Abel's wallet and found in his hotel room, it would have been a conclusive link corroborating Hayhanen's testimony concerning their relationship.

Monday, May 18

I had arrived in Atlanta. The taxi let me out and I stood looking at the massive stone walls, the towers, guards on patrol and the huge main gate. This was Atlanta Penitentiary: a bleak, stark, rock fortress. I remembered a description of a prisoner's first impression, in one of the inmate magazines Abel had sent me: "If he has never been in prison before, the very shape of the buildings scares him at first."

I met first with Warden Wilkinson, who told me that Abel was in good health and well-adjusted to his routine. Abel was continuing, as I had learned earlier, to get on well with the seven others in his cell, including a convicted kidnaper. The warden repeated, however, that so long as Abel was his charge, he would be alert to the possibility that some young inmate might try to kill the Soviet Colonel in the delusion that this would make him a popular hero.

The warden had arranged that I could meet Rudolf in a private visitor's room. He told us to take as long as we wanted.

Prison life had aged the Colonel. He looked gaunt, as if he had lost weight from his normally lean frame. Yet he carried himself well in his faded gray prison uniform. When we shook hands he smiled and this was the same natural Rudolf. He was in good humor; I suspected this was because the case seemed to be going well in the Supreme Court and he finally had a visitor.

I got him talking about his art work. He was still enthusiastic about his silk-screen experiments and reported with obvious pride that he was contributing many drawings to the prison magazine.

In an attempt at humor, I said, "Your present art studio is undoubtedly superior to the one on Fulton Street in Brooklyn."

The Colonel laughed and replied, "The light is much better, and so is the rent."

When I asked whether he had any friends among the prisoners, he explained there was only one man he had singled out.

"He's a very interesting fellow," he said, "and we spend a lot of time together."

Abel said this man was a former United States Army officer who had served with OSS during World War II and later had charge of a team collecting evidence of German concentration camp atrocities. Since I had been in charge of this project for the major Nuremberg trial against Goering and his associates, I should have crossed paths with Abel's friend, but I had no recollection of the man. Anticipating my next question, the Colonel said the fellow had been convicted of being part of a Soviet espionage ring in Germany following the war.

(When I got back to New York, I checked into the man's background and found that all his statements to Abel were true.)

We moved to a discussion of his case and Abel took me completely by surprise when he asked, "Do you think an application for my release on bail is advisable now?"

"After all," he said, "the Supreme Court on its own initiative has ordered a two-hour reargument. This establishes that there is a substantial doubt as to my having been properly proven guilty beyond a reasonable doubt. Isn't that a fair interpretation?"

I was convinced that application for bail would be a disastrous move and regarded as publicity-seeking. "I don't think," I said, "that in a capital case of this nature the application would have even a remote chance of success. The reargument, you realize, is still seven months away. Besides, who would provide the bail?" The Colonel said he was forced to agree with my logic.

Just as I had known he would, he asked again about his personal belongings. This led me to tell the story of Friday's meeting with the FBI and how his wallet had been searched for the first time, uncovering the damning microfilm. His face flushed as I spoke and he went completely silent.

"You have shaken me up quite a bit," he said after a moment. Then he was quiet again. "I don't ever remember leaving any such paper in that particular wallet," he continued, indicating quite plainly that he remembered the billfold.

"I'm very suspicious," he said. "I mean, after eighteen months, that they should suddenly find this. I'm not worried for myself. They can't do anything more to me. But since it was discovered in your law office, it could be an attempt to smear you in some manner and thus injure my defense, especially in light of the latest developments in the Supreme Court."

I did not agree with this and said so. The wallet had been entirely in the hands of government agencies from the time of Abel's arrest, and its discovery at this late date could be embarrassing only to them, not to me.

He said that he did not think the microfilm would mean anything to the government, for if the code was his own, he doubted that it could be broken. I explained to him that it appeared to be in Hayhanen's cipher.

There was no doubt that in some fashion Abel had been receiving information from the "outside." When I told him I planned to stop in Washington, D. C., on my way home, he said that he had learned there was a new exhibit dealing with his case on display in the FBI museum in the Department of Justice building. He suggested that I have a look at it.

"You might find something we could use in the reargument," he said. Then he added that FBI Director J. Edgar Hoover, in his recent book, *Masters of Deceit*, had written that Colonel Abel was arrested by Immigration officers "at the request of the FBI."

"That reinforces our contention, doesn't it?" he asked. "Maybe you'll find some similar boast in the exhibit. That man's vanity could be his undoing."

(Mr. Hoover's candid explanation of Abel's arrest did in fact become a useful part of our reargument brief to the Supreme

Court, but there was nothing in the FBI's Washington exhibit to which a reasonable person could object. With the display, when I reviewed it, was a prominent notice explaining that the case was on appeal to the Supreme Court. I toured the FBI Museum with a dozen other visitors and, unidentified, listened to an interesting discourse on the Abel case by one special agent Sullivan.)

Abel was supremely confident of the outcome of his appeal. In fact, I had never seen him so confident or so outspoken on the court battle. As I made ready to leave now, he said, "I'll see you next in the Detention Headquarters on West Street, on my way home."

When we shook hands, he added, "You are leaving me with a very happy memory of a very pleasant visit."

Warden Wilkinson later had a guard take me on a tour of the entire prison. It was a very worthwhile but sobering experience. Atlanta Penitentiary is a monument to American efficiency in the grim area of penology.

I saw the prisoners busy—making mailbags, uniforms and working in the laundry and machine shops—and I saw them at play, on the baseball field and lifting weights in the gymnasium.

In the late afternoon, I visited the commercial art department and found the Colonel presiding over a small private art studio in which he had several excellent oil paintings and some beautiful silk-screen work which he had produced, using new processes which he had devised. Clearly, he was making fine progress in his new medium. Also, the light in the studio was clearly superior to that in his former abode in Fulton Street, Brooklyn.

Monday, June 15

A short note from the deputy Supreme Court clerk had informed us the week before that the reargument of the Abel case was now put over from October to at least November, so as not to inconvenience or unduly tax the Solicitor General, who was scheduled to argue another matter on our October date.

I had immediately written a long protest of the delay to Chief Justice Warren, explaining that from the outset it had been the Government which had been so anxious to set a trial date, pick a jury and begin the trial. Now, with my client in prison, no one seemed to care. I suggested a conference to determine "what would best advance the cause of American justice here and abroad."

So at 4 P.M. on this day I was in Washington, and the Solicitor General and I met with Chief Justice Earl Warren in his chambers. J. Lee Rankin, the solicitor general, began by saying he was sympathetic to our position; but his other matter, involving the important rights of five states in the tidelands oil question, had been adjourned one year and the arguments would take a full week.

The case, United States vs. Louisiana, had actually been pending since 1955 and twenty-six attorneys from five states had made arrangements to be in Washington for the oral argument, set down for October 12.

Mr. Rankin said he would want additional time to rest and prepare himself for our case "because many issues in the Abel situation are novel."

When it was my turn, I pointed out that a case of human rights, with a man imprisoned, should take precedence over property rights. The Chief Justice appeared to be inclined to favor my argument but he indicated that if I insisted on my position, it would be professionally embarrassing to the many lawyers concerned. I mentioned my own commitments in my personal law practice.

I suggested that if the Court fixed a definite date, not long after the tidelands argument, we could have no reasonable objection. Chief Justice Warren then fixed November 9 for the reargument, assuring me there would be no further delays. He said he again wanted me to know all members of the Court were aware of the tremendous burdens which had been placed upon the Abel defense and were appreciative of my personal contributions.

The Solicitor General now stated that the FBI had information that Abel's letters to his "family" were conveying information to the Russians—and that permission to write to his family had been granted at my request. I quickly corrected him, pointing out that my function in the matter had been limited to transmitting Abel's request and I had not urged that it be granted on humanitarian or any other grounds. It had been a government decision, with full knowledge of all circumstances.

"I think," I said, "there's a quite a difference between the two courses of action." The Chief Justice interrupted to say, quite emphatically, "There is all the difference in the world."

Monday, July 20

I wanted the matter of my fee cleared up (I had pledged it to specific charities) and I had reminded Abel that "I believe it rather important to your case that your family forward the necessary funds before November. I will then be in a position to make the donations which I have pledged and this should further alleviate the atmosphere of emotional hostility which originally prevailed."

Now the late mail brought a letter stating that the Colonel's wife had the $10,000 and was waiting for me to advise her how the payment should be made. I instructed her to deposit the money in her Leipzig bank for the account of my firm's New York bank, which then would debit the account of the East German bank by $10,000.

Monday, July 27

On this day, to my surprise, an East German lawyer with the impressive name of Wolfgang Vogel, of Alt-Friedrichsfelde 113, Berlin-Friedrichsfelde, wrote me:

Dear Colleague:
Mrs. Hellen Abel from The Democratic Republic of Germany

has retained me to protect her interest. I am mainly to conduct the correspondence between Mrs. Abel and yourself. Kindly correspond with me exclusively in the future.

The lawyer announced that a first "honorary payment" to me of $3,500 was already on its way and "I personally assure you that all other expenses in this connection will be covered by my client as soon as you will acknowledge receipt of the above amount."

Within a matter of days, my bank (First National City) notified me they had received $3,471.19 from a Mrs. Hellen Abel of Leipzig. I sent a cablegram to Herr Vogel, reporting I had received a first payment of my "token fee."

The Colonel, meanwhile, wrote "the fact that only part of the money has been sent should not disturb you as I myself recommended my wife send a smaller sum at first, to see whether the transfer was successful."

Tuesday, July 28

The history of the case was that each plus was balanced by a minus. When things went smoothly, we should beware. On this day I received an unexpected letter.

"We wish to advise that this Department has determined, as a matter of policy, that Abel's privilege of exchanging written communications with anyone outside the United States, including his purported wife and daughter, should be terminated."

The Justice Department was cutting off Abel's mail privilege, believing that he was sending information to the Soviets. This apparently was what Solicitor General Rankin had been referring to when we met with the Chief Justice in June.

The letter from Justice concluded: "This determination was based on our opinion that it would not be in the national interest to allow Abel, a convicted Soviet espionage agent, to continue his correspondence with people in the Soviet bloc."

This prohibition was to incite the Colonel to anger, as nothing else did during the four years and five months that I represented him. He denied the charge, and denounced it.

"I must admit," wrote Abel, "that the phraseology of the government's letter evoked my profound admiration. The letter is a pearl."

Abel warmed up slowly, beginning with interpretation:

> This state of affairs may have an important bearing on the matter of payment of your fee, among others. I am sure my wife will be very disturbed by this action and this may well cause her to reconsider the wisdom of transferring a large sum of money when she has no information as to her husband's well-being. . . .
>
> That this is discriminatory against me is obvious, because there are many inmates here who correspond with their families in Europe, Latin America and other countries. I am strongly convinced that this ban is motivated not from the desire to prevent my transmitting information (after all, what would be of value after more than two years? The situation in U.S.P. Atlanta?) but to prevent any aid reaching me and to force me to "cooperate." The question of financial aid is important if a new trial is undertaken. The lack of funds would be a serious impediment to the proper conduct of my defense.
>
> It may be one of many other reasons but whatever it may be, it does seem to contradict the reason for granting writing privileges to prison inmates—that such correspondence has a beneficial effect. As far as I recollect from the newspapers, no such restrictions have been placed on the four Americans held in China for espionage.
>
> I would like you to initiate any steps you find necessary to reverse this order, bearing in mind all the implications it may have in the matter of the appeal now before the Supreme Court. I am sure you will agree with me that this unusual action merits careful consideration and that appropriate steps should be taken to counter it.

After first getting a formal ruling from the Justice Department, I had advised Abel, "Under our law, your correspondence is a privilege and not a right. I do not know of any practical steps which can be taken in the matter. The clear inference is that you have been communicating in some form of code and in my judgment it would be inadvisable for me to try to upset the determination."

In reply, Abel wrote his longest letter—two full sheets—vigorously opposing the idea he was sending information to East Germany. He accused the government of hypocrisy, in a rebuttal which, I thought, made several sound observations:

> Concerning my correspondence, I find it difficult to write objectively as it naturally hurts me to lose all contact with my family. I cannot help feeling that it is intended as an extra, additional punishment above that meted out by the judge.
>
> As you say, the exchange of letters between an inmate and his family is called a privilege; nevertheless it is an activity which is encouraged by the authorities and the Book of Rules for Inmates emphasizes this.
>
> Letters are censored and any containing material deemed improper are returned. Since my letters, sent by air mail, took from twenty-five to thirty days in transit, of which no more than five could be reasonably ascribed to the mail proper, it would seem that sufficient time was available for the most minute scrutiny. . . . The inference then is not that I used code to send messages to "people in the Soviet bloc"; but that I did not do so, since all letters were passed by the censors and mailed. Mail privileges are usually suspended for infractions of rules of prison conduct.
>
> I would like to point out further that my mailing privileges were granted me in the first instance by Washington shortly after my arrival here. The reasons now cited by the government were certainly existent then and surely should have been more potent then

since the passage of time would render these reasons less valid. I really cannot see what danger to the national security can result from my sojourn in the Atlanta Penitentiary, where my contacts with the outside world are non-existent. It is reasonable to assume then that the danger (if any!) would be a product of my "activities" prior to my arrest in June 1957—more than two years ago. Any "information" that old is not information any more. . . .

On the moral side there can be no justification, in view of the widely stated attitude of the government of the United States regarding the superiority of its behavior as compared with that of the Chinese government, for instance. . . .

I would like you to reconsider this whole matter and give me a considered opinion as to the merits and further, would it be more proper, should a case be brought to court, that it be prosecuted by a lawyer other than yourself, so that no animus fall on you. Please do not construe this as an expression of dissatisfaction—quite the contrary! I am thinking of the matter in connection with the main issue, and do not wish to cause any embarrassment to you whatsoever. . . .

Monday, September 14

We simply could not risk another court action, wherein the Government would publicly accuse Abel of sending coded information to the Soviets, just before the reargument of his appeal. While sympathetic, I could not see either the Court or the public rising up in indignation because Colonel Abel's mail privileges had been restricted. For all I knew, he might be slipping information into his letters—something so simple as the fact he wasn't "cooperating." I wrote in reply:

While I appreciate your discomfiture, it is my best judgment that any move to resist the withdrawal of your correspondence privileges would be ill-advised at this time. Indeed, it could even be calculated to lead you into such a move as you suggest.

We are in a weak position, since I cannot believe that any court will order the prison to permit you to correspond with people in the Soviet bloc. Since this is so, the only purpose served by such a proceeding would be to permit the Government, just prior to rearment before the Supreme Court, to confuse the issue with allegations concerning your conduct in prison. . . .

Approaching the Supreme Court reargument with a strong position, strengthened by our new brief, I hate to contemplate the commencement of any proceeding which would permit the Department of Justice to attack you with any new material not in the trial record.

It may require some patience on your part, but I believe that your best interest will be served by your abiding by the present ruling until the reargument has been held.

Despite Abel's fear (or threat) that the embargo on his mail might interfere with payment of my fee, a second and final check was cleared on this day. Mrs. Abel forwarded the remaining amount ($6,529.81). I filed a formal motion in Federal Court, Brooklyn, for authorization to accept the funds (with an explanation of their origin) and a statement detailing how I intended to divide the fee.

"It is my belief," I wrote, "that in a land of plenty, such as the United States, the most effective means of combatting totalitarianism lies in the furtherance of sound moral training and a true understanding of justice under law." Accordingly, I stated that the money would be donated by me in this fashion: $5,000 to Fordham College; $2,500 each to Columbia and Harvard Law Schools. I was graduated from Fordham College and Harvard Law, while my two assigned assistants (two for trial, one for appeals) were both Columbia Law graduates.

When reporters called to press me for additional details, I said, "There is more to the practice of law than making money." A lawyer friend said to me the next day, "Why didn't you add, 'but not much more'?"

As I later wrote the Colonel, "My giving away the defense fee has served to make the public aware, I feel, that this is a test of American justice."

Whether he liked it or not, the Soviet officer was receiving a primer course in American law.

Monday, October 19

During this period I received three letters from East Germany, as Frau Hellen Abel suddenly became a regular correspondent. As usual, they were crudely constructed and highly emotional. The woman lamented the ban on Abel's correspondence, the court delay and described her alleged emotional sufferings.

I never considered that these letters were from Rudolf's wife and therefore the pleas and plaints ("So much depends on you—I shall not exaggerate if I say that it is a matter of life and death to me and my family—and I implore you . . .") fell on cynical ears. I regarded the letters as the amateur and transparent work of a Soviet intelligence unit. To me, the letters meant only one thing: someone over there was very much interested in the future of my client.

During this period I was unaware that the "real" Mrs. Abel was writing her prisoner husband (just prior to the government's ban on his mail) letters quite different than those sent me by the KGB's ersatz Hellen Abel. Much later, I was able to compare the letters. Hellen Abel wrote Rudolf in Atlanta:

> I find satisfaction, though a sad one, in my attempt to alleviate your fate (hiring a lawyer, paying the fee). . . . Our life goes on as usual. The weather is fine but is dark and dreary in my soul. . . . You write you are fifty-seven. I am not young either and this may be a reason for my mood and counts for the foul weather in my soul. We all grow older; even my cat is seldom going out for rendezvous and stays more at home. . . . Despite my bad moods, we do our best to get ready for your return and this fills our life.

Meanwhile, the letters to me, postmarked Leipzig, were heavy in tone and sounded like this:

It is with so much impatience and anguish that I have been waiting for some news concerning the outcome of the re-argument of my husband's case. So many dreary days have passed and I am still ignorant of what is going on. . . . This expectation is getting badly on my nerves. I have no sleep, no appetite and feel nervous and restless and that is, I think, the reason why I have fallen ill and must keep to my bed. My daughter feels miserable too.

P.S. If you see my husband, do not tell him of my illness.

Monday, November 9

"The case of Rudolf Abel," said the Washington paper, "is providing a rare spectacle of the protection afforded a defendant, whatever his crime, by the American Bill of Rights. . . .

"He is entitled under the Constitution to the same rights in his trial as any American citizen and is receiving them in full measure before the Supreme Court. . . . For the second time today, the Court will listen to legal argument on whether the constitutional rights of the Russian colonel were violated when he was arrested. . . ."

It was still early and I sat up in bed in my Washington hotel room reading the morning papers. I had already reviewed my notes on the oral argument, and since the Court did not convene until noon, I would have time to go over them again after breakfast.

But as I read this news account, I was reminded of a dinner the week before with an old friend and businessman client. During this casual meeting, I had caught a good measure of abuse because, as my martini-drinking companion put it, "You have wasted all that time—thousands of good working hours—on that Russian spy's defense.

"That was time," he lectured me, "you should have been devoting to the problems of American businessmen, or some other worthwhile cause."

My nearsighted friend would never understand why the Constitution protected Abel, until some night when he or one of his family was arrested for drunken driving and perhaps vehicular homicide. Then he would seek the best lawyer in the country to defend him and demand every constitutional right to which he was entitled. Many people never think about rights and privileges until they personally feel the need of them. Otherwise they denounce lawyers and judges for finding "loopholes" or "technicalities" in the law.

When the Department of Justice arrested Abel with their alien detention writ, and later convicted him on evidence so obtained, they had violated his rights under our Constitution, I still thought—and think. Similar writs, called writs of assistance, were used by the British to harass the Americans in the 1770s. Significantly, John Adams said that when the great Boston lawyer, James Otis, denounced these writs in open court, "American independence was then and there born."

Standing before the Supreme Court on this day, I again argued that the administrative warrant (returnable to themselves and held secret), used to take Abel into custody, was a subterfuge to permit the Immigration and FBI agents to seek his cooperation and obtain evidence of espionage.

"For the Court to uphold the conviction," I said, "would be to let government officials ignore the requirement for search warrants in any criminal case also involving deportation charges."

When each oral argument was concluded, and throughout the arguments, the Court fired dozens of questions. In answer to a query from Justice Whittaker, the Solicitor General agreed the search would have been illegal if its real purpose had been to uncover espionage evidence. But, said General Rankin, the agents were truly looking for materials to support the deportation charge. Many tongues were in their cheeks, I thought.

In what seemed to be an afterthought, the government lawyer said the items found in the Hotel Latham had little significance balanced against the mass of evidence introduced at the trial. I reminded the Court that the original "raid" on Abel's hotel room had led to the discovery of most of the evidence which later showed up in the trial court.

To my amazement, the Government suggested that some of our present arguments were never advanced before Judge Byers and therefore the Supreme Court should decline to consider them. I strongly resisted this line and produced a copy of our original brief in the District Court which made all the same points.

(I later wrote Abel, "The Government resorted to this unusual argument out of apparent desperation. It was an obvious effort to permit the Court to circumvent the issue, since the Court undoubtedly would like to affirm the conviction but finds it extremely difficult to refute our legal arguments.")

As to the question of whether the two FBI agents had entered Abel's room illegally, Mr. Rankin said they had moved into the room without being invited. Chief Justice Warren then asked, "They used a little stronger language than that, didn't they? They forced their way in—or pushed in?"

The Solicitor General conceded the point.

When two hours had run their course, the Court took the case under advisement a second time.

Years ago, when the small-town lawyer traveled to the country seat to plead a major case, a few friends and relatives made the journey with him, and there was a certain holiday atmosphere to these expeditions. Nine close friends had come down from New York to hear the Abel case. Ann and Frank Bushey headed a group from Manhasset, Long Island; Elizabeth and Frank Van Orman came from Short Hills, New Jersey. Two hours after the argument, we were on the train headed back to New York, in a car which fortuitously was all our own. One of the group had been provident enough to pack a bottle of Scotch and he had waited until now to break it open. As we rolled toward New York, exchanging views and quips on the oral arguments, I felt more and more like the old-time country lawyer returning from a trial at the county seat.

Abel had let two of my letters go unanswered. He was obviously still smarting under the government's order restricting his correspondence, for he now wrote, "I regret the delay and can only say in explanation that I seem to have lost my appetite for writing."

His letter was to the point: "At present I am engaged in producing Christmas cards for the inmates and the Warden. The irony of the situation, I am sure, will not escape you . . . I made no attempt to send cards to my family.

"P.S. Would it be possible to ask your secretary to buy a package of goodies to be sent me for Christmas?"

Rudolf's card, which arrived Christmas week, was striking and very different from last year's. It was done in blue and black and pictured three devout shepherds on the side of a hill outside Bethlehem, staring into a sky with "the star." "Noel" was across the face of the card. One of my partners, a devout Catholic, said to me, "You're gaining on him."

1960

U-2 pilot Francis Gary Powers in 1960, before he was shot down in Soviet airspace. (Courtesy of Dereu & Sons Mfg. Co.)

Monday, January 11, 1960

The FBI earlier this week completed a thorough and final search of Abel's property. Everything worth packing was then loaded into two great cases, insured for $1,750, and shipped to Leipzig. The balance of his things (lathes, tools) were sold for $100, which did not begin to cover the $244.82 shipping charges to East Germany for the bulk of the lot.

Reporting to the Colonel, I wrote, "After every form of bureaucratic delay I have disposed of all your possessions. . . . After finding a variety of people who wanted us to pay them to remove the heavy equipment, we were able to salvage $100 on it. I enclose a copy of the bill of lading, together with the packing list. . . . This should conclude the matter."

I was being overly optimistic. In his next letter, Abel wrote to say that in going over the list he had missed two articles—"my guitar and a Speedgraphic camera 3 1/2" X 4 1/2" without a lens."

We checked with the FBI and learned the guitar "was irreparably injured in the course of examining it for evidence of microdots. The Speedgraphic was adjudged valueless and was not shipped. You appreciate that a decision had to be made as to those items which were of sufficient value to warrant the payment of shipping charges."

Abel made one more try. "Regarding the guitar," he wrote, "I imagine that any attempt to obtain redress would involve formidable legal procedures much more expensive than the instrument itself. . . ."

I assured him that to try to litigate the matter would be both expensive and inadvisable "because of the allegations which the government was sure to make."

Tenacity, though, was Rudolf's middle name. It was March before our correspondence no longer concerned itself with the guitar and Speedgraphic.

Monday, January 25

Eleven months earlier we had argued before the Supreme Court for the first time. Each Monday, of course, was decision day in the high tribunal. About noon, it had become a ritual for me to drop my business and go over to the Lawyers Club to bolt down lunch and watch the teletype, waiting for word from the Supreme Court.

I complained in a letter to Abel on this day that I envied his equanimity. Judging from his last letter, he seemed to be more concerned about his guitar than the Court decision.

To this, he replied, "I am naturally wondering when the Supreme Court will publish its decision; at the same time I try not to let it affect me too much. At times I succeed. Other times it has me worried. As you say, the time is more propitious this year. The political situation is more relaxed both internally and externally and it makes it more hopeful from our point of view. . . ."

I also touched on his correspondence problem: "I think that all we can do is exercise the Christian virtues of patience, fortitude and hope. At first it must seem to be rather easy for me to be giving such advice to a man in prison, while I have my freedom. Actually, however, because of the nature of the case, almost no day passes without my receiving inquiries, attempted humorous sallies (some good-natured and some not) and other reminders of my participation in your defense. I received an anonymous letter from Houston, Texas, the other day in which I was told that a man who steals the truth by sophistry is worse than a common thief. I just have to expect this sort of thing."

Saturday, February 20

Frau Abel, describing herself as "the unhappy simple woman whose heart is broken," sent me an appeal for clemency and mercy addressed to Chief Justice Warren. It was in keeping with the maudlin standards established in her previous writings:

> . . . An unknown to you, a sick and broken-hearted woman, takes the liberty to waste some of your precious time to ask you to help her in that matter that is the question of life and death. . . . Unfortunately I know neither all the circumstances nor the extent of my husband's guilt . . . but I am sure that he could not have done anything criminal for there are few people in the world so honest, kind and noble as Rudolf is. It seems to me that the point of the problem lies not in him but rather in those abnormal, tense relations which have existed between the countries of East and West. My husband—a simple, common and very good man—is only a victim, a plaything of ruthless destiny . . .

The letter was typed on plain white writing paper and ran to five hundred ill-chosen words. There was one note of interest:

> Quite recently I happened to hear that in September 1955 three American citizens were handed over to American authorities in Berlin. They were, as I heard, convicted in Russia for their anti-governmental activities and released before their terms . . . I believe that their families in America understood that it was the manifestation of humanity. Is America a less humane country and is it not clear that one good action calls forth another? . . .
>
> I shall pray for you to the end of my days.

That I should forward this letter to the Chief Justice was of course, out of the question. There was only one place I would send it—to the Justice Department for study and analysis. Then I replied to Frau Abel:

> With respect to your personal appeal to Chief Justice Warren, I do not believe I should forward it to him. In my opinion, it would do no good and, very possibly, grave harm to your husband's case. If the decision should be in his favor, the least likely reason for any such result would be the slightest sympathy on the part of the Court for your husband's predicament.
>
> As to your reference to the transfers of American personnel in 1955, these are matters which more properly should be addressed to the attention of our State Department. . . . The only cases which have received prominent publicity and public interest here are those of Americans now being held by Red China.

Monday, March 28

JUDGMENT UNITED STATES AGAINST ABEL AFFIRMED TODAY.

The telegram, received in New York at 3:59 P.M. and relayed by phone to my office, was signed by Chief Clerk James R. Browning of the Supreme Court of the United States. The message was passed to me on the back of an envelope while I was speaking on nuclear energy insurance problems before the executive committee of the National Board of Fire Underwriters.

At about the same time, Abel was writing me from Atlanta, "I have just heard over the radio that the Supreme Court by a 5-4 decision upheld the findings of the lower courts. I am eagerly awaiting your opinion, especially in view of the closeness of the voting. I believe there could be an appeal for a new hearing in view of the 5-4 vote.

"I can appreciate your chagrin at the result but I believe that there are alleviating circumstances that soften the blow."

Incredible Rudolf. After two years and nine months—stretching from the summer of 1957 to the winter of 1960—he had just lost his case in the Supreme Court by one vote and now was extending me his sympathy. But in the next breath he said, "Would it be possible for you to come to Atlanta for a personal conference to discuss possible legal moves? I have one or two things in mind that are best discussed . . ."

For myself, I had mixed emotions. I was relieved that it was over—especially for my family. I was disappointed we had not won, but I was pleased that we had gone all the way and satisfied we had done our best.

Over a year before, when we had first argued the case in Washington, I had prepared a short statement for release whenever the case should be decided by the Court and regardless of the outcome. Now reporters began to call my office, some clearly in the expectation that I would denounce the Court's decision as a "miscarriage of justice." My office issued the year-old statement, unchanged:

> The very fact that Abel has been receiving due process of law in the United States is far more significant, both here and behind the Iron Curtain, than the particular outcome of the case.
>
> Mr. Donovan added he would make this same comment, regardless of the decision. When asked how he felt about today's decision, he simply said, "Tired."

There were three separate opinions by members of the Supreme Court. This, of course, was an indication of the battle which must have been waged in their conference room and, perhaps, brought about the second oral argument. Moreover, the language of the opinions was sharp.

Justice Felix Frankfurter, under whom I had studied at Harvard (we dedicated our yearbook to him when he was appointed to the Court), wrote the majority opinion. Justices Tom C. Clark, John Marshall Harlan, Charles E. Whittaker and Potter Stewart concurred.

Justice William J. Brennan filed a dissenting opinion, in which Chief Justice Earl Warren and Justices Hugo L. Black and William O. Douglas joined; Justice Douglas also wrote a separate dissent, in which Justice Black concurred.

Ten years before, in a noted search-and-seizure case (United States v. Rabinowitz), the Supreme Court had held that Federal law officers making a valid criminal arrest without a search warrant might search the suspect and his premises, even though they had time to get a warrant. Justice Frankfurter had strongly dissented from the Rabinowitz decision of 1950. However, in his decision in the Abel case he said the Court was not being asked to reconsider that case and thus it would be "unjustifiable retrospective lawmaking" to do so.

Both dissenters took pains to include the Rabinowitz case (even to quoting Justice Frankfurter's 1950 opinion) in their opinions, inferentially jabbing at their fellow justice for abandoning his former views. He had written that "petty cases are even more calculated" than the proverbial hard cases "to make bad law." Justice Douglas began his opinion:

"Cases of notorious criminals—like cases of small, miserable ones—are apt to make bad law. When guilt permeates a record, even judges sometimes relax and let the police take shortcuts not sanctioned by constitutional procedures. That practice, in certain periods of our history and in certain courts, has lowered our standards of law administration. The harm in the given case may seem excusable. But the practices generated by the precedent have far-reaching consequences that are harmful and injurious beyond measurement. The present decision is an excellent example."

Justice Brennan borrowed this quotation from Justice Frankfurter in the Rabinowitz case to buttress his own opinion: "'Arrest under a warrant for a minor or a trumped-up charge has been familiar practice in the past, is a commonplace in the police state of today, and too well-known in this country . . . The progress is too easy from police action unscrutinized by judicial authorization, to the police state.'"

Speaking for the majority, Justice Frankfurter rejected the claim that the arrest had been a pretense. He said, "At the worst, it may be said that the circumstances of this case reveal an opportunity for abuse of the administrative arrest. But to hold illegitimate, in the absence of bad faith, the cooperation between INS and FBI would be to ignore the scope of rightful cooperation between two branches of a single Department of Justice concerned with the enforcement of different areas of law under the common authority of the Attorney General. . . . [This had been precisely the reasoning of Judge Byers in the District Court.]

"We emphasize again that our view of the matter would be totally different had the evidence established . . . the administrative warrant was here employed as an instrument of criminal law enforcement to circumvent the latter's legal restrictions, rather than as a bona fide preliminary step in a deportation proceeding. The test is whether the decision to proceed administratively toward deportation was influenced by, and was carried out for, a purpose of amassing evidence in the prosecution for crime. The record precludes such a finding by this court."

Justice Douglas saw it differently: "With due deference to the two lower courts, I think the record plainly shows that FBI agents were the moving force behind this arrest and search. For at least a month they investigated the espionage activities of petitioner. They were tipped off concerning this man and his role in May; the arrest and search were made on June 21. The FBI had plenty of time to get a search warrant . . . The administrative warrant of arrest was chosen with care and calculation as the vehicle through which the arrest and search were to be made . . . Thus the FBI used an administrative warrant to make an arrest for criminal investigation both in violation of the Immigration and Nationality Act and in violation of the Bill of Rights. . . .

"The issue is not whether these FBI agents acted in bad faith. Of course they did not. The question is how far zeal may be permitted to carry officials bent on law enforcement. As Mr. Justice Brandeis once said, 'Experience should teach us to be most on our guard to protect liberty when the government's purposes are beneficient.' . . . The facts seem to me clearly to establish that the FBI agents wore the mask of the INS to do what otherwise they could not have done. They did what they could do only if they had gone to a judicial officer pursuant to the requirements of the Fourth Amendment, disclosed their evidence, and obtained the necessary warrant for the searches which they made.

"The tragedy in our approval of these short cuts is that the protection afforded by the Fourth Amendment is removed from an important segment of our life . . ."

In his majority opinion, Justice Frankfurter said there were safeguards against indiscriminate use of the Immigration Service's detention writ. He specifically pointed to the fact that an application for this warrant must be made to an independent responsible officer (the district director of INS), to whom a prima-facie case of deportability must be shown.

Justice Brennan, however, attacked this procedure, saying, "These arrest procedures, as exemplified here, differ as night from day from the processes of an arrest for crime. When the power to make a broad, warrantless search is added to them, we create a complete concentration of power in executive officers over the person and effects of the individual . . . They may take any man they think to be a deportable alien into their own custody, hold him without arraignment or bond, and having been careful to apprehend him at home, make a search generally through his premises.

"I cannot see how this can be said to be consistent with the Fourth Amendment's command; it was rather, against such a concentration of executive powers over the privacy of the individual that the Fourth Amendment was raised . . .

"Like most of the Bill of Rights, it [the Fourth Amendment] was not designed to be a shelter for criminals, but a basic protection for everyone; to be sure, it must be upheld when asserted by criminals, in order that it may be at all effective, but it 'reaches all alike, whether accused of crime or not.'"

Needless to say, I agreed with the dissenters on the proper rule of law, while understanding the reluctance of a court to free the defendant. However, I refused to be drawn into public criticism of the Court's decision, reiterating my statement that Abel had received due process of law even though we had lost our case.

Tuesday, March 29

From all across the country, the editorials came. They were written, I am certain, without benefit of the three opinions and some were exceedingly depressing. Most of them completely missed the point we—and the four minority justices—had striven so hard to make. Furthermore, some of them showed little understanding of the high court's function; the writing was built on emotion.

"The dissenters ignored either innocence or guilt," said one especially awkward piece. Another rabble-rouser wrote, "In protecting the life of a great nation against Communism officers cannot be expected to be too technical. If they had waited to get a search warrant they might not have secured the evidence to convict the spy."

The Fourth Amendment was the very heart of the search-and-seizure question and there never was any doubt that the constitutional protection applied to aliens, as well as every citizen. Despite this, we had editorials declaring:

> It is a national disgrace that four members of the Supreme Court wanted to free this man . . . These four judges would confer on a Communist spy the special protection the Constitution gives to United States citizens . . .

> It is a dangerous situation indeed when a Soviet spy, apprehended with the materials of his trade in his possession, can almost be freed on a technicality . . .

> Freeing of a master Russian spy on a *mere technicality* would have been a grave miscarriage of justice . . .

The Supreme Court, of course, does not deal in technicalities. It is difficult to comprehend how mature Americans can equate the Fourth Amendment with the cliché "mere technicality."

There were two editorials which did not play the anti-Court tune. One of these, in the Washington *Post and Times Herald*, was nonetheless critical of the decision—but for an entirely different reason:

> The Supreme Court decision . . . may have enhanced national security; but it certainly did not enhance the security of Americans against unreasonable searches and seizures. The relaxation of Fourth Amendment standards was applied in this instance to an alien—and an odious, dangerous alien at that. But history has pretty plainly indicated that constitutional shortcuts sanctioned in regard to aliens soon come to be sanctioned in regard to citizens. . . .
>
> It is essential that spies be apprehended and brought to justice. But is at least equally essential that the decent privacy of American homes be protected against arbitrary intrusion by over-zealous policemen. It would be ironic indeed if the court had jeopardized their protection in upholding the methods used to convict a Soviet spy.

Finally, there was the sober comment by the Worcester, Massachusetts, *Telegram:*

> There is a special significance in this case of Colonel Abel. The Fourth Amendment, under which his appeal was made, stands at the opposite extreme of the police state philosophy to which the Soviet Union subscribes . . . Although our courts may not always speak in unison on this issue, or with perfect wisdom, the fact that they may deliberate on it, openly and in freedom, is not to be lightly dismissed. When even a Soviet spy can, on constitutional grounds, command a sober review by the highest court in the land, it testifies to the underlying strength and integrity of our democratic foundations.

Tuesday, April 5

The Colonel looked gaunt and beat; his clothes hung loose. There were dark circles under his deep-set eyes. Prison has made him an old man, I thought. It was almost a year since I had last seen him, and when they led him into the room I was startled by this seeming physical deterioration.

"I'm all right," he said quickly. "It's just the heat down in Georgia. It has knocked me out and I lost ten pounds."

To facilitate our meeting, the Department of Justice had courteously agreed to bring the Colonel to New York City and hold him in the West Street house of detention while we conferred. Abel had asked for a prompt meeting, following the Supreme Court decision, and I simply could not be relieved of pending court engagements. He explained they had made the long trip from Atlanta by car, driving mile after mile through a broiling South. They had stopped only in Washington, where the Colonel was put up in its Federal prison.

"I'm beginning to see more and more of the inside of your American prisons," he said. Even in Atlanta he had not lost his light touch.

He began then by reporting that despite his poor appearance, things were going well in Atlanta. He said he was now in a cell with only three other inmates; this proved to be a more comfortable and satisfactory way of life. He explained that he continued to occupy most of his time with art work—he was teaching several classes—and passed the long hours in his cell with mathematical exercises.

It was on both our minds, so I asked, "What did you think of the decision?"

He hesitated, smiled wanly and said, "I was not surprised. I did not believe the case would be decided purely on the law. I regard it as a political decision because, quite frankly, I think that your arguments on the law were irrefutable."

We discussed the idea of applying for a rehearing before the

Supreme Court. I told him that while I felt it a futile move, it was about all that was left to us.

"Then I'd like you to explore it," he said. "As long as there is a course of action open to us, I want to take advantage of it."

We skated onto thin ice once more as we moved to a discussion of the possibility of applying for a reduction of his thirty-year sentence. I had recently discussed this with Department of Justice officials and so I was prepared.

"This can only be done," I said, "if the Court knows you are actually cooperating with the Government. I can give any other reason for making the application in open court, but under our practice the judge must know you're cooperating. Otherwise, the original sentence will not be changed."

He shook his head. "That is out of the question. Never will I do it," he said. "In that first half hour, when I sat on the bed that morning in the Hotel Latham, I decided then. I am firm in my decision."

"Under the circumstances," I added, "it would be idle, then, to bring such a motion before Judge Byers. In fact, it could even prove prejudicial to your future rights."

Abel just shook his head—and said nothing more.

I told him I had been receiving letters which purported to be from his wife but I frankly did not believe they were from any such person. He shrugged his shoulders.

The language of these letters, I said, indicated that this "Hellen Abel" considered me some sort of an evangelist seeking to convert his soul—and if this was not the case, then she must look on me as a simpleton for taking the case in the first place and pursuing it with such perseverance.

Rudolf laughed appreciatively.

"Do you really have a wife and daughter?" I asked, baiting him just a little.

"Of course I do," he said heatedly. But he left it there, neither adding nor explaining further.

In other words, while emphasizing that he did have a family quite interested in his fate, he was not contradicting my statement

346

that the letters I had been receiving were from an official source—not his family.

"Do you think your government will take steps to bring about your release, now that all hope of legal procedure is exhausted?"

"I simply don't know," he replied. "I think my biggest problem is that there is no American of sufficient importance in jail in Russia."

I allowed the conversation to break off and then, beginning slowly, drifted into a long story. I told him how I had been introduced to a CIA consultant who was formerly the Russian counterespionage chief in Vienna, explaining that this "defector" was extremely interested in Abel's future.

"He claims," I said, "that should you ever return to Russia you'll be considered politically unreliable; you'll be subjected to lengthy interrogation—for several years, perhaps—and if you're cleared, you'll be placed in a job where you can do very little good, and no harm.

"This all stems," I continued, "from a complete Soviet disbelief in the American judicial process. In fact, this man claims that if we had won the case in the Supreme Court it could have been very bad for you. If Immigration had deported you, the KGB certainly would have deduced that you had talked and agreed to become a double agent. This is all part of the Oriental distrust for Western ways, the defector said."

Abel listened, watched me closely all the while and when I had finished, he sat silent. I thought he took it well. Finally, he said, "This is always possible. I believe, in fact, this might have been true five or six years ago. It is no longer true."

Since 1953, he said, there had been "tremendous reforms" accomplished in his country and he believed the secret police in Russia now had less power than their counterpart in a democracy because their activities had been deliberately and forcefully curtailed.

"I don't believe my reliability will be questioned any more than that of an American officer returned home under similar circumstances."

Having said this, he changed the subject and asked me to renew—strongly renew—his application for the privilege of writing to his family. "It has been last August since I've heard from them," he said, "and I still believe this is unfair and unjust."

We talked about a friendly guard in the West Street prison who, I had found out that day upon inquiry, had quit since my last visit. "Couldn't stomach it," said the head guard. Abel remembered him well and said he understood. "I could be a prisoner for many years," he said, "but never a guard. It takes a special, unimaginative type to herd other human beings."

Wednesday, April 20

I filed the petition for rehearing, calling upon the five justices of the Supreme Court who had voted to affirm "to rigorously examine their judicial consciences." Tom Debevoise had recently become Attorney General of Vermont and thought it best not to appear in the papers, although he endorsed my effort. One of my partners, however, was shocked by my approach to the Court and sternly informed me that despite my zeal I should be held in contempt.

My petition stated that it was made on behalf of the millions of United States residents subject to the Immigration and Naturalization laws whose personal liberties were now "severely and unjustly curtailed by the decision in the Abel case." The paper was only four paragraphs long.

At long last, the case seemed to be ending.

Sunday, May 1

At 4:30 A.M. (Moscow time) Francis Gary Powers, a thirty-year-old American pilot from Pound, Virginia, lifted his glider-winged "Utility 2" plane off the runway at Peshawar, Pakistan, and headed for the Soviet border. Powers had flown twenty-seven missions totaling five hundred air hours in the U-2, but the "silent overflight" across the Soviet Union was the most rigorous of all his assignments. Powers later admitted to being "scared and nervous."

A lonely and grueling flight, it began at Peshawar, a border town not far from the Khyber Pass, and was planned to end 3,788 miles later at Bodo, Norway. Almost 3,000 miles along the route was over Soviet territory. The flight was always made at upwards of 70,000 feet where the pilot would breathe only pure oxygen and every movement demanded great exertion. The flight took eight hours to complete.

Called the "Black Lady of Espionage" by the Russians, the U-2 was a spy plane flown by CIA pilots. It was equipped with cameras, tape recorders, radars and radios. Powers' principal mission was to get photographs of missile sites near Sverdlovsk.

When he was twenty miles southeast of the Soviet industrial center, he changed his course. He made a 90-degree turn to the left. There was a noise, a flash (an orange or reddish glow), and the plane began to fail. After recovering momentarily, it nosed into a dive. Powers lost control, was thrown "outward," and then bailed out. He did not attempt to destroy the aircraft (a destruction button was near him) and did not use a self-destruction drug provided but not required. When he touched down by parachute on Soviet soil, he was captured and within a matter of hours was a prisoner under interrogation at Moscow's famed Lubianka prison, 2 Dzerzhinsky Street.

In time, Francis Gary Powers and the May Day U-2 incident became the Soviet Union's greatest propaganda triumph since the cold war had begun.

Wednesday, May 11

In answer to Soviet charges that the United States had been guilty of "deliberately spying" with its U-2 overflights, President Eisenhower suggested at his news conference that the Russians review the case of their own Rudolf Ivanovich Abel and the evidence of his guilt produced at the trial.

The President admitted the flights, took full responsibility for them, and now he defended them, declaring, ". . . ever since the beginning of my administration I have issued directives to gather, in every feasible way, the information required to protect the United States and the free world against surprise attack . . ."

For those with poor memories, he then reviewed the Abel case and used the KGB Colonel as an example of the Soviet Union's spy missions to this country.

Pictures and stories of Abel appeared in newspapers all across the country again. Six weeks after the Supreme Court had presumably laid the case to rest, it was back on the front pages. And the New York *Daily News* editorially proposed "An Abel for a Powers" swap.

The editorial stated, "It is safe to assume that Abel is of no further value to our government as a source of information about Red activities. [He never had been.] After the Kremlin has wrung all the propaganda it can out of Powers . . . such a trade looks like a natural."

Monday, May 16

The Soviets, however, had only just begun to squeeze young Powers for propaganda purposes. In Paris, Premier Khrushchev, pale and trembling with anger, demanded the United States apologize and condemn those responsible for the "inadmissible provocative actions of the United States Air Force." Short of this, he would walk out on the Big Four summit meeting which was about to commence.

The four heads of state sat together three hours and five minutes and could agree only that they should adjourn. Eisenhower refused to apologize, of course, and the summit collapsed before it ever really began.

In Washington, the Supreme Court ruled the Abel conviction must stand. The court denied our petition for rehearing in a brief

350

order. "The action came," said one of the papers, "in the midst of an international crisis over the crash of the U-2 some 1,200 miles inside the Soviet borders."

Wednesday, June 8

At the center of the international crisis was the shy, quiet son of an aggressive onetime coal miner, now a shoemaker. Oliver Powers, who never went beyond the fifth grade, said of his boy, "He always done what he was told but he was an adventuresome boy. I wanted him to be a doctor, but he said he'd rather be a pilot."

Writing from prison, Powers said he was being treated "much better than I expected. I get more than I can eat and plenty of sleep . . . I also get to walk in the fresh air every day that it doesn't rain. One day I even took a sun bath."

Allen Dulles, his chief as director of the CIA (Dulles retired in the fall of 1961 and was succeeded by John A. McCone), described Powers as a fine pilot, an excellent navigator and an exceptional photographer. He was only incidentally a spy. In this sense, then, it was rather absurd to compare him to Colonel Abel, but in the months ahead their names would be continually and almost inextricably linked. In addition, Powers was editorially assailed for failing to take his life and for not destroying his plane. The wreckage of the U-2, carefully reassembled, was being exhibited in Moscow's Gorki Park as a symbol of the "American bandits."

Sunday, June 12

Abel had written only one short letter since March, and this was to urge me to press for reinstatement of his mail privileges since "there seems to be some evidence that Powers is writing to his family." But this day's mail brought a letter from him that was electric with excitement.

"I received a letter from Mr. Powers, the father of the U-2 pilot," he began. A copy of the letter and his reply followed:

Dear Colonel Abel,

I am the father of Francis Gary Powers who is connected with the U-2 plane incident of several weeks ago. I am quite sure that you are familiar with this international incident and also the fact that my son is being currently held by the Soviet Union on an espionage charge.

You can readily understand the concern that a father would have for his son and for a strong desire to have my son released and brought home. My present feeling is that I would be more than happy to approach the State Department and the President of the United States for an exchange for the release of my son. By this I mean that I would urge and do everything possible to have my government release you and return you to your country if the powers in your country would release my son and let him return to me. If you are inclined to go along with this arrangement I would appreciate your so advising me and also so advising the powers in your country along these lines.

I would appreciate hearing from you in this regard as soon as possible.

Very truly yours,
(signed) Oliver Powers.

Abel had replied:

Dear Mr. Powers,

Much as I appreciate and understand your concern for the safety and return of your son, I regret to say that, all things considered, I am not the person to whom your request should have been directed. Obviously, this should be my wife. Unfortunately, by order of the Department of Justice, I am not permitted to write to my family and so cannot convey your request to them directly.

The Colonel never missed a chance to slap the Justice Department over the restriction on his mail. Even this shoemaker from

352

the Virginia hill country had to hear of it. Rudolf would have made a good politician in our country.

In his message to me, which followed, Abel asked that I send copies of the letters to Vogel, his wife's lawyer in East Berlin, and bring Mrs. Abel up to date on all developments.

I had previously written Abel that I was going to Europe on business, and this led him to suggest "there might be some benefit if you could meet my wife's lawyer . . . you could give him a much clearer picture of what is going on than any exchange of letters can do.

"Hoping you have a good trip."

Abel clearly sensed a deal was now possible. The Russians had found some bait.

I made copies of the letters available to the FBI in New York and the CIA in Washington and with the government's advice released a summary of the Powers and Abel letters to the press wire services. This put the story back on page one (POWERS-FOR-ABEL SPY SWAP SOUGHT; U.S. STUDIES PROPOSAL BY PILOT'S FATHER) but Justice and the State Department quickly issued "no comment" statements. One of those high-ranking but anonymous sources was careful to explain, however, there were two obstacles to the trade: 1) Powers was still to be tried for espionage; 2) The Russians had never acknowledged Abel as their agent, let alone a Russian citizen. For the Soviet to enter into negotiations for Abel would be to admit they used spies.

For this very reason, Abel was displeased with the news stories and sent me a sharp note to this effect. He wrote, "I am not in a position to initiate or participate in negotiations for an exchange. The copies of O. Powers' letter and my reply were intended only for the information of my wife. I want it made known to Mr. Vogel that the news release was not at my initiative . . . I am still prejudiced against any publicity and believe the best policy is not to do anything to raise it."

Overall, the publicity produced salubrious results. Editorials supporting the proposed exchange appeared in newspapers in Providence, Atlanta, Philadelphia, Dayton, Denver, Winston-Salem, Orlando, Fla.; Terre Haute, Ind.; Roanoke, Richmond and New York. The sentiment, summed up, was "We would like to see Francis Gary Powers back in this country." Meanwhile, of course, the wire-service stories were being carefully studied in Moscow, per our plan.

At ten the next morning, my son John and I sailed for London on a business trip, aboard the *Nieuw Amsterdam*.

Friday, June 24

The Department of Justice on this day lifted the restrictions on Abel's correspondence. A telegram to this effect reached me at my hotel in London. With the news in hand, I called at the American Embassy and learned that under these new circumstances it was no longer necessary for me to look for a meeting with East German lawyer Vogel while in Europe. Abel, I was told, could now write to his wife and her lawyer, and they could deal with the problem of an exchange any way they saw fit. I meanwhile was advised that all American Embassies were being alerted to my presence in Europe and that if I should hear from Vogel (say, in Switzerland) I should immediately notify the nearest Embassy.

For the remainder of the trip—which was to take us to Zurich, Paris, Dublin and back to London—we relaxed and pretended I had no Russian client who called himself Abel. In Paris, however, I spent a delightful half hour with American Ambassador Amory Houghton at his invitation, and we discussed the case generally.

Wednesday, August 17

A public trial in Russia, I have always thought, can be likened to a medieval morality play. It is a theatrical performance—presented with the definite purpose of edifying the general public by exhibiting the triumph of good over evil. In the trial of Francis Gary Powers, the obvious purpose was the furtherance of current themes of Soviet propaganda. Like any other good theatrical production, it was well rehearsed.

Powers was confined and held incommunicado 108 days. On his thirty-first birthday, ironically, he was dressed up in a double-breasted blue suit and brought to trial (under Article 2 of the Soviet Criminal Code) as a spy. If convicted, he could be put to death, or sentenced to from seven to fifteen years in prison.

The trial setting was perfect: the Hall of Trade Unions where, during the 1930s, most of the notorious purge trials took place. Inside, the hall gleamed under a fresh coat of paint and forty-four crystal-bead chandeliers helped to light the huge "courtroom."

It was patently that the Soviets had encouraged and aroused public interest. There was a refreshment stand (coffee, tea, soda pop, sweet rolls and salami sandwiches) on the main floor and about two thousand spectators, called to their seats by a theater bell, had the aid of ushers. It was more like a Broadway opening night than the commencement of a trial of a man charged with a capital crime.

With the pilot's parents, Oliver and Ida Powers, and his wife Barbara in a special block of seats, the cast was complete. The television cameras began to record the extravaganza and Powers stood up to speak: "Yes, I plead guilty."

The court, made up of the three-member military collegium, received the plea and then directed the prosecutor, Roman A. Rudenko, Procurator-General of the Soviet Union (whom I remembered as a prosecutor at the principal Nuremberg trial), to begin the questioning.

The three military judges were simply other actors in the drama. Decisions on the conduct of the trial and its outcome had been taken at the highest level of the Communist party. The whole show required serious advance preparation. Its propaganda purposes and probable effects had to be studied in the light of public reactions within Russia as well as the Soviet satellites.

All criminal justice, of course, is inherently imperfect since it is an attempt to effect divine judgments in a human society. However, with its procedural safeguards and the right of trial by jury, criminal law in the United States is well designed to achieve abstract justice. As for Soviet criminal law, we must distinguish between cases that affect the security of the state and other offenses. With respect to the latter, I believe that a reasonable attempt is made to achieve abstract justice, within the framework of Byzantine jurisprudence, on which Soviet law is largely based. But where state security is involved, in the Soviet or any other absolute dictatorship, human rights are suppressed or obliterated to the degree believed to be required by national interests. The security of the state is given a value transcending the natural and constitutional rights which a defendant always has in a free society.

Mikhail I. Griniev, fifty-five years old, was Powers' court-assigned counsel. His defense of Powers was totally inadequate. In America it would have been said that defense counsel "sold out" his client. Griniev urged that the American pilot was merely a tool, an accomplice to a foul crime (as Rudenko had characterized the overflight), while the United States was the real culprit. Powers was led into some strange admissions, including the fact that he had never voted in an election in the United States.

He also delivered a contrite speech:

"The situation I am in now is not too good. I haven't heard much about the news of the world since I have been here, and I understand that as a direct result of my flight, the summit conference did not take place and President Eisenhower's visit [to Russia] was called off. There was, I suppose, a great increase in tension in the world, and I am sincerely sorry I had anything to do with this. Now that I know some of the consequences of my flight I am profoundly sorry I had any part in it."

Griniev announced the defense would not challenge the facts or the "assessment of the crime" by the state prosecutor.

All of which was to be expected. Like the judges, the defense lawyer was carrying out his assigned role in the play. His plea for Powers was probably prepared by a propaganda committee. That is one reason, for instance, he was never seen in consultation with his client during the trial. It would have been pointless and might even have proved to be a risky interference with the pacing of the drama.

To me, this phase of the trial was especially galling. It was my belief, and I was not alone here, that under our system an intellectually honest defense of Powers could have been offered.

As there is a three-mile limit in maritime law, and beyond that all enjoy freedom of the seas, so at some distance upward there must be freedom of space. Russia had never agreed to an international convention for determining the limits of sovereignty in space, and it could well have been argued that since the United States had made U-2 flights for several years with Russia's knowledge but without hindrance, Russia did not effectively control the air space over her borders at the cruising altitude of the U-2. Therefore, this region was free in the sense that the sea is free beyond the three-mile limit, and Powers committed no crime against the sovereign state of Soviet Russia.

The trial in the Hall of Trade Unions continued three days, and when they had done with it, Powers was sentenced to 10 years' confinement—3 years in prison and 7 years in a labor camp.

"The result of the Powers trial," wrote Abel, "was to some extent surprising. I had not expected great severity—I thought that a sentence to ten years in a penitentiary would have been imposed. However, a three-year penitentiary term and seven years in a labor camp was in my own view quite lenient when one considers the case, especially as Powers could be released in five years and maybe even earlier if he were to be deported. I cannot see how anybody could classify this as 'very severe' in comparison with the thirty years I received. What adjectives could be used to describe it? I wonder if Judge Byers could find the proper words?

"I sometimes wonder what would have happened here—in Congress, in the press, on the radio and the TV—if something comparable to the U-2 incident had occurred in Kansas with some Russian pilot as the villain in the piece?"

Saturday, September 10

With the Powers trial out of the way, Mrs. Abel moved back into the picture. After three months, she wrote to offer comment on the exchange of letters between Oliver Powers and her husband:

> My daughter and I passionately desire Rudolf to be released from imprisonment and join us as soon as possible but the means suggested [the trade] seem to us not only unreal but even dangerous. My husband's letter says that the pilot's case has nothing to do with him. Therefore, we do not understand why this question has arisen. To contemplate our further steps, I shall obviously have to meet with my lawyer in East Berlin. . . .

There was nothing to do now but play the waiting game and look for the trade winds to shift.

When the Supreme Court refused to grant us a rehearing, we paid Abel's $3,000 fine—part of the sentence imposed by Judge Byers—and asked his wife to send an additional $5,000 to cover any future expenses. Rudolf needed $250 a year for basic personal needs. "Mrs. Abel" wrote she was busy selling things and borrowing money to meet her husband's obligations.

Sunday, December 4

It was time again for the colonel's annual Christmas message and request:

"I shall be sending you a Christmas card in the near future," he began and then explained his wants. "I would like four pounds of plain milk chocolate and for the book, I would like a text on the theory of Quadratic Forms, or Leonard E. Dickson's *Introduction to the Theory of Numbers.*"

Ever Mr. Meticulous, he also jogged us about renewing his newspaper and magazine subscriptions.

1961

1961

Wednesday, January 4, 1961

At the summit conference Khrushchev had suggested the meeting might better be postponed eight months—with the clear inference that President Eisenhower, who had served two terms and could not succeed himself, would then be gone. On November 8, John Fitzgerald Kennedy had been elected President, and the Soviet Premier had made it known he wanted the U-2 "to become a thing of the past"; he hoped "a fresh wind will begin to blow" with the coming of a new American Chief of State.

These pronouncements, of course, did not escape the friends of Colonel Abel, and so I was not surprised when in his first letter of this new year, Rudolf wrote, "Incidentally, in one of her last letters my wife suggested that I appeal to the new President. I stated that I did not think it possible, in the present circumstances, for me to do so but suggested that she do so herself, much in the same way as the relatives of Powers and others have done . . . I would be indebted to you if you could find it possible to offer her some counsel on this matter."

My advice to Frau Abel was to address a simple, non-legalistic petition to the White House, but I cautioned her to send it only after the new administration had had time to become settled in its new responsibilities.

Per usual, I kept our Government up to date.

On the 21st of the month, President Kennedy was inaugurated. Four days later, the new Chief Executive held his first press conference and announced the release of Air Force Captains Freeman D. Olmstead and John R. McKone, the RB-47 pilots who had been shot down by a Soviet fighter July 1, 1960. Their reconnaissance plane had been flying over the Barents Sea and they were the surviving members of the six-man crew. This was Khrushchev's good-will gesture to the new administration. The air was clearing, slightly.

Wednesday, February 8

Mrs. Abel's petition for clemency was neither simple nor nonlegalistic. It was offensively emotional:

Mrs. Hellen Abel
c/o Mrs. E. Forster
Leipzig 22 Eisenacherstr. 24
Germany

To His Excellency Mr. John F. Kennedy
  The President of the United States of America

February 8, 1961

Dear Mr. President:
  Please would you forgive my distracting you from your important state affairs for considering my personal matter, but really it is a matter of life importance to me.
  I am the wife of Rudolf I. Abel who was convicted to thirty years of penitentiary in 1957. . . . My name is Hellen Abel. I was born in

362

Russia in 1906. I am a teacher of music and live in Germany with my daughter Lydia Abel . . .

After the fate separated me from my husband more than ten years ago, I have suffered all the time bitterly waiting for his return. I do not know all the circumstances of my husband's case but I am convinced that he could not have done anything immoral or criminal. Believe me, he is a very honest, noble and kind man. I know him better than anyone else. I am sure that he was defamed and muddled up by some wicked people for the purpose unknown to me. . . . Not a single exact evidence of his guilt in stealing secrets of value to the United States has ever been produced. Why was he punished so severely? I am writing about it not because I try to persuade you of his being innocent—I realize that this is beyond my power—but I am writing to ask Your Excellency to be humane and merciful to my miserable husband even if you are quite sure of his being guilty. . . .

I was inspired by the good news which I learnt from the newspaper that two American pilots Olmstead and McKone were released in Russia and handed over to the American authorities. This raised my hopes that the question of my husband's release before time might be considered by you favourably. I am sure that in case of your being merciful to my poor husband this action would be generally understood not only as evidence of your humaneness and kindness but also as a proof of Your Excellency's desire to contribute to the beginning of a new era of peace in the history of humanity. It is quite certain that such a humane action cannot but affect favourably the fate of some Americans who got into trouble abroad and cannot return home. . . .

I beg of you, Mr. President, to comply with my petition . . .

> With utmost respect,
> Very sincerely,
> Yours
> (signed) Hellen Abel.

The message was clear to me: Khrushchev was angling for a Kennedy release of Abel to reciprocate for the release of the RB-47 fliers.

Over the years the FBI had made several business trips to Atlanta to call on Rudolf. From time to time they sounded him out on "cooperating." This was routine; they were checking to see if he was going soft in prison. They had to know, and now, with the possibility of a trade, it was only logical that our counterintelligence have another crack at him before possibly releasing him.

Additionally, they had two pretty good levers with which to apply new pressure. There was the matter of the pending petition to the President and a London spy trial—called "the Secrets trial"—during which his name popped out.

Five persons, including two Americans, were convicted of stealing naval secrets for Russia from the top-secret British base at Portland, where the Royal Navy's underwater weapons research was conducted. The Americans, Morris and Leona Cohen, were identified as professional Soviet spies and onetime associates of Colonel Abel.

When Abel was arrested in the Hotel Latham, he had had photographs of the Cohens in a briefcase. These were the pictures, meaningless at the time, marked "Shirley and Morris." Five thousand dollars in cash had been attached by a rubber band to the photograph, presumably for delivery.

The Colonel wrote me of the most recent FBI visit, beginning casually, "Incidentally, I had a visit from the FBI. They were interested in getting information from me and used both the London trial and my wife's petition as wedges, hinting that my recalcitrant attitude would be detrimental. *Needless to say, I refused.*

"In one matter (the London trial), I made a statement. They said they might prosecute some people and on that basis said that I should tell them what I know of these persons so as to perhaps exonerate them. In reply I stated that I doubted that there could be a case against these people but if there were I might meet with their defense counsel to see of what assistance I could be."

It did not appear that the Colonel was going soft. He seemed unusually belligerent.

He closed the letter with a word of advice for his lawyer, who had been litigating around the country in recent months. "I sometimes wonder," he wrote, "whether the pace you are setting yourself (or is it that you are caught up in the tide and have to go on?) is worth the reward!"

I appreciated his concern, but, considering the mailing address from which this advice emanated, I was amused. My wife Mary, however, emphatically agreed with Abel.

Monday, May 8

The "heartsick" Mrs. Abel had gone back to work. After waiting three months for word from President Kennedy, Frau Abel opened up the subject of a trade again. This time, she had something to say:

> Thinking over the question whether there is something that could be done to precipitate the solution of the question, I remembered of the letter sent to my husband last year by the father of the pilot Powers. I have not read it but if I am not mistaken, he suggested to my husband that some mutual action be taken to help his son and my husband be released. Rudolf wrote to me then that Powers' case had nothing to do with him and I did not consider myself that any benefit could come of it for us or the Powerses. . . .
>
> I wanted to write about it to Mr. Powers at once but was afraid that all the affair could be given publicity which would influence unfavourably the fate of my petition. Not knowing how to act, I have decided to ask your advice . . . what should be done to accelerate our case?
>
> Please, do not leave my letter without reply.

Immediately communicating with our government, I wrote, "I think it is perfectly evident that for the first time we have an offer to exchange Powers for Abel."

What was in my mind, as I wrote the letter to Washington, was the bleak day of November 15, 1957, when I had stood before Judge Byers in Brooklyn Federal Court and pleaded for Abel's life on the ground, among others:

> It is possible that in the foreseeable future an American of equivalent rank will be captured by Soviet Russia or an ally; at such time an exchange of prisoners through diplomatic channels could be considered to be in the best national interest of the United States.

We were moving now, but it would be slow progress. In the next nine months I was to receive three more letters from Mrs. Abel. The Colonel, meanwhile, was informed of all communications. A friend in Washington advised me to be patient, explaining, "What you lawyers in private practice do in three weeks, it takes us in government nine months to get done."

The Colonel moved, as always, with dispatch. He wrote, "I personally think this is a good move and should Mrs. Powers agree, it should help clarify the situation at an early date. I have written Mrs. Abel that I agree with her decision . . ."

Rudolf indicated that to him the only problem still to solve was to find a country which would grant asylum to him and Powers.

Thursday, May 25

Washington informed me that United States Pardon Attorney Reed Cozart had written Mrs. Abel that no basis existed for granting clemency to Colonel Abel. With a little coaching from the government, I framed an answer to Frau Abel, prominently mentioning the case of Igor Melekh, a Soviet United Nations official arrested for espionage last October 28. Melekh had been in the United States since 1955 and was working at the UN as chief of the Soviet translation section.

I wrote:

. . . I have read with interest the newspaper account of the release of Melekh (a Soviet national) who had been indicted but not court-tried for the crime of espionage. I also noted he returned to the U.S.S.R. While the news accounts said that the United States made no connection between Melekh and Mrs. Powers, in view of the similarity of the charges against them I suspect that the American officials expected some gesture by Soviet authorities. If none has occurred, it may be that U.S. officials would be disinclined to have any interest in such future gestures. In any event, I believe that the Melekh case indicates that the United States has an interest in the development of better relations between the two nations and I hope that the Soviet government has a similar interest.

Therefore, I would be willing to go to the Department of Justice to see what can be done for your husband along the lines of your request. However, I think there must be some indication of good faith on the part of the Soviet government as there was by the U.S. in the Melekh case. I suggest, then, that you contact the Soviet government to determine what interest they would have in effecting such a release. . . . If something is to be done in this matter, if should be done promptly.

Saturday, June 17

The letters kept coming. Less than a month had gone by, and on this day there was another in the now familiar pale blue envelope from Heartsick Hellen:

Having received this long awaited letter so important for me, I at once went to Berlin. I visited the Soviet Embassy and asked them to help me in the matter of getting the release of my husband as I personally could not do anything more for my husband's case. I was listened to attentively and requested to come again a few days later.

On my second visit I was told that my request was regarded

367

with sympathy and I was recommended to proceed with the efforts along this line.

In this connection I am sure that if my husband is pardoned, Mr. Powers will be amnestied too . . .

Wednesday, July 26

After discussion with the government, I wrote "Mrs. Abel":

After receipt of your letter [of June 17] I went to Washington and discussed the matter with the appropriate officials. As a result, I am of the opinion they are interested in the possibilities suggested in your letter although, as I had surmised in my previous letter, the Melekh case looms large in their thinking. The action of the government in dropping the charges against Melekh resulted in considerable adverse public reaction. Consequently, I can understand why these officials are reluctant to contemplate any additional action unless the Powers case is first resolved.

Under our law any action to grant clemency for your husband must be by the President. I believe that similar provisions for executive clemency are available under Soviet law which could make such action possible for Mr. Powers. I assume it was this type of action which was contemplated by officials with whom you discussed the matter.

I am hopeful that we may be ultimately successful in our understanding, but am convinced that, in view of the situation referred to above, officials here would not be willing to entertain a petition for clemency for Rudolf until Powers is back in the United States.

To make it patently clear we were not talking just to hear ourselves talk, I wrote the same letter to Abel, enclosed a copy of his "wife's" last exercise in sentimentality, and concluded, "I believe that I have done all which can be accomplished in your behalf. The next move, as you can see, is entirely up to Soviet officials. I have every reason to believe that upon the release of Powers you should receive executive clemency and deportation."

Thursday, August 17; Monday, September 11

There were two letters from Frau Abel of Eisenacher Strasse, No. 22, Leipzig. One was to Mrs. Barbara Powers, care of my office. Mrs. Abel quite obviously had grown impatient in July and so wrote, "You can hope to see your husband in nine years being still young, while for me every day of separation is an additional step towards death. We are already elderly people, our health is no good at all and we cannot hope to live long. Excuse me for this unintentional complaint . . ."

She then made her usual plea about Rudolf's being imprisoned for crimes which he could not possibly have committed, and reviewed her petition to President Kennedy, finally urging the Powers family to call on the American President "to take definite measures to deliver your husband. NOW BOTH YOUR AFFAIR AND MINE DEPEND COMPLETELY ON THE AMERICAN AUTHORITIES—whether they take some steps to make their pilot free or not."

And to me she wrote:

On your advice I visited the Soviet Embassy in Berlin and showed them your letter of July 26. I am glad to tell you that as before the Soviet representative showed great understanding of my case and reassured me of their willingness to help.

As to Melekh's case, they were surprised when I mentioned it. As I gathered from your letter this is now the only possible obstacle but they explained to me that it has nothing to do either with my husband's case or that of F. Powers and they flatly refuse to carry out negotiations on this question.

I gathered from our talk that there is only one possible way to achieve success now—THAT IS SIMULTANEOUS RELEASE

OF BOTH F. POWERS AND MY HUSBAND WHICH CAN BE
ARRANGED.

There it was. That was what I had been waiting to read. She
signed it, "Eager to get your reply . . ."

Wednesday, December 6

Rudolf wrote his usual year-end letter in which he confessed that
his imprisonment was "becoming something of an affliction." It
was his fourth annual Christmas message. He again reminded us
mortals on William Street to renew his subscriptions and again
asked for his four-pound ration of milk chocolate.

Reporting on his Christmas cards he said, "All in all, they are
quite good and show a steady improvement. Things here are much
the same. I trust you are in good health and wish you and your
family and your staff, who take care of my chores, the Merriest of
Christmases and the Happiest of New Years."

That was the last letter from Rudolf postmarked Atlanta, Georgia.

1962

(The following report concerns a mission under United States government auspices; there have been certain necessary deletions and alterations of detail, for reasons of security.)

Thursday, January 11, 1962

At the request of the United States government, I attended a meeting in Washington and was told it had been determined "on the highest level" that it would be in the national interest to effect a Powers-for-Abel exchange.

"If you are willing," they said, "we would like you to undertake a mission to East Germany to negotiate the exchange."

I readily agreed and we discussed the implications of the mission. The natural question, of course, was how great would be our sacrifice in releasing Abel, the "master spy." The answer appeared to be, not great at all. First, almost five years of imprisonment had demonstrated that Abel had no intention of "cooperating" with our counterintelligence forces. Next, since it is the function of an espionage agent not only to gather information but to transmit it to his principals as rapidly as possible, it could be assumed that by now Abel could submit current reports in Moscow only on life in United States prisons. Any information acquired before his arrest was already known to his principals. Finally, after his international publicity it was inconceivable that he ever again would be used outside the Iron Curtain.

"What of his value back home to evaluate intelligence from

373

here?" I asked. "With his knowledge of the United States, he would seem to be the ideal man to head the North American desk in KGB headquarters in Moscow."

"We don't think so," I was told. "If we took back such a man, abroad and isolated from us for so many years, there always would be a lingering question as to his undivided loyalty. You can't afford to gamble on such things. Now, if we would be hesitant to have such a man head a 'top secret' operation, surely the ultra-suspicious Soviet would be even more reluctant. Abel has been here almost nine years; his own assistant defected. The very fact we agree to release him would create a doubt in the Russian mind and they would worry that he had 'made a deal.' The great probability is that he would serve only to instruct others in techniques. Even there, at his age and in poor health, his usefulness is limited, if they decide to use him at all."

This analysis made sense to me.

It was agreed that since it was quite normal for me to travel to Europe on business, I would arrange a trip to London in the usual manner. I would send word ahead to friends, make a hotel reservation, travel by commercial aircraft, and screen the mission from both my office and my family.

I composed and sent from Washington a letter to "Frau Abel" in Leipzig, which said that there had been "significant developments" which warranted a meeting. I concluded:

My proposal is that I meet you at the Soviet Embassy in East Berlin on Saturday, February 3, 1962 at 12:00 noon. It is imperative that no publicity be given to this meeting by any party. Accordingly, if the foregoing meeting is satisfactory please cable me at my law office only the message "Happy New Year."

The Pardon Attorney in our Department of Justice had curtly rejected last May Mrs. Abel's plea to President Kennedy for clemency. I believed it necessary for me to carry an official letter which would convince the Russians that the United States government

374

would stand by my commitment to release Abel. Late this afternoon I was given such a letter, which I criticized as being so cautious in its wording as to be ambiguous. However, they declined to change it, and it was all that I carried into East Germany as evidence of my status and good faith. It was on Department of Justice stationery and read:

Dear Mr. Donovan:

With respect to the recent conference with you regarding executive clemency for your client, this is to assure you that upon the fulfillment of circumstances as outlined, the reason set forth in the letter to your client's wife as to why executive clemency should not be considered, will no longer exist.

Sincerely yours,
Reed Cozart
Pardon Attorney

Thursday, January 25

On this morning at ten o'clock, I received at my law office a cablegram from Berlin which read HAPPY NEW YEAR and was signed HELEN. The meeting in East Berlin was set.

I immediately made all arrangements for a journey to London and sent the necessary advance cables there. I explained to the family that my trip should be brief, and I promised British souvenirs to the children. Mary grumbled good-naturedly that I should find more clients with business in Brooklyn.

Saturday, January 27

I attended the annual luncheon of the International Association of Insurance Counsel at the Hotel Plaza. I told as many friends as possible of my impending trip to London, to discuss a merger between an unnamed American life insurance company and certain British interests. My friends were agreed that further combinations of American capital and British experience in international insurance would be desirable. I promised several wives of members to send them Liberty silk scarves.

One lawyer asked me, "What ever happened to that Russian spy Sobel, or whatever his name was?" I told him that Abel was now serving thirty years in Atlanta. He nodded sagely, reflecting satisfaction with the justice of the long sentence and quiet pleasure in my having lost the case.

After the luncheon I took a cab to the Harvard Club to meet a Washington contact for my final briefing. I gave him my detailed itinerary for the trip, and he informed me when I could expect official instructions in London.

He told me that the East Germans were holding a young American Yale student from Michigan named Frederic L. Pryor for trial on espionage charges. Before the Berlin Wall was erected, Pryor had been doing research in East Berlin to complete his doctorate thesis on trade behind the Iron Curtain. He dug too deeply, obtained some material regarded as confidential, and now the East Germans planned a propaganda trial. The prosecutor had publicly announced he would demand the death penalty for the young American. It was believed that the whole affair was being publicized in the hope of arousing American public opinion in favor of Pryor and thus compelling some form of recognition of the East German government by the United States.

Another young American student, Marvin Makinen from the University of Pennsylvania, had also been arrested for espionage, on the ground that he had taken illegal photographs of military installations while touring Russia. He had been tried by a Soviet court, convicted, and sentenced to serve eight years' imprisonment in Russia.

I was told the East German lawyer Vogel now claimed to represent both the Abel and Pryor families. The other day he sent a message to the United States Mission in West Berlin that Mrs. Abel was confident that Pryor and Makinen would be freed if the United States released Abel in exchange for Powers. However, our people regarded Vogel as untrustworthy. The government's advice to me was that while I should try to release all three Americans, my basic mission would be to exchange Abel for Powers. Beyond that man-for-man trade, I should use my own discretion and "play it by ear." I resolved to try for all three Americans.

My friend in the Harvard Club also advised that it had been determined I should go alone through the Wall into East Berlin. I reminded him that the original plan in Washington included my being accompanied by an American Mission officer fluent in German and Russian. The theory had been that, in addition to the companionship, some of his diplomatic immunity might rub off on me.

"I know," he said, "but plans have changed. There have been too many incidents at the Wall recently. You can understand that if anything went wrong on your mission in East Berlin, and an American Mission officer were involved, it could be diplomatically embarrassing to our government. After all, we don't recognize East Germany."

I digested this for a minute and then said that undoubtedly it was considered most remote that anything would "go wrong" while I was over there alone.

"Well," he said, "your situation is very different. There could be no embarrassment to the government since you will have no official status at all."

Possibly noting a quizzical expression on my face, he hastened to say that he had been instructed to assure me that if anything did "go wrong" a very grave view of the matter would be taken by our government "on the highest level."

In response to inquiries, I was advised to take no recording device or weapon on any part of the journey.

Tuesday, January 30

I arrived in London early in the morning after a routine flight from Idlewild by Pan American jet. I checked into Claridge's hotel and shortly thereafter was visited by a young, very competent "Mr. White," who alerted me to my departure for Berlin the following Friday. He told me that during the remainder of the journey I would be known as "Mr. Dennis," for security reasons. Then he gave me some West German marks and I gave him a morning bracer of Claridge's brandy.

Resting in the room, I kept going back to World War II when I used to stay in Claridge's with the late General Donovan. OSS had to keep a suite there because of its convenience to the governments in exile whose undergrounds we were supporting. Peter of Yugoslavia and Michael of Romania were housed on our floor, while we were continually visited by a most unlikely assortment of persons seeking to consult the General. Probably a few of them had introduced themselves to me as "Mr. Dennis."

Wednesday, January 31; Thursday, February 1

I spent two delightful days and evenings in London, visiting old friends in the insurance fraternity. I had lunch with David Evans, dinner with Jim Silversides, and an evening with the young David Coleridges. I explained to all that I must leave for Zurich on Friday but hoped to stop over in London on my way home. Meanwhile, I enjoyed a rewarding visit to the rare bookshops and left several items to be rebound by a London bookbinder.

Friday, February 2

Before dawn Mr. White arrived and I checked out of Claridge's. I asked the desk clerk to hold any mail for my return and sent Mary a cablegram, saying friends had invited me to take a holiday in Scotland. She had been urging me to arrange just such a rest.

At Connaught Square, still before dawn, we picked up a young lady representing British security. She quietly entered the back seat of our small car. For two hours White drove toward a British air base in the country, while we chatted about such irrelevant matters as the delights of kippered herring for breakfast, especially with a slice of smoked Scottish salmon on the side. It was pouring rain throughout our journey.

When we arrived at the air base, the young lady identified our car to a uniformed guard and then there emerged from the sentry box a faceless gentleman in dark civilian clothes, wearing a most proper bowler hat. He tipped the bowler to "Mr. Dennis" as he entered the back seat, deplored the unpleasant weather and then asked for my passport. Per previous instructions I opened it to the visa page—which did not show either my name or photograph—and he meticulously affixed an official stamp attesting that I had just left Great Britain. We drove ahead through the base and a few minutes later were at the side of a waiting American C-45. I quit the car with my bag. The young British lady waved through the rain and cheerily said, "God bless, Mr. Dennis." The faceless gentleman again tipped his bowler.

Captain MacArthur of the U.S. Air Force introduced himself and we took off immediately. "Mr. Dennis" was the only passenger. Over a breakfast of coffee and doughnuts, the Captain explained that because of foul weather our flight would have to be around Amsterdam to an air force base at Wiesbaden, West Germany. I passed the next three hours reading a newly published book, *My Life in Court,* by an American lawyer named Nizer.

We refueled at Wiesbaden, had sandwiches and coffee in the

plane, and then through the most miserable fog and sleet we made a two-hour flight along the narrow Corridor leading through East Germany to Berlin. We finally skidded into Tempelhof Airdrome, where our plane was met by an American named Bob, who had a small car parked nearby. By now it was snowing heavily. No one seemed to object as we quickly drove away.

We rode in silence to a darkened private house in a residential section of West Berlin. We entered, lighted the living room, closed the blinds, took off our snow-covered clothes and for the first time faced each other in clear light.

"Greetings," he said. "I'm sorry not to have talked much during our drive but I thought that after your flight from London you'd like to settle down and relax before we had a chat." He was tall, good-looking, around forty and had a quiet air of assurance.

"You'll live here alone. Every morning a safe German maid will come, fix your breakfast and make the bed upstairs. We've tried to make your life comfortable and you'll find everything from American cigarettes and twelve-year-old Scotch to current magazines.

"Suppose you unpack and relax for a few hours. I'll come by later, to take you out for dinner."

Three hours later we had an excellent meal together in a side-street restaurant. We talked about everything except my mission. Later we drove over to the Berlin Hilton hotel, crowded with commercial travelers, and Bob showed me its dimly lighted Golden City Bar. As we rode home through the snow, he explained that after my trip to East Berlin the next day I should call him from the Hilton at an unlisted telephone number which I was to memorize. The number, he said, would be manned day and night for this sole purpose while I remained in Berlin.

Back at my empty home I found my way upstairs and went to sleep in a cold bed, thinking of the warmth and music in Claridge's the night before.

Saturday, February 3

I awoke literally stiff with cold. Outside there was sleet falling upon the snow, with that depressing gloom that can shroud Berlin in unpleasant weather. However, my immediate concern was the frozen bedroom.

It took me an hour to analyze the mechanics of the house and the Germanic thrift which had dictated its building plans. It had two separate heating plants, one for downstairs and one upstairs, so that neither would be unnecessarily used. During the day, no occupant with common sense should waste fuel by warming the bedrooms; during the night, there was no reason for heat in the living room; by German logic, only a blockhead would keep all the house warm all the time, however extreme might be the winter in Berlin. To assure the efficiency of this diabolically clever scheme, the entrance foyer had two separate doors inside—one opening into the living room and the other into a stairway which led to the bedchambers above. The night before, Bob and I had neglected to turn on the upstairs heat, although the temperature was near zero.

I soon found I had developed a cold which settled in my back; it felt like pleurisy. When Bob arrived we ascertained I had no temperature and he promised liniment. We agreed it would be complicated for me to be examined by either an American Army or a German civilian doctor. We tried to picture—and quietly cursed—the dour German burgher who had built the house and now probably was sunning himself on a beach in Argentina.

Before Bob came I had taken a walk and found an old Catholic church. I was in time for eight o'clock Mass. The darkened church had few at the service, perhaps because of the weather. There were almost no young people, I noticed. Most were women and several old men wore black armbands, presumably for sons lost in World War II. The church was almost as cold as my bedroom.

After a good breakfast at the house, served by the silent German maid, Bob explained with maps the only routes still open through the Wall. The plan selected for my journey today was simple. The S-Bahn, or elevated railway, left West Berlin and passed over the Wall, allowing passengers to get off at Friedrichstrasse in East Berlin. It was, Bob said, a trip made daily by a few East German workmen with approved permits and even fewer "neutral" visitors. Once I left the train, I would use my own discretion in getting past the East German border guards and making my way to the Soviet Embassy on Unter den Linden. Bob explained that conditions at the East German border varied from day to day and could not be predicted. Occasionally the guards would refuse to permit any visitors; at other times they would subject them to interminable delays, perhaps accompanied by stripping and searching each person.

We drove through a snowstorm to the S-Bahn station in West Berlin, where I bought a round-trip ticket (for good luck, I told Bob). I climbed the stairs and boarded the first train.

I recorded the details of the trip in my formal report to Washington written late that night. Upon my return each evening I went to the Golden City Bar, called the unlisted number and would be joined by Bob. I meanwhile would have written in longhand a brief summary of the day. He would drive me home, send the summary to Washington at once, and after dinner would bring a stenographer to whom I dictated a detailed report. All the following "dailies" are excerpts from such reports. Other details are from my diaries.

At about 1115 hours I entered the S-Bahnhof at the Zoo station and took the train for a twenty-minute trip to Friedrichstrasse. On the way we passed over "the Wall," which was heavily patrolled by uniformed police (locally known as VOPOs, an abbreviation of their official titles). All were armed with carbines and side arms. In most places on the East Berlin side, dynamite and bulldozers had leveled the ground for almost two hundred yards behind the barbed wire.

At Friedrichstrasse I was permitted to pass by the first uniformed guard to have my passport inspected, but when I rounded a corner through a roped corridor I found approximately a hundred people herded in lines and waiting for passport clearance. After ten minutes only one or two persons had been processed for entry and the delay seemed to be deliberate.

Since it was almost 1130 hours I left my place in the line and marched up to the nearest VOPO. Glowering, I loudly told him in German that I had an appointment at 1200 hours at the Soviet Embassy. He clicked his heels and promptly escorted me to the head of the line.

Two uniformed customs officials questioned me as to how much money I carried. I showed them (20 West German marks). In reply to another inquiry, I stated that I was staying at the Hilton-Berlin hotel; this was per instructions from Bob. They finally had me sign a printed card containing my answers, which they called my "visa" and attached to my passport. There was no further interference and I was permitted to go out of the station into the biting cold of East Berlin.

I last had been in Berlin in the summer and fall of 1945. We had borrowed a Navy photography crew from Capt. John Ford's Field Photographic Unit in OSS. It was headed by Commander Ray Kellogg and included Budd Schulberg, his brother Stu and a dozen other Hollywood professionals. Our mission was to assemble captured Nazi films and other visual evidence which could be used in evidence at the war crimes trials in Nuremberg. The city of Berlin then was demolished and barren, as though starkly sketched by Goya. Hungry, despondent Berliners stayed off the streets out of fear of the Russian troops. The latter included a Mongolian regiment brought in to terrorize the Germans. We lived in a Berlin villa in the Wannsee region, surrounded by a special detail of United States infantry to guard against Russian deserters. Our bedroom ceilings were thick with huge flies, swollen from feasting on the bodies of dead soldiers floating in the Wannsee.

In February, 1962, East Berlin appeared to be unchanged. As far as one could see in any direction, the buildings were in ruins or disrepair. Shell holes were still in the sides of crumbling walls. The streets were strangely deserted and seemed filled with an oppressive fear. It was as though the Russians had decided in 1945 that East Berlin should continue a living death so the Germans would never forget.

Through the falling snow I made my way to Unter den Linden. As I rounded one deserted corner, there suddenly appeared a group of ten or twelve youths, in shabby trench coats or heavy turtleneck sweaters and without hats. Some had cigarettes dangling from their lips. They looked like a pack of wolves. I straightened up and with the grim face of an East German or Soviet official who needed only his attaché case for a weapon I walked through them. It seemed like a long minute. Later I learned that such gangs of homeless youths were wandering the streets of East Berlin night and day. They were scavengers, and West Berliners believed they were tolerated by the Soviet so that occasionally they could be used for violence; afterward their actions could be characterized as "hooliganism" for which there was no official responsibility.

When I reached Unter den Linden, I was appalled. Looking up and down what had been one of the great boulevards of the world, I could see almost nothing but desolation. A few stragglers trudged through the snow. I remembered when I had stayed on the avenue in a gay hotel, in the summer of 1936 during the Olympic Games. Germany had been at the height of a false elation upon regaining a position of world power, and few promenading then on Unter den Linden could have foreseen its ruins.

I located the Soviet Embassy but a receptionist, after checking, informed me in excellent English that I must proceed next door to the Consulate where my meeting would take place. I walked there, rang the bell and opened a formidable door.

"How do you do," said a smiling young woman in the foyer. "I am the daughter of Rudolf Abel. This is my mother, Frau Abel, and her cousin Herr Dreeves."

I shook hands with all three but said nothing. The "daughter" was around thirty-five years old, spoke English fluently and appeared to be very sharp. I took her to be Slavic. "Frau Abel" looked to be about sixty and a typical housewife. She reminded me of a German character actress. "Cousin Dreeves" never spoke, only grinned. He was a lean, hard-looking man about fifty-five; he kept closing and opening powerful hands and I mentally classified him as an Otto the Strangler type. He probably was from the East German police. All were shabbily dressed.

After a few minutes of silence, I was lighting a cigarette when Frau Abel abruptly rose and faced me. "How is my poor husband Rudolf?" she cried in broken English. When I said "fine," she burst into convulsive sobs which continued for several minutes. The daughter kept patting her on the back, while the cousin fetched her a glass of water. I sat there impassively.

"Why," suddenly asked the daughter, "was the last letter from my father on different stationery from his others, and why were both his last letter and your own postmarked Washington?"

After a moment I said, "My letter was mailed from Washington so it would not go through my law office. I wanted to prevent any chance of a leak. As for your father, I sent him a letter telling him about my trip to Berlin but at my request it wasn't delivered in the usual way. It was read to him in the warden's office at Atlanta. This was to eliminate any rumors among the other prison inmates, and his reply was forwarded to Washington to be mailed." The daughter seemed satisfied.

"Can you make the exchange?" asked the wife, again as though speaking a rehearsed line in a foreign movie.

"This very day," I said, "if everyone is reasonable and acts in good faith."

"How does my father get along in prison?" the daughter asked.

"He never looked better," I said. "It's a nice sort of prison and he has an artist's studio in which he paints all day long."

"Even a golden cage is a cage," observed the daughter, at which Frau Abel again burst into sobs. I began to wonder when this old-fashioned melodrama would end.

During our wait of about fifteen minutes, I smoked several cigarettes. Twice the daughter said loudly, "I would like a cigarette." I made no offer either time and Dreeves then would furnish her one. Each time she then would say, "I need a light" and when I again made no move Dreeves would light her cigarette.

At exactly 1200 hours a door to the anteroom opened, and there entered a tall, well-proportioned, neatly dressed man with rimless glasses. He introduced himself to all, with a self-confident air, as Ivan Alexandrovich Schischkin, second secretary of the Soviet Embassy.

"Do you speak German?" he asked me in English.

"Very poorly," I replied.

"Good," he said. "We both will do better in English."

He invited us into a private conference room, where he seated himself behind a desk and waved us to sit down. There were exactly enough chairs. From the time we entered the room until we left an hour later no one of the so-called family spoke a word, except that the daughter said "Yes" when asked if the family could return the following Monday for a second meeting. Schischkin accepted them as a star of the stage might regard necessary props.

I began by explaining to Schischkin that I was a lawyer in private practice, with many pressing matters, and that I had come at considerable sacrifice of personal time. I explained that I was required to earn a livelihood for my family and therefore could not stay in Berlin very long. I accordingly would require a prompt answer to my proposals.

"Of course," replied Schischkin, "I understand completely." His English was impeccable.

He asked me how I had reached Berlin from New York and whether the inclement weather had caused difficulties. I told him my normal law practice required an annual visit to London and that I had arrived there by commercial airliner. After a few days I had left for Berlin on a special military flight provided by my government. I added that my transportation and devious route to Berlin had been planned so that my whereabouts would be unknown except to a few high government officials.

"Where are you staying in West Berlin?" he asked. I told him that the United States Mission had provided a billet in a private house but I did not know its address or location.

"Secretary Schischkin," I said, "I have come to Berlin for only one reason. An East German lawyer named Wolfgang Vogel sent me a message that Mrs. Abel believed that if I could arrange the release of her husband, this would free Powers, the American student, Pryor, held in East Germany and the American student Makinen now in prison in Kiev. Upon this understanding I have obtained a pledge from my government that we will deliver Abel to any point you designate in Berlin, within forty-eight hours after an agreement is reached."

Schischkin drummed his fingers on the desk. I then passed him the letter from the Pardon Attorney in the Department of Justice. He read it carefully, placed it to one side and said, "Very vague." I replied that any lack of detail in the letter was deliberate so as to avoid loose talk by stenographers which might result in a "news leak." I then sat back in my chair.

After a pause Schischkin removed the rimless glasses, began to polish them and said, "Over a year ago these Abel people came to my office in the Consulate, because they are East Germans. I heard their story and told them I would intercede with the Soviet government, to see whether Powers might be exchanged for Abel. I later received a favorable reply from Moscow, because certain Fascist factions in the United States have sought to link this East German Abel with the Soviet Union. This falsehood has been a source of anti-Soviet propaganda in the United States. We would like to see this eliminated, in order to promote greater understanding between our two countries.

"However, as to these American students Pryor and Makinen, I have never even heard of their cases. You now have introduced a new matter and I would be wholly unauthorized to discuss it with you."

I expressed my amazement. The only reason for my trip to Berlin was the message from Vogel, supposedly quoting Mrs. Abel, I said. If Schischkin was not prepared to discuss this proposal, I would have no instructions from my government and could only return home.

"You would have *no* further instructions?" asked Schischkin quizzically.

"None," I said. "On the other hand, I would like to tell you of the preparations which have been made to deliver Abel here if Vogel's promise is carried out.

"I will communicate our agreement to Washington. Abel immediately will be sent here by military aircraft, accompanied by the United States Deputy Director of Prisons. He will be carrying a Presidential commutation of sentence, already executed by President Kennedy but requiring counter-signature by the Deputy Director. This will be done at the place of exchange (we suggest the Glienicke Bridge) after I attest that we are receiving the right men. A man to identify Powers is already in Berlin; the family of Pryor are here, as you may know; and persons who know Makinen are readily available. All that is needed is your agreement and Abel will be released to you."

Schischkin listened intently. Then he said, "Are you sure that such a document has already been signed by President Kennedy?"

"Absolutely," I replied. "It of course carries a condition that Abel can never re-enter the United States, on penalty that his present sentence would be reinstated.

"I would like to add another thought. Such an exchange has been advocated in our press for some while, and in my personal judgment, if you want Abel released now is the time to act. If we delay, the favorable climate could be changed by an international incident or our domestic politics."

"Do you believe," said Schischkin thoughtfully, "that these views you last expressed also represent the views of the United States government?"

"Definitely," I said.

Schischkin stated again that he was troubled by the fact that I carried no credentials except the "vague" letter from the Pardon Attorney. I told him that if required I could forward to him further

388

credentials from our Chief of Mission in West Berlin. "However," I said, "I would think it rather obvious that no busy private citizen would travel thousands of miles on such a mission if he lacked proper authorization."

I further displayed considerable annoyance that the matter was not being concluded then and there.

"After coming over here at personal sacrifice," I said, "if Vogel misled me with lies I feel strongly he is a downright rascal who should be severely punished by the proper authorities."

"I understand your point of view," Schischkin replied, "but under all these circumstances it is impossible to discuss your proposals today. I shall have to communicate with my government."

I suddenly turned upon Mrs. Abel and said angrily, "Vogel said you told him to make these statements. Was he telling the truth or not?" The woman looked frightened and bewildered, but remained silent.

Schischkin quickly interrupted: "There is nothing further to say now. However, I will state that I believe you are properly annoyed."

Schischkin then said he wished to keep for the present the letter from the Pardon Attorney. I asked whether he could not photostat it and let me retain the original.

"I am a Soviet Embassy official," answered Schischkin testily. "If I agree to return it, there should be no question in your mind."

I acquiesced and then suggested that in view of my pressing time schedule, we could adjourn the meeting while I obtained lunch somewhere in East Berlin. He meanwhile could radio Moscow for their agreement and we could conclude the matter later in the afternoon.

"This is Saturday," he replied. "To work in the manner you suggest would be entirely too fast. Couldn't you return here next Monday at five o'clock?"

I said yes, but that I could not remain long after Monday, reminding him that I required forty-eight hours to produce Abel. Meanwhile, if he should receive word from Moscow before Monday he could communicate with me through a West Berlin telephone number. I wrote down Bob's unlisted number on a card and passed it to him. He asked whether the number would be answered at night and on Sunday. I told him it would be answered at any time during my stay in Berlin. My government recognized that my time was valuable and had extended this courtesy to facilitate my task.

Schischkin then said reflectively to me, "So it is three for one they want."

I observed with a smile, "One artist is always worth more than three mechanics." With a smug look at my reference to Abel, he returned my smile.

"I should like to express a personal opinion," I said. "With the Abels now claiming East German citizenship, and Pryor being held by the East Germans, surely Pryor's release should ease any difficulty in Soviet Russia's explaining publicly what otherwise might seem to be undue concern for the East German citizen Abel." He nodded thoughtfully, as though this might be a new consideration.

Schischkin asked me whether I had had any trouble entering East Berlin. I told him how I had come and said my sole difficulty was the crowd at the railroad station. If I returned, I would appreciate his eliminating this annoyance. He said that such crowds were usually present only on Saturdays but if I regarded it as important he could arrange for special privileges. Why did not my government make a car available to me, which could cross through "Checkpoint Charlie"? I explained that I had traveled by the worker route so as to be unobtrusive and avoid the press. He seemed satisfied with this answer.

I offered Schischkin my professional card and, to be friendly, also gave him my card as vice-president of the Board of Education of the City of New York. He looked at it carefully and then commented, "This is very good work." I asked him for his card and he said with surprise, "Is that necessary?" I replied, "No, but desirable." He then gave me his engraved card, which I pocketed. We shook hands and I left the office, with "the Abel family" trailing after me. The conference had lasted an hour.

Once in the street, the so-called daughter said to me, "Don't you wish to see Herr Vogel?" I answered that this would be determined by the Soviet Embassy in due course. She then said, "Pryor is an East German matter and I don't see why this should involve my father."

"Vogel got me to come over here," I said, "supposedly on the authorization of your mother. If his message was false and unauthorized, he brought me over on a false alarm and he'd better stay out of my way."

She laughed and added, "If it's that much of a false alarm, he'd better stay out of our way, too!" They left me at the next corner, the daughter explaining they were staying in an East Berlin hotel.

I returned via the S-Bahn but with considerably more difficulty. My credentials were examined three or four times by armed police at various checkpoints in the station. There was little human traffic going west. At one point they kept my passport about ten minutes, dropping it into a slot in the wall of a booth for inspection. I waited in an anteroom and found a collection of East German and Soviet propaganda booklets on a shelf. I took two of each. When I finally was cleared, there was an hour's wait for a train.

Coming back over "the Wall," I saw heavily armed police posted along the elevated railway tracks, watching through binoculars for possible escapees. Several were women. Since a canal separates East and West Berlin at this point, which a refugee would have to swim after clearing the East Berlin barbed-wire fences, escape seemed most unlikely. Darkness was falling and searchlights from the East German side had begun to play upon the canal as we passed over it.

Sunday, February 4

I slept late in the morning, warmed by the strong liniment which Bob had produced for my aching back. I went to Mass in the nearby church, which was far better attended than yesterday. The weather, however, was still miserable. The night before, I had dictated my first detailed report, and the draft was delivered to me in the afternoon. I devoted considerable time to correcting it.

Bob brought me some newspapers in English, and the maid came by to cook a roast chicken in German style. It was almost like any quiet Sunday at home.

Monday, February 5

At 1700 hours (5 P.M.) I returned to East Berlin and the Soviet Embassy. This time there was no line awaiting entry at the border, and I had little difficulty making my way through the controls.

Crossing the Wall, I noticed on the East Berlin side various observation towers and machine-gun emplacements. With the vigilant guards on the elevated railway tracks, one might have thought they were fearful of an invasion, instead of an exodus. All railroad police and the guards at Friedrichstrasse station carried black hip holsters of a size and shape indicating a weapon equivalent to our snub-nosed .38 pistol. Except for a few supervisory officers, the guards appeared to be young peasants less than twenty years of age.

On the way to the Embassy at Unter den Linden, the only persons apparently at ease on the streets were those in uniform, especially Soviet Army officers. I walked up the deserted Unter den Linden toward Brandenburger Tor, remembering it in other days. The top of the monument to German military triumphs apparently was being used as an observation post. One could not get within more than a thousand yards of it, because of rope barriers with large VERBOTEN signs. I saw no evidence of heavy armor, such as tanks or bodies of troops, at any time in the entire district. Yet an unmistakable atmosphere of military occupation prevailed.

The Soviet Embassy was a large, white stone building with handsome classical lines and was in the shape of a shallow U. To the left was the Embassy entrance, while across the courtyard was a similar entrance to the Consulate. The front of the building was patrolled by Soviet Army sentries. A bell had to be pressed at the front door for admission to either the Embassy or the Consulate. When the receptionist admitted me, I would enter a foyer filled with Soviet propaganda; on the Embassy side there were photomurals of recent public demonstrations in Moscow, principally featuring Khrushchev.

In both buildings there were a number of doors from the anterooms, and mousy officials continually bustled in and out, carrying files. All Embassy personnel to whom I spoke, including the receptionists, appeared to be fluent in Russian, German and English. Their demeanor would be described as "correct," but I noticed that an air of superiority was used to keep German visitors in their proper place.

The center section of the entire building appeared to be dominated by a large hall or dining room; from the street there could be seen an enormous stained-glass window with elaborate decorations surrounding a hammer and sickle. The building was four stories high.

This afternoon I entered the Consulate shortly before the appointed time. In the anteroom were Miss Abel and Cousin Dreeves, who gave me one of his less attractive grins. At my request Miss Abel spelled the cousin's name, which was "Drews" (pronounced "Dreeves" in German). She informed me her mother had remained in their hotel room because she had been "very nervous" since our meeting Saturday.

"Have you received any good news?" she asked. I replied that this was a matter to be discussed only in the presence of Secretary Schischkin.

Schischkin suddenly appeared. He bowed stiffly to Miss Abel and Drews but cordially shook my hand. He then requested me to join him in a private conference in the inner office. He completely ignored my companions.

I presented to him a brief note from Alan Lightner, chief of the United States Mission to West Berlin, which stated I was authorized to travel to East Berlin in connection with business at the Soviet Embassy and that Lightner had been fully informed of the purpose of my trip to Berlin. The letter was on the stationery of the U. S. Foreign Service and was signed by Lightner as American Minister.

Schischkin remained standing and read the note aloud with care. Then he said, "While I never doubted your integrity during our meeting on Saturday, one must be careful about such things." I stated that in addition to meeting Mr. Lightner that morning I also had been introduced to his deputy, Mr. Howard Trivers, who believed that he had met Schischkin. Schischkin replied that he had no recollection of ever meeting Mr. Trivers although from time to time he did have "some dealings with Americans."

"More to the point," he said, "did you report on our last meeting to your government? What instructions have you received?"

"I reported at once," I replied, "and my only instructions were to return today in accordance with your request and hear what further message, if any, you have received from your government."

Schischkin sat down at the desk and then very formally opened a large leather portfolio, stating that he had received instructions from Moscow. In answer to my inquiry, he said there would be no objection to my recording the note verbatim. He then proceeded to read the following:

1. The Soviet Government has humane feelings and in this spirit agrees to exchange Powers for Abel.
2. This humane action on both sides and the elimination of a permanent source of anti-Soviet propaganda should contribute to better relations between our countries.
3. If the American Government is interested in the freeing of Makinen, who is now in Kiev, the Soviet Government is ready to exchange Abel for Makinen but a simultaneous exchange of both Powers and Makinen for Abel is impossible. It is up to the Americans to make their choice. If the matter is properly concluded and better relations result, further developments could occur.
4. As to the case of Pryor, this matter is out of the province of the

Soviet authorities and must be accomplished through the East German Government. This can be done through Mrs. Abel and her attorney Vogel, who already have communicated to Donovan that their petition has received favorable consideration by the East German Government.

Schischkin then stated that he had no further instructions. Mrs. Abel and I should proceed to devise a plan to effectuate the exchange, which the Soviet then would consider. Schischkin would say, however, as to the American suggestion of Glienicke Bridge (which I had mentioned at the last meeting), "Not bad."

I told him that I was most interested in the reference to Marvin Makinen. Could I assume that in the event the other releases were carried out, and better international relations resulted, the U.S.S.R. would grant clemency to Makinen in the early future? Schischkin said that he could not confirm my interpretation at the time but would make appropriate inquiry.

I told Schischkin I would communicate this counterproposal to my government and hoped to return with a reply within twenty-four hours. Schischkin suggested that in view of my sore back (which had been quite noticeable) it would be unnecessary for me to return in person. He suggested I send my government's reply through diplomatic courier to the Soviet Embassy.

Having delivered the formal message, Schischkin relaxed and in a conversational manner asked whether I had volunteered to defend Abel. I explained that Abel did not make the usual request that counsel be "assigned by the court" but rather, that the court assign "counsel recommended by the Bar Association." I told him that this had displeased the Federal judge, whose reaction was that Abel did not trust him. Schischkin smiled appreciatively.

He asked about my compensation in the matter. I explained that I had agreed with Abel on a fee of ten thousand dollars for the defense, and that I had had donated the entire amount to three universities. Schischkin commented that this was a "most commendable" action on my part.

"Tell me," I said, "why you permit the Embassy here to be surrounded by wrecked buildings and shell-shattered walls, unrepaired since World War II."

"We have not deemed it advisable," he replied, "to eliminate from Berlin all the ravages of war. Accordingly, we have made no effort to do it and have no intention of doing it in the immediate future."

I spoke of my last visit to Berlin in 1945 in connection with the Nuremberg Trials, while I was still in the Navy. Schischkin immediately wished to know my rank. When I said "Commander" he repeated it after me and seemed impressed.

I mentioned Marshal Nikichenko, who had sat in uniform as the Soviet military judge in the principal trial of Goering, von Ribbentrop, Kaltenbrunner, Streicher, etc. I had met Nikichenko many times during the London negotiation of the Axis War Crimes Treaty and later during the trial in Nuremberg. Schischkin said he knew Nikichenko by reputation, but hastily added he was not a lawyer.

When I rose to leave, he noticed that I did so with considerable discomfort and asked whether the muscular cold in my back had improved. When I said it had not, he laughingly told me he would recommend a medical prescription of "either cognac or vodka." I suggested that vodka would be preferable since it would not produce an alcoholic breath, and he agreed. I told him a current New York City story about the bank president who sent a memorandum to his vice-presidents which stated:

All vice-presidents who have been drinking vodka martinis at lunchtime are requested hereafter to drink plain whiskey. This bank would prefer to have its afternoon customers regard our officers as drunk rather than stupid.

Schischkin seemed to enjoy this very much and on this note escorted me back to the anteroom.

Outside the Embassy, Miss Abel and Cousin Drews inquired

as to what had transpired. I gave them a summary and Miss Abel said, "We must go immediately to see Herr Vogel, who has promised to remain in his office to see us." When I asked why Vogel could not have joined us at the Embassy, she stated that he had so many clients he could not leave his office. She kept referring to the office as his "bureau" in the French manner.

We hailed a cab and during the half-hour trip Miss Abel and I discussed possible procedures for the exchange. We finally agreed tentatively to establish Glienicke Bridge on Wednesday night, February 7, at ten o'clock. In the event of bad flying weather or any other contingency delaying the arrival of one of the prisoners, the meeting would be postponed to the following night, same place and time.

We finally arrived at Vogel's office and Cousin Drews paid the fare. When I left the cab and looked around in the semi-darkness, I was puzzled. Vogel's office seemed strangely situated for a supposedly prominent lawyer in any country. It was at 113 Alt-Friedrichsfelde, in what appeared to be a second-rate residential neighborhood. The building was set back some 75 yards from the sidewalk, with overgrown vacant land in front. The structure was recently constructed; it had two stories and was square with brick facing. As we approached, I noticed that the ground floor seemingly consisted of cheap living quarters, with thin blankets covering the windows instead of shades or curtains. We walked to the rear and opened a side door, with Miss Abel leading the way and Cousin Drews following me.

The entrance was poorly lighted. I made out a flight of stairs leading up a narrow hallway, with absolutely bare walls on either side. It seemed so unlike the approach to the office of any attorney that with Cousin Drews behind me as we climbed the stairs I grew apprehensive and looked over my shoulder once or twice. At such moments one is comforted by the thought that there is no point in worry since there is no place to run.

At the head of the stairs, Miss Abel pressed a buzzer and we were admitted to a small anteroom, which led to an even smaller waiting room. Several people were sitting there when we entered, but rose quickly and left. In a few minutes Herr Vogel appeared and ushered us into his own small but well-furnished office. He was about thirty-seven years old, dark-haired and good-looking with an ever-quick flashing smile. He wore a hand-tailored gray flannel suit, a white-on-white shirt, a figured silk tie with matching breast kerchief and elaborate cuff links. He looked like many successful sales executives in the United States.

Vogel immediately inquired in German whether I spoke that language well and I replied in English, "Very poorly." (In various ways during the day it was indicated they all believed I knew more conversational German than I would admit.) To my surprise, Cousin Drews volunteered to act as interpreter and translated for Vogel my summary of the developments in Schischkin's office. Vogel nodded and said he was pleased to present to me an official communication from the Attorney General of the East German Republic. This was in German and read:

> It is hereby certified that the petition for release of your client to American authorities can be granted if the conditions known to you are met by the Americans.
>
> Attorney General:
> Official: Windlisch
> State Attorney.

The message was obviously patterned after the letter from the United States Pardon Attorney which I had presented to Schischkin at our first meeting and which he had dismissed as "vague." I wondered for a moment how State Attorney Windlisch had seen the Pardon Attorney's letter.

The message was dated 5 February 1962 and was presented to me only in the original German. Drews said he could not translate it literally but could summarize it in layman's language. I asked for a photostat of the original, as well as an exact translation in

English. Vogel replied that they had no reproduction facilities and, after summoning a secretary, informed me that while she could translate the letter into French or Italian no one in the office could give an English rendering. At my request he did have the girl type a copy of the original German document, which he personally certified in writing as correct.

After some discussion of the letter, with Miss Abel indicating her pleasure that all barriers to the exchange had been removed, I told Vogel that in order to make my own plans I wanted a simple answer to a simple question: If the tentative plan for the Wednesday night exchange were approved by all concerned, did Vogel now guarantee that the East Germans would produce Pryor at the same time and place for the tripartite exchange? "Definitely yes," replied Vogel.

I then stated that I wished to be informed of his current status as attorney for the Pryor family. To avoid complications or prematurely raising their hopes, the Pryors should not be told of my presence in Berlin or the current negotiations. Vogel said he expected Mr. Pryor at his office the next day and would tell him whatever I suggested. I said he should tell Mr. Pryor his petition to the East German government was progressing as favorably as could be expected, and that if all went well Vogel might have a decision as early as the coming Friday. Vogel so agreed. I told him I would promptly notify my government of the entire day's developments and would send my reply to both Schischkin and Vogel before noon the next day (Tuesday).

Throughout the meeting I was reserved but friendly. Because of an indication in a message from Washington that they believed I had been very strong in censuring Vogel's conduct during the Schischkin meeting on Saturday, I made no reference now to Vogel's broken promises. At the conclusion of the conference, Vogel called us a taxi and we all shook hands with him as we left. At the head of the stairs I politely beckoned to Cousin Drews to precede me. He did.

Miss Abel and Drews accompanied me to the Friedrichstrasse station in the taxi. On the way, Miss Abel repeatedly inquired about my reaction to the day's developments, saying that her mother would be "anxious to learn the news." I told her that I honestly could not forecast the reaction of my government, because of Vogel's representation to us that he could deliver all three Americans in exchange for Abel. However, I said that if the promises made during the day were carried out in good faith and promptly, it was not beyond belief that my government would accept these terms.

I explained to her that since my government was anxious to aid all three Americans, it would continue to remain disturbed so long as any one of them was retained in custody. She said our government should remember that the East German authorities had stated that if Pryor were tried he would receive either a death sentence or a long term of years. I told her that while Powers was a primary and basic objective of my mission, this did not mean that at any time would our government abandon either of the other two Americans and that we would try to protect their interests to the maximum extent possible. At the Friedrichstrasse station Miss Abel and Drews left me.

I again negotiated the East German border controls, but this time they detained my passport at the primary checkpoint for a much longer period of time. Returning on the train with me was an odd assemblage of people: some poorly clad German workers, a young Chinese, a well-dressed Balkan professorial type with a spade beard, and a drunken Cockney right out of Piccadilly in a blue trench coat, accompanied by a shifty-eyed young German. From my arrival at the Zoo stop, I went directly to the Hilton Hotel, arriving at about 7:10 P.M. When I called Bob, he said they had been very concerned over my late return.

After dinner in a quiet café I returned home and prepared for bed. Suddenly Bob arrived. A message for me had been received on the unlisted West Berlin telephone number I had given only to Schischkin. It came from a West Berlin phone booth, with a man speaking in German:

400

Unexpected difficulties have arisen. Must speak with you urgently in my office at 11 A.M. tomorrow, 6 February.

Vogel.

Bob and I discussed the implications of the message. We both were suspicious. I felt strongly that if I returned to East Berlin the next day I should not visit Vogel but unexpectedly confront Schischkin with the message and demand an explanation. Bob agreed, so notified Washington and they approved the gambit late that night.

Tuesday, February 6

At 1000 hours I went back to East Berlin by the usual route and rang the doorbell of the Soviet Consulate. A harsh voice in German demanded my business and repeated this in a shout, but I could not understand where the voice came from. I finally found that it was from a slot above the doorbell and I said, "I would like to see Mr. Schischkin." After a pause, the voice said, "Do you speak English?" I said loudly, "I have been speaking it and I want to see Mr. Schischkin." A buzzer opened the door and I entered.

In the anteroom I found an African Negro, in a round astrakhan fur hat and wearing a coat with an astrakhan collar, stretched out sound asleep on a line of chairs. Shortly thereafter, the doorkeeper appeared and after telling me that I must wait he shook the African rather rudely, addressing him in a strange tongue. The African sat up but remained there, with hat and coat on, so long as I stayed. I found some new Communist propaganda in English on a desk and took two copies of everything.

About fifteen minutes later, Schischkin entered the room. He apologized for delaying me but expressed surprise at my "unexpected visit." He invited me into the private office. I then informed him that after leaving his office yesterday, in accordance with his suggestion I had accompanied Miss Abel and her cousin to the law offices of Vogel. I described the visit, showed him the letter from the

401

Attorney General of East Germany, and said that upon my return to West Berlin I had reported fully to Washington. I told him my report stated that although our government had been led to expect Powers, Makinen and Pryor in exchange for Abel, I would recommend acceptance of the present offer of Powers and Pryor since I believed from the Moscow message given me by Schischkin that with the improvement of relations between the United States and the Soviet, clemency for Makinen could be expected in the near future. Schischkin nodded. I said that subsequently my government had advised me of their willingness to accept the Soviet offer of Powers and Pryor for Abel, with our understanding that Makinen soon would be separately released.

Finally I told Schischkin of the mysterious telephone message from Vogel late the night before and how, when reported to Washington, it had disrupted all plans. I handed Schischkin a copy of the message and he said, "How very strange a message! What does it mean?" I said that this was one of my objects in visiting Schischkin this morning, since the message had come via the telephone number which I had given only to him, at our first meeting last Saturday.

"The Abel family were present when you gave it to me," said Schischkin blandly.

"The number was written by me on a card which I passed directly to you," I reminded him.

"Some people have sharp eyes," replied Schischkin.

I said I trusted that the Soviet had no intention of withdrawing the position expressed the day before in the message from Moscow. Relying on this in good faith I had completed arrangements with Vogel and Miss Abel, had recommended the plan to Washington and they had approved it. I added that everything was now in readiness to transport Abel to Berlin for the exchange.

Schischkin sat back in his chair and stated quite solemnly that the Soviet government was not in the habit of changing an expressed position. He now wished to reaffirm their willingness to

402

trade Powers for Abel, but to reiterate that the matter of Pryor was beyond the authority of the Soviet government.

"However," he said, "I wish to make a few personal observations. You tell me now for the first time that you have arranged with the East German government to release Pryor in return for your releasing Abel. Before that, you agreed with my government to release Abel in exchange for Powers. It seems to me you are like a trader who is trying to sell the same merchandise to two different buyers and is asking both for payment."

"That's ridiculous and you know it," I said. "I have been accepting your stated position that any action by the East German government is wholly beyond your authority or control. East Germany is granting clemency to Pryor in recognition of two facts: that the Soviet is releasing Powers because of its 'humane feelings' and the United States is responding by freeing Abel. In view of your government's stated position of the independence of East Germany, why is it any of your concern what the East Germans—or any other independent government—may decide to do in recognition of the commendable Soviet-U.S. accord? If for 'humane feelings' the East Germans decide to release Pryor or a herd of sheep, on the same bridge and at the same time as the Powers-Abel exchange, how is this a matter which concerns you or your government?"

Schischkin almost smiled, but made no answer.

"Let me make one thing clear," I continued. "If the deal we agreed on yesterday is now being repudiated, I will advise my government immediately. I can't state their position for them, but my personal recommendation will be that I return to New York and we abandon all negotiations on the matter."

Schischkin digested this for a moment and then said, "In my judgment, because of the message you have received from Vogel, you should go to his office at once. After you talk matters over with him, please feel free to return here later today if you wish." I asked him if he could not telephone Vogel and have him come to the Soviet Embassy, to expedite matters. He was sorry, Schischkin replied, but while he occasionally saw the Minister of Justice of East Germany on official business, it would be highly improper for a Soviet official to interview a private East German lawyer.

"I know from past experience that I should have an interpreter with me when I talk with Vogel," I said, "and you could be of great value in that way at a meeting here. Moreover, I would have to taxi alone to his office and couldn't pay the fare, since I have only a few West German marks and they are illegal currency over here."

Schischkin replied that he personally would be unable to act as an interpreter but that he was sure I would experience no difficulty. With respect to my finances, he said I should take a taxi and pay the driver in West German marks, since "although they are illegal, they will be gratefully accepted."

After a futile fifteen minutes waiting for a taxi outside the Embassy, I walked through snowdrifts to the Friedrichstrasse station and found a cab. We drove to Vogel's office, the taxi driver silently accepting my West German marks. At the office I found Drews alone. He explained that Miss Abel would not attend. She was upset over the latest difficulties reported by Vogel and moreover was "taking care of her mother."

Drews commenced to read a lengthy statement in English, which he said had been prepared by Miss Abel. I interrupted and suggested that I read and take the statement with me. Vogel objected and accordingly I said that I must copy the statement. The document, handwritten in English on cheap, lined paper read as follows:

Last night after we had departed I was summoned by Mr. Vogel and he told me bad news.

Mr. Vogel saw somebody from the office of the Attorney General and when he mentioned about your words that you had secured the consent of the Soviet Union for an exchange of someone else, that official was greatly surprised. He stressed the point that originally they agreed to the exchange of Pryor for Abel, that is, one person for one person. Now it appears that the terms of the exchange seem to be different and this man foresaw certain complications. DDR agreed to exchange Pryor for Abel but nothing more. This agreement should be followed to the letter.

If not, DDR [the East German government] feels free to act as it deems necessary and cannot give its consent to an exchange of one person for two persons, one being from a different country.

Mr. Vogel asked me to convey to you his concern for the matter, as he feels unable to postpone the trial of Pryor and in the Office of the Attorney General he was given to understand that in case of the American refusal to exchange Pryor for Abel they will start the trial and make a sensation out of it, as they have enough evidence to convict Pryor which as you understand might have negative results for the U.S.A. and for the Pryor family in particular.

When Drews finished reading, I became very angry and called the entire message "malicious nonsense." I said that both East Germany and Vogel were obviously acting in bad faith and that neither my government nor I had time for idle games with such people. I wished to state that any idea of an exchange of Abel for Pryor alone was out of the question; that unless East Germany adhered to the commitment officially made yesterday by the letter of the Attorney General, I must break off all negotiations at once and recommend to my government that I should return to New York. I said I had the impression that Schischkin and Vogel together were trying to make a fool of me and that I would not stand for it.

Vogel smiled nervously and said, "What is happening is a competition between Soviet Russia and East Germany, a sort of wrestling match, for the privilege of obtaining the release of Abel."

"What kind of a match would that be?" I retorted. "It would be like your Berliner Max Schmeling fighting a fly-weight."

"This may be," replied Vogel, "but I can assure you in good faith that such a struggle is going on. The Attorney General of East Germany has taken a firm position in the matter, as you see from his message."

"Nonsense," I said. "If Schischkin told the Attorney General of East Germany to walk across this floor on his hands he'd get down

405

and try. I repeat, I have no time for childish games. Either East Germany lives up to its official commitment, given me in writing yesterday, or I break off all negotiations and ask my government to bring me home." I stood up and began to put on my overcoat.

Vogel quickly pressed a buzzer on his desk. As though in a stage play, the door to his office opened and an assistant walked in. He stood stiffly before the desk and, head nodding like a parrot, announced that Vogel had just received a telephone call from the Attorney General of East Germany. The Attorney General, said the latest addition to our cast of actors, wished Vogel to appear in his office at 1300 hours (1 P.M.) for a further discussion of "the Pryor matter."

"This is good news," exclaimed Vogel, rising and looking at his watch. "Please remain here in East Berlin until my appointment is concluded. I promise I shall try my best to have the Attorney General change his mind."

I stated that since I had had an early breakfast I would like to be directed to a good hotel for lunch. After Vogel conferred with the Attorney General, he could meet me there. Vogel agreed and gave me fifty East German marks (I had explained that I had none) and Drews then asked if he could join me for lunch. I said, "Of course." On the way out of the office, Drews remained behind "to reserve a table in the restaurant" (which was largely unoccupied when we arrived). He was probably telephoning Schischkin. Vogel, looking over his shoulder to see whether Drews could see him, made a thumbs-up gesture to me and said, *"Nicht zurückgehen (no retreat)."* He obviously was trying to carry water on both shoulders. Drews then came downstairs and we entered Vogel's car, an attractive new sports model.

We started toward Friedrichstrasse for the restaurant, but after five minutes of driving, a black sedan suddenly raced from behind and forced us to the curb. Four large uniformed East German police, all armed, climbed from their car and surrounded ours. After a moment of shock Vogel got out, and there ensued several minutes of heated conversation behind our car.

When Vogel returned and started up the engine, I asked, "What did those clowns want?"

"I got a ticket for speeding," he replied.

For his answer I should have given him a ticket for perjury. However, if the object was to jar me before lunch I must confess it was somewhat successful.

He proceeded to drive us to the restaurant, the Johanneshof near Friedrichstrasse station, which was very pleasant. The printed menu was excellent but it turned out that they did not have many of the things which were on it. I had a good soup and a crisp salad, followed by cheese and coffee. Drews had some kind of stew.

Throughout the lunch, Drews was very polite but continually probed for my personal opinion whether a Pryor-Abel exchange would not be feasible. I told him that any such discussion was a waste of time. At one point he asked whether I reported to the State Department and upon my replying in the affirmative, he said, "Has this decision not to obtain the release of Pryor been cleared with Secretary of Defense McNamara, who is from Michigan and a friend of the Pryor family?" I told him that I did not know but that this would be highly unusual since such a mission as mine was only within the purview of the State Department.

Since leaving Schischkin at the Embassy, I had never referred to the fact that the Vogel telephone message delivered to me the night before had arrived via the unlisted number I had given only to Schischkin. Nevertheless, during lunch Drews volunteered that "after Vogel broke the bad news to the Abels last night, Miss Abel was lucky enough to remember the telephone number which you gave Schischkin and which she had memorized." He also volunteered that a business friend who was a foreigner happened to be in East Berlin at the time and, when he learned of their difficulties, agreed to take the message over to West Berlin to telephone it.

At one point, quite unexpectedly, Drews said to me, "Why do you think that on several occasions Schischkin has insisted upon seeing you alone and leaving us outside?" I told him I had no idea and he dropped the subject.

I commented to Drews that I felt "so sorry" for the Abel family and asked the names of Mrs. Abel and the daughter. He replied "Lydia" for the mother and "Helen" for the daughter. I asked whether Helen had ever married, and he replied, "Unfortunately, no." He immediately followed this by asking whether Abel had not discussed his family with me and I replied, "There never was any occasion for this." (The fact is that according to prior correspondence and records at the Abel trial, including microfilm letters seized in Abel's room at the time of his arrest, Cousin Drews's statements were completely false. He had reversed the names. Moreover, one of the letters introduced in evidence at the trial, apparently from Abel's daughter, had described her new husband at great length.)

Near the end of the lunch (about 3:15 P.M.) Drews excused himself "to go to the men's room," presumably to telephone. Shortly thereafter Vogel arrived and called for the check. When it came, I gave Drews the East German fifty-mark note which Vogel had given to me earlier and requested that he pay the check and keep the change. Drews produced a roll of bills and said, "You keep the fifty marks." I explained that I wanted to carry no East German money, to avoid any currency difficulties at the border. Vogel flashed his teeth and said, "It is fortunate you are so careful about currency matters, or else the East German government might have to exchange you for somebody." I smiled back, with equal good humor.

Drews paid the check (forty marks) and pocketed the change. Vogel thereupon announced that he had had a "terrific battle" with the Attorney General but had finally been "victorious." He said that all difficulties concerning the release of Pryor at the time of the Powers-Abel exchange had now been removed. The entire difficulty was because the Attorney General fiercely resented the fact that the preceding Saturday, upon my visiting East Germany, I had called upon Schischkin in the Soviet Embassy instead of first visiting Vogel and the Attorney General.

I pointed out that my last cable from the United States to Mrs. Abel had clearly stated I would be pleased to meet either her or "her representative" at the Soviet Embassy and that if Vogel had wished he could have been there. I also said that this new position of the Attorney General was strange in view of the official letter on his behalf, approving the release of Pryor, which had been delivered to me the day before.

Vogel replied that these matters were no longer significant; the one important fact was that the Attorney General now would consent to the release of Pryor. Vogel and I should proceed to the Soviet Embassy, and, after a conference with Schischkin, Vogel would report to the Attorney General that the deal had been approved by Soviet officials. He stated that he had already secured an appointment with Schischkin at 4 P.M.

I asked him whether this meant, without qualification, that all East German objections to the simultaneous exchange of Abel, Powers and Pryor had now been removed. He replied, "Yes."

We left the restaurant and proceeded at once to the Soviet Embassy, where we were received in the anteroom by Schischkin. He formally introduced himself to Vogel, as though a complete stranger, and then inquired how everything had been proceeding. Speaking in German, Vogel gave him substantially the same report which he had given me at the luncheon table, stating that all East German difficulties had been removed. Schischkin made no comment but then suddenly requested me to have a private meeting with him in the inner office.

After closing the door, Schischkin sat behind the desk and informed me that at the first meeting last Saturday, at which he had urged that Powers was a sufficiently important individual to be exchanged solely for Abel, he had asked me whether Powers was not a "national hero" in the United States because of his feats. I had replied that to judge by our public press in the United States, Powers was not regarded as a "national hero" but as someone who had performed an aeronautical mission for adequate compensation and whose conduct at his trial in Moscow left a certain amount to be desired. Also, that I had stated that there was a substantial view in the United States, especially by those responsible for United

States counterintelligence, that Abel should not be released under any circumstances since he might decide someday to talk.

Schischkin stated that he had communicated my remarks to his government and that this afternoon (Tuesday), he had received a new message from Moscow. He opened a portfolio and pretended to read it. The message stated that from my remarks on Saturday, it would appear to Moscow that the American government regarded Makinen as more valuable than Powers and that accordingly the offer of Powers for Abel should be withdrawn and that a firm offer of Makinen for Abel should be submitted.

I exploded at this point and, rising, said that Schischkin had taken these few remarks out of context; he knew full well that from the very outset the Powers-Abel exchange had been basic to the discussions and our obtaining of Powers was the *sine qua non* of any deal. I said that not only had Schischkin known this, and reaffirmed it to me that very morning (Tuesday), but that the Moscow message which he had read me the day before had recognized my position. It first and separately gave unqualified approval to the exchange of Powers for Abel and only later referred to Makinen as a possible American alternate choice. I reiterated that my instructions from the outset had been that there could be no deal without Powers and that the sole question was what the Soviets would offer in addition to Powers.

Schischkin blandly replied, "The message from Moscow this afternoon has superseded all my other instructions. I now am unauthorized to discuss any matter except exchanging Abel for Makinen."

I said that after the message read to me the day before, and Schischkin's oral confirmation of this commitment that morning, his latest announcement must mean that the Soviet was not seriously interested in obtaining the release of Abel.

"You have been playing chess with me since last Saturday," I said. "While I enjoy chess on occasion, I don't now have time for a game."

"Me?" replied Schischkin. "I play only volleyball."

I told Schischkin that whatever game he liked to play, I was interested at this time in only one question: Was yesterday's deal of Abel for Powers and Pryor still firm? If it was not, I would report this to my government and recommend that I immediately return home. Schischkin stated that this question was a new matter and that he must communicate with Moscow for instructions. He requested me to return tomorrow between 1400 and 1500 hours (2 P.M. and 3 P.M.) at which time he would read me the reply from Moscow.

I said that I saw no point in making another exhausting trip through the Wall to his Embassy, since I had given him my telephone number in West Berlin and he could communicate any reply to me at the proper time. Accordingly, I must decline to return to the Embassy and instead request that when Schischkin received further instructions he should telephone them to me. I added that if I had not heard from him by tomorrow night, I would request permission to return home. Schischkin said, "Very well," and told me I would receive a message tomorrow.

I left Schischkin in considerable heat and without shaking hands. Drews, who had waited in the anteroom, joined me as I left the Embassy and walked the entire distance to the S-Bahn at Friedrichstrasse with me. On the way he kept asking for my personal reactions so that he could "report to Miss Abel and the family." I told Drews that my basic reaction was that the negotiations on the non-American side since last Saturday had been conducted with irresponsibility and bad faith.

I added that if the "Powers plus Pryor for Abel" deal should fail, and my government accepted my recommendation that I return home, I would feel obliged to report to Colonel Abel that his "family" apparently were abandoning him and perhaps he should reconsider his position of "noncooperation" with the United States. I added, as significantly as I could "I am confident he will accept my judgment."

Drews said little. When we parted, he muttered, "Good luck in your return trip." I replied, "Thanks for lunch." It had been a long day.

I slept late and by noon there still was no word from Schischkin. My report on the events of the preceding day had been communicated to Washington and several reply messages had come. They carried two thoughts: one, I had been playing my role so strongly that I was endangering my primary mission to swap Abel for Powers; two, if I returned to East Berlin it would be at my own risk.

At 3:15 P.M. this message was telephoned to the unlisted West Berlin number:

> Donovan:
>   Unfortunately we got no reply today. We hope to get it tomorrow. Will inform immediately.
>
> Schischkin.

The game of chess was being played out, but it seemed to me that decisive action was necessary despite the caution urged by Washington. Unless a strong step now were taken by us, either the mission collapsed entirely or the Soviet would conclude that if they held out long enough, only Powers would have to be freed.

I discussed the events of the past few days with Bob and he suggested that we consult not only Lightner, the State Department Chief of Mission in Berlin, but also Gen. Lucius Clay, who was the personal representative of President Kennedy in Berlin with rank of ambassador. Since we could not jeopardize my quarters, the meeting was held at Bob's residence.

It was a depressing day, dark and filled with sleet. The open fire in Bob's living room felt good, especially with my nagging back. General Clay listened patiently while I reviewed the advice from Washington and my own estimate of the situation. I felt strongly that if I could regain the negotiating offensive, Pryor would come out with Powers. On the other hand, we all agreed with Washington that it would be foolhardy for me to go through the Wall and pay another unexpected call upon Schischkin.

We finally agreed upon a tactic which might carry the day. It was General Clay who wrote out the message which we dispatched to Schischkin:

> Received your telephone message and regret delay, as unfortunately the time which I can spend here is limited. As my back still bothers me, I would like to ask that you come to the residence of Mr. Howard Trivers of our mission between 4:00 and 6:00 P.M. tomorrow, Thursday, February 8, 1962. The address is 12 Vogelsong, Dahlem.
>
> Donovan.

Bob left to dispatch this by diplomatic courier. General Clay and I chatted about our last meeting, which had been up in Lake Placid, New York. He had been visiting the pleasant Adirondack camp of the late Carle Conway, chairman of the board of Continental Can Company. We agreed that we now were in another world.

Thursday, February 8

I was awakened at dawn by a courier from Bob. A message had just been received over the special West Berlin number. It read:

> Donovan:
>
> I got a favorable reply. Waiting to see you at my office at 4 o'clock today if your health allows you to come here.
>
> Schischkin.

Over breakfast, Bob and I considered the latest message. Should it be taken at face value? Was it another skirmish by Schischkin in his obvious war of nerves? Was it a trap set by Vogel or Drews, for whom the Soviet would disclaim all responsibility?

I believed I should take the gamble and go back, after sending confirmation to Schischkin. I told Bob I regarded the last few days as typical Pavlovian tactics.

Pavlov, the great Russian scientist, conditioned the reflexes of animals by offering rewards of food and then suddenly withdrawing them. This "first sweet, then bitter" approach was now applied by Russia in international negotiations, to demoralize opponents. I thought Schischkin's experiment with me was over.

Bob communicated with General Clay, who concurred in my decision. I thereupon sent this message, by courier:

Schischkin:

Will come at 1600 hours but because of health would appreciate your having car at station at 1530.

Donovan.

I arrived in East Berlin at 3:45 P.M. but found no car awaiting me. Because of the still-heavy snow, I took a taxi to the Soviet Embassy and offered the driver West German marks. He apparently believed I was trapping him into an illegal violation, perhaps because we had arrived in front of the Embassy, and protested vehemently. I led him into the Soviet Consulate and told the doorman to take care of him. The doorman paid him off in East German marks.

A minute or two later, Schischkin appeared and invited me into the private office. When I entered, a small table had been set up, on which were a bottle of Armenian brandy, German mineral water, cookies, and a bowl of fine apples, with lovely crystalware and silver. Thank you, Professor Pavlov, I thought.

Schischkin immediately poured the brandy (which he described as "our best" and "very expensive") and suggested a toast of "good luck." After clinking of glasses, he stated that he had received a favorable reply from Moscow and that the entire deal had been approved. He explained this meant Powers would be exchanged for Abel and that simultaneously the East Germans would release Pryor. However, he stated, while the release of Pryor by the East

414

Germans would be simultaneous with the Powers-Abel exchange, the two actions should not occur in the same place since East Germany is a separate government.

I told him I thought that this was an unnecessary complication of the matter. While I had no objection to such a procedure, I failed to see why it would not be more convenient to have all three men brought to the same spot. He said that he believed he must insist upon this.

I told Schischkin I would recommend to my government the acceptance of the foregoing. In so doing I wished to make clear my understanding that if relations between our two countries improved, an act of clemency for Makinen could be expected in the near future. Schischkin stated that he had communicated my "thoughts" on this to his government, which approved them in principle.*

With respect to the time and place, Schischkin at first suggested, with a straight face, the Soviet Embassy in East Berlin, as a "convenient location." I told him that in my judgment this would be highly improper and that the exchange must occur at some border point. He withdrew the suggestion.

Schischkin said he was open to any proposal on timing but that he thought the following Saturday would be the best day. When asked about the hour he said, "The earlier the better." I first suggested noon, but he said, "Why not earlier?" When I suggested 0730 hours he thought this would be excellent, since there should be few people moving about at that time.

He said that after reviewing the matter he did not believe that the Glienicke Bridge would be the best place because barbed wire had sealed it off. I told him that my information was that it remained open to traffic. He asked whether I had actually seen the bridge. I said that I had postponed any inspection trip until the agreement for exchange was definite. Schischkin said that they

*During 1962 and early 1963, I sent to Schischkin and others repeated reminders of the pledge. On October 11, 1963 Makinen was released by Russia. An American priest held 23 years was also freed. Two Soviet citizens facing espionage charges in the United States were deported in exchange.

believed that the Oberbaumbrücke near Warschauer Strasse would be preferable, since it is a border-passing point used only by West Germans. I told him that pending a review of the matter by my government, I saw no objection to this. He said that at the same time Pryor could be released at the "Checkpoint Charlie" crossing on Friedrichstrasse.

He inquired how many people should attend the Powers-Abel exchange I stated that I believed the official party should not consist of more than a half-dozen. He indicated agreement.

Schischkin said that Moscow had requested I personally intervene with my government to try to assure a minimum of anti-Soviet propaganda when the exchange became publicly known. I replied that because of our guarantees of freedom of the press, this was an extremely difficult matter. He said that they appreciated this fact but that they would like to suggest that the United States government issue a brief statement, saying that Powers had been released by the Soviet government at the request of his relatives and because of the desire by the Soviet and the United States to improve relations between the two countries. He suggested that no announcement be made simultaneously concerning the release of Abel, and that after a few months (which he later shortened to a few weeks) the United States government could announce that in recognition of the Soviet act and in the same spirit, Abel had been released. He said that he saw no reason for any United States government reference to the Pryor matter, but that in any event it was completely an East German affair.

I told him that while I could give assurance (as I had stated in our first meeting) the United States government did not intend to make propaganda out of the exchange, he must realize that the situation would be delicate at best and we could guarantee nothing. I said I stated this so that if my government had to issue a clarifying statement he would not regard us as having acted in bad faith. He appeared to be satisfied but requested that I return at noon the next day for further "discussion of details." I agreed.

He poured us each another brandy, closed his portfolio, and

began to relax a bit. I asked him how many languages he spoke and he said "only four"—Russian, German, English and Swedish. He told me he had attended the University of Moscow during World War II. He was just completing his tenth year abroad and now would like to tour his own country, since except for Moscow he had been only to the Crimea, on brief vacations. He said that he had one daughter. He told me there were seventy different languages in the Soviet Union and more than a dozen separate nationalities. No effort was being made to have common tongues, except that everyone had to learn Russian.

I told him that in our country there had been too few linguists, because of our geographical isolation and the common use of English. I explained that we were making efforts to remedy this situation by having children taught foreign languages, including Russian, while young.

"You should study Russian," he said.

"In my country," I replied with a smile, "only the optimists study Russian. The pessimists study Chinese." He laughed, but nervously.

I informed Schischkin I had been advised that the Bureau of Prisons had moved Abel temporarily to New York. I wished to warn that it seemed probable that his arrival would become known to the New York newspapers, leading to speculation about an exchange. (It never did.) I told him about the fascinating grapevine of information which flows through even maximum-security prisons, relating how Abel had informed me in Atlanta that a new exhibit concerning his case had just been installed in the FBI Museum, in the Department of Justice building in Washington.

Schischkin declared that problems with the American press were very difficult and in Russia they had no such problems with their newspapers. "I'm sure of that," I said. He asked about my family and I described them. He asked my age and when I replied "forty-five" he said, "I regret to state this but you look much older." This was a statement I would not contest at the time.

We had more brandy, cut up an apple, and at the conclusion of our visit he called an Embassy car and chauffeur. Despite the cold and renewed sleet, he insisted upon escorting me out the door and across the sidewalk to the waiting car.

I returned through the usual channels and arrived in West Berlin at 1810 hours. I gave a message for Washington to Bob at the Golden City Bar, saying that the deal was complete and "the package there" should be transported immediately. Later I visited General Clay at his residence and he was pleased with the report.

Friday, February 9

I met Schischkin at the Embassy about 1200 hours (noon) and reported the general concurrence of the United States government to accept Powers and Pryor for Abel, with the expectation of clemency for Makinen in the near future. Schischkin stated that a review of the traffic on Oberbaumbrücke this morning had led them to return to my original proposal of Glienicke Bridge. However, because of a 25-mile trip to the bridge for the Russians, they could not make the exchange before 0830 hours.

As to Frederic Pryor, Schischkin argued at length that Pryor should be released to his family in Vogel's "law office" in East Berlin. I flatly refused to agree to Pryor's release in any location in East Berlin. Schischkin finally agreed to his release at the Friedrichstrasse border point, simultaneously with the Powers-Abel exchange. I told him Pryor would be met there by a car with a two-way radio, which would notify us at the bridge. He nodded. I urged Schischkin, in his self-interest, to release Pryor today so as to keep the deals separate, but Schischkin replied that this would be contrary to his instructions.

Schischkin said that the principal concern of the Soviet was over any official statement issued by the United States. He said they would not hold us responsible for what the press might do, but he emphasized the importance of the text of our official statements for future relations between our countries. I replied that no statement in Berlin was contemplated and that I could assure

Schischkin there would be no official propaganda by us and nothing discrediting the U.S.S.R. Two points were all-important to the Soviet: no use of the word "exchange" and nothing in our official statement connecting Abel with the Soviet. I replied that I would communicate these views to my government.

(Subsequently by cable I strongly urged that our official statement be drafted to avoid the two points, for the following reasons: first, we should not jeopardize the hope of early clemency for Makinen, which could depend on proper conclusion of this deal; second, any such language in an official text was quite unnecessary since the entire press would describe it as an "exchange" and link Abel with the Soviet. This would not be our responsibility, so long as it was not in our official statement.)

"An ideal statement by the United States," said Schischkin, "would mention clemency for Abel as a result of the petition of his family and because of his age, making no reference to the Soviet Union." He expressed a wish that our official statement concerning Abel be released later, but I refused to make any such commitment. The Soviet government's announcement, he said, would relate only to Powers and ascribe their clemency to consideration for his family and a desire to improve relations between the United States and the Soviet Union. No Soviet official statement, now or in the future, would refer to either Abel or Pryor.

Schischkin said he would attend the Powers-Abel exchange with two Soviet officials. Lightner, the Deputy Chief of Prisons and myself, together with the three Soviet representatives would meet in the center of the bridge at 0820 hours for assurance that all was well. Two guards then would bring the respective prisoners forward, and, when identified, each man would be released to the opposite side. The officials would shake hands, then all would leave. He drew a sketch of the meeting, which I pocketed. I agreed to the plan as sensible, but said it must be reviewed by my government. If we proposed any change, I would communicate at once with Schischkin. Upon his inquiry, I assured Schischkin that no reporters or press photographers would be permitted at the exchange.

I returned to West Berlin at 1330 hours. Bob took me to see Major General Watson, commanding the United States armed forces in Berlin, for a discussion of security plans for the following morning. General Watson was one of four men in West Berlin who knew I was there. "Mr. Dennis" arrived quietly and entered General Watson's heavily guarded headquarters by a rear door. While I was waiting in the General's anteroom, an affable colonel walked in, must have thought I was a visiting Congressman, and pleasantly said, "I'm Colonel Foote, how are you?" Mr. Dennis shook his hand and said coldly, "How do you do." I could sense he thought I was a boor.

Late that night Bob told me Abel had arrived in West Berlin and, if I wished, I could see him. I told Bob that sleep was more important to me just then and arranged to be awakened early.

Saturday, February 10

I rose at 5:30 A.M. and wearily packed. It was my eighth day in Berlin and, if all went well, my last. After breakfast, I went with Bob to the United States military compound. The small guardhouse, where Abel was held in a maximum-security cell, had been emptied of other prisoners and was heavily guarded. Inside I met the Deputy Director of Prisons, who turned out to be Fred Wilkinson, the warden of Atlanta Penitentiary when I visited Abel there. He had recently been promoted. Over coffee, we discussed final arrangements and then I asked permission to meet alone with Abel.

Rudolf rose when I entered the underground cell. He smiled, held out his hand and said, to my surprise, "Hello, Jim." He had always addressed me as "Mr. Donovan." He seemed thin, worn and suddenly old. But he was gracious as ever and offered me an American cigarette, saying a bit wryly, "I shall miss these."

We talked in a relaxed way. I asked him whether he was apprehensive about returning home and he quickly replied, "Of course not. I've done nothing dishonorable." He knew all about Francis Gary Powers but had never heard of Frederic Pryor's case. I outlined the exchange arrangements and he thought they seemed to be sensible. He said he had never heard of Schischkin, although our people had informed me that in their judgment I had been negotiating not with the "Second Secretary of the Soviet Embassy in East Germany" but with the chief of the KGB in Western Europe.

As the time neared for our departure, he took my hand and said with great sincerity, "I never can thank you enough for your hard work but, above all, for your integrity. Your hobby, I know, is collecting rare books. In my country such cultural treasures are the property of the state. But in some way I shall arrange for you to receive an appropriate expression of my gratitude, within the next year."

I drove with Bob from the prison to our appointed rendezvous at Glienicke Bridge. When we arrived, it was clear but bitter cold. United States military police were in evidence everywhere at our end of the bridge. They had relieved the West German border guards, whom I discovered in the sentry box, sipping coffee and looking both puzzled and vaguely apprehensive. They obviously were uninformed of our mission. Abel arrived about 8:15 in a car filled with guards. One of them, who later marched out on the bridge with Abel and Wilkinson, was one of the largest men I have ever seen. He must have been six feet seven inches tall and weighed perhaps three hundred pounds. I never did find out who he was, but presumably he came from the Federal Bureau of Prisons.

At exactly 8:20 I walked to the center of the bridge, flanked by Alan Lightner of the State Department Mission in Berlin and a young civilian who had been a comrade of Powers during his U-2 flying days. Schischkin meanwhile was walking toward us from the other side, accompanied by two civilians. He and I stepped out alone at the center of the bridge, formally shook hands and gave mutual assurances that all was ready in accordance with our agreement. I then introduced him to Alan Lightner and he introduced me to a "Mr. Pryzov" or some such name.

We then beckoned toward our respective ends of the span and a trio walked forward from each side. Ours comprised Abel, Deputy Director Wilkinson and the "man mountain" guard. The Russian trio consisted of Powers, with a fur shako on his head, and two men who looked like retired wrestlers. Both Abel and Powers were carrying overstuffed bags.

Schischkin announced to me rather precisely that since Pryor had been released by the East Germans at Friedrichstrasse, the exchange of Powers for Abel now could take place. I told him I must confirm this and called for confirmation from our end of the bridge. Someone finally yelled back to me, "No word on Pryor yet."

Schischkin said my side was in error and that we must complete the exchange immediately before civilian traffic appeared at the bridge. I replied, "We wait right here until my people confirm that Pryor has been released." I explained that we had told Pryor's family the night before there might be a favorable development and early this morning several security officers had driven them to "Checkpoint Charlie" to identify and greet their son.

"My information," said Schischkin, "is that Vogel accompanied Pryor to the border crossing and the young man then was released."

"Perhaps Vogel is arguing with Pryor about his legal fees," I suggested with a smile. "This could take months."

Schischkin roared with laughter and said, "I yield to you as a lawyer. No doubt you've had the same experience many times."

Now relaxed, Schischkin told me it had been a pleasure to meet me and that I should take a more active role in government affairs. "We need men with understanding," he said. I told him high income taxes would prevent that for many years to come. "I understand," he said, "and this is why you have so many men with inherited wealth in your government." I asked him if he thought men with inherited wealth should lounge on beaches instead of contributing their services to the common good. "No," he replied, "but you have too many."

Suddenly we heard a cry from our end of the bridge: "Pryor's been released." It was 8:45. I motioned to Wilkinson, who produced an official-looking document and countersigned it. (Identification of both prisoners had meanwhile been confirmed by friendly waves.) At signs from Schischkin and me, Powers and

Abel moved forward with their bags and crossed the center line. Neither looked at the other. Powers said, "Gee, I'm glad to see you," and grasped the hand of his former comrade. They walked to our end of the bridge.

Abel paused. He asked Wilkinson for the official pardon, saying, "I'll keep this as sort of a diploma." Then he put down the bag, extended his hand to me and said, "Goodbye, Jim." I replied, "Good luck, Rudolf." Schischkin stood aloof, then put out his hand and said to me, "How long will you and Powers remain in Berlin?" I shrugged and, thinking of the Corridor journey ahead, replied, "I think we're entitled to a few days' rest here, don't you?" "Of course," he smiled. "Goodbye and good luck." We parted.

At our end of Glienicke Bridge I paused briefly to thank Bob, Lightner, Wilkinson and the Colonel in charge of security. Then I entered a sedan in which Powers and his U-2 comrade already occupied the rear seat. As our car raced toward Tempelhof Airdrome I was introduced to Powers, who seemed dazed. At the airdrome was waiting, engines warmed, my old C-45 with Captain MacArthur. We jumped aboard, took off at once and headed for Frankfurt. There was little said until MacArthur came back and announced we had cleared the Corridor and were in West Germany. Then we all shook hands and laughed. MacArthur warmly congratulated me but never spoke to Powers.

The plane had a flight surgeon aboard, who took Powers to the cargo space for a physical examination. At Frankfurt we were quickly transferred to a Super-Constellation which, we were informed after takeoff, was the plane assigned to the Commanding General of the Air Force in Europe.

Once aloft, we all relaxed. The plane was magnificently equipped, with plush bunks and a galley. A white-jacketed steward promptly asked if we would like a drink and something to eat.

"I'd like a martini," said Powers. "You know, a couple of weeks ago in my cell I dreamed one night about a martini." I asked for a double Scotch.

I sat down at a table opposite Powers and smiled at him. He

wanted to know all about me, especially whether I had been sent by his "Paw." It quickly developed that his "Paw" back in rural Virginia dominated the thinking and affections of Francis Gary Powers. I explained to him that I had never met his dad but had once spoken to him on the phone many months ago, to assure him that anything I could do to help his son would be done.

"You're a lawyer," said Powers, "and you know, I may need a lawyer when I get back to the States."

"Well, Frank," I said, "if you think I've been representing your interests well during the past few weeks, you can regard me as your counsel. My annual retainer will be one smoked Virginia ham, delivered each Christmas holiday."

He laughed his appreciation.

We talked for the next few hours, with his former U-2 friend joining in. Powers was a special type, I thought. People at home had been critical of his performance when downed and later when tried in Moscow. Yet, in charity, suppose you wished to recruit an American to sail a shaky espionage glider over the heart of hostile Russia at 75,000 feet, from Turkey to Norway. Powers was a man who, for adequate pay, would do it, and as he passed over Minsk would calmly reach for a salami sandwich. We are all different, and it is a little unfair to expect every virtue in any one of us.

I went up to the cockpit, met the Colonel piloting the plane and heard American news broadcasts about the exchange on Glienicke Bridge. It was the middle of the night back home but the White House had issued a communiqué at a hastily called press conference. The Colonel and his crew shook my hand and were more than friendly. I noticed they avoided Powers.

Over a few drinks I asked Powers about his trial in Moscow and especially his confinement beforehand. He had been held over one hundred days incommunicado prior to the opening of the public trial.

"Gee, I felt alone," he said. "They never beat me or anything but it was just being alone and never knowing what might happen. They kept a light on in my cell, and in the middle of the night

424

they'd wake me up to go down to the same room where I gave the same answers to the same questions by the same man. After a while, it gets you."

The scene was familiar to anyone who had once read Arthur Koestler's *Darkness at Noon* about the Moscow Trials in the 1930s.

Following the trial, Powers said, life in prison was cold, drab and solitary. He was in a building with other "political prisoners," as distinguished from common criminals. After a time he was fortunate enough to get a cellmate, a Latvian serving a long term for "counterrevolutionary activities." Powers was taught to weave rugs and occasionally was allowed to read two publications in English, the London *Daily Worker* and the United States-published *Nation*. I expressed some surprise at the Russian selection of the latter, which many regarded as left-wing but which frequently took points of view highly critical of the Soviet Union. Powers had no explanation.

"I thought more about politics and international things than I ever did before," he said. "For example, it just doesn't make sense to me that we don't recognize Red China and let her into the United Nations." It did not seem a proper occasion on which to discuss the point.

He told us that one day, walking around the inner prison courtyard for exercise, a ball of bread dough landed at his feet. He picked it up and took it to his cell. Inside was a paper on which was printed in English, "I have important information for the President." He did not know from which cell it was thrown and never did establish contact.

All of us slept for hours between conversations. We refueled at the Azores, held to our course and finally the captain came back to announce that we were approaching Powers' destination, an isolated air base in the Carolinas. I was to continue to Washington.

When we landed in the Carolinas, Powers gathered the pitiful mementos of prison life he had been permitted to bring out of Russia: a few small rugs he had woven, some cheap toys made by other prisoners, and his rough prison clothes. He said, "Goodbye, Mr.

Donovan," as he stepped off the plane. I think he added, "Thanks." I never saw or heard from him again.*

Sunday, February 11

I attended late Mass at a church in the Georgetown section of Washington, D.C. As I was leaving the church I met Mr. Justice William Brennan of the Supreme Court. (In the Abel case he had written the opinion for the four Justices who dissented. The majority opinion, upholding Abel's conviction, was written by Mr. Justice Felix Frankfurter, my old professor in Harvard Law School).

"I thought," said Mr. Justice Brennan, "the radio last reported you somewhere over the Atlantic."

I assured him I had been in church in body as well as in spirit, then gravely said, "Please do me one favor, Mr. Justice. Present my highest personal regards to Mr. Justice Frankfurter and tell him I finally have found an effective way to set aside a judgment of the Supreme Court of the United States."

Tuesday, March 6

On this day the Central Intelligence Agency issued a report on Francis Gary Powers which stated, in substance, that he had reasonably performed his assigned U-2 mission to the best of his ability and had now brought back information of value to the United States. On the same date Powers publicly testified before the Senate Armed Services Committee, which concurred in the conclusions of the CIA. Important to him, he was granted his back pay.

*On December 20, 1963, as I was reading the galley proofs of this book, there arrived in my office a Christmas card: "Wishing special folks like you the best of everything." Written on the card was: "Thanks for all you did. Hope the Virginia ham arrives safely. Francis Gary Powers." Accompanying the card was a 12-pound smoked Virginia ham.

. . .

Shortly thereafter Frederic Pryor arrived in my New York office, accompanied by his mother, father and brother. It was our first meeting. The family graciously presented me with a small crystal paperweight containing an actual piece of rubble from the Berlin Wall and an inscription, signed by the entire family, which reads:

> This is a piece of the Berlin Wall, from behind which you delivered Frederic on February 10, 1962. The gratitude of the Pryor family will last long after this Wall is a thing of the past.

In August, 1962, there was an incident at the Berlin Wall in which an escaping East German youth was shot by VOPOs and left to die within full view of West Berlin spectators. At the height of this crisis a Soviet courier came to the border crossing at Friedrichstrasse and asked for an American Mission officer. He gave him an envelope and package, addressed to me at my William Street address in New York. The enclosed letter read:

> Dear Jim,
>   Although I am neither a collector of old books nor a lawyer, I believe that the two old books printed in the XVIth century and dealing with law that I was lucky enough to find are sufficiently rare to be a welcome addition to your collection. Please accept them as a mark of my gratitude for all that you have done for me . . .
>   I trust that your health will not suffer from overwork.
> Sincerely yours,
Rudolf.

The accompanying package contained two rare, sixteenth-century, vellum-bound editions of *Commentaries on the Justinian Code*, in Latin.

The Abel case was closed.

THE WHITE HOUSE
WASHINGTON

March 12, 1962

Dear Mr. Donovan:

You have by this time become aware of the resolution of the case of Francis Gary Powers. It must be a source of great gratification to you, and I want you to know that I consider the return of Mr. Powers and the results of the review of the case valuable contributions to the national interest.

So far as I am aware, the type of negotiation you undertook, where diplomatic channels had been unavailing, is unique, and you conducted it with the greatest skill and courage. The additional release of Frederic L. Pryor and the openings left for negotiations concerning Marvin W. Makinen could only have been accomplished by negotiation of the highest order.

I wish to thank you for the service you have rendered.

With every good wish,

Sincerely,

Mr. James B. Donovan
Watters & Donovan
161 William Street
New York, New York

July 16th 1962

Dear Jim,

Although I am neither a collector of old books nor a lawyer, I believe that the two old books printed in the XVth century and dealing with law that I was lucky enough to find are sufficiently rare to be a welcome addition to your collection. Please accept them as a mark of my gratitude for all that you have done for me.

As I was writing this, I was happy to receive your letter of June 22nd (delayed somewhat en route) in which you write about sending my belongings.

For this I am very grateful to you and as soon as they arrive, I will confirm their receipt.

I trust that your health will not suffer from over work.

Sincerely Yours,

Rudolf

A letter from Rudolf Abel to James B. Donovan after his release.
(Courtesy of the author's estate)

ACKNOWLEDGMENTS

The author acknowledges his gratitude to his family and law partners for their patience; Chief Judge Charles S. Desmond, who provided a foreword in the original edition; Bard Lindeman for his able aid in preparing the manuscript; Mrs. M. McInturff for her constant help; all who aided in the court defense and the mission to East Germany.

INDEX